NAT
TURNER

NAT
TURNER

A Slave Rebellion in History and Memory

EDITED BY

KENNETH S. GREENBERG

OXFORD
UNIVERSITY PRESS

2003

OXFORD
UNIVERSITY PRESS

Oxford New York
Auckland Bangkok Buenos Aires Cape Town Chennai
Dar es Salaam Delhi Hong Kong Istanbul Karachi Kolkata
Kuala Lumpur Madrid Melbourne Mexico City Mumbai Nairobi
São Paulo Shanghai Taipei Tokyo Toronto

Copyright © 2003 by Oxford University Press, Inc.
Introduction and chapters by Kenneth S. Greenberg © Kenneth S. Greenberg
"Nat Turner and Sectional Crisis" © Louis P. Masur
'The Event' in "Nat Turner's Slave Rebellion" © Herbert Aptheker
"Symptoms of Liberty and Blackhead Signposts: David Walker and Nat Turner" © Vincent Harding
"Styron's Choice: A Meditation on History, Literature, and Moral Imperatives"
© The University of Texas at Arlington

Published by Oxford University Press, Inc.
198 Madison Avenue, New York, New York 10016

www.oup.com

Oxford is a registered trademark of Oxford University Press

Library of Congress Cataloging-in-Publication Data

Nat Turner : a slave rebellion in history and memory / edited by Kenneth S. Greenberg.
p. cm.
ISBN 0-19-513404-4
1. Turner, Nat, 1800?–1831.
2. Southampton Insurrection, 1831.
3. Slaves—Virginia—Southampton County—Biography.
4. Turner, Nat, 1800?–1831—Influence.
I. Greenberg, Kenneth S.

F232.S7 .N46   2002
975.5'552—dc21   2002070087

1 3 5 7 9 8 6 4 2
Printed in the United States of America
on acid-free paper

For Judi,
Laura, Amy, and Lisa

and

For Frank Christopher and Charles Burnett

CONTENTS

PART FOUR: MEMORY

The Nat Turner slave rebellion erupted in Southampton County, Virginia, during the early hours of 22 August 1831. It was directed by an extraordinary 31-year-old man who was inspired by a series of heavenly visions to lead his people in a great battle to destroy slavery. Seven conspirators, initially armed with a variety of farm implements, attacked Turner's home farm, the Joseph Travis residence, and killed all the white inhabitants in their sleep. During the next 24 hours, the rebels moved rapidly from farm to farm, killing every white man, woman, and child they encountered; gathering horses, guns, and recruits; and ultimately generating consequences that touched the entire nation and that continue to influence American race relations to the present day.

The revolt was short, lasting little more than a day. Although panic spread throughout the South, the major violence was confined to Southampton County. The number of people directly involved was limited—60 to 80 active rebels who killed no more than 57 to 60 whites, and an infuriated white population who retaliated by summarily executing scores, if not hundreds, of blacks. Yet Nat Turner and the revolt he initiated have become an important part of American historical memory. Whenever Americans have attempted to understand the meaning of the Southampton revolt of 1831, they also have had to grapple with the meaning of slavery and race relations in our society.

The present volume gathers the best recent scholarship on Nat Turner, a few classic works in the field, and transcripts of two interviews conducted for the documentary film *Nat Turner ~ A Troublesome Property*. Part One, "The Search for Nat Turner," begins the volume with two essays that focus on a set of issues that are fundamental to any analysis of the subject. Every historian who deals with the world of Nat Turner encounters a set of sources that are notoriously obscure and difficult to interpret. They include newspaper accounts, letters from white eyewitnesses or from people who spoke to white eyewitnesses, trial records, government documents, folk memories, *The Confessions of Nat Turner* (a published pamphlet produced as a result of conversations between Turner and local lawyer Thomas R. Gray), and a scattering of other materials.[1] With the exception of African-American folk memories, every one of the routes into the mind and world of Nat Turner is through sources produced by people who deeply hated the rebels and their leader. Such sources must be analyzed with great care.

The first essay in this volume, "Name, Face, Body," begins by asking three basic questions never before seriously considered by historians. What was Nat Turner's name? What did he look like? What happened to his body? The impossibility of definitively answering any of these questions begins the volume with a powerful commentary on the impenetrability of the sources available to historians. It sets an appropriately skeptical tone for any attempts to understand Nat Turner and his world. Some questions are not answerable, and honest scholarship requires an admission of failure when it is appropriate.

The second essay turns to a close analysis of the single most important document produced by the Nat Turner slave rebellion: *The Confessions of Nat Turner.*[2] This document was the creation of a complex collaboration between Nat Turner and lawyer Thomas R. Gray. Turner had eluded capture for almost 70 days after the rebellion. He was caught on 30 October and then brought to the Southampton County jail to await trial. At various times between 1 and 3 November, Gray visited Turner in his jail cell and questioned him about his motives and his role in the rebellion. Within a few weeks, Gray published Turner's *Confessions,* a document that has come to be regarded as the most direct route into the mind of the nation's most famous slave rebel. But *The Confessions* has always been difficult to analyze and to interpret because it contains two voices. Nat Turner certainly spoke to Thomas R. Gray when they met in that jail cell in early November 1831, but Gray wrote the published pamphlet and clearly added his own voice to Turner's. Readers of *The Confessions* have hitherto found it virtually impossible to unravel the intimately intertwined strands of the two voices in that document.

David F. Almendinger, Jr., is the first historian to attempt the kind of painstaking analysis required to help us understand the double-voiced narrative of *The Confessions.* Through a careful reading of eyewitness accounts of the rebellion published in contemporary newspapers, Almendinger determines their authorship and point of view. This enables him to read *The Confessions* knowing what Thomas R. Gray had written and read prior to its production. Almendinger's method permits him to identify new facts and ideas in *The Confessions*—facts and ideas that could not have come from Gray or any other white observer. Overall, he concludes that the content of *The Confessions* was primarily supplied by Nat Turner and not by Thomas R. Gray.

Part Two consists of two stories of the rebellion. They are included here to give readers a glimpse of the radically different interpretive frameworks that have separated and continue to separate scholars of the Nat Turner rebellion. We have always been, and we remain today, a nation deeply divided over how to remember slavery and slave rebellions. One symptom of our division is evidenced by the almost total absence of public historical monuments to commemorate slave rebels like Turner. Another symptom is embodied in the deep and bitter interpretive debates that divide the scholarly community.

The first essay in this section is a chapter of Herbert Aptheker's master's essay completed in 1937 at Columbia University.[3] It is included here for a variety of reasons. First of all, it occupies a key position among the relatively few history books that deal extensively with the Nat Turner rebellion. William Sidney Drewry was the first modern historian to take up the subject of Turner. Drewry was a native of Virginia and grew up near the area of the rebellion. He completed his doctorate at Johns Hopkins University in 1900 and immediately published his dissertation under the title *Slave Insurrections in Virginia (1800–1831)*. Drewry was a careful historian who read extensively in primary sources and actually spoke with local black and white residents who had direct contact with people who were alive in 1831. However, Drewry's dissertation was seriously marred by racial stereotypes and assumptions common among white Virginians of the late-nineteenth and early-twentieth centuries. He presented a vision of slavery as a benign and benevolent institution, an image of the slaves as contented workers who rarely rebelled, and a stereotyped portrait of Nat Turner as a "wild, fanatical Baptist preacher."[4]

When Herbert Aptheker entered graduate school in the mid-1930s, Drewry's image of slavery and of Nat Turner still prevailed in the academy. But Aptheker arrived at Columbia with a deep personal animosity toward segregation and the racial assumptions that lay behind it. He had also begun to be influenced by Marxist thinking that rooted American slavery in a larger story of class conflict. Hence, Aptheker's master's essay reflected a radically different set of ideas. Slavery was not benign—it was exploitive. Slave rebellions were not isolated and infrequent events directed by fanatics. They were common and were led by intelligent men like Nat Turner—men motivated by a clear and simple desire for liberty. Although Aptheker's master's essay was not published until 1966, all of these ideas reappeared in his more broadly focused Ph.D. dissertation, published in 1943 as *American Negro Slave Revolts*.[5]

Aptheker's view of slavery and slave rebellions did not immediately win over mainstream historians, although it did inspire a small group of pioneers working in the field of what was then known as "Negro History." In fact, he remained marginalized for many years in part because of his deep involvement with the American Communist party during the height of the Cold War, and in part because of his Marxist theoretical framework that attracted significant criticism. But in the 1960s, during the era of the civil rights movement, Aptheker experienced renewed interest in his research on Nat Turner, an interest that eventually led to the publication of his master's essay. In fact, many African Americans of that era turned to Aptheker's work on Turner as they searched for examples of heroic leaders who attacked slavery and who might serve to inspire a new militant resistance to more modern forms of racial oppression.

Part Two also contains a second and very different Nat Turner story, written by historian Thomas C. Parramore. Parramore, a professor emeritus at Merideth College in Raleigh, North Carolina, had first written about Nat Turner in his carefully researched 1978 history of Southampton County.[6] Since that volume was a county history commissioned by the local historical society, it was not widely reviewed or read by professional historians. Yet its chapters on Nat Turner are so detailed and well researched that they merit an important place in modern writing on the subject. Perhaps the greatest contribution of this 1978 study is Parramore's discovery that previous historians had erroneously mistaken the elder Thomas Gray for his son Thomas R. Gray. Parramore conclusively demonstrated that it was the relatively young 31-year-old lawyer Thomas R. Gray who entered Turner's jail cell in November 1831 and shortly thereafter published *The Confessions*. Moreover, Parramore's diligent research unearthed information about the rapidly declining social and economic status of the younger Gray. He had even become estranged from and disinherited by his father. These facts led Parramore to posit a complex and fascinating relationship between Turner and Gray. The outcast Gray might have felt an affinity for the outcast Turner—an affinity that became evident in *The Confessions*. Parramore went so far as to suggest that the lawyer and the rebel had, in a sense, "conspired to create" *The Confessions* and that "it was the vein of compassion and identity" that Gray felt toward Turner that gave the document "its enduring power and haunting validity."[7]

The Parramore selection included in this volume is a newly commissioned work. It draws on his earlier research, but it also contains new emphases and conclusions. While Parramore reiterates his core argument about the relationship between Turner and Gray, his central theme shifts to a harsh critique of Turner as a rebel leader, a critique that sometimes echoes conclusions reached by William S. Drewry 100 years earlier. Parramore contends that the rebellion was poorly planned and poorly executed. After his initial attack on the Travis house, Turner "frittered the night away" with "useless" military drills. Moreover, according to Parramore, Turner could not control the excessive drinking of his men. When the rebel leader finally began to move, his attack route meandered aimlessly from house to house, circling around itself and allowing time for whites to organize resistance. Overall, Parramore argues that Turner was a religious mystic who could not lead, who lacked the personal will to kill anyone, and who was incapable of setting the appropriate example of ferocity to inspire his men.

Part Three includes six essays that place Nat Turner in a variety of contexts and communities. The first essays in this section offer two radically different readings of Nat Turner's connections to the African-American community. The positions they advocate represent the polar extremes of a conversation that has been endlessly repeated since Nat Turner first began his rebellion in 1831. Vincent Harding's essay on David Walker and Nat Turner first appeared as a chapter in his 1981 classic history of African-American resistance, *There Is a River: The Black Struggle for Freedom in America.*[8] Harding writes with passion, elegance, and conviction about the religious inspiration of Nat Turner. But the core of Harding's position is that Nat Turner was not alone and isolated in a remote part of Virginia in 1831. He was part of a vast river of African-American resistance, extending deeply into the past and future and broadly across the nation. Black abolitionist David Walker had written his *Appeal* in Boston shortly before the Turner rebellion. It called for militant black resistance to slavery and was widely circulated throughout the region surrounding Southampton County, Virginia. Even though there is no clear evidence that Nat Turner ever read Walker's *Appeal*, Harding suggests that Turner and Walker were linked because they were part of the same vast river of struggle. Turner did not have to read Walker's words to understand that "the God of Walker's *Appeal* had always been in Southampton County."

Patrick H. Breen's contribution is part of his doctoral dissertation recently completed at the University of Georgia. Breen makes no attempt to link Nat Turner to the African-American community outside of Southampton County. Instead, he narrows his gaze to the confines of the local community. Through a careful reading of *The Confessions*, Breen suggests that, as a youth, Nat Turner had been highly respected and integrated fully into the world of the black community of Southampton County. But once Turner's religious visions took a more mystical and radical turn, the African-American community rejected him. That many blacks in Southampton County ultimately joined Turner at the moment of rebellion did not necessarily signify that they accepted his leadership or religious vision. The community was diverse, and individuals could think for themselves. Those who joined the rebellion frequently did so for their own reasons and not because they blindly followed Turner's leadership. In Breen's vision of Southampton County, Nat Turner stood at the margin rather than at the center of the black community.

The next two essays place Nat Turner in different comparative contexts. James Sidbury's "Reading, Revelation, and Rebellion" offers an analysis of the different ways in which the three great American slave-rebel communities of the nineteenth century—the communities of Gabriel, Denmark Vesey, and Nat Turner—read and interpreted the Bible in varying ways. Sidbury's main point is that there was no single "slave church" or "invisible institution" that united the African-American community within the institution of bondage. He focuses on three communities separated by time and space in order to study the varied "secret local worlds of the sacred," worlds in which unordained and isolated preachers created local variations of the dominant Christian message. Sidbury identifies complexity and variation where others had described a monolith.

The selection by Douglas R. Egerton broadens the comparative context even further in order to answer the question of whether Nat Turner was an aberration among slave rebels. Was Turner uniquely irrational, incompetent, and incapable of leading his people in a successful rebellion? Egerton's method of answering this question is to place Turner in a broadly comparative context—measuring his visions, plans, and accomplishments against not only United States' rebels like Gabriel and Denmark Vesey, but also against the rebels of Jamaica, Guyana, and Cuba. Egerton concludes that, while there were important differences among the slave rebellions of the western hemisphere, the similarities were overwhelming. Turner was no deviant among slave rebels. He shared their religious visions, their plans, and their tactics and strategies. Even if he was not consciously aware of it, Nat Turner was part of a tradition of hemispheric resistance to slavery—a tradition remarkably similar to the vast river of resistance identified by Vincent Harding.

Louis P. Masur's contribution is derived from his recently published *1831: Year of Eclipse.*[9] This essay places Nat Turner in the context of the sectional crisis of the nation. The Turner rebellion exacerbated the developing split between North and South on the issue of slavery. Southerners came to fear that northern abolitionists like William Lloyd Garrison might have incited and might continue to incite slaves to rebellion. They came to distrust a nation that could tolerate the speech and activities of such dangerous individuals. Masur also describes the extraordinary debate about the gradual abolition of slavery that was generated by the Turner rebellion within Virginia. Governor Floyd, joined by many allies from the non-slaveholding western part of the state, came to believe that the only way to protect the state from future insurrections was to eliminate slavery. This belief led to a bitter debate within the Virginia legislature about a variety of proposals for gradual abolition. Although the abolition schemes were defeated in the end, it is clear that the Turner rebellion inflicted wounds on the nation that would not be healed easily.

Literary scholar Mary Kemp Davis offers the final contribution to this section of the book. Davis is the author of *Nat Turner Before the Bar of Judgment,* an important volume about images of Nat Turner found in six novels written between 1856 and 1967.[10] In this selection, she turns her attention to a topic that hitherto has been neglected sorely by historians and other scholars of the rebellion—the role of black women. Davis combs the documents of 1831 in search of black women and finds them mentioned in many places. While only one woman was tried and executed as a rebel, and another may have ridden with the rebels, Davis discovers that African-American women engaged in a wide variety of activities related to the rebellion. They supported the rebels, betrayed them, testified at their trials, performed a variety of heroic acts, died at the hands of whites, and helped or hindered whites who tried to escape. Looking at the rebellion with a focus on black women gives Davis a different lens through which to view the events of 1831. She discovers a complex community of women divided in their reactions to the rebellion. She reexamines the work of William S. Drewry, and, while acknowledging his racial bias, she recognizes him as one of the few scholars to have paid any serious attention to black women. Finally, she offers a discussion of the women in Nat Turner's family. While Davis's discussion of the black women of the rebellion may raise more questions than it answers, it does begin the examination of a new and potentially very fruitful topic for scholarly analysis.

The primary concern of Part Four is American memory of the Nat Turner rebellion, with special focus on the controversy surrounding William Styron's 1967 novel *The Confessions of Nat Turner*.[11] The Styron controversy led to a bitter and divisive racial conversation that generated deep anger—anger that has not yet dissipated. Styron's novel initially met the kind of critical praise about which most writers can only dream. But a significant group of black intellectuals was deeply disappointed and offended by Styron's *Confessions*. Ultimately, under the editorship of John Henrik Clarke, this group published a collection of highly critical essays entitled *William Styron's Nat Turner: Ten Black Writers Respond*.[12] Styron had claimed that his novel was consistent with the known historical facts, but the black critics noted a pattern of distortion that diminished the stature of Nat Turner as a heroic historical figure—and, by implication, also diminished the stature of the black freedom fighters of the 1960s. They particularly objected to Styron's portrayal of a Nat Turner who burned with sexual desire for a white teenager, who had a homosexual encounter with another slave, and who despised the weakness and docility of his fellow slaves. Overall, they argued that Styron's Nat Turner bore no resemblance at all to the historical rebel leader and that he was little more than a reflection of Styron's own racial and sexual fantasies about black people.

Charles Joyner's essay "Styron's Choice" was originally delivered in 1996 as a lecture at the University of Texas at Arlington.[13] It offers a good summary of the historical and literary issues at stake in the debate between William Styron and his critics. It also proposes a series of careful judgments that will be certain to please and to annoy all participants from that 1960s controversy.

Two interviews follow the Joyner essay. They were both conducted as part of a documentary film entitled *Nat Turner ~ A Troublesome Property*. Beginning in 1997, I joined with producer Frank Christopher and director Charles Burnett to create a film about Nat Turner in American history and memory. During the course of film production, we conducted interviews with nearly all the people involved in the 1960s debate over William Styron's novel. That experience led me to several conclusions. Most significantly, I was deeply impressed by the formidable intellectual and moral power of all participants on all sides of the controversy. At first I distrusted this reaction. How could I sympathize simultaneously with so many mutually inconsistent ideas and judgments?

I pondered this issue at great length and finally realized that my film colleagues and I had experienced the debate over William Styron's novel in a way that made it appear quite different to us from the way it had appeared to those who had experienced it firsthand in the 1960s. We certainly asked questions about the substantive issues that separated William Styron from his critics, but, more importantly, we also asked questions about the larger political and biographical contexts that gave life and meaning to those issues. Any reader of the vast volume of material produced by the debate over Styron's Nat Turner might get the mistaken impression that it was a conversation about the validity of historical research or about the relation between history and fiction. But our interview questions asked people to set their ideas about Nat Turner within the context of their life experiences. The two interviews presented here, one with William Styron and one with Dr. Alvin Poussaint, clearly demonstrate that the confrontation between Styron and his critics was not merely a clash of facts but, rather, a clash of worlds. Nat Turner appeared to Styron through the lens of his experience as a white liberal in segregated Virginia, his admiration for Dr. Martin Luther King, Jr., and his friendship with James Baldwin. In contrast, Dr. Poussaint experienced Nat Turner through the lens of experiences in left-wing and integrated summer camps and his deep involvement in the civil rights movement at the moment of the birth of "black consciousness." A careful reading of these interviews demonstrates that William Styron and Dr. Alvin Poussaint were unlikely to understand each other because they lived in such different worlds. Their debate was less about Nat Turner than it was about themselves and the worlds in which they were rooted.

The epilogue follows Nat Turner into Hollywood, the place where all famous Americans are destined to end their lives. It tells the story of why Nat Turner's face has not yet appeared in movie theaters, and it brings the volume full circle. The culture that obliterated Nat Turner's name, face, and body in 1831; the culture that cannot agree on an appropriate historical monument for the rebellion; the culture whose historians and literary figures repeatedly engage in bitter battles about the memory of its most significant slave rebel—such a culture cannot portray Nat Turner coherently on film. Even in our fantasies, we have been unable to restore the name, face, and body of a man who lost them all so many years ago.

A few final words about how I edited this volume are in order. My overall approach has been to let authors speak in their own voices. This has not been an easy task. I have been studying Nat Turner for the past seven years, and I disagree with many conclusions reached by these authors. The world of Nat Turner scholarship is messy and confusing. If I had tried to clean up all of the inconsistencies, errors, and contradictions generated by my colleagues, I would have produced a radically different book—but it would have been a book that I had authored rather than edited. Readers must be alert to the fact that inconsistency extends even into the stylistic formatting of the essays. A few essays that appear in this volume have been published previously. They are reproduced here as *reprints*, exact duplicates of the way they looked when they first appeared in print. Hence, the essays by Herbert Aptheker, Vincent Harding, and Charles Joyner include formatting styles, especially in the notes, that are inconsistent with each other and with the Oxford University Press style adopted for the newly written essays.

Many people helped and inspired me as I worked on the construction of this book. I want to express my deepest gratitude to the contributors. They have evidenced a professionalism and patience that has won my admiration and respect. My friend Catherine Clinton, and my Oxford editor Susan Ferber have been enormously helpful—Catherine in getting the project into the right hands at Oxford, and Susan for gently and skillfully managing the book through to publication. I would also like to thank my filmmaker colleagues, Frank Christopher and Charles Burnett. Their intelligence, skill, and deep moral commitment inspired me as we worked together on *Nat Turner ~ A Troublesome Property*. Dean Michael R. Ronayne at Suffolk University created the kind of supportive atmosphere that makes it possible to engage in serious scholarship. My colleagues in the history department at Suffolk—Sharon Lenzie, Susan Keefe, Lauri Umanski, John Cavanagh, Michele Plott, Robert Allison, Robert Bellinger, and Robert Hannigan also generously listened, gave advice, and encouraged me every step of the way. Judi Greenberg, Laura Greenberg, Amy Greenberg, Lisa Greenberg, Roslyn Marino, Howard Greenberg, Jean Guttman, the Berwicks, the Guttmans, and the Jacobsons all helped in ways that might surprise them.

I would also like to thank Mary Pat Buckenmeyer, Michael Chapman, Rick Francis, Kitty Futrell, Vivian Lucas, Cheryl Pare-Ikley, and Bruce L. Turner for their generous help at various stages of this project. I owe a special debt of gratitude to James McGee, whose painting graces the cover of this volume. It is a painting that reflects the inspiration of Lavenia McGee, the entire McGee family and friends, and the ancestors that have spoken to him across the generations.

Kenneth S. Greenberg
Suffolk University
Boston, Massachusetts

PART ONE

THE SEARCH FOR
NAT TURNER

—

ONE

Name, Face, Body

—

KENNETH S. GREENBERG

W hat was Nat Turner's name? What did he look like? Where is his body? We can ask these simple questions about any major historical figure and usually expect to discover simple answers. But Nat Turner was no ordinary "major historical figure." He was a slave rebel, deeply and passionately hated by the white people of Virginia who captured and hanged him in 1831. Both his position as a slave and his position as a man who threatened the core values and institutional structures of the antebellum South have made him a difficult figure for historians to reconstruct. The men who tried and hanged him, and then dissected his body, may have done their job of obliteration so well that it will never be possible to put the pieces back together again—neither the pieces of his body nor the pieces of his character and identity. Nat Turner may be destined to live forever in our memory as the most famous, least-known person in American history.

Historians do not readily accept the idea that their knowledge of the past may be limited. They are too often subject to the hubris common among men and women who work in quiet libraries or sit at desks and believe that they can reconstruct a dead world from the shards of a pot, or that they can reconstruct the life of a slave from a few marks on a page. Humility, deep humility about the limits of our knowledge, seems a better way to approach the reconstruction of a man like Nat Turner.

Consider Nat Turner's name. At first glance, the issue may not seem complicated. Nat Turner's name was, obviously, "Nat Turner." No historian has ever asserted otherwise. If only things were that easy in the world of American slavery and race relations. It is worth examining this matter in some detail, for the inquiry can tell us a great deal—perhaps not about Nat Turner, but certainly about who we were and are as a nation and as a people in continuous racial division and turmoil.

Names have always been one of the most important points of contest and conflict between blacks and whites in America. And battles over names are never trivial matters. It is of great consequence whether you are called "black" or "colored," "Negro" or "African American." It is of great consequence whether you are Cassius Clay or Mohammed Ali. To name a piece of the world is to define it and to assert control over it. Moreover, our naming systems create order for us in the universe. Hence, how we name ourselves and what we name ourselves carry symbolic meanings that cut to the very heart of who we are as individuals and who we are as a people. We assert our dignity and our place in the social order through our names. It is little wonder that many cultures attribute magical significance to a person's name, or that the naming of a child is often accompanied by a religious ritual, or that religious conversion or entry into adulthood is frequently marked by the assumption of a new name.

Almost universally, the process of enslavement typically began with an attempt to rename a newly enslaved person. This is one of the ways in which masters asserted the destruction of a slave's old identity and the imposition of a new one. One witness on a slave ship anchored off the coast of Africa in 1797 noted that the first African man and woman brought on board were always renamed "Adam" and "Eve"—new names for newly created people. Once the slaves were on a plantation in the Americas, many masters also attempted to rename them. Robert "King" Carter, one of the largest eighteenth-century planters of the Chesapeake area, remarked, "I name'd them here" and instructed that the overseers should take "care that the negros . . . always go by ye names we gave them."[1]

Enslaved people resisted this renaming practice in countless ways. The modes of resistance varied with time and place. During the early years of North American slavery, many enslaved people retained their African names among themselves—especially on large plantations on which masters could not easily manage every detail of slave life. These old names often persisted secretly; or sometimes a new name became accepted because it resembled a name with African associations. Moreover, in large areas of the South, enslaved people successfully asserted the authority to name their own children—and in so doing linked them to a larger network of kin and ancestors.[2]

To understand that the naming of slaves was contested terrain is to set the stage for an appreciation of the problem of Nat Turner's name. It is best to begin with the recognition that, legally, in nineteenth-century Virginia, as in virtually all slave societies, a slave had no surname. This was no trivial matter. The denial of a legal family name was one of the most powerful symbolic ways in which masters asserted their dominance while simultaneously affirming the slavish condition of the people they owned. One of the distinguishing features of slavery, in the minds of masters, was that a slave had no binding legal relationship with kin. Enslaved husbands and wives, and enslaved parents and children, could make no legal claims on each other. The central relationship recognized under the law was the relationship of master and slave. That is why masters had the legal freedom to sell slaves away from their own families.

The denial of a legal last name was also part of the larger process by which masters excluded slaves from participating in the culture of honor reserved for the master class. It was only free people who could express honor and respect for each other by using last names. It was only free people who could further embellish their names with honorific titles such as Mr., Colonel, or Sir. Slaves, at least in the minds of masters, possessed only a simple and humble first name.[3]

So the man who would one day become widely known as Nat Turner was most commonly known as "Nat" among the people who owned him in Southampton County, Virginia. This was the name used in the few legal documents that mention him before 1831. He was referred to as "Nat" in the 1822 inventory of the estate of his deceased master.[4] And "Nat" was almost certainly the name used for him in the common speech of white people of the county.

Actually, there is a possibility that he was occasionally called Nat Turner before 1831. Sometimes slaves became associated with the family names of their masters in legal documents of the era. For example, the trial records of the participants in the 1831 rebellion repeatedly referred to slaves with formula phrases such as "*Daniel* a Negro man slave the property of Richard Porter," or "Moses, the property of Thomas Barrow."[5] This kind of linkage was essential, and not just for demarcating the lines of property. Southampton County was a community in which many enslaved people shared a common first name, and the only way to differentiate them from one another, at least for whites, was to refer to the name of the master. For example, the trial records of the rebels of 1831 refer to many slaves with exactly the same names: three Bens, three Daniels, three Davys, three Harrys, three Joes, three Nathans, three Stephens, four Henrys, four Jims, four Nelsons, and seven men named Sam.[6] This proliferation of names has been a source of confusion for historians, and it must also have confounded many in antebellum Southampton County. Outside the courtroom, whites typically shortened legal formulations such as "*Daniel* a Negro man slave the property of Richard Porter" into the simpler "Porter's Daniel"—and, on occasion, even "Daniel Porter." Perhaps Nat Turner became associated with his surname in just this manner.[7]

However, Nat Turner had been sold to Thomas Moore in 1822. When Moore died in 1828, Turner became the property of his son, Putnam Moore. Yet there is no evidence that anyone ever called him "Moore's Nat" or "Nat Moore." Moreover, shortly before the rebellion, Joseph Travis had married the mother of Putnam Moore. Although Travis was the family name associated with the household in which Nat Turner was enslaved in 1831, there is little evidence that Nat Turner ever became "Nat Travis."[8]

How did "Nat" become so closely associated with the Turner name? Nat Turner was born in 1800, the slave of Benjamin Turner. When Benjamin died in 1810, Nat Turner became the property of Benjamin's younger brother, Samuel Turner. Nat Turner seems to have kept his association with the Turner family name even after Samuel Turner died in 1822 and he was sold into the Moore family. It is difficult to know how much of this association with the Turner name was imposed by whites and how much was created by Nat Turner himself, his family, or other members of the black community. We know that, during the time of slavery, some African Americans chose surnames that they either kept in secret or overtly asserted and that had been informally accepted by communities of black and white people.[9] We have no evidence that Nat Turner did this, but it is certainly possible. We also know that when slavery ended and African Americans could select their own legal last names, they sometimes chose the family names of their original owners rather than a completely new name or the name of a more recent owner. We can, at least in part, understand this as an assertion of the autonomy of newly freed people—as an act that involved going back to an original name with which they felt a connection—perhaps a surname that linked them to kin in the community.[10] So, if we read the values expressed by this post-emancipation naming practice back into the time of slavery, we can see that, ironically, Nat and Turner may have become connected with each other by some combination of an assertion of black autonomy and of white mastery. In other words, Nat Turner might have chosen his name for his own reasons, and whites might have chosen the same name for different reasons. Of course, this is all just speculation, since we really know nothing definitive about the use of the name "Nat Turner" before the moment of the rebellion.

However, this is only the beginning of the story of Nat Turner's name. The person many people call Nat Turner today was actually referred to by many other names during and after the rebellion of 1831. The newspapers of Virginia devoted a large amount of space to the insurrection. They relied on correspondents who were residents of Southampton County or who traveled to the county with militia units. A reader of Virginia newspapers published in the aftermath of the rebellion was exposed to a wide variety of names for the leader of the rebellion. Some accounts certainly called the rebel leader "Nat," but he was more frequently known as "Nat Turner." Also, quite often, his name appeared as "Gen. Nat Turner," "General Nat Turner," "Gen. Nat," "The Preacher-Captain," "The General," or "Capt. Nat."[11]

It is important not to misunderstand this widespread use of honorific attachments to Nat Turner's name in the Virginia newspapers of 1831.

Such titles were not intended to honor the man, but to mock him. For white Southerners, an inflated title next to the name of a slave was the functional equivalent of naming him after a great warrior or leader of the ancient world. To call a slave "Cato," "Caesar," "Hercules," or "General" was to create what appeared to masters as an oxymoron designed to generate contempt rather than respect.[12] One can sense this intention in the way several newspapers noted that Nat "calls himself General."[13] In their view of the world, a real man of honor achieves his position by being honored by others; only a man with no honor must resort to bestowing a title upon himself. One can also sense the mockery in the way newspapers would, in a single article, switch between calling Nat Turner "General" or "Captain" or "Nat"—something they would never do to local white leaders like Colonel Trezvant or General Broadnax.[14] When these newspapers really wished to use a title to honor a man, the title had a stability and consistency lacking in those that they attached to Nat Turner. No newspaper ever referred to Colonel Trezvant or General Broadnax by their first names alone or suddenly switched their rank to captain.

It must also be noted that when newspapers referred to Nat Turner as "General" or "Captain" they were not inventing the titles themselves. These were actually honorific titles awarded to Nat Turner by the black community. It is possible to gain some understanding of 1831 African-American names for Nat Turner from the trial records of the rebels. These records are not exactly an unmediated source of African-American voices. Although many blacks did testify at the trials, a white clerk transcribed and often paraphrased the testimony. Still, it is startling to discover that no African-American voice (even if filtered through a white person) called the rebel leader "Nat Turner," and hardly anyone called him "Nat." Typically, he was "Captain Nat" or "General Nat"—names that were simultaneously honorific and intimate, using both a military rank and a first name.[15] Moreover, unlike white use of the titles "General" and "Captain," the African Americans who called him those names really intended honor, and not mockery. In a world so deeply divided along racial lines, even a single name, such as "General Nat," was really two names with two meanings, depending on whether or not it was uttered by a black or a white voice.

The official legal documents of the rebellion tell a different story of Nat Turner's name. Here we can sense another kind of struggle. Since a slave had no legal surname, the courts and other legal authorities could not simply call him "Nat Turner." They certainly couldn't use "General" or "Captain," since they didn't want to sanction titles they considered fraudulent. On the other hand, the name "Nat" probably didn't seem entirely adequate for a man who had become so famous and was already so widely known as "Nat Turner."

One can see the struggle to use and not to use the name "Nat Turner" in several official sources. The trial court reached an awkward solution by calling him "Nat alias Nat Turner"—thereby simultaneously denying and affirming his surname.[16] The reward notice issued by Governor Floyd for the capture of Nat Turner shows similar evidence of a struggle. It begins with reference to "Nat, otherwise called Nat Turner" and then calls him "Nat" elsewhere in the document.[17] The Governor's Council, an important advisory group meeting in Richmond, demonstrated the same ambivalence. In one session they call the rebel leader "Nat or Nat Turner," in another they decided he was "Nat alias Nat Turner," and in a third he became just "Nat Turner."[18] Edward Butts, deputy sheriff of Southampton County, evidenced a similar problem with Nat Turner's name. When local white farmer Benjamin Phipps captured and delivered the rebel leader, Butts gave him a receipt for "Nat Turner," but it was "Nat" whose death by hanging he certified several days later.[19]

However, the single most influential "naming" of Nat Turner cannot be found in newspapers, trial records, or official government records. It is contained in Thomas R. Gray's *Confessions of Nat Turner*. The published document containing *The Confessions* consists of several elements: Thomas R. Gray's introductory remarks addressed to the reader; court documents certifying the authenticity of the confession; the confession itself—purporting to be in the voice of Nat Turner, yet actually containing the voices of both Gray and Turner; asides embedded in the confession and addressed to the reader in Gray's voice; a copy of Nat Turner's trial record as reinvented and modified by Gray; and lists of whites killed and slaves tried in the rebellion.[20] As one might expect in a document with so many elements, Nat Turner is given several names throughout the different texts—"Nat," "Nat Turner," and "Nat, alias Nat Turner." But the central point to be made about *The Confessions of Nat Turner* is not that it contains multiple names, but that it actually marks the triumph of a single name: Nat Turner. Here, a reader can find no references to "Captain Nat" or "General Nat"; here, the court unequivocally addresses the rebel leader as "Nat Turner," and not as "Nat, alias Nat Turner"; and here, in the list of slaves tried for the rebellion, every slave but one is given only a first name. The only slave with a surname is "Nat Turner." And, most importantly, on the cover of *The Confessions*, the name "Nat Turner" is presented in large bold print at the center of a title.

The publication of *The Confessions* is a key naming moment in the life of Nat Turner—even though it occurred after his death. Yet, as with everything else connected with Turner's name, it generates more questions than it answers. Consider the possibilities. Who did the naming? Nat Turner certainly didn't write *The Confessions* directly, and he certainly did not select the title. So it was Thomas R. Gray who named Turner in this document. But Gray did not invent the name "Nat Turner." Many others had already used it. Perhaps, as I have already suggested, Nat Turner himself initially selected the name. Or perhaps the whites who owned him chose it. Or perhaps it was the result of a kind of negotiation between Turner and his owners.

Or maybe we should look at it in a different way. Nat Turner's actions as the leader of a rebellion may have compelled Thomas R. Gray and the white community to distinguish him from other slaves by acknowledging his surname—even as they tried to obliterate his body and his memory from their landscape. White Southerners might continue to hate him, but Turner himself had forced them to hate him as "Nat Turner," and not as "Nat." Perhaps one of the greatest achievements of the Nat Turner rebellion went unnoticed by all of the people who lived through it: Nat Turner had not just killed people; he had named himself and permanently changed the way anyone could talk about him.

While there is no evidence that an explicit goal of the rebellion was to change the name of Nat Turner, there is considerable evidence that the larger issue of names and naming was very much in the minds of many African Americans who participated. No participant directly discussed the issue, but the indirect evidence is highly suggestive. We have one surviving published narrative from an escaped slave, John Brown, who spent his early years in Southampton County. While he did not live in the immediate area of the rebellion, he was close enough to have been connected to the same social world as many of the rebels. When he sat down to write the story of his life, nearly 25 years after Nat Turner's hanging, he began his narrative with a discussion of his name. "When in Slavery," he tells us, "I was called Fed. Why I was so named, I cannot tell. I never knew myself by any other name, nor always by that; for it is common for slaves to answer to any name, as it may suit the humour of the master."[21]

This sensitivity to the issue of names in slavery must have been on the minds of the rebels when they named "Hark," one of the key people who joined with Nat Turner in planning the rebellion, "Captain Moore" or "General Moore"; or when they referred to "Davy" as "brother Clements."[22] They must have known exactly what they were doing when they changed the name of Methodist minister Richard Whitehead before they killed him. Whitehead was at work in the fields with a group of his own slaves when the rebels approached. They stopped some distance away and called to him. But instead of addressing him as "Mr. Whitehead," they called him "Dick." The minister should have sensed that this language change indicated that his "white head" was in danger. But he came forward and was promptly dispatched.

The long and complicated saga of Nat Turner's name did not end with his death. In subsequent years, the battle continued on many fronts. In public discourse among southern whites, the name "Nat Turner" nearly vanished in the wake of the rebellion. For example, in early 1832 the Virginia House of Delegates debated the expediency of ending the threat of future insurrections by instituting the gradual abolition of slavery. Yet, among the many speeches delivered on this topic, it is virtually impossible to find the name of the man who triggered the debate. They are full of references to the "Southampton Tragedy" or the "Southampton Affair"—but not to "Nat Turner."[23] This method of naming, used by many other southern whites in subsequent years, had the effect of shifting attention away from the agency of the man who was at the heart of the rebellion—turning it into a kind of uncaused disaster.

Black abolitionists, coming from the opposite side of the political spectrum in antebellum America, also moved away from the name "Nat Turner." But their motives were quite different. Some time after the rebellion, they began to call its leader "Nathaniel Turner." These abolitionists were men who clearly understood the importance of names and naming in the context of American slavery and race relations. Henry Highland Garnet knew exactly what he was doing when he praised "the patriotic Nathaniel Turner" in an 1843 speech to the National Convention of Colored Citizens in Buffalo, New York.[24] The great Frederick Douglass, throughout his long political career, nearly always referred to the leader of the 1831 rebellion as "Nathaniel Turner"—and very occasionally called him "General Turner."[25] Charles Lenox Remond explained the reason for this naming practice in an 1844 speech he delivered in Boston. "Sir," he announced to the audience in a talk full of praise for the rebel hero, "*I will never contemptuously call him Nat Turner*" (emphasis in the original). In other words, the black abolitionists recognized that the name "Nat" was a diminutive form of the name "Nathaniel," and they would not diminish the rebel leader by using the shortened form of what they believed to be his real name. This is a point that both the black and white residents of Southampton County would have completely understood. The trial records show that there were other slaves named "Nat" involved in the rebellion and that there were even some men named "Nathan"—but the full name "Nathaniel" had apparently been reserved for white residents like "Nathaniel Francis." So, the black abolitionists awarded Turner what they considered his *real* name—the name he deserved, rather than the name others might have used for him, or even the name he might have used for himself.

Generally, during the years after slavery ended, the name "Nat Turner" became the conventional way of referring to the slave rebel. This marks the ultimate triumph of the name highlighted by Thomas R. Gray in *The Confessions of Nat Turner*. However there have always been interesting variations and challenges. There is a powerful tradition of African-American folklore about Nat Turner within Southampton County. In this context, Nat Turner is sometimes called "Prophet Nat." More often he is referred to as "Ole Nat," and the rebellion itself is sometimes called "Ole Nat's Fray." In interviews conducted in the 1930s by workers of the Federal Writers Project who recorded the words of Virginians who had once been slaves, the name "Ole Nat" appears several times. Cornelia Carney tells her interviewer that "White folks was sharp . . . but not sharp enough to git by ole Nat"; and Allen Crawford informs another that "Ole Nat was captured at Black Head Sign Post."[26]

This usage must have developed long after the rebellion, since Nat Turner certainly was not old in 1831. He was only 31. The "ole" must be in reference to a man long dead and in the past. The use of "Nat" here is a way of indicating an easy familiarity with the man—although it was a familiarity which did not always signal admiration. "Ole Nat" could be conjured up in African-American folk tradition as a smart, heroic figure, or as a figure who was frightening and threatening.[27]

Another informative use of names for Nat Turner occurs in William Sidney Drewry's *Slave Insurrections in Virginia*. Drewry was a white resident of Virginia who grew up in and around Southampton County in the late nineteenth century. *Slave Insurrections in Virginia*, published in 1900, was based on his Johns Hopkins doctoral dissertation and has become an important and influential work among all subsequent students of the Nat Turner rebellion because Drewry spoke directly with people who had memories of the rebellion, and he worked diligently in the archives of Southampton County. But the way he refers to Nat Turner reveals just how deeply he was trapped in the racial conventions of his time and place. While Drewry makes an occasional reference to "Nat Turner," most commonly he describes the rebel leader as "Nat," evoking a racial condescension that dates back to the time of slavery. When Drewry occasionally calls him "general," the word appears uncapitalized and in quotation marks—to signal to a reader that Turner was not a real general. Even more striking, virtually every white person named in the book, with the exception of John Brown, is given a title—either Mr., Mrs., Colonel, or General; no black person ever receives a title, and most are identified only by their first names. Such a naming practice offers a strong clue that a modern audience needs to read this book with great care. It can still be read usefully—but only if a reader understands its limitations. It presents a view of the rebellion seen through the eyes of a white man trapped in the racial conventions of the nineteenth century.[28]

One other significant period in which Nat Turner's name was an issue was during the 1960s controversy surrounding William Styron's Pulitzer Prize–winning novel *The Confessions of Nat Turner*. The problem of Nat Turner's name in William Styron's novel never reached the level of public discussion reserved for the issue of Turner's sexuality. In fact, any reader of the prodigious amount of writing generated by that controversy might easily remain unaware of the name difficulty. But the problem of American race relations runs so deep in the culture that every issue involving race that is a subject of public discussion is always evocative of a host of other issues not so fully discussed. The public discussion about William Styron's novel seemed to center on a host of factual questions. Did Nat Turner have a wife? Could he have lusted after the beautiful and very white Margaret Whitehead? Did Turner have ambivalent feelings about the black community? Why did he personally kill only one woman during the course of the rebellion? Did he display courage during the rebellion?

Of course, what made and still makes the controversy over Styron's novel one that reveals so much about American race relations is that it never really was about what it seemed to be about. It was about something much deeper, and the name issue can offer us just a glimpse of the hidden complexity. Some recent remarks made by Dr. Alvin F. Poussaint point the way. During the 1960s, he was one of ten black intellectuals who wrote essays, published as *William Styron's Nat Turner: Ten Black Writers Respond*, attacking Styron's novel.[29] During an interview, Dr. Poussaint reflected on his work in the years just before he encountered William Styron's novel.[30] Between 1965 and 1967, he had been very active in the civil rights movement, serving for two years as Southern Field Director of the Medical Committee for Human Rights in Jackson, Mississippi, in support of workers involved in voter registration. It was during this period that Dr. Poussaint experienced a deeply disturbing encounter involving his own name—and, symbolically, the names of many other black people in America.

Dr. Poussaint began his narration of this encounter by describing a street scene in a small Mississippi town.

> I was walking with my secretary, and a police car pulled up next to me and they jumped out. They ran up to me and said, "Where are you going, where you going, boy?" I said, "To my office." They said, "What's your name, boy?" I said, "Dr. Poussaint." So, [the officer] moved closer to me and he said, "What's your first name, boy?" I stared at him. He put his hand on his gun and said, "What's your first name, boy?" My secretary was from Hattiesburg, Mississippi, [and she] kept yanking on my other arm, "Tell him your first name, tell him your first name." [The officer] kept coming forward, kept making more threatening moves, said, "Tell me your first name, boy." Finally, I said, "Alvin." He said, "Thank you, Alvin, now go on get out of here. Next time we are taking you down to the courthouse." I mean, I was . . . diminished, psychologically, that he had forced me into doing what he wanted me to do, to demean myself right in front of him to let me know that he was a police officer, I was a doctor. He was the superior one and I better get that message.[31]

This type of encounter was not unique to the experience of Dr. Poussaint. It not only linked him to many other African Americans of our era, but to many others, extending into the deep past—back to the newly captured people renamed Adam and Eve on a slave ship, back to the men and women renamed on the plantation of Robert "King" Carter, and back to Nat Turner. And so, when Dr. Poussaint first read William Styron's novel, he was extremely sensitive to issues involving names and naming in American race relations. As he later described it, "I was very, very aware and conscious of that practice of dehumanizing black people by not giving them their full name, only calling them by their first names, that is what the slaveholders did with their slaves. . . . This was part of white supremacy practice and racial etiquette to do that. So, in the book, when [William Styron] is referring to Nat Turner only as 'Nat,' it just stirred up memories of that. I said, I wonder if Styron maybe is doing that in some unconscious way because he also is part of this culture that sees black people in terms of their first names and not their full names."

In his published essay, Dr. Poussaint began his critique of the novel by first quoting Styron's introductory reference to "Nat." And then he rhetorically asked, "Is this familiarity by the author part of intuitive white condescension and adherence to southern racial etiquette? Is this reference and the entire book an unconscious attempt to keep Nat Turner 'in his place'—to emasculate him? Would the novelist expect Nat Turner to address him as 'Mr. Styron?'"[32]

It is deeply ironic and quite startling that Dr. Poussaint's critique of Stryon's novel appeared in a volume of the collected essays of African Americans in which Nat Turner is constantly referred to as "Nat." While Dr. Poussaint himself carefully called the slave rebel only by two names, his essay was surrounded by others that repeatedly referred to Nat Turner as "Nat"—even using titles for their essays such as "You've Taken My Nat and Gone" or "Nat's Last White Man." Of course, as Dr. Pousssaint and the other black intellectuals clearly understood the matter, the name "Nat" had a completely different meaning when affectionately and intimately used by 1960s African Americans who clearly admired the rebel leader than when it was used by the white writer William Styron.

The name issue, as it appeared in this critique of William Styron, tells us much about why the entire Styron controversy generated such passion and seemed (and still seems) so intractable. It gives us a peek at the way language becomes fractured in a racially divided society. The name "Nat" was at least as fractured in 1967 as the name "General Nat" had been in 1831.

But in 1967 the name "Nat" had an additional element of instability. From everything we know about William Styron, it seems clear that he did not *consciously* intend to use "Nat" in a derogatory way.[33] Even Dr. Poussaint did not accuse Styron of a conscious intention to demean Nat Turner by using only his first name. And so "Nat" entered the conversation between William Styron and his critics quite thoroughly fractured—not just split into a word of double meanings, but also into one of unintended and unconscious meanings.

The shattering of language and meaning is both a cause and consequence of a shattered social world. Dr. Poussaint's experience of being compelled to name himself "Alvin" in a small Mississippi town shaped, for him, the meaning of "Nat" as it emerged from the mouth of William Styron. It was a meaning not consciously intended by the author, but it was also a meaning that Styron could not control since it was rooted so deeply in Dr. Poussaint's experience. In a world in which experience, language, and meaning had been so deeply fragmented, conversation and communication became virtually impossible.

It is now easy to see that the simple question "What was Nat Turner's name?" does not have a simple answer. He was called "Nat" by masters before 1831, by nineteenth- and twentieth-century whites adhering to the values of southern racial etiquette, by William Styron, and by twentieth-century African Americans who identified with him and considered him a hero. He was "Nat Turner" to some masters, to some antebellum southern newspapers, to Thomas R. Gray in *The Confessions of Nat Turner,* and to most modern scholars. He was "Nat alias Nat Turner" at his trial. He was "General Nat" in the view of followers who sought to honor him, and "General Nat" in the view of whites who hoped to demean him. He was "Nathaniel Turner" in the eyes of black abolitionists. And he was "Prophet Nat" or "Ole Nat" in the folk memory of many African Americans. But we don't know what Nat Turner's mother and father called him; and we don't know, and we can never know, what he called himself.[34] So, in what sense can we say that we know Nat Turner's name?

Now let us turn to another simple question. What did Nat Turner look like? Do we have an image of the man? Strong evidence suggests that someone drew a portrait of Nat Turner during the few days that the rebel leader sat in his jail cell awaiting trial and execution. The *Norfolk Herald* of 14 November 1831, reported that Thomas R. Gray had taken Turner's confession "which he intends to publish with an accurate likeness of the brigand, taken by Mr. *John Crawley,* portrait painter of this town [Norfolk], to be lithographed by *Endicott and Swett,* of Baltimore." However, copies of this lithograph and this edition of *The Confessions* have never been found.[35]

The closest we can come to knowing what Nat Turner might have looked like would be to examine a reward notice issued by Virginia Governor John Floyd. During the 70 days that Nat Turner eluded capture, he was pursued by white Virginians in one of the most massive manhunts in the history of the state. The governor desperately wanted to catch the notorious rebel, and so he requested a detailed description by residents of Southampton County who knew him well. William C. Parker responded with a written sketch of the man: "He is between 30 & 35 years old—five feet six or eight inches high—weighs between 150 & 160 rather bright complexion but not a mulatto—broad-shouldered—large flat nose—large eyes—broad flat feet rather knock-kneed—walk brisk and active—hair on the top of the head very thin—no beard except on the up-per lip and the tip of the chin. A scar on one of his temples produced by the kick of a mule—also one on the back of his neck by a bite—a large knot on one of the bones of his right arm near the wrist produced by a blow—." Governor Floyd then issued an official reward notice based on this portrait, but with a few minor changes. He referred to the rebel leader as "Nat" and omitted the causes of Turner's scars and knot.[36]

This is an interesting description of a man. Several things can be said about it. Most importantly, we need to understand it as being exactly what it was. It was a "wanted" poster. It was written by a white resident of Southampton County and was designed to be useful to the men seeking to capture Nat Turner. That is why it lingers over certain details such as scars and knots. Given the powerful desire to capture Nat Turner, we can be certain that this description offers a "true likeness" of the man, but it is a true likeness seen through a particular set of eyes—the eyes of the master class in search of a fugitive. It was a "true likeness" intended for a specific purpose at a specific time.

Think about this. Suppose you were to conjure up an image of yourself as you might be sketched on a "wanted" poster. Now imagine yourself as you appear in family photo albums, or as you might be described by a friend or a member of your family. A "true likeness" can vary quite a bit depending on who is producing it and for what purpose. Would Nat Turner's family and followers have described him as having "broad flat feet rather knock-kneed?" Would they have lingered over his scars and knot? His mother might have commented on his resemblance to another member of his family; his followers might have detected a dignity missing in a "wanted" poster. We will never see or be able accurately to imagine such images; nor will we ever know how Nat Turner might have described himself.

The reward notice also raises the issue of Nat Turner's skin color. It tells us that Turner had a "rather bright complexion" but that he was "not a mulatto." It is difficult to know the precise meaning of such a description. Clearly, in 1831 in Virginia, skin color was of vital importance. It was a central way of distinguishing African Americans from white people as well as from each other. Hence, it served as a key part of a description that would be used to capture a fugitive. To note that Turner was "bright" but not "mulatto" most likely meant that he was light skinned, but not so light as to be obviously of mixed racial background.

The portion of Nat Turner's description regarding his skin color has had an interesting history since Governor Floyd first issued his reward notice. Almost as soon as Floyd described Nat Turner as "bright," there emerged powerful social forces working to darken his color. It happened almost immediately. As soon as Nat Turner was captured, an eyewitness reported that he had seen Turner and that "[h]e answers exactly the description annexed to the Governor's Proclamation, except that he is of a darker hue, and his eyes, though large are not prominent—they are very long, deeply seated in his head, and have rather a sinister expression." This description was obviously written by someone who was very familiar with the Governor's reward notice. Yet he saw something different in his actual encounter with Turner. For this man, the real Nat Turner appeared far more threatening than the officially described Nat Turner—and the "sinister" eyes and "darker hue" seem part of a reinterpretation that turned the rebel leader into a much more frightening figure.[37]

Many others have made a similar "reinterpretation" of Nat Turner's skin color—although often for quite different reasons. For example, in Harriett Beecher Stowe's 1856 novel *Dred*, the title character is a slave based on the historical Nat Turner, and yet she imagines him as "a tall black man, of magnificent stature and proportions. His skin was intensely black and polished like marble." Stowe chose to envision the slave rebel as an exotic figure, very black and very noble.[38]

William S. Drewry, the turn-of-the-century local white historian who repeatedly called Nat Turner "Nat," darkened the rebel leader's skin for quite different reasons. He described Turner as a "stout, black Negro of the pure African type."[39] This is extraordinary, since Drewry was very familiar with the original sources and almost certainly was aware of the reward notice and its reference to Turner's "bright complexion." There is no evidence that Drewry consciously lied about this matter. More plausibly, given his racial sensibilities, he could not help but see Nat Turner as a man who committed horrible atrocities and therefore as a man who must have been very black.

John W. Cromwell, the African-American teacher, writer, and activist, also darkened Nat Turner in his 1920 article published in the *Journal of Negro History*. He tells us that Turner "was of unmixed African lineage with the true Negro face." While such a description does not explicitly address the issue of skin color, it strongly suggests a black color and certainly makes no mention of a "bright complexion." Stephen Oates, the most recent major biographer of Nat Turner, also presents Turner as very dark. He tells us that Turner's "fierce eyes, broad shoulders, and brisk knock-kneed walk made him seem larger than he was. At 30 years old, Nat stood around five feet seven and weighed about 150 pounds. He now wore a mustache and cultivated a tuft of whiskers on his chin. He was a striking man, this coal-black Prophet, with his whiskers, moody expressions, and trembling, articulate voice." What is most startling about this description is that it clearly paraphrases Governor John Floyd's description of Turner in several particulars and yet it changes Turner from a man who was "bright . . . but not a mulatto" into a man who was a "coal-black Prophet."[40]

What is going on here? It seems clear that the darkening of Nat Turner was determined by multiple factors in the culture. White racist writers wanted Nat Turner to be very black, since it reinforced the racial stereotype of the slave rebel as an African savage. African-American writers who admired Nat Turner wanted him to be very black because they saw him as a noble representative of the race. Other writers darkened Turner for a mixture of these reasons and others.

The issue of skin color reappeared in altered form during the 1960s confrontation between William Styron and the "Ten Black Writers." One of the most striking features of that controversy is that at no time did either Styron or his critics refer to the face of Nat Turner. Styron wrote his novel in the first person, creating an imagined world as seen through the eyes of Nat Turner. Such a point of view never required that he actually describe the man. In fact, Styron apparently never had an image of Turner's face in his own mind as he wrote the novel.[41] Moreover, since so much of the black criticism attacked Styron's imaginings, Turner's face never appeared in their work either. Of course, the critics offer multiple references to "black Nat Turner," and it was the "blackness" of Nat Turner that they were defending against what they saw as Styron's attempt to "whiten" him. Yet, while the phrase "black Nat Turner" may have implied a dark skin color to many readers, it was centrally intended as a larger statement about race and culture, and not about the actual physical features of the man.[42] In fact, the controversy of the 1960s offers us a view of the real Nat Turner as a man with a "blank" face rather than as one with a "black" or a "bright" face.

James McGee, a man who is today a "keeper of the memory" of Nat Turner and his fellow rebels in the black community of Southampton County, adds an additional layer of meaning and significance to the issue of Nat Turner's complexion. McGee has no formal training as a historian and little formal education of any kind. Yet he is an extraordinary historian and artist—a brilliant man who listens to and takes seriously the oral traditions of his community. It was he who first brought to my attention the "bright complexion . . . but not a mulatto" reference in Governor Floyd's reward notice. To my knowledge, he is the first scholar to have paid any significant attention to that phrasing.

James McGee believes that Floyd's description of Turner is evidence that has been overlooked by professional historians but has been widely recognized in the folk traditions of Virginia's African-American community: it is evidence that Nat Turner was the son of his master. Benjamin Turner had raped Nat Turner's mother.[43]

When James McGee first read that Turner was "bright" but "not a mulatto," he understood it as a double statement. McGee believed that the white community of 1831 was anxious to capture Nat Turner and hence was compelled—just this one time—to describe his true "bright" color. And yet this same community felt equally compelled to cover up a possible implication of this color. They had to deny that Turner was of mixed racial background, assert that he was "not a mulatto," in order to avoid casting a shadow over the reputation of a man they regarded as a benevolent master. McGee had noticed the tension in the two parts of the description—"bright," but "not a mulatto"—and, given his intimate experience of southern race relations, was quick to draw the conclusion that the phrasing was intended to hide the fact that a master was the father of the most famous slave rebel in American history. In this same context, McGee was not at all surprised to discover that Turner became known by the surname of his first master. They were kin.

What should we make of this analysis? First, it is important to note that James McGee developed his understanding of the written description of Nat Turner because he was willing to take seriously the oral traditions of his community. These oral traditions gave him a way of listening to black voices unmediated by white interpretations. Given his experience of southern race relations, McGee had learned to approach written documents with great skepticism. He took the oral record seriously and used it to probe written words and to discover meanings otherwise buried. He knew all about the ways in which people "transformed" descriptions of skin color in order to conform them to racial stereotypes.

Second, there is a lesson in this analysis for historians who do not take seriously the folk traditions of the black community. Virginia today has many African Americans who believe they are descendants of Nat Turner. If one searches for these people in written accounts, it is very difficult to find them. They are an extraordinary group of people whose voices should be heard. The historical profession and our larger community are greatly diminished if we do not listen to them.

Third, it is important to recognize that we must be very careful to consider all of the facts before we actually conclude that Nat Turner was the son of his master. James McGee has opened a line of thinking that we must consider seriously. However, there are many ways to read the sources—both the written and oral ones. After all, in *The Confessions*, Nat Turner does tell us twice (through the pen of Thomas R. Gray) that his father was a slave. When Turner was a child, both his mother and his father encouraged him to believe that he was "intended for some great purpose." Later, we learn that Turner's father "escaped" from slavery to "some other part of the country."[44] As with virtually every subject connected with the Nat Turner rebellion, the evidence moves us in more than one direction simultaneously.

Now let us turn to the question of Nat Turner's body. What happened to it? Where is it? We know that Nat Turner was hanged in Jerusalem, Southampton County, Virginia, on 11 November 1831. One newspaper account of the event claimed that "General Nat sold his body for dissection, and spent the money on ginger cakes."[45] Part of this description is almost certainly true and part is certainly false.

It seems likely that Turner's body was dissected after death. Dissection of executed slaves served a dual function in antebellum Virginia. The white community saw it as a sign of contempt and an additional humiliation to the person executed. Hence, dissection or some other kind of bodily mutilation was a common fate of slave rebels. Moreover, dissection served the educational needs of medical students and doctors desperate for bodies to probe. In fact, at the very moment of Nat Turner's execution there existed an unusually high demand for cadavers at the medical department of the University of Virginia. Between September 1831 and February 1832—the period during which Nat Turner was hanged—16 graves had been robbed in Richmond and their contents sold for shipment to Charlottesville. Doctors were definitely on the prowl in Virginia in 1831.[46]

However, the report that Turner sold his body for "ginger cakes" is certainly false. No one paid him for the use of his body when he was alive. Why would they do so upon his death? This kind of report was likely just another way to humiliate and dishonor the slave rebel.

Since 1831, there have been a variety of reports regarding the ultimate fate of Nat Turner's body. We can be certain that something terrible happened to it, but the exact nature of that terrible something remains lost. First, consider William S. Drewry's 1900 description of the fate of Nat Turner's body. He tells us that Turner was skinned, that his skin was made into a purse, that the flesh was turned into grease, and that his head and body were permanently separated. Drewry's information on this matter carries some degree of credibility since he knew the residents of the county intimately, had spoken to people who had lived through the rebellion and its aftermath, and could actually describe the fate of specific body parts. Eyewitnesses had told him that they had seen Nat Turner's skull and that it "resembl[ed] the head of a sheep, and [was] at least three-quarters of an inch thick." He quite specifically informs us that Turner's "skeleton was for many years in the possession of Dr. Massenberg, but has since been misplaced"; and that "Mr. R. S. Barham's father owned a money purse made of his hide."[47]

James McGee tells of a chilling boyhood memory that corroborates one part of Drewry's account. In 1949, in a still-segregated world, in a state still uncomfortable with a full presentation of its racial past, Southampton County was celebrating the bicentennial of its founding with a gala celebration at the athletic field of the white high school in the town of Franklin. The main event was an extraordinary historical pageant organized by the Junior Chamber of Commerce and the Woman's Club. As the young James McGee and other black children watched a history of the county unfold before them from a vantage point literally and symbolically outside the fence that surrounded the field, they were treated to a series of displays and tableaux depicting an early Indian village, pioneers, "the gentlemen of '76," the coming of the railroad, the "War Between the States," the Gay Nineties, Iwo Jima, and much more. What they did not see at this celebration was a depiction of Nat Turner or any mention at all of the existence of slavery.[48] As James McGee remembers it, there was only one small hint of the terrible memories that lay buried in the county. A table of historical artifacts had been placed on display for anyone to examine at the armory nearby. And on that table, McGee later recalled, amidst a variety of artifacts associated with the 1831 rebellion, he saw a purse—a purse with a label stating that it had been made from the skin of

Nat Turner. William S. Drewry had described this object in 1900, and James McGee saw it nearly 50 years later.

None of this is conclusive proof that the purse ever existed. When terrible events happen in a community, morbid imaginings can sometimes surround the real horrors. James McGee himself is aware of the possibility that boyhood memories may be distorted, or that a false label might have been placed beside a purse as part of some sadistic joke. Still, these multiple reports of a purse made from the skin of the rebel leader are disturbing and suggestive.

Aside from the question of Nat Turner's skin, there is also a fog that surrounds Drewry's report of the fate of Nat Turner's head and skeleton. There is considerable evidence that Turner's body is buried somewhere in the town of Courtland (formerly Jerusalem) in Southampton County and that his head may be somewhere in the city of Wooster, Ohio. Strange as this may sound, there are several completely independent pieces of evidence supporting such a claim. The first clue can be found in the memoir of Frances Lawrence Webb, born in 1868 close to the border of Southampton and later a resident of the town of Franklin. Drewry had claimed that Turner's skeleton was not buried, that it had been in the possession of Dr. Massenberg before it had been "misplaced" some time before 1900; and he also implied that Nat Turner's head had been seen relatively recently in the county. Yet, in her memoir, Frances Lawrence Webb, known as "Miss Fanny" to her friends, tells a different story. Nat Turner's "headless body" was buried near the spot where he was hanged, and "[h]is skull, which was found in possession of a local physician at the close of the War Between the States, became the property of the Provost Marshall who dominated the county in the days of reconstruction, and was given by him, as a precious relic, to one of the Northern Universities, where possibly it still remains."[49]

The idea that Nat Turner's head could have ended up at some northern university may, at first, seem rather bizarre. And yet other clues, independently generated, point in the same direction. On 27 August 1902, *The Democrat*, a newspaper in the town of Wooster, Ohio, contained an article about an extraordinary "relic" saved from a fire at the College of Wooster: the skull of Nat Turner. The story had been generated by a visit from Joshua James Herring, a traveler from North Carolina who had close ties to Southampton County. Herring had heard about the head from a local resident and wanted to know more. The newspaper told about Herring's visit and included a plausible story about how Turner's skull had somehow found its way to the college. The head reportedly had arrived in town for some unknown reason during 1866—a date consistent with the time period suggested by Frances Lawrence Webb. It first had been placed on display in the office of Dr. Leander Firestone. My recent check of census and local biographical records confirms that Dr. Firestone was, in fact, practicing medicine in Wooster in 1866 and had a special interest in anatomy. Moreover, the skull had come with an affidavit of authenticity, signed by residents of Southampton County with family names common to the area. Dr. Firestone had used the skull in discussions with medical students at the college. By the time the college burned down in 1901, the head had been placed in its museum collection, and it became one of the few objects tossed clear of the conflagration.[50]

One other independent piece of evidence suggests that the head of Nat Turner was at the College of Wooster well into the twentieth century. This evidence is contained in the papers of William Styron. Styron received many letters from readers in response to his 1967 novel on Nat Turner. One was from a dentist who remembered an early visit to Wooster. As a boy (probably some time during the 1920s), he had visited the biology building at the college. There, he found "all kinds of glass cases filled with all kinds of marine life preserved in pallid eternity by formaldehyde"; he found "fossils of all kinds" and "Indian relics"—and, most horrific of all, he found a human head with a paper pasted across the forehead stating: "This is the skull of Nate [*sic*] Turner. A Negro slave who lead an unsuccessful revolt against the white owners in 1831." This correspondent told Styron that, as a result of that initial visit, he had become fascinated with the object and returned repeatedly to view it, last observing the head in 1948—just a year before James McGee may have encountered a different body part of Nat Turner in Southampton County.[51]

So Nat Turner's head may very well be somewhere in Wooster, Ohio, today. Maybe and maybe not. As always in the Nat Turner story, there are other possibilities and clues pointing in other directions. During the course of the slave rebellion, militia units cut off many heads. "Henry" was decapitated. One cavalry company reportedly cut off the heads of 15 rebels. One or more heads may have been displayed at a location in the county known as "Blackhead Signpost." There are reports that several of these heads were not buried and that whites carried them around as trophies. It seems clear that in 1831, more than one African-American head was in circulation within Southampton County.[52] So when a head emerges from the shadows at a later time, the authenticity is always uncertain. The heads of Southampton County are not catalogued according to modern archival standards. Any heads that circulated within the county, within the state, or within the national circuit of "phrenologists" could have been falsely labeled at any time. The head of "Nate Turner" displayed in Wooster certainly belonged to some human treated in the most inhumane way possible, but it may or may not have belonged to the historical Nat Turner.

Even if there was only one Southampton County head, it has never been described the same way twice. Drewry said it "resembl[ed] the head of a sheep, and [was] at least three-quarters of an inch thick." The newspaper editor in Wooster in 1902 characterized it as "a large skull, of fine contour, of well developed brain, of a man 34 years old." And William

Styron's correspondent tells us that it was "quite large and complete with jaw bone and large white teeth. The bone itself was gray and pitted like weathered concrete." Were all these men describing the same object, or two, or three?

Moreover, I have contacted many people who attended the College of Wooster in the 1940s. Other than the one report in the letter to Styron, no one else has seen the "Nate Turner" head. Several respondents thought it was inconceivable that such a head could have been placed on display at the college as late as 1948. Others noted that they had daily entered the building in which the head was supposed to have been on display—and they never saw it. One had been active in the early civil rights movement and believed that such an object, if it really did exist, would have caused an uproar on campus.

Also, within the papers of William Styron there quietly rests another letter, from another gentleman—a man from Elkhart, Indiana. "I have in my possession a skull," he volunteers, "which I believe to be that of Nat Turner. . . . The skull was given to me by my father who inherited it from his. My grandfather was a doctor who practiced in Richmond, Virginia, around the turn of the century. The skull was given to him by a female patient whose name is not known. She claimed to have gotten it from her father who was a physician in attendance when Nat Turner was executed." And, as always, this skull came with yet another description: It was "in poor shape and minus the lower jaw and all the teeth. There is a large fracture all across the crown and the top has been separated from the remainder."[53] Nat Turner's head certainly gets around.

And then there is John W. Cromwell's description in his 1920 *Journal of Negro History* article. He tells us that Turner's body was given to the surgeons for dissection, that he was "skinned to supply such souvenirs as purses, his flesh made into grease, and his bones divided to be handed down as trophies." Moreover, Cromwell claims, "It is said that there still lives a Virginian who has a piece of his skin which was tanned, that another Virginian possesses one of his ears and that the skull graces the collection of a physician in the city of Norfolk."[54]

So it seems quite clear that Nat Turner's head is in Wooster, Ohio; or Elkhart, Indiana; or Southampton County, Virginia; or Norfolk, Virginia; or perhaps in some other place.

It should come as no surprise to discover that if you visit Southampton County today you will not be able to visit the grave of Nat Turner. Local historians, both African American and white, can point out the general area of the abandoned lot and paved-over roadway where the rebels, and perhaps parts of Nat Turner, may once have been buried. But the absence of any physical marker at all stands as a cultural marker that something terrible happened here, that something has been so utterly destroyed and scattered that it can, as yet, have no place of memory.

We do not know the name of Nat Turner. We do not know what he looked like. We cannot find his body. The horrible and disturbing lesson to be learned from our absence of knowledge about all of this is that we cannot escape from our past. We live in a world, and have long lived in a world, that is deeply fractured—a world in which the body parts, images, and name of one of the most important figures in American history have been shattered into a thousand fragments. And all our efforts may never suffice to put the pieces back together again.

It is a troubling legacy of slavery and the way it has destroyed our knowledge of enslaved peoples that one of the most important African Americans of the nineteenth century may be lost to us in a deep way. The world that dissected Nat Turner's body after he was hanged may also have permanently damaged our ability to reconstruct him in our histories. Our search for Nat Turner repeatedly directs us down a hallway lined with endless mirrors in which we are forever destined to see little more than the reflections of our own faces.

TWO

The Construction of *The Confessions of Nat Turner*

DAVID F. ALLMENDINGER, JR.

> I began a cross examination, and found his statement corroborated by every circumstance coming within my own knowledge or the confessions of others whom [*sic*] had been either killed or executed, and whom he had not seen nor had any knowledge since 22d of August last.
>
> Thomas R. Gray, *The Confessions of Nat Turner*, 1831

Long before he first met Nat Turner in the Jerusalem, Virginia, jail, Thomas R. Gray began to assemble evidence on the Southampton rebellion and its leader. For ten weeks after the events of 21–23 August 1831, while Nat Turner remained at large, Gray immersed himself in factual details about the uprising. By the time Nat Turner was finally captured, on 30 October, Gray knew more about the rebellion than any man alive, except perhaps the leader himself. For that reason, during the first three days of November, Gray got permission to enter the jail and write down the leader's own statement. By 5 November, when Nat Turner came to trial, Gray had completed the manuscript of *The Confessions of Nat Turner*, the most authoritative account of the rebellion to that day. Two days later he was in Richmond looking for a publisher. He was able to work swiftly because he had prepared himself single-mindedly for the moment that he might meet the leader and because he had begun to construct the manuscript before that moment arrived.

It helped Gray's efforts, too, that he had connections and that he did not have to work alone. Though he had been an attorney for less than a year, he already belonged to a circle of influential men in Jerusalem. These included a half dozen lawyers, the county clerk, the sheriff, and 20 justices of the peace, who attended with varying regularity the monthly sessions of the county court. From this courthouse circle there emerged three individuals who, in the last days of August 1831, began their own inquiry into the rebellion. Gray was one of these three. They worked unofficially, since the court neither called for their inquiry nor appointed them to that task. Yet, since each of the three had duties in the trials that followed the rebellion, their investigation, in fact, proceeded within the court and drew upon the evidence produced there. At least one of the three had begun to gather evidence by Saturday, 27 August, when he handed to John Hampden Pleasants, senior editor of the *Richmond Constitutional Whig*, a preliminary list of white people killed in the rebellion. Pleasants, the only newspaperman to report from the scene, included the list with his first dispatch.[1] The editors of the *Norfolk Herald* heard about the inquiry less than a week after the rebellion; on Monday, 29 August, the paper reported that a "judicial investigation" would soon take place and would bring forth "a correct story of this most extraordinary affair."[2] By that day, the investigators were questioning prisoners at the jail and interviewing witnesses. On 30 August, according to General Richard Eppes of the militia, "investigations were going on as to the conduct of the blacks who were confined in the jail of Jerusalem."[3] Soon, preliminary information began to reach the public through a series of anonymous letters from Jerusalem addressed to newspaper editors in Raleigh, Richmond, and Norfolk. The investigators continued to work anonymously through the remainder of summer and into the middle of fall. Eventually, their findings—complete with certificate under seal from the court—appeared as Gray wrote them in *The Confessions of Nat Turner*.

The most prominent of the three investigators was James Trezvant, the congressman from Southside Virginia and a magistrate on the Southampton County court in 1831. Forty-eight years old and completing his third and final term in Congress, Trezvant had lived in and around Jerusalem for 25 years.[4] He had been an influential man at the courthouse since 1815, when he was appointed the commonwealth's attorney, or prosecutor, for the county court. He became one of the two commanding officers of the Southampton militia in 1818, when he was promoted to colonel. He resigned both positions in 1825 to take his seat in the U.S. House of Representatives.[5] At the time of the rebellion, though he had not prosecuted a case or commanded the militia in six years, Colonel Trezvant remained one of the most powerful men in the county. He lived on his "new plantation," as it was called in court minutes of 1827, two miles southwest of town and on the road from Jerusalem to Cross Keys, a crossroads settlement ten miles to the southwest.[6] The farm of Joseph Travis, where the rebellion started, was another five miles beyond Cross Keys.

On the morning of Monday, 22 August, when the express rider arrived from Cross Keys with news of the uprising, Trezvant was among the first to hear the news. It was Trezvant who, in turn, dispatched a second express to Petersburg with a letter appealing for arms, ammunition, and force. The *Richmond Compiler* reported that Trezvant's message was brief, identifying neither victims nor insurgents nor offering any interpretation of events. "The letter of Col. Trezvant was evidently written in great haste—It required some little time to decypher it," the *Compiler* reported. "To remove any sort of doubt of its authenticity, Mr. Gilliam of Petersburg had certified that he knew Col. T's hand writing and that it was genuine."[7] With this account in the 24 August *Compiler*, James Trezvant became the first member of the courthouse circle to be identified by the press in connection with these events. Over the next ten weeks, he became the leading magistrate at the Southampton trials, sitting at proceedings for 29 of the 48 people brought before the court for trial or hearing in connection with the rebellion. His importance was confirmed after Nat Turner was captured and brought to Jerusalem. The principal responsibility for conducting Nat's preliminary examination on 31 October—for nearly two hours—fell to Colonel Trezvant.[8]

The second key figure was attorney William C. Parker, a newcomer to the courthouse circle. Born on the Northern Neck of Virginia, Parker was 39 years old in 1831. He arrived in Southampton in 1826 and qualified as an attorney that year. In 1827 he paid tax on just four slaves over the age of 12 and still owned no land.[9] Over the next four years, he established himself in his profession and by the summer of 1831 had gained appointment as the commonwealth's attorney for cases heard in the district circuit superior court.[10] In earlier years, Parker had acquired a reputation for bold deeds, a reputation borne out by his actions during the week of the rebellion. The editor of the *Richmond Compiler* knew of him already as "an active officer of the last war on the Canada lines, and a man of as much intrepidity as of address." In the uncertain days between Monday and Saturday, Parker, though not then a militia officer, took command of the white defenders of Jerusalem. On Friday, according to the *Compiler*, he rode into the countryside "at the head of a party of 20 or 30 mounted persons" in pursuit of fugitive rebels.[11] When the *Compiler* identified him on 29 August, Parker became the second of the courthouse circle to be linked in the press to affairs in Southampton. By the middle of September, he had organized a volunteer company of cavalry, the "Southampton Greys," and by the first of October, he was styling himself "Captn. of Cavalry" in petitioning the governor for carbines and pistols.[12] In the trials that followed, Parker placed himself in the thick of things. Though a prosecutor in superior court, he nonetheless acted as defense attorney in county court for 14 accused rebels. His first appearance as counsel came on 31 August, in the first Southampton trial; his last appearance came on 5 November, at the trial of Nat Turner.

The third investigator, Thomas Ruffin Gray, was the youngest of the three principals. Gray was 31 and had turned to law as his profession only within the previous year, having experienced, as he later said, "every vicissitude of fortune."[13] A native of Southampton, he grew up about ten miles north of the courthouse at Round Hill, the farm owned by his father, Captain Thomas Gray, the county's leading horse breeder. In 1821, when his father gave him 400 acres between Round Hill and Jerusalem, the opportunity opened for young Gray to follow in his father's footsteps.[14] He built a house in 1824, married by 1826, and took up farming. In 1827 he paid tax on eight horses and 23 slaves above the age of 12. That same year, he became a justice of the peace of the county court. Then his fortunes declined. In the next four years, Gray, his father, and his younger brother, Edwin, suffered financial reverses that forced them to reduce their holdings. In 1830 Gray sold more than half of his farm.[15] In the spring of 1831, he was assessed for not a single slave or horse, though his father still paid taxes on five of each.[16] At some point between 1828 and 1830, after the death of his young wife, Gray took possession of a house that his father had owned in Jerusalem, and moved into town.[17] He qualified as an attorney on 20 December 1830, resigned his seat on county court that day, and took up his new profession.[18] On the morning of Monday, 22 August, Gray was residing in Jerusalem. From that day forward, he was drawn into the affairs of the rebellion. Like Parker, he provided counsel for slave defendants, receiving the first of his five assignments on 31 August, the first day of court deliberations. Two of the defendants assigned to him on 3 September, Moses Moore and Jack Reese, would give extraordinary evidence.

Four other men with links to the courthouse circle became involved in the inquiry. Though none of these four was so deeply engaged as Trezvant, Parker, and Gray, they did help to gather and interpret evidence. Meriwether B. Brodnax, the 32-year-old attorney for the commonwealth in county court, interviewed witnesses and defendants, recorded depositions, and drafted charges.[19] Another figure, James Williamson Parker, 31 years old and a judge on the county court, was up to his neck in the rebellion and trials.[20] Parker's gate stood just beyond Trezvant's plantation on the Cross Keys road, where Barrow Road joined from the west.[21] On the afternoon of 22 August, Nat Turner's men fought their first skirmish with white volunteers in Parker's field. Nine days later, on the first day of the Southampton trials, Parker sat as a judge. Altogether, he sat on trials for 18 slaves and on hearings for four free blacks. At the examination of Nat Turner on 31 October, Parker joined his neighbor Trezvant as a second interrogator, and on 5 November he sat with nine other judges at Turner's trial.[22]

In addition, James S. French, a 24-year-old Jerusalem attorney, became involved as soon as news of the uprising reached town. According to an account published years later, French borrowed a colt and joined the first group of volunteers to leave town in search of the rebels, following their track from Cross Keys northward and then eastward to James Parker's field, where they confronted the rebels.[23] Whether French took part in this episode or not, the rebels then engaged the volunteers in combat. The volunteers retreated toward Parker's gate, where they were rescued by a second party arriving from Jerusalem. Together they returned and dispersed the rebels.[24] French certainly became connected to the investigation through his many assignments as defense counsel for minor figures in the rebellion.

Finally, Theodore Trezvant, the Jerusalem postmaster, became attached to the inquiry as its public observer. Trezvant, 41, was a younger brother of the colonel. Although he had no position in court, he followed the trials and picked up information through his brother. When John Hampden Pleasants of the *Richmond Constitutional Whig* came to town with the Richmond cavalry, Pleasants recruited the postmaster as a correspondent.[25] Newspapers in Richmond, Norfolk, and Raleigh eventually published as many as six of his reports, usually identifying him as the source.

The investigation began at once, turning for evidence to the surviving rebels locked in the county jail. Until Nat Turner could be caught and questioned, these prisoners were the most promising sources. Four of them had witnessed almost the entire rebellion. One of these was Hark who, like Nat Turner, was about 31 years of age and a slave of Joseph Travis. Hark had assembled Turner's initial followers at Cabin Pond, less than a mile north of the Travis house, on Sunday and remained with the rebels until he was shot from his horse on Tuesday morning. At the time of his arraignment on 3 September, he knew more about the origins of the rebellion than any other witness. Recognizing his importance, the court appointed William C. Parker as his defense counsel.[26]

The second such prisoner was Sam Francis, a slave of Nathaniel Francis, about the same age as Hark and Turner, and one of the four men in whom Nat Turner originally confided. When Sam was brought to jail on 30 August, according to one report, he denied that there had been "any thing like a general concert among the slaves."[27] The court assigned his defense to Thomas R. Gray.

The third prisoner was Jack Reese, about 20 years old, the brother of Hark's wife, and slave of a Travis neighbor, Joseph William Reese.[28] Jack protested that he had been an unwilling rebel, claiming that Hark had brought him to Cabin Pond and then prevented him from slipping away until the rebels had left Catherine Whitehead's farm. Willing or not, Jack had heard in full Nat Turner's plan and then had witnessed the first seven assaults.[29] The court assigned his defense to Gray.

Finally, there was Moses Moore, about 15 years old and also a slave at the Travis farm. Moses had not been at Cabin Pond, but he had observed the seven who did meet there as they arrived Sunday night in the Travis yard. A few hours later, he said, he was awakened and compelled to go with them. He accompanied the main body of rebels all day Monday, from shortly after midnight through the afternoon skirmish at Parker's field.

He held horses taken along the way and, in that role, became a witness at all but two of the places at which the rebels took lives.[30] At the arraignment on 3 September, the court assigned his defense to Gray also.

The investigators had varying success with these prisoners. Hark and Sam apparently divulged little before their trials on 3 September or their executions six days later. Jack Reese, by contrast, confessed in front of his guards that he had been present at Cabin Pond and gave an account of the meeting there.[31] Gray's defense, supported by testimony from Moses Moore, nearly spared Jack's life. When the magistrates voted by a majority of one to recommend commuting Jack's death sentence, they no doubt took into consideration the value of his testimony. His account of the dinner at Cabin Pond gave Gray and the other investigators their first idea of Nat Turner's motive.

Moses Moore also gave evidence freely, starting before the trials got under way.[32] Altogether, Moses gave evidence concerning at least 12 defendants, the highest number for any witness, black or white.[33] So valuable was his testimony that the court—for two months—repeatedly postponed his trial, proceeding finally on 18 October, when they had no other defendants remaining. Gray called as witness a guard who testified to being present "on several occasions" when Moses was examined "sometimes for the Commonwealth and sometimes on behalf of the prisoners." The guard said Moses spoke "freely and voluntarily after being Told that he was not compelled to give Testimony & that nothing which he said would be of any advantage to him." The court recommended, and the governor accepted, a commuted punishment for him.[34] His testimony would prepare Gray and the court to meet Nat Turner in early November.

What investigators learned in the weeks before Nat Turner's capture was revealed in six anonymous letters written in Jerusalem between 31 August and 1 November 1831 and published by newspapers in Raleigh and Richmond. Each letter contained evidence about its author's experience and attitude, thereby indicating its author's probable identity. Together, these documents recorded the progress of the inquiry to the point at which the investigators met their most important witness. Together, too, they shed light on the construction of *The Confessions of Nat Turner.*

Two of the letters were written on Wednesday, 31 August, and drew upon evidence obtained from prisoners in the jail. The first of these, 380 words in length, was written before that day's trials and appeared on 8 September in the *Raleigh Register.*[35] The second, containing 1,410 words, was written after court adjourned; it appeared on 3 September in the *Richmond Compiler.*[36] The editor in Raleigh identified his correspondent simply as "a member of the Bar of Southampton county." The author must have been Colonel James Trezvant. The editor in Richmond said only that his account was by "a resident of Jerusalem" who had "much to do, both in a military and civil capacity; both in arresting and bringing to punishment the bandits." This author was undoubtedly William C. Parker. Each of these August letters recounted the skirmish at Parker's field from the perspective of the second group of volunteers, who arrived from Jerusalem in time to rescue the first. Each author referred to pressing duties in court on Wednesday. The Raleigh correspondent, writing before court convened, explained that he was "engaged in duty" and must be brief. The Richmond correspondent, writing after court adjourned, also mentioned pressing responsibilities. "I write to you in great haste," he said, "as my military duties and my duties in Court, require all my attention."

There were striking differences in the letters that indicated authorship by two different men. They differed in organization, in their estimates of the number of prisoners, and in the spelling of the word *jail.* They contained no common sentences or paragraphs, the earlier text not providing a pattern for the later one, as it might have if the same busy man had written both. The letters also recounted some unique experiences. Only the Raleigh correspondent revealed how he had learned of the rebellion: "The first intimation I had of the insurrection," he recalled, "was by an express from the scene of slaughter, on Monday the 22d, requiring assistance." The same author then had volunteered "with several others" and participated in what he alone described as "a tedious ride, post haste, of several hours." This man alone mentioned the express from Cross Keys.[37] This man thought the ride tedious. This must have been Trezvant, the judge, the man who dispatched the relay express to Petersburg, the former colonel now approaching 50.

The Richmond correspondent, unlike Trezvant, had commanded counterinsurgents before the militia organized itself. He wrote of being in Jerusalem at 1 A.M. on Tuesday, after the skirmish at Parker's field, and receiving intelligence about the rebels. "I had then under my orders here about 60 men," he said. During daylight on Tuesday, 23 August, he had ridden by the farm of Levi Waller, where he saw "in one room ten dead persons, women, boys and girls, from helpless infancy to hoary age." He had commenced a letter on Wednesday, "anticipating" this editor's desire to be "correctly informed of the events which have recently occurred in this county." But he interrupted that letter on receiving news that the rebels were embodied in the upper part of the county, "whither I repaired with a small number of mounted men." By the time he completed his letter, the court had met and sentenced "one to be hung on *Monday next.*"[38] This man had known the editor well enough to anticipate the request. This man mentioned his still-pressing military duties as well as his duties in court. This man alone claimed to have acted boldly, with men taking his orders before the militia arrived to defend Jerusalem. This man therefore must have been the intrepid Captain Parker of the Southampton Greys, the counselor whose defendant, Daniel Porter, had been sentenced that very day.

These two letters indicated that while not much was yet known, Trezvant and Parker both could identify Nat Turner as the leader of the rebellion, and both could attribute Nat's inspiration to his interpretation of recent solar events. Both dismissed Nat Turner as a "fanatic." Parker knew Nat Turner to be literate and religious. Trezvant understood him to have been "digesting" the idea of insurrection for years, basing this conclusion on testimony from "several blacks who have been examined" and on a statement by Nat's wife, whose name he did not provide.

As for the rebellion, Parker now knew that the "ringleaders" had gathered their first recruits on Sunday at a dinner "in a remote field." He thought that they had started at about midnight at the Travis house and that Nat Turner had entered that house first, but he did not know what had happened inside. Parker revealed none of his sources in the Richmond letter, but he must have learned most of this from Jack and Moses. He clearly learned nothing from Sam Francis or Hark, the two witnesses in custody who had entered the Travis house. While he mentioned no other assaults, Parker already knew that the rebels had attacked "house to house," not simultaneously. Trezvant and Parker agreed on the number of victims, placing the number of whites killed at 64 (an estimate less accurate than the one John Hampden Pleasants had obtained four days earlier from another source in Jerusalem). Trezvant estimated the number of rebels at about 40, Parker at 40 to 50. Though neither man raised the matter of slavery as a possible motive, each was being drawn unwittingly in that direction when he considered the apparent scope of the insurrection. Trezvant said he now believed that "the plot was a general one—at least through many of our adjacent counties." Parker agreed, saying he feared that "the scheme embraced a wider sphere" than he had first supposed.

On the question of motive—the most important matter in developing a theory of the rebellion—Trezvant noted the "indiscriminate" carnage but declined to speculate about anything beyond banditry (which he rejected) or fanaticism. Parker pressed a bit further, noting as a "remarkable" fact about the behavior of the rebels that "not a single instance of mercy or pity, or relenting, occurred throughout the whole of their proceedings." "Their *object*," he said, "seems to have been, to produce unusual consternation and dismay, by indiscriminate massacre." In a passage bearing striking similarity to the testimony of Jack Reese, Parker quoted Nat Turner himself as having said that they would "kill and slay as they went."[39] Then he too drew back and made no connection between this suggestion of terror and the institution of slavery.

Over the next two weeks, Parker and the others became less hesitant and less like-minded in their speculations, a change that became evident after the appearance of a third anonymous letter from Jerusalem. This one was addressed on 17 September to John Hampden Pleasants at the *Richmond Constitutional Whig*, in which it appeared on 26 September.[40] This document revealed important developments in the inquiry.

The *Richmond Constitutional Whig* letter, 4,079 words in length after editing by Pleasants, was more than twice as long as the previous two letters combined. Its author filled his report with new details and speculation, creating the most comprehensive account of the rebellion to that point. Had *The Confessions of Nat Turner* never appeared, the *Richmond Constitutional Whig* letter would have become the authoritative account. The author was someone other than Trezvant or Parker, though he too had been close to the court proceedings. He praised the court for "listening with unwearied patience to the examination of a multitude of witnesses, and to long and elaborate arguments of counsel," and he complained about the pressures of time. "Professional duties," he wrote, "prevent me from bestowing as much attention to the drawing up of this narrative as I would wish." He too had examined witnesses, and their testimony had led him to conclude that "not more" than ten slaves had killed all of the white victims. "In support of my opinion, I have examined every source for authentic information," he said. "Every individual who was taken alive has been repeatedly questioned; many of them, when their stay in this world, was exceedingly brief—and the answers of all confirm me in my belief." He too had been in Jerusalem on Monday morning when the express arrived from Cross Keys, and he too had volunteered to pursue the rebels. .

Other evidence in the *Richmond Constitutional Whig* letter indicated that this was the work of a third anonymous author in Jerusalem. This correspondent had experienced different events and had a different perspective. This man had ridden not with Trezvant and Parker but with the first party of volunteers, who had crossed the river at Jerusalem and headed southwest, straight to Cross Keys, in search of the rebels. There they had picked up the trail "and pursuing them, we found the blood hardly congealed, in the houses they had left." He did not mention the skirmish and rescue at Parker's field, but he did note that within "two and a half or three miles of Jerusalem" the progress of the rebels "was arrested." This *Richmond Constitutional Whig* correspondent had spent Monday night— "the whole night"—not with William C. Parker in town, but out in the county, pursuing the rebel force. Fortune, he said, "seemed to sport with us, by bringing us nearer together, and yet, making us pursue separate routes." On Tuesday morning this author had retraced the entire rebel route, "a distance of 20 miles." Like Parker, he reported stopping that day at the farm of Levi Waller, where he encountered the first white survivor, a girl of about 12. "She gave me a minute account of the tragedy there acted," he said, "having witnessed it from her place of concealment." Parker mentioned no such survivor in his account, but one other author in 1831 did so: Gray referred to her near the end of *The Confessions of Nat Turner*.[41] The *Confessions* also contained an account of the skirmish at Parker's field, which Gray tried clumsily to present in the voice of Nat Turner. He failed to disguise the true perspective as that of a white man riding with the first party of volunteers.[42]

Other details in the *Richmond Constitutional Whig* letter would reappear in *The Confessions*. The most striking similarly between the two documents is that of their lists of white victims. Each list proceeded through the names with almost an identical sense of chronological order, reversing only Arthur and Anne Eliza Vaughan. The spellings of names agreed in all but four cases. The lists agreed on the total number of white victims and concluded with an identical expression of that total: "amounting to 55." They were, in fact, two later versions of the list that had been handed to editor Pleasants on 27 August in Jerusalem. Their compiler, who now provided this account to the same editor, must have been attorney Thomas R. Gray.[43]

The *Richmond Constitutional Whig* letter indicated what Gray had learned six weeks before the capture of Nat Turner. Gray agreed with previous characterizations of Nat as a religious fanatic but denied that he had been a preacher. "He exhorted, and sung at neighborhood meetings, but no farther." In the Travis neighborhood, Nat had "acquired the reputation of a prophet" or Roman sibyl, an interpreter of signs in the heavens and of characters drawn in blood on leaves. Gray agreed with James Trezvant that the idea of rebellion appeared not to be recent, based on evidence obtained from the same woman. " 'Tis true," Gray said, "that Nat has for some time, thought closely on this subject—for I have in my possession, some papers given up by his wife, under the lash." The papers were "filled with hieroglyphical characters, conveying no definite meaning." On the oldest paper, Gray found drawings of a crucifix and the sun, and the numbers 6,000; 30,000; and 80,000. The reference to hieroglyphs and numbers reappeared in *The Confessions*, recounted in the voice of Nat Turner.[44] Gray had obtained even more evidence of this kind: "There is likewise a piece of paper, of a late date which all agree, is a list of his men; if so, they were short of twenty." He said that Nat pretended to know how to make gunpowder and paper, facts that also found their way into *The Confessions*.[45]

By the date on the *Richmond Constitutional Whig* letter, Jack Reese had been dead five days. It must have been Jack who led Gray to a theory about Nat's plan for the rebellion. Gray's statement of that theory appeared near the middle of the *Richmond Constitutional Whig* letter, in his account of the meeting at Cabin Pond. There he supported Parker's impressions about the dinner and the plan, but Gray had new information. Gray now disclosed, with what proved to be only one error, the names of all seven men at the dinner.[46] He knew that Nat had taken aside each of the other six and held "long conversations" developing his plan. One man—almost certainly Jack Reese—had objected. Nat then had asserted that the plan was practicable, that their numbers would increase "as they went along." They would attack by surprise and with a speed that would "strike additional horror."

Gray now communicated Nat Turner's motive in terms that Trezvant and Parker had hesitated to employ. Nat had imagined, he said, "the possibility, of freeing himself and race from bondage." Five paragraphs later he added bluntly, "His object was freedom, and indiscriminate carnage his watchword." Nat's inspiration, he said, might have originated "something like three years ago," after a whipping he received from his previous master "for saying that blacks ought to be free, and that they would be free one day or other."

Gray demonstrated, too, that he now could place the events of Sunday through Tuesday morning in sequence, basing this chronology on information he must have acquired from Jack and Moses. He did not yet know who had killed anyone in the Travis house. He did know, however, that all five occupants had been "dispatched" with a broadax, "and one blow seems to have sufficed for two little boys, who were sleeping so close, that the same stroke nearly severed each neck." An infant, "with its head cut off," had been found in the fireplace. These details apparently came from direct observation: Gray must have visited the Travis house before the bodies were removed, when he was retracing the route. He knew, too, that the rebels had divided their forces at the Whitehead farm and then united again, details he must have acquired from Moses. And he now could estimate that there had been about 40 insurgents, based on the best evidence and on what he said he "actually saw."

Gray's interpretation in the *Richmond Constitutional Whig* letter revealed that two points of dispute within the inquiry had emerged by mid-September, and that on each point Gray was dissenting from the majority view in ways that minimized the scale of the rebellion. He disagreed, first, on the extent of the conspiracy. He rejected earlier speculations put forth in the Raleigh and Richmond letters about an extensive "concert." "I have heard many express their fears of a general insurrection," he said; "they are ignorant who believe in the possibility of such a thing." He theorized that Virginia slaves, unlike the free blacks of Saint Domingue, were incapable of general insurrection. "Is it possible," he asked, "for men debased, degraded as they are, ever to concert effective measures?" Gray also dismissed earlier speculations that the rebels had been planning the uprising for a long time. He noted that they had begun without guns. "If the design had been thought of for the least length of time," he argued, "they certainly would have made some preparation." These differences between Gray and the others would continue until Nat Turner could be questioned.

The early theory of a general concert was revived just one week after Gray completed the *Richmond Constitutional Whig* letter. It reappeared in an attachment to a fourth anonymous communication from Jerusalem, this one addressed to Thomas Ritchie, editor of the *Richmond Enquirer*.[47] Ritchie had written to this correspondent, whom he referred to as "a friend in Southampton," for news on 13 September. His friend had been out of town attending the superior court in Greensville County on Friday,

16 September, and received Ritchie's request only after returning to Jerusalem.[48] He began his reply five days later, on Wednesday, 21 September. This friend must have been William C. Parker, the new prosecutor in the superior court, whose duties had taken him to Greensville.

Ritchie's correspondent reported on the trials in Southampton and neighboring counties, noting in particular the alarming testimony of a young slave woman who claimed she had "heard the subject discoursed about among her master's slaves, and some of the neighbouring ones, for the last eighteen months." As he wrote the main body of his letter, he discounted her claim and argued against the theory "that there was a 'concert or general plan' among the Blacks." On a related matter, concerning a "plan of defence against a similar attempt in the future," he made a suggestion that revealed his identity in another way: he recommended creating "volunteer corps" that might ride regularly through the countryside to give an impression of power.[49] This was the captain of the Southampton Greys. "A Volunteer company has been raised here," he reported, "composed of the most intelligent and respectable gentlemen." Then, in the brief attachment he wrote on Saturday, 24 September, he changed his mind about conspiracy. The slave woman's testimony had shaken his confidence. "If her tale is true," he wrote, "the plot was more extensive than we had previously believed."

This wavering was characteristic of Parker, not of Gray, who ridiculed the notion of a general conspiracy from beginning to end. Gray, furthermore, could not have been the man who attended the court in Greensville on 16 September, for he was ill at home. On each day from 12 to 20 September, he was attended by Dr. Orris A. Browne, who billed him for six doses of medicine and nine visits, including one "in rain" on the sixteenth.[50] This indecision was Parker's.

The scale of the plot remained a question until 31 October, when Nat Turner was brought before the two magistrates for preliminary examination. At that examination, Nat Turner himself began to influence interpretations. On 8 November, editor Ritchie of the *Enquirer* published extracts from the fifth and sixth anonymous letters. Each of them was written after the examination, and each came from an anonymous correspondent in Jerusalem. Ritchie identified the first and longest of these as "from the pen of the gentleman to whom we have been so much indebted for the previous details of this murderous insurrection." Apparently, he was referring to the correspondent whose previous letter appeared in the *Enquirer* on 30 September and who had attended the Greensville court. The author of this new letter identified himself explicitly as someone other than Gray since he referred to Gray in the third person. These identifications point to William C. Parker as the author.[51]

This gentleman revealed that he, too, had been present at the preliminary examination and had joined the questioning. Parker, who was about to be named Nat Turner's counsel, might have been a likely participant alongside the two magistrates. If Parker was indeed the author of this letter, he had shifted toward Gray's interpretation of the rebellion, but he was still wavering. Adopting Nat's own explanation of motive, this man had asked Nat how "the idea of emancipating the blacks entered his mind." This motive had underlain Gray's explanation all along. He reported, too, that the plot had originated "not until rather more than a year ago" and that Nat had conspired with only "five or six others." Still, he reserved some doubt, noting that all of the conspirators "seemed prepared with ready minds and hands to engage in it."

This long excerpt from the sixth Jerusalem letter provided some new, clarifying details about the rebellion, though these soon proved to be less than complete. According to this report, after entering through an upstairs window of the Travis house, Nat had passed through Joseph Travis's chamber. Then, he had opened a door to admit the others, returned to the chamber, and delivered the first hatchet blows, "both to his master and mistress, as they lay asleep in bed." Nat's examination also had provided information about rebel tactics. According to the letter, Nat had said that "indiscriminate massacre was not their intention after they obtained a foothold, and was resorted to in the first instance to strike terror and alarm." This appeared to be comforting news. "Women and children would afterwards have been spared, and men too who ceased to resist."

Immediately below this document, Ritchie published an extract from the sixth letter, also written on 1 November by a man with information about Nat Turner's examination. He reported having "just had a conversation with some gentlemen who saw him yesterday." This correspondent must have been postmaster Theodore Trezvant, reporting what he had learned from his brother and James W. Parker, the two examining magistrates. "Nat states that there was no concert of an insurrection," he reported. Until the day before the uprising, no more than two people other than Nat Turner knew of the plan. One more detail emerged about the Travis killings: "He admits he struck his master first with his hatchet, who called on his wife when he received the fatal blow from one of his associates."

Below this excerpt, Ritchie published two sentences from a seventh anonymous Jerusalem communication. This note, written before Nat Turner's trial on 5 November, reported briefly that Nat Turner was making "a voluntary confession" of his motives "to Mr. Thomas R. Gray, who intends publishing them, in pamphlet form, for the satisfaction of the public." Immediately after this, Ritchie added an editor's note in which he reported having been informed "by a gentleman from Southampton" that Nat Turner had been tried "on Saturday last" and that the evidence had been persuasive. This gentleman, traveling through Richmond just two days after the trial, must have been Gray himself, in search of a printer. "The testimony was clear and conclusive as to his guilt," Ritchie reported, "and he will be hung on Friday next."

As to Nat's guilt, Gray had persuaded himself long before the first jailhouse interview. He had learned enough in August and September from witnesses at the trials and survivors in Cross Keys to draw that conclusion. He had seen with his own eyes the evidence at specific places, and, in addition, he could draw upon the pool of information that had been accumulating in Jerusalem. By the middle of September, he had enough evidence to sketch a general outline of Nat Turner's life and to reconstruct an almost-correct chronology of the rebellion.[52] With these sources on hand, he began to take down the confession on 1 November.

Much of what Gray knew before that date found its way into *The Confessions of Nat Turner*. In the foreword, headed "To the Public" and written entirely from his own point of view, Gray rehearsed familiar theories about the leader's "gloomy fanaticism" and the "entirely local" scope of the rebellion.[53] This was followed by the major part of the work, presented under the heading, "Confession." Here Gray assumed the role of amanuensis, writing down Nat's recollections of his life as a slave, touching on facts known for weeks: Nat's reading and writing, his experiments with gunpowder and paper, his revelations and prophecies, his interpreting of signs and hieroglyphics, and his rising influence among neighborhood slaves.[54]

He also recorded Nat's account of the baptism with a white man in 1826 or 1827, which Gray had already discovered through Parker and probably from the white man himself.[55] He took down the history of Nat's discontent, an attitude Gray had inferred from the report of Nat's whipping in 1828 for remarks Nat had made about blacks and freedom.[56] After the recollections, he recorded the most important part of the text, Nat's narrative of the rebellion.[57] Though full of new details, this narrative fit consistently into the general sequence of events that Gray had assumed in writing the *Richmond Constitutional Whig* letter in September.

Then, after the narrative, Gray returned to his own point of view for a "cross-examination" of the witness. He found Nat's statement "corroborated by every circumstance coming within my own knowledge or the confessions of others whom [sic] had been either killed or executed, and whom he had not seen nor had any knowledge since 22d August last."[58] He concluded with a commentary on the uprising and an account of Nat's trial, neither of which derived from the interviews.[59] Finally, he appended two lists, one identifying the 55 white persons killed in the rebellion, the other naming the slaves and free blacks brought to court in Southampton.[60] Neither list was entirely new, earlier versions having appeared on 15 September in the *Norfolk American Beacon* and been attributed to "a source entitled to a most implicit credit." Gray, the probable compiler of both lists, must have appropriated them for *The Confessions*. This was the manuscript of 8,494 words that Gray finished in five days and then carried to Baltimore, where he had it printed before 22 November.[61]

The Confessions had been in print no more than two weeks before it gave rise to skepticism that never died. The author of a review appearing on

2 December in the *Richmond Enquirer* was the first to say that he did not believe that Nat Turner could have spoken in the words that Gray wrote down.[62] The pamphlet's "culprit" was speaking in language "far superior to what Nat Turner could have employed." The reviewer expressed no doubts about the content of the pamphlet, but Gray's rendering of Nat's expression gave him pause. It was eloquent, even classical. "This is calculated to cast some shade of doubt over the authenticity of the narrative, and to give the Bandit a character for intelligence which he does not deserve, and ought not to have received." The reviewer accepted the confession as a legal document, questioning neither the method by which Gray obtained it nor Gray's account of how it had been read to some members of the court.[63] The reviewer was not troubled by the lack of a witness for the interviews or by the apparent lack of signature for the defendant, who could both read and write. He doubted only that a slave could have spoken in such a style, and he feared this lapse might lead others to doubt the authenticity of the confession within *The Confessions.*

Even this skeptical reviewer acknowledged, however, that in all other respects, the confession appeared to be "faithful and true." In fact, there is considerable evidence within the document of its accuracy in portraying Nat Turner; there are numerous signs that Gray rendered at least the content faithfully. After all, Gray did not produce a mere compilation of earlier documents. Most of the material in *The Confessions* was new, not borrowed. Except for some short, familiar phrases and the two lists of names, Gray incorporated no previously published written matter. No whole sentences or paragraphs from earlier accounts reappeared. This was new writing with significant, new information, particularly in the recollections and narrative.

The recollections dealt with events both internal and external, beginning with Nat's recalling a memory from age three or four when he first sensed that he was destined for something greater than slavery. The telling of this memory brought forth new details of vital history: his exact age (31 on 2 October); the name of his first master (Benjamin Turner—known earlier, but not published); and the presence at the Turner house of his mother, father, and grandmother. It brought to light, too, the piety of his grandmother and of his first master, "who belonged to the church," and the "religious persons who visited the house," whom he often saw at prayers. Members of this pious group had once observed that according to Turner, "I had too much sense" to be raised a slave, "and if I was, I would never be of any service to any one as a slave." Further details revealed new evidence about Nat's intellectual development. He had learned to read with such "perfect ease" that he had "no recollection whatever of learning the alphabet," although he did recall the occasion on which "the family" (of Benjamin Turner) discovered that he could spell. As an adult, he had embraced austerity in his "life and manners," never becoming addicted to stealing, always cultivating a reputation for superior judgment, and always holding conjuring in contempt. He had fasted, prayed, attended religious meetings, and reflected upon Scripture; twice Gray quoted him (perhaps imprecisely, and without chapter or verse) reciting the same passage from the Sermon on the Mount. While praying at his plow, he had experienced the first of nine revelations of divine spirits. Two years after this, he had had a second revelation, and then a third, which induced him to prepare followers for some purpose. At about the time of the third revelation, he ran away from an overseer and remained in the woods for 30 days, after which the spirit had ordered him to return. He recalled specific times for two of the remaining revelations, one falling in 1825 and the other on 12 May 1828. After the ninth revelation came the two solar events of 1831, which he had interpreted as signs from "the Spirit" that he should slay his enemies with their own weapons.[64]

The sequence of these memories matched the chain of ownership for Nat Turner. While he did not mention all of his masters and mistresses by name, the events he recounted were consistent with the order of their tenure over him. Nat's memories of being inside the master's house came from his early life with Benjamin Turner (his master from 1800 to 1809). His vision at the plow must have occurred after he became a field hand for Benjamin's elder son, Samuel G. Turner (from 1809 to 1822) and his first wife, Esther Francis Turner (dead by 1817), the eldest sister of Nathaniel Francis.[65]

Nat's period under the overseer must have come after Samuel's death in 1822, when he fell into the hands of Samuel's second wife and widow, Elizabeth Reese Williamson Turner (killed in the rebellion). His revelation in 1825 and the baptism that "the white people" had tried to prevent (together with the whipping Gray mentioned in the *Richmond Constitutional Whig* letter) must have occurred after he was passed to Thomas Moore (1823 to 1827) and his wife, Sarah Francis Moore (also killed). Sarah Moore was the second sister of Nathaniel Francis to become mistress over Nat Turner. Nat's four years with Thomas Moore, apparently a time of rising antagonism toward whites, brought four visions that he described in violent, apocalyptic terms. The revelation of 12 May 1828 continued in this vein, with the spirit instructing Nat to pick up Christ's yoke and "fight against the Serpent."[66] This vision occurred a year after Thomas Moore died, after which Nat had been passed to the widow Moore and her seven-year-old son Putnam, now his legal owner (also killed). Two years later, at "the commencement of 1830," Nat was living with Joseph Travis (also killed), the "kind master" who married Sarah Moore (in October 1829) and settled at her farm.[67] These recollections are consistent with known facts.

In November of 1831, there were at least five people from Cross Keys who might have provided Gray with information about Nat Turner's life.[68] These included the second son of Benjamin Turner, John Clark Turner, who was born in 1801 and had lived at his father's farm with Nat Turner until 1809.[69] There was also Sarah Francis, who was the mother of two of

Nat's mistresses and who, as one of the religious persons visiting the Turner house, had known Nat Turner as a child.[70] As well, there was Sarah's son, Nathaniel Francis, who had known Nat Turner for at least 20 years. Among the slaves in Cross Keys were Moses Moore (received into the penitentiary at Richmond on 30 October) and the unnamed woman Gray identified as Nat's wife.[71] Each of these people might have known parts of this history, which Gray could then have pieced together himself. However, to describe the visions in a sequence consistent with vital history, Gray needed either to contrive a fiction with incredible care or—more simply—to obtain the authentic account by the one source whose memory had stored a lifetime of animosity against those who had stood in the way of freedom.

For readers in 1831, the question of authenticity mattered most in the next section of *The Confessions*, wherein Gray presented Nat Turner's narrative of the rebellion. This narrative—3,119 words in length and amounting to more than a third of the pamphlet—immediately became the standard account. Like the recollections, it presented events from Nat Turner's point of view. Except for parenthetical insertions (clearly marking Gray's comments), it imparted only what Nat could have known and made no claim that he had witnessed everything. Even with these limitations, the narrative disclosed at least 116 factual details about the uprising that had never appeared in print.[72]

The Confessions contained the fullest account of events during the rebellion's initial assault, which ocurred inside the Travis house. Nat Turner had entered his master's chamber with Nathaniel Francis's slave Will, whose presence among the insurgents had not been mentioned in earlier accounts.[73] When Nat failed to kill Joseph Travis with a hatchet, it had been Will who stepped forward. Will "laid him dead, with a blow of his axe, and Mrs. Travis shared the same fate, as she lay in bed."[74]

In this account, Nat did not identify the killer of the two boys in the house, Putnam Moore and Joel Westbrook, Travis's apprentice. He did reveal, however, that it had been Will who returned to the house with Henry Porter to kill the infant child of the Travises, "sleeping in a cradle," whom they had forgotten until they had gone some distance from the house.[75] After the Travis disclosures, the account moved to revelations concerning assaults at the next four farms. Will and his axe accounted for at least eight, and perhaps 12, of the first 13. Will's dispatching of the Reverend Richard Whitehead inspired Nat to give him a title: "Will, the executioner."[76] All of this came as new information.

Revelation followed revelation. Nat accounted for the single killing that he had performed, that of Margaret Whitehead.[77] He recounted how, after dividing his forces, he had ridden alone to muster a detachment. (Here, in presenting a complicated series of actions, Gray maintained Nat's perspective flawlessly.) Nat explained how he had planned the attack on the Waller farm so as to "strike terror to the inhabitants." He disclosed that he had taken a position at the rear of the attackers, which explained why he had not witnessed any killings after leaving the Whitehead farm, "except in one case." The exception was Mrs. William Williams (the former Rebecca Ivy, about 18 years of age), who nearly escaped, but was caught, carried on horseback to the body of her husband, and shot.[78] He revealed that at Parker's gate he had argued with his men that they should not waste time going to the house but should advance directly to Jerusalem.[79] Old fragments from earlier sources fit consistently into the pattern of new details that Gray learned from the ultimate witness.

Gray's closing commentary confirmed prevailing suspicions about Nat Turner, now a proven fanatic. In the cross-examination, Gray reported, Nat admitted that he had failed to organize a general conspiracy and agreed to the "impracticability of his attempt."[80] Thus, while the rebellion may have been brewing in Nat's mind for some time, it had never involved large numbers of conspirators. These conclusions served Gray's original purpose of reassuring a frightened community.

Still, there were details that made it difficult to extract assurance. Of all the events narrated by Nat Turner, the killing of the Travis child must have reassured Gray's readers least. Gray wrote down Nat's account of what happened in just one sentence: "[T]here was a little infant sleeping in a cradle, that was forgotten, until we had left the house and gone some distance, when Henry and Will returned and killed it."[81] Gray knew more about the Travis child than this sentence indicated. In *The Confessions*, he did not mention the condition of the child's body as he had seen it at the Travis house and as he had described it in the *Richmond Constitutional Whig*: removed from its cradle, lying beheaded in the fireplace. These details by themselves indicated that the killer had expressed some motive beyond mere rigor in executing a plan. They indicated, too, that the infant had not been killed by accident and perhaps not in fury. They suggested, instead, that this body had been left as a sign to be read by those who would discover it: slaveholding was now a capital crime that corrupted blood and for which there could be no plea of innocence or commutation of punishment. Gray had examined this sign in August. "Five were murdered at this house," he wrote in the *Richmond Constitutional Whig*, "several never changed their positions; but a little infant with its head cut off, was forced to exchange its cradle for the fire-place."[82] Information added by Nat Turner in November, though obscured by Gray's use of the passive voice, clarified the meaning of the sign. This child, not more than a year old, had been killed not to prevent escape or to keep an alarm from being raised. It had been killed for another purpose, with a deliberation that surpassed ruthlessness.[83] Its killing signified terror.

The word *terror* appeared twice in *The Confessions of Nat Turner*, both times in Nat's account of the assault on the Waller farm. In the first reference, Nat described his tactic of approaching at full speed "to carry terror and devastation wherever we went." In the second, he explained that this tactic had been directed at the immediate victims to "prevent their escape and strike terror to the inhabitants."[84] In the preceding summary of his plan, there may have been an additional allusion to terror, when he reported, "until we had armed and equipped ourselves, and gathered sufficient force, neither age nor sex was to be spared."[85] In each of these cases, Nat used the word in its oldest meaning: the state of being greatly frightened, or paralyzed with sudden fear.[86]

His reference to the Travis evidence, however, indicated that some among the rebels had a different idea. Those who returned for the child had meant to instill something more than a fear that paralyzed the immediate victim. By their actions at the Travis farm, they conveyed an intention to plant an enduring dread in the entire population. This idea reappeared in the killing of Rebecca Ivy Williams. Gray did not indicate that Nat Turner himself had defined the idea in these broader terms. Perhaps Nat had not known about it or understood it. Or perhaps he was conveying it through inference, as when he denied any knowledge of an insurrection in North Carolina but asked if Gray did not think "the same ideas, and strange appearances about this time in the heaven's [*sic*] might prompt others, as well as myself, to this undertaking."[87]

This was new evidence that Gray chose not to emphasize in constructing the record of Nat Turner's confession. He included it, but he let it pass without parenthetical comment in the narrative and without remark in the cross-examination, drawing no connection to the earlier evidence about the child in the fireplace. Since he could not have forgotten what he himself had seen in late August and written about in September, he must have decided at this point that reticence was the safer policy. For good reason, he must have chosen to put the earlier evidence aside, knowing that these details, if linked, could terrify and inflame a white population whose fear it was his purpose to calm. As he constructed the record, only those readers who remembered his description in the *Richmond Constitutional Whig* could have understood the embedded meaning of the new revelation, had they chosen to do so. Only they could have understood what Gray must have perceived the moment he heard Nat's account of the Travis child: that Nat Turner had not seen everything (true to his subsequent admission), and that the leader must have known less about some particulars than Gray himself. Gray must have realized then that the investigation had given him an advantage in dealing with this witness—if not in seeing the whole event, then certainly in being able to verify particulars. He did not intrude then, however. After all, his interest lay in not raising questions about the significance or authority of the witness. Gray insinuated nothing beyond the ken of the witness at that point, therefore, and he drew no attention to his own deep command of detail. For good reason, this too he put aside. He adhered instead to another of his purposes, that of persuading readers about the centrality of the fanatic and the authenticity of his confession.

PART TWO

STORIES OF THE REBELLION

———

THREE

The Event

———

HERBERT APTHEKER

It may at once be said that there are features of the Turner revolt that are still uncertain and probably will remain so. Any statement purporting to give the precise number of Negroes who took part in the revolt, or the exact number of victims, white or Negro, is to be suspiciously regarded. What appear to be fairly good approximations may be made.

It is thought, however, to be possible with the available evidence, to answer other and more important questions. The causes and the purposes of the event may be discerned. Whether what is today to be seen in this connection is all that really existed over one hundred years ago cannot be said, but causes and purposes are yet visible and appear to be sufficient to explain the revolt. Similarly, there are many results that appear, some more clearly than others, which will be discussed later.

Concerning the Turner revolt there is unanimity on two things, and only on two things. First, all agree it took place, or, at least, started (whether it was local or not will be dealt with later) in Southampton County and, second, that the leader was Nat Turner. The former has been sufficiently described, but what sort of person was Nat?

A: Nat Turner, The Man

The year eighteen hundred was a fateful one for American slavery. It was then that John Brown was born, that Gabriel's revolt occurred and that

This essay is a chapter from Herbert Aptheker's Master's thesis completed at Columbia University in 1937.

Vesey purchased the ownership of his own body, and it was then, too, on October 2, that Nat Turner was born.[1] He was, then, almost 31 years old at the time of the revolt. The following description of him was given,[2] together with the announcement of a reward of $500 for his capture, by the Governor of Virginia, John Floyd: "Nat is between 30 and 35 years old, 5 feet 6 or 8 inches high, weighs between 150 and 160 pounds, rather bright complexion, but not a mulatto, broad shoulders, large flat nose, large eyes, broad flat feet, rather knock-kneed, walks brisk and active, hair on top of the head very thin, no beard, except on the upper lip and the top of the chin, a scar on one of his temples, also one on the back of his neck, a large knot on one of his bones of right arm, near the wrist, produced by a blow."

Very naturally, William Lloyd Garrison in commenting upon this description, pointed[3] to these scars as explaining Turner's actions. But the Richmond *Enquirer*[4] assured its readers that Turner got two of his bruises in fights with Negroes and one of them, that on his temple, through a mule's kick. Of course Drewry[5] accepts the explanation of the southern newspaper and also points out, correctly, that Turner stated his last master, Joseph Travis, had been kindly.[6] But Nat had had other masters like Benjamin Turner and Putnam Moore, and he had[7] (though Mr. Drewry[8] omits mention of this) run away from one of these (which is not certain[9]) after a change in overseers. Moreover, Drewry's[10] own description of Nat does not aptly characterize one who is given to fighting. "From childhood Nat was very religious, truthful and honest, 'never owning a dollar, never uttering an oath, never drinking intoxicating liquors, and never committing a theft.'"

As a matter of fact, whether Turner's scars were caused by the kick of a mule or the whip of a white man, or both, it seems fairly clear that his motivation was not personal vengeance. The question of motivation, both of Nat and of his followers, will shortly be discussed in detail. Here suffice it to say that the conclusion of that examination will be that Nat Turner sought the liberation of the Negro people.

But, to return to the personality of Turner: An examination of the evidence reveals a highly intelligent man who finds it impossible to accept the status quo and discovers his rationalization for his rebellious feelings in religion. James C. Ballagh's[11] descriptive phrase "well-educated" is not well chosen for it implies formal instruction. Nat himself[12] was unable to account for his ability to read and write, though this is often ascribed to his parents' instructions. But it is certain that he was literate and that he read and reread the Bible. He also appears to have been gifted mechanically. It is possible that he owed part of his revolutionary spirit to his father, who, when Nat was a boy, ran away and was never recovered. But the supreme influence in his life undoubtedly was religion, as he understood it. Nat, himself, thought this was largely due to the many religious people who surrounded him in his youth, particularly, he says, his grandmother. These people noticed his ". . . uncommon intelligence for a child, remarked I had too much sense to be raised, and if I was I would never be of any service to any one as a slave." Since there is no disagreement on this point one more quotation will suffice. "As I was praying one day at my plough, the spirit spoke to me, saying, 'Seek ye the kingdom of Heaven and all things shall be added unto you.' *Question* (by Thomas Gray)—What do you mean by the Spirit? *Answer:* The spirit that spoke to the prophets in former days—and I was greatly astonished, and for two years prayed continually, whenever my duty would permit—and then again I had the same revelation, which fully confirmed me in the impression that I was ordained for some great purpose in the hands of the Almighty."

Drewry states[13] that Turner was an "overseer" and U. B. Phillips describes him as a "foreman." Neither one nor the other tells where he got his information. Perhaps Drewry heard this from one of the people he interviewed as to their recollections of Nat going back some seventy years—not very good evidence. Phillips' choice of a word is better, for while a slave might be a foreman, he was never an overseer. But where his information was obtained is unknown. Nothing has been seen to substantiate either Drewry or Phillips.

Phillips' terminology is in another respect an improvement over Drewry's and here appears to be well-founded. Drewry thinks that Turner was a "Baptist preacher," but Phillips states that he was a "Baptist exhorter."[14] While it is a fair assumption that Turner did not adhere to a complete theological system, he did practice one distinctive feature of the Baptist faith, i.e., baptism by immersion, as he himself states[15] in discussing the case of a white man, Ethelred T. Brantley, whom Turner prevailed upon to cease "from his wickedness."

Some[16] have said with Drewry that he was a preacher; others,[17] fewer, have denied this. It is clear that Turner was not a regularly ordained minister, or, indeed, a properly enrolled member, of any church,[18] but that, being admired and respected by his fellow slaves,[19] he often spoke to them on the Sabbath get-togethers. The word "exhorter" accurately describes Nat Turner. It is important that the contemporary accounts of the revolt referred to him, generally, as a preacher; this helps explain certain laws enacted after the Revolt. One evidence of this contemporary opinion will be quoted. This piece of evidence[20] is selected because, so far as is known, the source has never been used, and because it is of excellent quality. Clearly the writer did not expect posterity to read it and it was written less than one week after the event. The letter is addressed to Thomas Ruffin, then Judge of the Supreme Court of North Carolina. It was written by one E. P. Guion and dated, "Raleigh, Sunday August 28th, 1831." The part pertinent here runs as follows: "It is strange to me that men can be so blind and Infatuate as to be advocates of Negroes Preaching to negroes no doubt that these veery Slaves would have Remained quiet but for this fanatic Black that has excited them in this diabolical deed some of them were wounded and in the aggonies of Death declared that they was going happy fore that God had a hand in what they had been doing they also had a story among them that the English was to assist them."

B: CAUSE AND MOTIVE

What were the causation and the motivation of the Turner Revolt? The former, which, it is felt, is more deep-seated, more prolonged, more objective than the latter, has been displayed in some detail in the preceding pages. This cannot be *proven*, as can a result in chemistry, but it seems correct to say that the Turner Revolt was not merely a remarkable coincidence agreeing with the temper of the half-decade preceding it. Rather, just as the laws, petitions, plots, revolts, intrigues of that period were manifestations of the times, of economic depression, of sociological maladjustment, of uncertainty, of fast and vast changes, and in turn helped create the spirit of those times, so the Turner Revolt appears to be a manifestation of this spirit, and a direct and indirect influence itself in developing the spirit and accounting for the events in the time immediately following its occurrence.

The evidence concerning the motivation of Nat Turner and of those who fought with him is fairly definite. Yet contemporary and later writers have offered varied hypotheses as to the motivation. These take three forms. It is said (1) that the motive is unknown, (2) that plunder was the object, (3) that liberty was sought; some here saying only because of the incitations of the abolitionists, others maintaining that the desire for liberty needed and had no such extraneous creator but sprang from the brains and the hearts of the Negroes themselves.

The early newspaper accounts[21] at times stated that "Their ultimate object. . . . (is) not yet explained." But in a work written[22] over fifty years after the event one is again informed that Turner's ". . . motives remain unknown."

The second explanation was widely adopted by contemporaries. The papers[23] of the time kept referring to the Negroes as "banditti" and to Nat Turner as the "bandit" and Governor Floyd, in his message to the Virginia Legislature of 1831–32, refers to "a banditti of slaves."[24] A North Carolina paper printed a letter telling of the discovery of a plot led by a Negro called Fed. Said the writer:[25] "Fed's plan, I have no doubt, was like that of Nat in Virginia, to obtain whatever money he could from the negroes, and more by plunder, then make his escape, and leave his poor deluded followers to shift for themselves." Niles also, at first, reported[26] that ". . . it is believed to have originated only in a design to plunder and not with a view to a more important object. . . ." Writing some weeks later Amos Gilbert observes[27] the confusion in the Southern papers on this point. "It appears from the southern papers that an insurrection recently took place

with some colored people of Southampton County Va.; or rather perha[
that some fugitive slaves had killed a number of persons in their pursuit
of plunder."

But the majority of the less immediate contemporary accounts and almost all of the later commentators agree that "a more important object,"
liberty, did exist. Some state this implicitly when they excoriate the abolitionists for having, as they affirm, brought on the revolt; others, observing no proof of that, often add a saving statement about the possibility of
Turner's having read or met the abolitionists.

Governor John Floyd in his message of December 6, 1831, already referred to,[28] states that Negro preachers and northern abolitionists were
responsible for the Revolt. Mrs. Lawrence Lewis,[29] a niece of George Washington, in a letter dated Alexandria, October 17, 1831, writes to her
friend, the Mayor of Boston, Harrison Gray Otis that ". . . to the Editor of
the 'Liberator'. . . . we owe in *greatest measure* this calamity." W. Gilmore
Simms,[30] in his review of Harriet Martineau's book on the United States,
objects to her statement, which he quotes in part, and not quite accurately, to the effect that the Revolt happened before the "abolition movement began." "Our author," says Mr. Simms, "confounds cause with effect.
She should have said that the Southampton insurrection broke out before
the secret workings of the abolitionists had been generally detected or
suspected."

A. B. Hart[31] declares that the Walker pamphlet ". . . may possibly have
influenced the Nat Turner insurrection of 1831. . . ." This very guarded
statement is cited by H. A. Herbert to substantiate his[32] idea that northern
agitators were responsible for the Revolt. It is very possible that Professor
Hart made his statement on the basis of the opinion of Benjamin Lundy[33]
who believed that Nat Turner ". . . had probably seen . . ." the pamphlet
and thought it ". . . probable . . . that the conspiracies (the Turner conspiracy and those that followed) were instigated chiefly by the before mentioned pamphlet of David Walker, if in fact they owed their origin to any
publication whatever." R. A. Brock[34] is also of the opinion that abolitionist
propaganda directly influenced Nat Turner. This gentleman is cited by
W. S. Drewry[35] who agrees with him. Carter G. Woodson also at least implies that abolitionist literature was important in bringing on the Revolt.[36]

Others, fewer, deny that there is discernible any connection between
this propaganda and the outbreak of the Revolt. First in this group is, of
course, William Lloyd Garrison himself,[37] who persistently and truthfully
denied advising the Negroes to use force and declared: "We have not a
single white or black subscriber south of the Potomac." As James Ford
Rhodes states:[38] "The assertion that slavery is a damning crime is one
thing; the actual incitement of slaves to insurrection is another." Yet, while
S. E. Morison[39] recognizes that ". . . Garrison always disclaimed any intent
of inciting slave insurrection" he thinks that the Turner Revolt was described by him ". . . in so truculent a manner as fairly to justify the Southern

suspicions of his motives." The word "truculent" is not too strong. In the *Liberator*[40] first giving an account of the Revolt is this paragraph: "Ye patriotic hypocrites! ye panegyrists of Frenchmen, Greeks, and Poles! ye Christian declaimers for liberty! ye valiant sticklers for equal rights among yourselves! ye haters of aristocracy! ye assailants of monarchy! ye republican nullifiers! ye treasonable disunionists! be dumb! Cast no reproach upon the conduct of the slaves, but let your lips and cheeks wear the blisters of condemnation." Certainly this is truculent, but not merely because of its exclamation marks. Nothing is more fierce, more uncompromising than truth.

The fact is that never has an iota of evidence been submitted to show that any abolitionist propaganda, of the Walker, Garrison, or milder type, had any connection whatsoever with bringing on the Turner Revolt.[41] Certainly one may say with A. B. Hart that it is "possible" the Walker pamphlet influenced Turner. It is also possible that some study of Napoleon influenced Turner and he decided that "... I was ordained for some great purpose in the hands of the Almighty."[42] There is as much proof for the one possibility as for the other. So when Burgess[43] states that "we shall probably never know whether there was [a connection between the propaganda and the event] or not," everything depends on what is meant by "know." The statement that there was no such connection is at least as justified as much of historical knowledge.

The previous writers, who asserted the abolitionists were responsible for the event, imply thereby that liberty was sought. And the origin of this seeking may clearly be seen in the mind of Nat Turner. It dawned and arose and filled his consciousness without having received any direct, definite extraneous stimulation. Thomas Gray's so-called *Confessions* tells the story. Here one learns that Nat Turner was able to read and that he read and lived through within himself the stories of the Bible. He was intelligent and well enough treated to want to be better treated.[44]

Certainly, Nat ran away and stayed away for thirty days. But then he returned for "... the Spirit appeared to me and said I had my wishes directed to the things of this world, and not to the kingdom of Heaven, and that I should return to the service of my earthly master...." But the other Negroes, the rank and file, as it might today be put "... found fault, and murmured [*sic*] against me, saying that if they had my sense they would not serve any master in the world."[45]

Turner stated,[46] further, that "... on the 12th of May, 1828, I heard a loud noise in the heavens, and the Spirit instantly appeared to me and said the Serpent was loosened, and Christ had laid down the yoke he had borne for the sins of men, and that I should take it on and fight against the Serpent, for the time was fast approaching when the first should be last and the last should be first. *Question:* (by T. Gray) Do you not find yourself mistaken now? *Answer:* Was not Christ crucified...." This last answer does not agree very well with the letter[47] from Mr. T. Trezvant to the editors of the Norfolk *Beacon*, of October 31: "He [Nat Turner] acknowledges himself a coward . . . he acknowledges now that the revelation was misinterpreted by him . . . he is now convinced that he has done wrong, and advises all other Negroes not to follow his example." It is possible that the mob which, it is said,[48] pricked, punched, and barrel-rolled Turner after he was caught, sought words like that from him, but the words of Nat Turner already given, and those to follow refute this propaganda from Mr. Trezvant, the purpose of which is given in his last sentence.

Turner waited for a sign from his God. This came to him in the form of a solar eclipse of February 1831. Nat then told four companions that it was time to prepare for the Revolt. And what day was selected?—July 4th. This moved William H. Parker to exclaim:[49] "This national holiday, hallowed as a day of liberty and peace (!) consecrated to the memories of the brave, patriotic heroes of the Revolution, was to be set apart for the complete destruction of the lives of their sons, and their property by a band of ferocious miscreants. Shame, shame! to thus pervert that sacred day and stain it with gory deeds!" How complexion affects reason!

But Nat Turner was ill on July 4th. Very naturally, then it was necessary to wait for another sign. And, again, the peculiar appearance of the sun, this time on Saturday, the 13th of August, when it had a "greenish blue color,"[50] seems to have been accepted as the sign. According to Drewry, Nat Turner exhorted at a meeting of Negroes in the southern part of Southampton not in North Carolina (as has been said)[51] where some of the Negroes ". . . signified their willingness to co-operate with him by wearing around their necks red bandanna handerchiefs. . . ." The same author states that these Negroes also showed their "rebellious spirits" by trying "to ride over white people."[52] No reference is given and the ring of this is false. It is, however, certain that there was a meeting of conspirators in the afternoon of Sunday, August 21 and it was then decided, as was done, to start the Revolt that evening.[53]

Nat was the last one to arrive at this meeting, purposely, as he stated. He seems to have appreciated the value of a dramatic entrance. He noticed a newcomer in the group: "I saluted them on coming up, and asked Will how came he there, he answered, his life was worth no more than others, and his liberty as dear to him. I asked him if he meant to obtain it? He said he would, or loose [*sic*] his life. This was enough to put him in full confidence." Such was the banditry of Nat Turner! And Turner, contrary to another of Mr. Trezvant's statements, did not believe he had "done wrong." As his lawyer stated, Turner pleaded not guilty ". . . saying to his counsel, that he did not feel so."[54]

There is what appears at first to be further evidence to substantiate the thesis that desire for liberty was Turner's motive. This is the speech which, according to G. W. Williams,[55] Turner made to his followers just before the Revolt started. The closing sentences reveal the gist of this: "Remember that ours is not war for robbery nor to satisfy our passions; it is a *struggle for freedom.* Ours must be deeds, not words. Then let us away to the scene of action." This, it is believed, accurately describes Turner's feelings, but the entire speech flowed from Mr. Williams' oratorical powers, not Turner's.

It appears, then, that Nat Turner's main object was not plunder. But what about his followers? If one may judge by the conversation between Will and Turner previously quoted he may fairly say that among the original conspirators liberty loomed as the primary, perhaps as the sole, aim. And if Mr. Guion,[56] in his letter to Judge Thomas Ruffin, was accurate, it appears that this same desire animated some, at least, of the scores who later joined the Revolt.

But it is a fair assumption that not all who took part in this movement were solely or primarily motivated by the desire simply for freedom. If it were otherwise, the Nat Turner Revolt would be absolutely unique. It appears that money was taken,[57] but not even an approximation as to the amount is possible. It is also not certain whether the money was taken for itself or as a means to furthering the Revolt. Drewry[58] is certain that ". . . each negro meditated returning home within a few days to take possession of his master's home." It would be interesting to know how Mr. Drewry knows what "each negro meditated" in 1831, but quite possibly this idea existed among some of them. Drewry, indeed, tells of one gentleman, Mr. Colin Kitchen (and this depends upon the latter's memory going back seventy years), who found, after the suppression of the revolt, that his house and its possessions had been taken over by one of his slaves.

It has often been said[59] that a large number of the Negroes who took part in the Revolt did so only under compulsion. As Higginson pointed[60] out, it was to be expected that, once the movement had been crushed, this would be offered as an extenuating circumstance. How many, then, if any, joined the Revolt only under duress cannot be said.

C: THE LIGHTNING STRIKES

No attempt will here be made to give a detailed picture of the proceedings of the revolt. Accuracy is impossible, and the importance of it is very questionable. Moreover, the attempt has been made by Drewry[61] who devotes forty pages to it. This is really too detailed, for the reader is told[62] that one infant was temporarily spared because it "sweetly smiled" at the assailant. Violence is too horrible to need any such artistic touches, and that such embellishments are not of an historic nature needs no demonstration. This was a revolt and as Lincoln Steffens remarked to Eugene Debs, who was strongly deprecating the violence of the Bolshevik Revolution:[63] "True 'Gene. That's all true that you say. A revolution is no gentleman." Here Nat Turner, himself,[64] may be quoted: ". . . He [Nat Turner] says that indiscriminate massacre was not their intention after they obtained foothold, and was resorted to in the first instance to strike terror and alarm. Women and children would afterwards have been spared, and men too who ceased to resist."

Certain phases of the event will be examined. Attempts will be made to answer such questions as: How many Negroes took part? How many people were killed *before* the Revolt was suppressed? Was there any connection between the poorer whites and the Negroes? How was the Revolt suppressed?

The first question may be answered only approximately—indeed, Nat Turner, himself, did not venture more. It appears that between sixty and eighty Negroes took part in the Revolt. But it is to be noticed that most of the contemporary figures were very much higher than this, thus making the extreme terror that ensued more understandable. The highest estimate[65] observed places the number at "six or eight hundred." Other contemporary accounts[66] put the number at from 150 to 300, but there is only one later writer, so far as is known, who gives the number as within that scope. J. B. McMaster[67] gives the number as two hundred.

There are, on the other hand, contemporary estimates, which fall within the range suggested as being probably accurate. From what Turner himself says[68] it is apparent that he thought his followers amounted to from 60 to 80. The Governor of Virginia[69] thought that there were no more than seventy slaves implicated at any time. The editor of the Richmond *Whig*, when he visited Southampton,[70] decided that ". . . the insurgents never exceeded 60. . . ." According to the Richmond *Compiler* of August 29th,[71] only about fifty Negroes took part. In the letter of E. P. Guion, already partly quoted, it is said:[72] ". . . it was thought that not more than sixty negroes at the most was [sic] in the Rebellion. . . ."

In comparing the two classes of evidence the second is clearly preferable and has been followed by all later writers,[73] with two exceptions. One has been mentioned. The other, who goes to the opposite extreme, is James C. Ballagh who states that ". . . the band grew . . . finally, to forty."[74] Why that low number is selected is not explained. It appears, then, that probably from sixty to eighty Negroes fought with Nat Turner.

The number killed before the Revolt was put down, may, again, only be approximated, but more closely than the other. Whether any Negroes were then killed is not clear, but if any were the number was small. A contemporary report states that at one of the last encounters, that at the home of a Dr. Blount,[75] the Negroes left ". . . one killed (we believe) and one wounded. . . ." Drewry states[76] that at the engagement which occurred at Parker's Field ". . . several of the Negroes . . ." were killed, but, as usual, no reference is given. Some,[77] on the other hand, have denied that any Negroes were killed while the actual Revolt was in progress.

In the *Confessions* Thomas Gray gave the names of the whites killed. His list amounts to fifty-five. The same total is given in the pamphlet by Samuel Warner[78] and it is the figure given by a number of later writers.[79] Drewry[80] reprints the list given by Gray and states that one overseer is omitted. No list gives the name of Shepherd Lee, 24 years old, who, in a genealogy of the Lee family[81] of York County, Virginia, is mentioned as "... killed in 1831 in Nat Turner's Insurrection...." This brings the number killed to fifty-seven. Very often, however,[82] a figure in the sixties is given. Only three figures higher than this have been seen.[83] Miss Martineau states that "upwards of seventy white, chiefly women and children ..." were killed. This figure, as she states, was gotten from hearsay. James K. Paulding asked a planter of eastern Virginia to describe conditions. This planter refers to Turner, and there is a footnote, apparently by Paulding, as follows: "The leader of the insurrection in Lower Virginia, in which upwards of a hundred white persons, principally women and children, were massacred in cold blood." The highest estimate, two hundred killed, appeared in one of the earliest contemporary guesses. It appears that more than fifty-five but less than sixty-five whites were killed in Southampton County within the approximately forty hours that the revolt raged.

D: WERE THERE WHITE ALLIES?

Some of the first contemporary accounts[84] stated that the revolt was led by a few whites, in no case more than three. Governor Floyd[85] in his message of December 6, 1831, hinted that the rebellious spirit was "not confined to the slaves." The close friendship between Nat and a white man, E. T. Brantley, has been mentioned. T. W. Higginson tells[86] what appears to be a story he invented of Nat Turner, at a meeting of Negro conspirators, sending some eavesdropping poor whites back to their homes with words of good advice, who then "... were better friends than ever to Prophet Nat." Drewry states[87] that Turner "... is said to have passed the home of some poor white people because he considered it useless to kill those who thought no better of themselves than they did of negroes." The tradition of Turner's behavior here may be accurate.

Better evidence has been unearthed by Mr. James H. Johnston.[88] This is a letter forming part of Governor Floyd's collected papers on "Slaves and Free Negroes." Although the letter is of considerable length it will be given in full for it is of great interest. The letter is addressed to:

> 'Ben Lee in great haste
> mail speadily
> Richmond swift.'
>   Chesterfield County
>   August 29, 1831.

My old fellow
Ben—

You will tell or acquaint every servant in Richmond and adjoining countys they all must be in strict readiness, that this occurance will go throug Virginia with the slaves and whites if there had never been an association—a visiting

with free and slaves this would never had of been. They are put up by the
free about their liberation. I've wrote to Norfolk Amelia, Nottoway and to
sevel other countys to different slaves bob and bill Miller Bowler john fergu-
son—and sevel other free fellows been at Dr. Crumps—and a great many
gentlemens servants how they must act in getting their liberation they must
set afire to the city beginning at Shokoe Hill then going through east west
north south Set fire to the birdges they are about to break out in Goochland
and in Mecklenburg and several other countys very shortly. Now their is a
barber here in this place—tells that a methodist of the name edmonds has
put a great many servants up how they should do and act by setting fire to
this town. I do wish they may succeed by so doing we poor whites can get
work as well as slaves or collord, this fellow edmonds the methodist says that
judge J. F.—is no friend to the free and your Richmond free associates that
your master Watkins Lee brockenberry Johnson Taylor of Norfolk and several
other noble delegates is bitterly against them all—servants says that billy hick-
man has just put him up how to do to revenge the whites—edmonds says so
you all ought to get revenge—every white in this place is scared to death
except myself and a few others this methodist has put up a great many slaves
in this place what to do I can tell you so push on boys push on.

Your friend Williamson Mann.

There appears to be no reason to question the authenticity of this letter, but to determine its meaning and to evaluate it are difficult. It appears
probable that Ben Lee was a Negro slave, the name Lee coming from his
"master Watkins Lee." This gives meaning to the phrase "edmonds says
you all ought to get revenge." This and other phrases in the letter, as the
one telling of his having written to "different slaves," indicates the existence, on how great or small a scale cannot be said, of a common feeling
among the poor, the exploited, slave or free Negro or white.

But nothing Nat Turner ever said, so far as what he said is known,
would indicate that there was this unity in the movement he led, and it
appears certain that no white people were concerned with the carrying
out of the Revolt itself. The letter does substantiate Floyd's statement
about the existence of a rebellious spirit among some of the poorer whites,
which, as will later be shown, seems also to have existed in North Carolina,
and indicates that this spirit was *aroused by* the Turner Revolt. Some results
of this will be observed when the effects of that event are considered.

E: Defeat and Capture

The quick suppression of the Revolt may be explained by the poor arms
and almost, if not quite, total lack of ammunition possessed by the Negroes; the fact that some, apparently, became drunk; all were fatigued;
and the separation of the forces, against the advice of Turner, when on
their way to the county-seat, Jerusalem (now called Courtland); and, at

the final test, the superior force and arms of the whites. It is, however, to be noticed that, notwithstanding the fact that two of the reasons some Negroes hoped for success were beliefs that the British would aid them and that there were but 80,000 whites in the country,[89] had Nat Turner been successful in capturing Jerusalem, with its arms and ammunition, he might have prolonged the conflict for many days; perhaps, with guerrilla warfare, for weeks.

Mr. R. P. Howison wrote:[90] "But when within a few miles of the place, (Jerusalem) they were met by a small body of white men, armed with guns generally loaded *with birdshot*, and at the first discharge, the cowardly wretches turned and fled to the swamps behind them." U. B. Phillips similarly wrote that[91] sixty Negroes were dispersed by eighteen whites, ". . . armed like themselves with fowling pieces with birdshot ammunition. . . ." But the factors mentioned and soon to be demonstrated sufficiently explain the defeat of the Negroes without resorting to the charge of cowardice; and the example Howison and Phillips select to substantiate that charge is fallacious.

After riding and fighting all Sunday night and Monday morning, Turner brought together his force and started out for Jerusalem. A few miles from that town they passed the gate of the estate of a wealthy farmer, a Mr. Parker. Some of the Negroes wished to recruit his slaves, and over the objections of Turner, set out for the home about half a mile from the gate. Some of those starting out appear to have been under the influence of Southampton cider (it has been mentioned that products of the orchard were important in the economy of the country) and they appear to have taken more refreshments from Mr. Parker's well-stocked cellar. Nat Turner became impatient and, leaving, as he stated, seven or eight men at the gate, went to fetch his tardy followers.[92] It was this handful of slaves which was attacked by eighteen whites and, according to Drewry,[93] who certainly is not sympathetic, the Negroes were armed ". . . with few rifles, fowling-pieces loaded with bird shot being the general weapon. The negroes were also in want of ammunition and used gravel for shot, Nat insisting that the Lord had revealed the sand would answer the same purpose as lead." This is substantiated by the Richmond *Compiler*[94] of August 29: "They had few fire arms among them—and scarcely one, if one, that was fit for use." This group retreated, but was re-enforced by the returning Turner and his companions. Now the whites retreated, but they, in turn, were re-inforced by a body of militia which dispersed the slaves. Turner, with a much reduced force, appears to have still made sporadic raids, but this engagement at Parker's Field was the critical one and by Tuesday, the 23rd, the Revolt was crushed. Soon three companies of federal troops (which, as previously stated, had been recently stationed at Fort Monroe for this purpose), with a field piece and 100 stands of spare arms with ammunition had arrived, at the request of the Mayor of Norfolk, J. E. Holt.[95]

General Eppes,[96] commanding the forces at Jerusalem, reported to the Governor that he had taken forty-eight prisoners. Other[97] estimates place the number at the low fifties. There is uncertainty, too, as to what was done with these men. The Samuel Warner pamphlet, published a month after the Revolt, gives the names, owners and dates of executions of nineteen slaves, but in the Gray pamphlet, seventeen slaves are given as having been executed (four free Negroes are mentioned as having been sent for further trial; it appears that three of these were hung). Eight of the Negroes Warner gives as having been hung are listed by Gray as having suffered transportation.[98] The lowest estimate of the number hung is eleven,[99] given by U. B. Phillips, but most later[100] accounts follow quite closely that given by Thomas Gray.

Nat Turner successfully eluded his pursuers from the end of August to October 30, when he was caught, armed only with an old sword, by Benjamin Phipps. During those weeks there had been rumors that he was caught, that he was a runaway in Maryland, that he was drowned, but he had never left Southampton.[101] He left his hiding place only at night for water, having supplied himself with food.[102] On November 5, the honorable Jeremiah Cobb pronounced the sentence of the Court,[103] which closed as follows: "The judgment of the Court is, that you be taken hence to the jail from whence you came, thence to the place of execution, and on Friday next, between the hours of 10 A.M. and 2 P.M. be hung by the neck until you are dead! dead! dead! and may the Lord have mercy upon your soul."

And on November 11, 1831, Nat Turner went to his death, calmly and apparently unafraid,[104] in the city of Courtland, then known as Jerusalem, in Southampton County, Virginia. But, though Jeremiah Cobb exclaimed dead! thrice, and even had he so exclaimed three hundred times, Nat then, at the moment of his execution, only began to live.

———

FOUR

Covenant in Jerusalem

———

THOMAS C. PARRAMORE

Nat Turner, a slave on the farm of carriage-maker Joseph Travis, met his cohorts by prearrangement on the afternoon of Sunday, 21 August 1831, at nearby Cabin Pond. They had talked for months about rebelling against the whites, and Nat had called the meeting to make final preparations for it. Present were Hark Travis and Will Francis, who, like Nat, were said to be Methodist "exhorters" (lay preachers). Nelson Williams, Sam Francis, Jack Reese, and Henry Porter were also present.[1]

Following extended discussion, they agreed to begin the revolt that night by killing the Travis family and then all other whites they found until they felt strong enough to spare at least women and children. The revolt, initiated by Nat's hatchet and Will's axe, would move from farm to farm, its members recruiting other rebels and confiscating arms and horses.[2]

Nat, known as "General Cargill" or "General Jackson," would lead. His principal subordinates would be known as "General Nelson" or "General Gaines," "General Porter," and "General Moore." (Hark Travis was better known to blacks as Hark Moore, from the surname of a former master, Thomas Moore.) Jack Reese, married to Hark's sister, begged off owing to illness but was induced by Hark to stay. The discussion concluded around 10:30 P.M.[3]

Walking through the woods to Travis's, where the family had gone to bed, the group, joined at the great house by Travis's slave Austin, spent some hours drinking cider from Travis's press, perhaps to fortify themselves against the grim work ahead. At last, at around 3:00 A.M., Hark placed a ladder under an upstairs window, and Nat silently climbed it, then crept downstairs to unbar the door. He called on his henchmen to initiate the killing, but they replied that he must set the example by starting it himself.[4]

Nat and Will slipped into the upstairs bedroom in which Travis and his wife Sally slept. In the dark, Nat swung a (possibly deliberate) glancing hatchet-blow at Travis's head. Travis lept up, calling his wife's name, but Will felled him with one blow of his ax and Sally with another. Twelve-year-old Putnam Moore (Nat's legal owner) and Joel Westbrook (Travis's coach-making apprentice) were all but decapitated in an upper bedroom by members of the group.[5]

Nat and Will found four operable guns and some powder and shot; the rest of the group armed themselves with grubbing hoes and axes. Perhaps to assert their seniority among hosts of expected recruits, they put feathers in their caps and red sashes around their waists and shoulders. Testimony later offered in the trial of a suspected rebel stated that the insurgent leaders wore "light breeches and the others dark ones."[6]

Nat led his men out into the yard and lined them up in an improvised formation, guiding them through his own version of drills of the county militia. He then marched them off toward Salathiel Francis's farm, a quarter-mile southeast. They took Travis's several horses and took a slave boy named Moses Travis to hold them. (Presumably, they wanted to keep the horses quiet until Francis was dead.) The band avoided the nearby home of Giles Reese, who owned inhospitable bulldogs that might signal the rebels' approach. En route, they realized that Travis's infant son Joseph had been overlooked, so Nat sent Will and Henry back to kill him, which they did by dashing his head against a fireplace.[7]

Salathiel Francis was asleep in his one-room abode, as was his slave Nelson. Sam and Will, slaves of Salathiel's brother Nathaniel, called for Salathiel, saying that they had a letter for him from their owner. Francis opened the door and, although he was a strong man, he was quickly overcome and killed by his assailants. Francis's terrified slave Nelson, fleeing out the back door, was shot but made his way to Nathaniel's farm to rouse the family.[8]

Moving southeast, the rebels, some of them mounted, bypassed the home of a widow Harris, allegedly because her slave Joe made sparing her a condition of his joining them. A mile further, the nine men came to widow Piety Reese's at about 5:30 A.M. An unlocked door made it a simple matter to dispatch both her and son William in their beds. James Balmer, the farm's overseer, was in the house and fell under a hail of hoes and axes. Badly hurt, he feigned death and survived.[9]

By this time, it was first light, about 6:00 A.M. Three miles south of Reese's, they came to the farm of Wiley Francis who, somehow fore-warned, remained defiantly at home, having sent his daughters and wife to the woods. He armed his slaves, who, stationed in his yard, seemed ready to offer resistance to the rebels. Duels with fellow slaves not figuring in his scheme, Nat dismissed Francis as not worth taking the time to kill and moved on.[10]

One report contends that Nat was telling slave women to "keep things in order until the tenth of March next," a date with perhaps mystical significance for him—the date when he would return, presumably with their menfolk. It was critical that he find large numbers of male slaves to join him, but, in the four hours since he had left Travis's house, he had added only two, owing, at least in part, to the small size of the farms raided. This could be remedied at larger plantations, so the rebels swung northeast toward an area of more well-stocked estates.[11]

Arriving at the farm of Mrs. Elizabeth Turner, Nat's former owner, they saw her overseer, Hartwell Peebles, at the brandy-still. Henry, Sam, and Austin veered toward him, the latter shooting him dead. At the great-house, Will dismounted at a gallop, raced to the front door, and split it open with his ax. Mrs. Turner and Mrs. Sarah Newsom, sisters, stood weeping in a front room as Will's ax struck the former dead. Nat pummeled Mrs. Newsome's head with his sword until Will again dealt a fatal blow.[12]

Nat led his eight mounted men on to the next farm north, the widow Caty Whitehead's. A few still on foot were sent by a path to Henry Bryant's, a few hundred yards northeast, from whence they would then make their way to Whitehead's. This party made short work of Bryant, his wife Sally, their child, and Sally's mother. But the rebels had little gunpowder and were beginning to mix sand or brandy with it, unwittingly diluting its strength.[13]

As the mounted rebels swept down a lane toward Whitehead's, they noticed the widow's son Richard, a Methodist minister, at work with slaves in a field beside the lane. Will halted beside the fence, called him over, and, when he came, severed his head from his body with his ax.[14]

As his horsemen reached the Whitehead yard, Nat saw a figure run past the garden; he gave chase but found that it was a slave girl. Turning back toward the house, he noted that the killing was already far advanced. Mrs. Whitehead's three daughters and an infant grandson were hacked to death, and she herself, found bathing the child, was being dragged out. As Nat came up, Will cut off her head, again with his lethal axe.[15]

Nat noticed another daughter, Margaret, hiding in a corner formed by a projecting cellar entrance. She tried to flee, but he overtook her and, after several ineffective blows with his sword, killed her with a fence rail, his only murder during the revolt. Hubbard, a slave, hid a fifth daughter, Harriet, between a bed and mat; when the raiders left, he led her to safety in some woods. She was rescued the next day by soldiers. Most of the Whitehead slaves ran off, but the rebels succeeded in bullying Jack and Andrew into joining. Both later slipped away.[16]

Nat again divided his men. One band moved to the farms of Howell Harris, a mile northwest, and Trajan Doyel, a few hundred yards further. The other went north to Richard Porter's farm, with orders to rejoin Nat and the others at Nathaniel Francis's. Doyel was killed in the road by his mill, but Harris, forewarned by a slave girl, escaped. Meanwhile, Doyel's slave Hugh reportedly ran to the neighboring house of Elisha Atkins and led Mrs. Atkins and her child into hiding.[17]

Nat next led his foot soldiers to Richard Porter's, two miles north of Whitehead's. The family was gone, but he enlisted several slaves there and, doubling back to meet his cavalry, learned that they had found the Harris farm deserted.[18]

Although Nat may not yet have recognized it, his rebellion was already disintegrating. Despite their having killed 23 whites with no loss to his 16 or so recruits, his situation was precarious. The flight of Atkins and others meant that word was outrunning the rebels' line of march; organized resistance was sure to appear, and many slaves, as at the Salathiel and Wiley Francis farms, were fearful or contemptuous of the rebels and refused to join.

In fact, few uprisings have ever been so ill prepared and unplanned. As far back as February, Nat and his key men had talked of revolt, initially setting 4 July as the date to begin, but Nat, ill, as he said, from forming and rejecting plans, postponed it. The Cabin Pond meeting on 21 August was held, he admitted, "to concert a plan, as we had not yet determined any."[19] The final plan, six months in the making, seems to have been to seize weapons and kill a great many white people with them.

To achieve successive surprises, Nat should probably have struck before midnight and moved quickly along a predetermined, preferably straight, course. The county seat at Jerusalem, apparently not yet envisioned as his destination, could have been reached before dawn. But he frittered the night away at Travis's conducting useless drills and perhaps overcoming the effects of excessive drinking, thereby making it possible to strike only two other tiny farms in the last hours of darkness.[20] Choosing routes as he rode, he had all but doubled back from his first course, giving whites in the vicinity a chance to collect their wits.

Perhaps reverting to an old policy of not mixing with those he influenced, or having found that he lacked a killer's instinct (as when he asked others to launch the carnage at Travis's), Nat began falling behind, usually reaching farms after they were raided. He was present, therefore, at only one subsequent attack. His stolen "fine-dress," light sword, silver-tipped and ivory-handled, may have been useful as a symbol of authority, but it was too dull to be otherwise serviceable—and may also have been deliberately misused. (He may have been forced to kill Margaret Whitehead because he had black witnesses.) There is no evidence that either he or most of his men were familiar with guns and ammunition, evidently preferring their hoes and axes. These were fatal shortcomings for those who were expected to set examples of exuberant ferocity.[21]

Nat also seems not to have pondered the likely interference by county militia and troops from Norfolk, Richmond, and elsewhere. He may not have anticipated that many slaves and free blacks, loath to abandon their families, would reject his cause (if, indeed, they fully understood what it was) or would be induced to join only under threats of death. A number of slaves even risked their own lives to aid white families. He also failed to anticipate that he could not prevent his men from quaffing cider and brandy and wasting time in plunder.

As the alarm spread, some whites speculated that Nat's destination was the Dismal Swamp, not far east, or the county seat at Jerusalem—though his meanderings gave no clue as to his destination, if he had one in mind. Others thought he meant to go to Norfolk, hijack a ship, and sail to Africa: but it is unlikely that any of his men had ever seen a vessel larger than the tiny boats on Southampton's narrow Nottoway River or knew anything about sailing.[22]

A slave of General Meriwether B. Brodnax, district militia commander, later declared that they were headed for the free states to "make proselytes and return to assist their brethren," a purpose consistent with Nat's alleged assurances that he would return in March. But there is no evidence of this plan in Nat's confession nor any indication that he had any idea how far or in what direction he would have to travel to realize it. He seems to have had little or no notion of distances or routes beyond the periphery of Southampton County and was reported to have assured his men that America's white population numbered only about 80,000.[23]

The truth was that Nat, despite his intellect, fierce will, and indomitable courage, was a lifelong mystic and, it seems, was incapable of devising a feasible plan. As one white observer put it, Nat hoped to free "himself and his race . . . by supernatural means."[24] He relied on sheer faith, and the help of fellow blacks inflamed by his passion, to reap the harvest of the signs and portents that nourished his understanding. Fate chose ill in making him not only the catalyst of liberty but field marshal as well; his Mazzini lacked a Garibaldi. And, in the end, it might appear that Nat understood all this before he decided to rebel.

The revolt lurched on aimlessly from one farm to the next. From the abandoned homestead of Richard Porter, the rebels proceeded to Nathaniel Francis's, just missing Francis and his mother, who had gone to Travis's to see what was wrong. At the Francis house, the rebels found two visitors, Mrs. John R. Williams and her infant, and killed both. Two young wards of Francis, nephews Samuel and John L. Brown, and Francis's distiller, Henry Doyel, were also killed. Lavinia, Francis's wife, eight months pregnant, hid under clothes and blankets in a closet and escaped detection. Returning home, Francis met a slave boy who said that Nathaniel's family was dead. Dred Francis and three boys, Nat, Tom, and Davy, enrolled with the rebels after being told that they would be shot if they tried to escape.[25]

While the slaughter was taking place at Whitehead's, John R. Williams, called "Choctaw" because he wore his hair Indian-fashion, was just starting to teach a class of children at his small school in the vicinity of Cross Keys, southeast of Whitehead's. Warned of the rebel approach, he dismissed the class and ran over to Whitehead's, finding the grounds strewn with mangled bodies. As he raced home, one of his slaves met him and told him that his child and wife Louise had also been slain.[26]

Jordan Barnes, a neighbor of Nathaniel Francis, got word of the Whitehead raid from his hired slave, Jack Reese, who, still unwell, had fled from the rebels. It was probably Barnes who later claimed to have "just had time to escape out of the back door as the negroes entered the front."[27] Peter Edwards, whose farm was next attacked, also had enough notice to escape with his family, leaving his slaves behind.

With five recruits from Edwards's farm, the rebels moved north to Militia Captain John Thomas Barrow's. Residing three-quarters of a mile north of Edwards, he too had heard of the uprising from a neighbor. He prepared to flee, but his pretty wife Mary is reported to have insisted on finishing her toilette. He fired his musket from a window at the rebels and ran for a rifle. As his front door was forced, he hurried Mary out the back and broke the stock of his rifle over the nearest rebel. Mary was briefly detained by her slave Lucy, but made her escape when another slave woman intervened. Barrow, fighting for time for his wife, was soon dead, his throat cut with a razor wielded by a rebel reaching through a window.[28]

Newit Harris, a farmer just northwest, was hustled into hiding by his slave Ben, who tended Harris's still. Harris's daughter-in-law, Mrs. Robert Musgrave, was approaching the farm with her infant child and a schoolboy nephew, George Musgrave. Ben met and took them to a cornfield, where the lady fainted. "Aunt Edie," another Harris slave, revived her, stuffed a handkerchief in the crying infant's mouth, and led them to where Harris was hiding.[29]

Nat overtook his men at Harris's, where some were deep into the proprietor's brandy. The elated rebels, now about 40 in all, greeted their leader with hurrahs. He ordered them to remount at once and head northwest to the Barrow road that led toward Jerusalem, the county seat. It seems to have been only at this point that Nat decided that Jerusalem, falsely reported to have a cache of militia arms, might be a secure bastion against white attacks. He ordered that his force hereafter approach each farm at full gallop, shrieking and shouting to maximize the terror.[30]

Some three miles further toward the Barrow road, Nat came to Levi Waller's. It was 10:30 A.M., and Waller was at his still when he learned of their approach. He sent his son Tom to bring the local teacher, William Crocker, and his pupils, including two of Waller's own children, to the Waller farm for protection.[31]

When the rebels arrived, Waller, remarkably, was still at work. Dred and other riders saw him fall behind weeds in the garden but failed to find him, perhaps owing to a diversion created by Waller's blacksmith, Alfred. While a massacre and decapitation of children and adults ensued, Waller, hiding behind currant bushes within 200 feet of the house, witnessed the worst carnage of the rebellion. At later trials, he recounted that he had fled to a swamp, remained some time, and crept back to see what was happening. The rebels were drinking his cider as though there was no hurry.[32]

In the meantime, Sam, Daniel, and Aaron had entered a log house, found Mrs. Waller hiding there, and cut her throat. Her daughter Martha and schoolgirl Lucinda Jones were among 11 slain children tossed onto a grisly pile. As Crocker fled across a cornfield, he was observed by the rebels but was saved when schoolgirl Clarinda Jones abruptly appeared between Crocker and the rebels and was shot. She feigned death and was later saved.[33]

"Yellow Davy," Waller's slave, rode off with the rebels "in great glee," evidently joined by Alfred. Nat regrouped and moved east. In his haste to reach Jerusalem, he bypassed the farm of 75-year-old Thomas Gray, the county's leading horse breeder.[34]

Along the way, the rebels reached the home of William Williams, where they demanded that his wife show them where to find him. She may or may not have pointed him out in a fodder field, where he was at work with two hired boys, Miles and Henry Johnson. But she was forced to ride behind a rebel and witness the death of all three before being shot to death beside her husband's corpse.[35]

It was late morning when the rebels reached the next farm east, that of Jacob Williams, who was measuring timber in a nearby wood. Edwin Drewry, overseer of the nearby James Bell farm was with a slave loading corn at Jacob's when he cried: "Lord, who is that coming?" He was quickly caught, shot, and, reportedly, disemboweled before the rebels advanced to Williams's house and killed his wife and three children. At the nearby home of Caswell Worrell, Jacob Williams's overseer, Mrs. Worrell and her child were also cut down. Worrell took in the scene from a distance and fled to safety.[36]

At the next farm, a quarter-mile southeast, Mrs. Rebecca Vaughan was in the yard giving "directions to a servant who was peeling peaches for dinner." As she returned to the house, she saw the rebels coming up the avenue and ran screaming inside. Nat's men dismounted in the yard, aiming guns at the house. Mrs. Vaughan appeared at a window pleading for her life and was shot twice. Her 18-year-old niece, Ann Eliza, reputed "beauty of the county," ran downstairs and was slain by a stalwart rebel named Marmaduke. Fifteen-year-old Arthur Vaughan was shot near the still, the last white killed in the revolt—less than half a day after it had begun.[37]

Owing to the inefficiency with which the revolt was executed, virtually all of Southampton County was now on tense alert. The first white warned was probably Nathaniel Francis, who lived just northwest of Whitehead's and was told in early morning by a slave boy of Travis, and by the wounded Nelson, Salathiel Francis's slave.[38] Others spreading alarms included, at least, Levi Waller, Wiley Francis, "Choctaw" Williams, Jordan Barnes, Peter Edwards, Mrs. John Thomas Barrow, Drewry Bittle, Mrs. Robert Musgrave, William Crocker, Caswell Worrell, and numerous loyal slaves.

By early Monday afternoon, white Southampton, though gripped by terror, was largely organized for defense and preparing to retaliate. Tiny communities—Boykins, Jerusalem, Branch's Bridge, Cross Keys, and others—overflowed with noncombatants seeking safety. Jerusalem was "full of women, most of them from the other [west] side" of the Nottoway River, which formed an imposing barrier to the rebels. Others slept in nearby "clusters of pines, with a blanket to each, and a pallet for the children." According to one report, "For many miles around . . . , the country is deserted by women and children."[39]

Southampton folklore abounds, perhaps excessively, in instances of loyal slaves aiding masters and mistresses in the crisis and rebels drinking to stupefying excess. No property had been burned, possibly to avoid columns of smoke that might reveal the rebels' location. All sources agree, possibly from propriety, that no rapes of white women occurred.[40]

Thus far in the rebellion, searches of houses had reportedly turned up between $800 and $1,000 in cash, and an impromptu pay scale seems to have been worked out based on rank. The paymaster, "General" Henry Porter, was to distribute ten dollars a day for generals, five additional for himself, and a dollar each for privates, an inducement to make enrollment in the revolt more attractive. At the end of the uprising, Nat's own funds, probably in his possession all along, are said to have amounted to four shillings, six pence, or about 75 cents.[41]

As Nat's army neared Jerusalem, he felt that his force, by this time fully mounted, might seize the bridge across the Nottoway at Jerusalem. Three miles short of the span, the 40 or more rebels came to the gate of planter James W. Parker's lane. Some of Nat's men insisted, against his judgment—an indication that he may have been losing control—that they could gain recruits there. So Nat and six or eight others kept nervous vigil while the rest galloped across a cornfield toward the house, half a mile away.[42]

Nat probably sensed that, with Jerusalem so near, it was an untimely moment for his forces to divide. When the raiders did not promptly return, he set off to hurry them and was leading them back from the deserted house when he saw several mounted whites coming from the direction of the gate. The small party he had left there was scattering in confusion.[43]

The attackers were a white patrol, led by Captain Alexander Peete, who had ridden out from Jerusalem in late morning and picked up the insurgents' trail at Levi Waller's. Pursuing it, the group came upon the rebels near Parker's, where the first armed engagement of the insurrection took place. Upon spotting the rebels at the gate, Peete, owing to the fact that his men were armed only with fowling pieces and their powder was wet from a shower, ordered his force to hold its fire until within 30 paces of the rebels.[44]

The battle at Parker's field opened with the kind of mischance that sometimes thwarts even the best-laid plans. Attorney James Strange French, riding an unbroken colt lent to him by a Jerusalem innkeeper, had not caught up with the scouts when he saw the rebels across a bridge ahead of him. He halted, but the neighing of horses caused his mount suddenly to dash forward onto the bridge. With admirable presence of mind, French fired his shotgun, though yet a 100 yards from the rebels, and cried out: "Here they are, boys, here they are." Charging, he briefly routed the startled rebels.[45]

Moments later, a second, smaller patrol of whites appeared nearby. This one, headed by attorney William C. Parker, a veteran of the War of 1812, had followed roughly the same route through this part of the county as had the first.[46]

As the first white patrol approached, Nat, who quickly restored order among his men, saw his advantage in numbers, if not in firepower, and thrust out for a sorely needed victory. Without allowing time for reloading, he ordered a charge, shouting, "Fire, and Goddamn them, rush!" The attackers overran several whites, striking one or more from their horses and wounding two others while the other whites retreated over a small hill.[47] The gates of Jubilee and Jerusalem appeared to have swung open.

Cresting the hill, however, Nat was dismayed to find the second white patrol rallying and reinforcing the first. The sight of this second party, and the first stopping to reload, again threw the rebels into disarray, though several plunged on into the whites' fusillade. But Nat's men were now seriously outgunned and demoralized. Dred's arm was shattered, and Hark's horse shot from under him. Nat caught the reins of an unmounted horse until Hark could claim it. Shouting to those of his men nearest him, Nat retreated, any rational hope of freeing his people now gone.[48]

Leaving behind four men dead and several captured, Nat carried away five or six wounded, in an orderly retreat. But, in the hope that he might yet find a way to prevail, he led his remaining 20 or so men down a private road toward Cypress Bridge, three miles below Jerusalem, where he might not be expected, and could attack Jerusalem from the east. Overtaking two more of his men, he was told that the rest had disappeared.[49]

Nat's course toward Cypress Bridge took him past the home of Mrs. John Thomas (her son George later a Civil War Union general). A mounted local white, James Gurley, kept track of the rebels as they marched and alerted farms and nearby militia, who took positions at Cypress Bridge to discourage an attack there.[50]

Frustrated and desperate, Nat headed south toward the Travis farm in search of more recruits. His route passed several vacant farms before swinging erratically north on the Belfield road, perhaps because he learned that all of the bridges ahead of him were guarded. After dark, he arrived at a wood near a farm belonging to Thomas Ridley and ordered a rest. The Ridley manor house was guarded by militia.[51]

Nat had just fallen into an exhausted sleep when he woke to a scene of alarm; whites were said by his pickets to be about to attack. He sent men to reconnoiter, but they found no one; their own return to camp reignited the bedlam. More rebels appear to have fled at this time, reducing Nat's forces to less than 20. These he gamely rallied and led his men a mile southwest toward Dr. Simon Blunt's, a farm with a large slave force.[52]

On Tuesday, 23 August, dawn was just breaking as the rebels crashed Blunt's front gate, 80 yards from the house. Nat apparently thought the Blunts had fled, probably leaving most of their slaves behind. But gouty old Dr. Blunt waited at the house with his 15-year-old son Simon, neighbor Drewry W. Fitzhugh, overseer Shadrach Futrell, and two boys, armed with six guns and ample ammunition. Some Blunt slaves waited in the separate kitchen to aid in the defense. The white women were in upper rooms.[53]

Hark Travis, in the lead, fired as he neared the house, testing whether or not anyone was inside. He was answered by Simon Blunt and Futrell, who were hiding on the front porch and receiving reloaded guns through a window. The first shotgun blast hit and unhorsed Hark. Badly hurt, he took refuge in a cotton patch and was soon afterward captured. In the following minutes, several other rebels were also wounded.[54]

Meanwhile, Mrs. Blunt handed her youngest child to her slave Mary and told her to flee. Mary and other slave women rushed across the garden, but Barrow's slave Moses, dropping his gun, cried, "Oh God damn you, have I got you," and, despite a game leg, lept the garden fence in ardent pursuit of Mary, only to abandon the chase and find temporary refuge in a small house nearby. He was apprehended there about 15 minutes later by Dr. Blunt's slave Frank.[55]

The resistance forced the raiders back, and the Blunt slaves, sallying forth, seized several, including Moses and Hark. Nat and the rest headed for Newit Harris's but ran into a white patrol there. In a flurry of shots, several rebels, including the redoubtable Will Francis, were killed. Others, including Elizabeth Turner's slave Nathan and another slave named Jacob, retreated to the woods to await nightfall. Nat and four others fled into another wood.[56]

Collecting himself once more, Nat dispatched Thomas Ridley's slaves Curtis and Stephen south on mules after dark to the vicinity of Cross Keys for recruits. These two decided not to return to Nat but had the misfortune to come across an armed white farmer, John Clark Turner. They told him they had absconded from the rebels, but he arrested them and handed them over to the enraged "Cross Keys Blues," a panicked and bestial militia company.[57]

Nat Turner, hiding with Richard Porter's slaves Nat and Jacob, dispatched them to look for Henry Porter, Hark, Nelson, and Sam and take them to Cabin Pond, where he proposed to meet them. He could not know that the first two were, or soon would be, captured, and that Nelson had unwisely fled to his master's farm. Nat and Jacob went the next day, the 24th, to Waller's to try to induce others to come with them. The Waller slaves, however, seized them for delivery to the whites. When they failed to return, Nat made his way alone on foot to Cabin Pond. The next day, he dug a cave under some nearby fence rails. His rebellion had been crushed.[58]

A small, separate band of potential rebels had emerged on 22 August. It was initially led by William "Billy" Artis, a free black who had earlier been attached to Nat's force but may have lost track of it after the Parker's field fight. He was able to recruit Benjamin Blunt's slave boy Ben and two other unidentified boys. This group fell in during the day with another free black, Thomas Haithcock, and two more boys, Caty Whitehead's slaves Jack and Andrew. Haithcock, proposing that they all join Nat, rode off with them to search for the rebels.

Haithcock, perhaps reflecting the anguished indecision of many blacks, soon lost stomach for the enterprise and turned himself and the four boys in to farmer James Powell. Finding them "very humble," Powell handed them over to the Cross Keys Blues. Artis and Ben had gone their own ways, the first and, probably, the second as well, to their graves.[59]

Another rebel party, composed of those who hid in some woods after the fight at Blunt's, talked of seeking revenge on Blunt that night. But a slave boy left them and reported the scheme to Blunt, who sent to Jerusalem for reinforcement. A company of 11 answered the call and stayed all night. Pandemonium, created by a false alarm the next morning, led a militiaman at Blunt's accidentally to shoot and kill a slave "of good character" belonging to Mrs. Fitzhugh.[60]

The Monday afternoon battle at Parker's field was the opening of a savage white counteroffensive. By nightfall, cavalry, infantry, and artillery were reaching Southampton from Richmond, Norfolk, Petersburg, Greensville, Bellfield, and other Virginia towns, as well as from Gates and Hertford counties in North Carolina.[61]

By Saturday, 27 August, six days after the revolt broke out, the whites had killed at least 38 blacks. Two days later, Jerusalem's jail held 48, with only Nat Turner, Sam Francis, and Billy Artis still at large; Sam was caught on 1 September. Blacks were still being "taken in different directions, and executed every day."[62]

A cavalry troop from Hertford County, North Carolina, reached Cross Keys, the village nearest Monday's slaughter of whites, by sunset on Tuesday and found there about 1,500 refugees.[63] Despite the fact that only three or four rebels were still afield, the place was a madhouse. Tales of white atrocities in Cross Keys were no doubt as exaggerated as early reports of hundreds of slaves in arms and hundreds of whites killed. But the whites there, both military and civilian, were taking revenge on virtually any black they found, some having "a strong disposition" to kill every prisoner.[64]

At Cross Keys, Nathaniel Francis was reunited with his wife, Lavinia, but the deaths of his sister-in-law, two small nephews, and his distiller had left him temporarily unhinged. Finding among the refugees his slave Charlotte, who had tried to kill his wife, he dragged her to a tree, tied her to it, and publicly shot her. He next found and embraced his slave Easter, who had saved Mrs. Francis, whereupon a mob "almost killed" him "for defending a negro woman," and then murdered her. Francis later claimed to have killed between ten and 15 blacks.[65]

A patrol of Hertford and Southampton men left Cross Keys on Wednesday to search for Nat Turner, Billy Artis, and any other blacks they might encounter. At Whitehead's, they came upon a horrible scene of whites "chopped to pieces" and "trees, fences and house tops covered with buzzards [and hogs] preying on the carcasses." A Whitehead slave appeared and began relating how he was forced to join the rebels, but Southampton men, identifying him as one of those at Parker's field, emptied their guns into him.[66]

Another militia group found Jack and Andrew, Nat's recruiters, at Waller's. Both were shot without inquiry, as were seven more during the day. "The heads of these negroes," said John Wheeler, father of one of the Hertford County officers, "were stuck up on poles, a warning to all who should undertake a similar plot."[67]

Among the prisoners at Cross Keys was Jim, who confessed his role in the revolt to his master, Peter Edwards, and was taken to Captain Joseph Joiner, a militia officer, to be held for trial. Joiner tied Jim "and placed him against a house," whereupon "a party rushed up and shot him dead." At Edwards's farm on the 25th, whites found rebel Austin "in the yard by himself perfectly defenseless," and killed him.[68]

Another prisoner at Cross Keys was Henry Porter, rebel "general" and "paymaster." Because of his role as a leader of the revolt, Henry's hamstrings were cut, his ears and nose cut off, and he was "burnt with red hot irons." He was then stuck "like a hog," decapitated, and "spiked to a whipping post for a spectacle to other negroes." When "General" Nelson was brought in, he too was beheaded. Both heads were taken by soldiers to Norfolk as trophies, while others were spiked on posts at various crossroads.[69]

Other units were equally indiscriminate and brutal. Richmond troops reportedly spent four days killing rebels "like so many wolves." A Norfolk paper reported many rebels "shot down in the roads, their bodies strewing the highway." Patrols took Richard Porter's slaves Jacob and Moses, who "confessed they had been engaged with other insurgents," and killed them on the spot. Porter's slave Aaron, said by Levi Waller to have "actively engaged with other insurgents at my house," surrendered and was shot. "Choctaw" Williams, his family dead, was "almost insane with grief" at Branch's Bridge and "wished to kill every negro . . . in sight." James Trezvant shut Jerusalem's post office and went "out killing negroes"; armed men were needed to thwart white attacks on the county jail. Northerner Oliver Smith told of slaves, with "the flesh of their cheeks cut out, their jaws broken," used as "a mark to shoot at."[70]

Hysteria continued to rage for days. Levi Waller's slave Alfred was taken by Peete's militia, which, too hurried to secure him, was "compelled to hamstring and disable him, and in this situation he was found . . . by dragoons from Greensville County, who shot him."[71] On 2 September, the body of Billy Artis, who committed suicide, was found beside a road. A slave sent on a horseback errand by his master was overtaken by soldiers who thought him "an enemy fleeing, . . . and killed both man and horse." Another's "ears were cut off, & after rubbing the wound with sand, they tied him on a horse" and set it loose in the woods. Arriving Richmond troops reportedly asked a black if this was Southampton County and killed him when he answered "yes."[72]

At length, cooler heads recognized that indiscrimate killing was denying the county court key witnesses and slaveowners valuable property. By 1 September, militia major Pitt Thomas had gone to Cross Keys and ordered that the local militia cease and desist, and the violence abated. Dred, who lost an arm at Parker's field, surrendered to Nathaniel Francis who, surprisingly, turned him in. It still required an executive order to disband the Cross Keys Blues. In terms of lives lost in the ten days of rebellion and retribution, at least 100 blacks, and possibly several times that figure, were killed, though no more than a handful had taken any part in the uprising.[73] More than slave barbarity, the ghastly depths to which their masters might sink was displayed for the world to ponder.

A few captured suspects died of wounds before they could be brought to trial. Marmaduke, owner unknown, was "an atrocious offender," the reputed killer of Miss Vaughan. At Jerusalem jail, a visitor on 24 August wrote that Marmaduke "might have been a hero, judging by the magnanimity with which he bears his sufferings." Another suspect, named Tom, "desperately wounded and about to die," gave jailors a "full confession" and declared that the slaves were, in general, "well affected and even fearful of their masters . . . as it was related to him." Benjamin Blunt's slave Anthony begged to be killed instead of transported out of state at an advanced age—and was reportedly granted his wish.[74]

Some whites were appalled by the massacre of blacks, one holding that "if the conduct of the blacks was outrageous, that of the whites was most Barbarous towards many . . . who were arrested, . . . they cut off the foot of a negro whom they had taken up in confusion, & found at last that he was innocent." Oliver Smith wrote of the dead blacks that "they and the Lord only know, whether they were guilty or innocent!" and reported that whites "take any suspicious one and kill him, without judge or jury!"[75]

Ripples from Southampton spread out from Virginia all over the South. At Riddicksville, North Carolina, Benjamin W. Britt reportedly shot a slave for "disobeying Mr. Britt's imperative 'Stop.'" Another was killed at Murfreesboro for "behaving imprudently" while driving the carriage of a lady and her children. A black man walking north along a Murfreesboro street was shot by eight or ten men, his head mounted on a post, and his body thrown into a gully.[76]

Eleven slaves were killed in a September alarm in Duplin and New Hanover counties, North Carolina. Whites in Halifax town led a free black "to the View," evidently a threat of hanging, intended to elicit a confession: not getting one, they shot him anyway. Trials and convictions were held in Nansemond and Sussex Counties, Virginia; eight were hanged in the latter and three sent to trial in Southampton, where two of them were executed. There were rumors of slave plots from Delaware to Georgia and as far west as New Orleans.[77]

Besides the 58 whites killed in Southampton on 22 August, others succumbed to the horror of the ordeal. In Murfreesboro, old Thomas Weston came out on his porch on the first morning to learn the news and dropped dead when he heard it, as did two others nearby. In Northampton County, militiaman Shepard Lee was killed during a false alarm.[78]

Much of the damage was psychological. In Sussex, a young woman was "frightened out of her senses" and "perfectly deranged for four days," while planter William Harrison was "very dangerously sick, perfectly crazy" and near death. Levi Waller, witness to the massacre at his farm, was "raving distracted—he goes about saying how they killed them! and then shakes his sides and laughs!"[79]

The 50 or more slaves and five free blacks lodged in the four cells of Jerusalem's jail were assigned counsel and tried over the course of several weeks by five to eight magistrates and a judge. On the testimony of witnesses, mostly black, 18 prisoners were hanged and 14 transported out of state by a panel of 12 freeholders. Thirty-two were acquitted, discharged, or released without trial. Lucy Barrow, who took "a very active part" in the revolt, was the lone woman convicted, riding defiantly to the gallows on her coffin.[80]

Meanwhile, white patrols were directed by Governor John Floyd to search for Nat until they found him. The rebel chieftain was described by Floyd as five feet six or eight inches tall, weighing 150 to 160 pounds, and of "rather bright complexion," though not a mulatto. His shoulders were broad, his nose large and flat, his legs somewhat knock-kneed, and his walk "brisk and active"; he had thin hair and a beard on his upper lip and chin. This description was modified by the *Richmond Compiler*, which described Nat as being "of darker hue" and having prominent eyes that were "deeply seated in his head" and "a rather sinister expression."[81]

Nat Turner remained hidden on the Travis farm for weeks and, later, on the Nathaniel Francis farm. He considered turning himself in but either could not summon the will or was yet unready to do so. When farmer Benjamin Phipps found him around midday on Sunday, 30 October, Nat, cold and shoeless in a brush cave, threw down his ineffectual sword and surrendered. He was conducted to Jerusalem the next day, reaching it at 1:15 A.M. on the 31st. A crowd of whites accompanied him but, owing to a strong guard, kept their distance.[82]

Nat claimed that he had stayed at the epicenter of desolation, hounded by searchers, because the roads were too well patrolled, even at night.[83] But this explanation seems evasive since only improbable good luck enabled him to hide so long. More likely, he stayed because deserted nearby farms kept him in provisions. Also, he may have known no place beyond Southampton that offered better security. Ignorant of any locality but his own, he could not have held out for long.

Even so, Nat's withdrawal may have given him a precious opportunity. The rebellion, which he must have known all along would fail, had earned him a wide audience and laid bare to it the frenzied fear and malice engendered by the ownership of slaves. His surrender might now provide him with a forum to send his message far abroad. If he could remain hidden for a time, he could compose and memorize a testament that might cause those it reached to reconsider the institution of slavery. But the circumstances under which such an apologia could be made must, if possible, be carefully chosen to allow him to deliver it without distraction.

In the Jerusalem jail, Nat was interviewed at length in the early hours of 31 October by magistrates James Trezvant and James W. Parker before an audience of curious whites and at least one free black prisoner. Nat may have welcomed the chance to rehearse and test his ideas in front of parts of his intended larger audience.[84]

Those present at Nat's rehearsal drew contradictory conclusions. To Trezvant, Nat seemed coherent, fully rational, straightforward, and even penitent, displaying "much shrewdness of intellect, answering every question clearly and distinctly, and without confusion or prevarication." He acknowledged being led "by the influence of fanaticism," stated that the revolt originated "entirely with himself," and claimed that he was "destined by a Superior power to perform the part which he did" but said that "the revelation was misinterpreted by him." A self-confessed "coward," he was now "convinced that he ha[d] done wrong."[85]

Dr. Isaac Pipkin of Murfreesboro, on the other hand, found him vague and confusing. Nat, he wrote, gave "a history of his mind for many years past; of the signs he saw, the spirits he conversed with, of his prayers, fastings and watchings, and of his supernatural powers, in curing diseases, controlling the weather, &c. . . . How this idea came or . . . was connected with his signs, *etc.*, I could not get him to explain in a manner at all satisfactory . . . I examined him closely," but "he alway[s] seemed to mystify."[86]

On the next day came the opportunity that may have fulfilled Nat's primary aim for inciting the revolt. With the court's (and, presumably, Nat's) permission, attorney Thomas R. Gray questioned him at length at the jail the first three days of November. Assuming that Gray attended the interrogation on 31 October, or reviewed transcripts from it, he could anticipate much of what Nat would say. He could also draw on the September court record and the testimony of many white witnesses to reconcile ambiguities in Nat's revelations and sketch a coherent profile of the man to enlighten a bewildered public.[87]

Nat appears to have recognized at once that the young attorney was a God-sent medium for his own purposes. The verbal seduction that had been his forte since childhood could here be employed without distraction to explain his life and justify his cause. In fact, in ways even Nat could not recognize, Thomas R. Gray was an ideal conduit through whom the tortured voice of chattel slavery could now address the world.

Gray's summary and gloss of Nat's address form what many believe to be the most powerful document wrought during two and a half centuries of American slavery. Composed primarily using three or four days of notes, a version of it was read to Nat on the stand and verified by him—so far as he understood the classical-school idiom in which Gray dressed Nat's words.[88] So carefully crafted and well scripted were Nat's revelations that Gray never had to prompt him and intervened only rarely to clarify certain points.

Tried and convicted by his admissions, Nat was hanged in Jerusalem at noon on Friday, 11 November, reportedly having sold his body for dissection to buy ginger cakes. He offered no "words of contrition" and "hurried his executioner in the performance of his duty." He died bravely and stoically; "not a limb nor a muscle was observed to move."[89] He could, perhaps, take with him to his grave a serene knowledge that those who termed his rebellion a failure did not reckon with the timeless power and influence of his final testament.

Prior to Nat's hanging, Gray left for Richmond with a polished account of the confession. When presses there refused to print it, probably owing to its perceived inflammatory character, he went on to Washington where he got a copyright on 10 November. A reputed 50,000 copies were run off a few days later by a Baltimore printer. The confession was on sale in Norfolk and elsewhere by 22 November for 25 cents.[90]

The Confessions of Nat Turner is an indispensable but troubling document for historians. Its power and apparent candor evoke a fascination that has brought William Styron a Pulitzer Prize and has generated a catalogue of plays, poetry, documentaries, novels, and historical studies. It remains the single most reliable source of information relating to the revolt. But it is the complex motives and attitudes of both Nat *and* Gray that are, or should be, at issue. Gray's pamphlet reveals much about both himself and his subject. Those who would know Nat must also know his amanuensis.

Gray opens with a preamble expressive of his contempt for the captive, "a gloomy fanatic" with a "dark, bewildered, and overwrought mind" seeking "to grapple with things beyond its reach." Nat was "bewildered and confounded" by portents that appeared to him, and surrendered ignominiously without a struggle.[91] This was the Nat of popular white perception.

Gray's postscript, however, offers this astonishing and eloquently ungrammatical passage: "The calm, deliberate composure with which he spoke of his late deeds, the expression of his fiend-like face when excited by enthusiasm, still bearing the stains of blood and helpless innocence about him; clothed with rags and covered with chains, with a spirit soaring above the attributes of man: I looked upon him and my blood curdled in my veins."[92]

The ignorant and depraved Nat of the preamble is reborn in the postscript as one who, "for natural intelligence and quickness of apprehension, is surpassed by few men I have ever seen" and possessed of "a mind capable of attaining any thing." In response to reports that Nat's motive was money, Gray responds that he was "never known to have a dollar in his life, to swear an oath, or drink a drop of spirits." The cowardly Nat of the preamble disappears and the rebel is extolled as admirable for "the decision of his character," a view that comports with Nat's conduct at the gallows.[93]

The postscript thus transforms the lurid early depiction of Nat into that of a nuanced and impassioned man, his cause a holy crusade. Clearly, Gray's preamble was composed before the interviews, the rest after some hours in Nat's presence. As a result, Nat may have died recognizing that he had won in a jail cell the victory that eluded him on the battlefield. Gray appears, in fact, to have fallen under Nat's spell; something in the slave's testimony must have resonated strongly in the interrogator.

Some suspected this at once. On reading Nat's confession, Boston emancipationist William Lloyd Garrison called dryly on southern legislatures to "offer a large reward for the arrest of Gray and his printers." The pamphlet, he prophesied, would "serve to rouse up other leaders and cause other insurrections, by creating among the blacks admiration for the character of Nat and appreciation for his cause."[94]

Gray's motives in offering the world a valiant martyr, rather than a deranged murderer, are worthy of inquiry. For this purpose, it is important to consider Gray's relationship with his own father. The elder Gray's will, dated 6 September 1831, left his son, lately admitted to the Southampton bar, nothing of his large estate. Rather, it directed that, should the son try in any way to interfere with its provisions, "it is my desire that the portion . . . bequeathed to my Grand Daughter Ellen Douglas Gray

[Thomas R.'s daughter] may be equally divided between my son Edwin and my Daughter Ann Gray."[95] This willingness to cut off his grandchild to spite her father betrays a profound rift between Thomas Gray and his son.

The elder Gray's animus may have been cause or result of his son's precipitate fall from respectability. In 1829 Thomas R., who lived on a substantial farm ten miles north of Jerusalem, owned 21 slaves and 800 acres of land; in 1830, 16 slaves; and in 1832, one slave and 400 acres. After selling a house and lot in Jerusalem in 1833, he had neither land nor slaves and was taxed only for a horse.[96]

The circumstances suggest the existence of a common filial pathology of rebellion by son against father and, by extension, against the manacles of authority at large. In addition, the son had lately lost his wife, Mary, possibly in childbirth, leaving him with a daughter he could not support. The county court in 1832 placed her in the custody of Gray's wealthier and more responsible colleague, William C. Parker.[97]

But this was not all. By 1831 Gray had resigned the respected office of justice of the peace, though remaining a commissioner of Indian lands and overseer of the poor, minor county offices awarded before his collapse in 1830 and 1831. At the September trials, which provided a chance for at least short-term financial recovery, he represented just five slave rebels, earning 50 dollars, less expenses, from the heaviest county court docket on record.

Not long afterward, Gray moved to Portsmouth, where he practiced law. It does not appear that he ever sought or received a share of his daughter's legacy. In accounting for Gray's attitude toward Nat, one cannot rule out a sense of indebtedness, conscious or not, toward Nat for ridding him of a despised father who had, in his view, effected his downfall by denying him his inheritance, and hence his position in society, at a critical moment in his career.[98]

The younger Gray was left with no gods and no pretensions. A "scoffer at religion," he had what his parson, eulogizing him in 1845, graciously called an "independence and fearlessness of mind." He "disdained alike concealment and restraint—what he tho't on any subject, as of any individual, that he said in or out of his presence." This trait was borne even into church, Gray having "invaded" it "with unhallowed lips"—evidently meaning that he debated doctrine openly with the pulpit. Both Nat and Gray, then, were acknowledged rebels, one against slavery and white society, the other against his God, his father, and his community.[99] Two such men, unconsciously or consciously recognizing their mutual mind-set, might find themselves bonded, even in the dismal shadows of a jail cell.

This portrait of Gray is that of a deeply conflicted man, one whose only known published work, *The Confessions*, may be read as a rebuke to the Shepherd for leading His lambs astray. It was Nat's good fortune that he encountered in Southampton's jail a white man who may have identified with his sense of oppression. *The Confessions* can thus be interpreted as a joint enterprise, a covenant perhaps, calling for the abolition of over two centuries of affliction.

As Nat may have hoped, it was his carefully prepared and rehearsed confession, made possible and universally credible by his rebellion, that focused American and world attention on the evils of slavery and helped to foment the Civil War. By his fortunate choice of a narrator of his story, he insured that his cause would not be forgotten and, in the end, would triumph. Gray had amply repaid his debt to Nat Turner.

PART THREE

COMMUNITIES AND CONTEXTS

FIVE

Symptoms of Liberty and Blackhead Signposts
David Walker and Nat Turner

———

VINCENT HARDING

I speak Americans for your good. We must and shall be free . . . in spite of
you. You may do your best to keep us in wretchedness and misery, to enrich you and your children, but God will deliver us from under you. And
wo, wo, will be to you if we have to obtain our freedom by fighting.

David Walker, 1829

I heard a loud voice in the heavens, and the Spirit instantly appeared to
me and said . . . I should arise and prepare myself, and slay my enemies
with their own weapons . . . for the time was fast approaching when the
first should be last and the last should be first.

Nat Turner, 1831

There was much about America in the 1820s that made it possible for
white men and women, especially in the North, to live as if no river of
struggle were slowly, steadily developing its black power beneath the
rough surfaces of the new nation. Indeed, the newness itself, the busyness,
the almost frenetic sense of movement and building which seized America, were all part of the comfortable cloud of unknowing that helped
preserve a white sense of unreality. Nor was the incessant movement of
the majority simply imagined. Every day hundreds of families were actually
uprooting themselves from the more settled areas of the East and seeking
their fortunes beyond the Appalachians, even beyond the Mississippi

This essay is a chapter in Vincent Harding, *There Is a River: The Black Struggle for Freedom in
America* (Harcourt, Inc., 1981).

River. Other whites from Europe and the British Isles were landing regularly at the Eastern ports, making their way into the seaboard cities and
across the country to the new West, providing an intimation of the waves
of immigrants soon to come. Thus the sense of movement in America was
based on a concrete, physical reality.[1]

Naturally, much attention and energy were invested in the political,
economic, and social institutions being developed and refined to serve
the new American society. The national government was defining its own
sense of purpose and power. Courts, banks, corporations, systems of transportation, and religion—all were being molded, reshaped, and reexam-
ined, set in motion to serve a nation of settlers intent on dominating a
continent. Because of that goal, the natives of the land were receiving
their share of attention, too—much to their regret. Relentlessly, the collective white behemoth pushed them from river to river, back into the
wilderness, smashing the cultures of centuries as if the Anglo-Americans
and their cousins were agents of some divine judgment in the land.[2]

As a matter of fact, major segments of white America were possessed
by just such visions of divine action in their midst, saw America as a Promised Land, as a staging ground for the earthly manifestations of the coming (white) Kingdom of God. Such godly visions, built strangely on the
deaths of significant portions of the nonwhite children of this Father,
contributed their own peculiar busyness to the blurring of American vision. For from the stately church buildings of New England (many built
on profits from the Trade), to the roughhewn meeting houses of the
Northwest and the sprawling campgrounds of the South, men who considered themselves agents of God proclaimed the need of the people to
prepare the way for His Coming. Whatever the differences in their theology or lack of it, from Unitarians to Hard-Shell Baptists, they were
united in their sense that the God of Israel was among them in a special
way, and busily announced the various implications of that presence
among the (mostly white) people. Partly as a result of such holy activism
and fervent conviction, various sections of the nation were periodically
swept by paroxysms of religious ardor, and the enthusiastic style of evangelical Protestant revivalism set its mark on large sectors of American life.

It was a time for building, whether canals or corporations or Kingdoms
of the Saints, a hectic time of new buildings when busy men and over-
worked women might understandably ignore certain dark and troubling
movements among them. It was a time that some called the "Era of Good
Feelings," when party strife among whites seemed less pronounced than
during the earlier founding periods. But the harsh and bitter debate
which was then being carried on in Congress and across the country over
the expansion of slavery's territory spoke to a different reality, one which
often seemed about to break out and threaten all the white kingdoms.[3]

Meanwhile, down in the kingdom that cotton was building, there was
just as much movement, building, and expansion, but of a somewhat dif-

ferent quality. Louisiana had become a state in 1812. Alabama entered the Union in 1817, and Mississippi two years later. Within the decade from 1810 to 1820, the population of the Alabama-Mississippi area alone had increased from 40,000 to 200,000 persons, including more than 70,000 enslaved Africans. Since the official closing of the Atlantic slave trade to America, the internal traffic in human bondage had burgeoned; Virginia served as its capital, while the nearby slave markets of Washington, D.C., provided an appropriate commentary on the state of American democracy. With the rise of this domestic trade, which eventually took hundreds of thousands of black people from the seaboard breeding and trading grounds into the interior of the developing South, new sectional bonds were established across that entire area, helping to create a self-conscious South that was tied together in many ways by the chain of black lives.[4]

The nation had committed itself to slavery, and the South was the keeper. In the 1820s the Southern black population grew from 1.6 million to more than 2 million persons, comprising some 40 percent of the section's total population, and ranging as high as 70 to 90 percent in some plantation counties and parishes. In this kingdom that cotton was building, enslaved black people were everywhere, and it was at once harder and easier for white men and women to deceive themselves. But there was no escape from the realities represented by the radical black presence in America. Thus private and public writings from the South continually referred to deep levels of fear—fear of insurrection, fear of death at black hands, fear of black life, fear of blackness, fear of repressed and frightening white desires. Usually it came out in references to "an internal foe," or "the dangerous internal population," or "the enemy in our very bosom," perhaps revealing more than the writers ever knew.[5]

Yet even in the South, even there where all the busyness of America could not shield white men and women from the stark black reality, it was still possible not to see where the objective enemy really was. In the 1820s, in Virginia's Southampton County, who would have chosen Nat Turner for the role?

On the surface, Nat Turner appeared to represent much of that development which allowed men who called themselves masters to rest in the rightness of their ways. The ascetic Turner seemed to have imbibed deeply all the best elements of evangelical Southern white religion, all the proper anesthesia against the knowledge of who he had been, what he had lost, and what there was to regain. He did not use tobacco or liquor, he seemed to live a perfectly disciplined life among men as well as women (though not all owners would think well of *that* fruit of the Spirit); by and large, he caused no real trouble for the keepers of the status quo. Indeed, around 1821 the young black man had vividly demonstrated to whites the exemplary advantage of his high standing among the other Africans by returning voluntarily to Samuel Turner after having run away for about thirty days. Such a faithful black exhorter and singer of spiritual songs was of great value in the eyes of the white world. Of course the eyes of the white world did not see into the deepest level of Nat's real relationship to the black community, or into his real relationship to his God. Therefore whites could never have predicted that Nat, once harshened and honed in the burning river, would be possessed by a driving messianic mission to become God's avenging scourge against the slaveholders and their world.[6]

After his birth in 1800, the first community Nat Turner knew was that of his mother, father, and grandmother, a family not far removed from Africa but held in slavery by one Samuel Turner. Had they considered themselves or young Nat simply to be "slaves," he would never have become a Messenger. Rather, from the outset they taught him that he was meant for some special purpose (and therefore so were they), and they led him in that path. For instance, the immediate family and the surrounding black community were evidently convinced—as was Nat—that he had learned to read without instruction. Soon they were fascinated by his experiments in the ancient crafts of Africa and Asia: pottery, papermaking, and the making of gunpowder. Perhaps this was seen as another manifestation of the esoteric knowledge the community was convinced that he possessed—knowledge that included events and times before his own birth. Meanwhile his grandmother Bridget, a "very religious" woman, instructed him in what she knew from the Scriptures and other sources, nurtured him in the songs of nighttime and sleep.[7]

We are not sure of all that Nat learned from his immediate family, but his father taught him at least one thing: slavery was not to be endured. While Nat was still a child his father had joined the ranks of the fugitives. (Who can imagine the conversation in that family before his father ran away into the shadows of history? How much of their substance did Nat carry to his own grave?) From the rest of the community of captives Nat learned the same lesson, which was often taught in the captives' own flight from slavery, in spite of the high costs involved. He knew of the injustices suffered by his community. He learned its ritual songs and prayers, and the stories of heroes like Gabriel. But Nat claimed that his most profound lessons came in his own lonely, personal struggles with the spirit, whom he identified as "the Spirit that spoke to the prophets."[8]

By the time he was 25, Nat had wrestled many times in the night with the Spirit of his God, the God of his Fathers. He had been pressed especially hard by the words: "Seek ye first the Kingdom of God and all things shall be added unto you." As he attempted to plumb the meaning and mystery of that promise, he had been driven into his own month-long experience of the wilderness, but then had returned to the Turner farm. Steadily he became more convinced that the Kingdom he sought was not the one preached by most of the white men he had heard. Instead, he saw the promised Kingdom of righteousness as one which would somehow be realized on the very farms and fields of Virginia, a Kingdom in which the power of the slavemasters would be broken. What made the vision chilling and exhilarating was his vivid awareness of being a chosen instrument for the bringing in of this Kingdom.[9]

Still, the way forward was not yet really clear, and Nat Turner went about his life and work, waiting. By this time Turner was a familiar figure in Southampton County and the surrounding areas. Of about average height, muscular in build, coffee-tan in complexion, with a wide nose and large eyes, he walked with a brisk and active movement among his people, marked within himself and among them as a special man. On Sundays and at midweek meetings he exhorted and sang in black Baptist gatherings. At one point, word spread that Nat Turner had cured a white man of some serious disease and then had baptized the white believer and himself in a river. Such a story only added to his renown.[10]

None of these developments, none of this high regard, moved Turner from his central purpose and passionate search. He waited and worked and married but knew that all these things were only a prelude. Then in 1825 a clearer vision came: "I saw white spirits and black spirits engaged in battle, and the sun was darkened—the thunder rolled in the Heavens, and blood flowed in streams—and I heard a voice saying, 'Such is your luck, such you are called to see, and let it come rough or smooth, you must surely bear it.'" Again, one day as he worked in the fields Nat claimed to have "discovered drops of blood on the corn as though it were dew from heaven." On the leaves of the trees he said he found "hieroglyphic characters, and numbers, with the forms of men . . . portrayed in blood." Through this African imagery the white and black fighters had appeared again, but this time the meaning was even clearer in his mind. What it signified to Nat was that "the blood of Christ had been shed on this earth . . . and was now returning to earth." Therefore, he said, "it was plain to me that the Saviour was about to lay down the yoke he had borne for the sins of men, and the great day of judgement was at hand."[11]

On one level, Turner was obviously living within the popular nineteenth-century Euro-American millenarian religious tradition, marked by a belief in the imminent return of Christ to rule his earth. Often, for persons thus convinced, a terrible and sometimes beautiful urgency caught fire and burned within them, annealing and transforming their being.[12]

But the burning within Nat Turner came from an at once similar and very different fire. That became evident in the spring of 1828, when the fullest description of the Kingdom he sought, and of his own role in its coming, were spoken to Nat's third ear. With very rare exceptions, white American evangelical religion could not contain such a Word, had no ear for it. On May 12, 1828, Nat said, "I heard a loud voice in the heavens, and the Spirit instantly appeared to me and said the Serpent was loosened, and Christ had laid down the yoke he had borne for the sins of men, and that I should take it and fight against the serpent, for the time was fast approaching when the first should be last and the last should be first." As if to clear away any lingering doubt he might have had, Nat heard the spirit's clear instructions, that at the appearance of the proper sign "I should arise and prepare myself, and slay my enemies with their own weapons." After that he waited, he bided his time.[13]

> *Oh praised my honer, harshener*
> *till a sleep came over me,*
> *a sleep heavy as death. And when*
> *I awoke at last free*
>
> *And purified, I rose and prayed*
> *and returned after a time*
> *to the blazing fields, to the humbleness.*
> *And bided my time.*[14]

For 28 years Nat Turner had been nurtured by the black community, instructed by signs on the leaves and in the skies. Now he was clear about who the enemy of righteousness was and who were the servants of the devil; he had only to wait for the sign. But it may have been difficult to wait: about this time, it seems, Turner was whipped by Thomas Moore, his present owner, "for saying that the blacks ought to be free, and that they would be free one day or another."[15]

A bustling, growing, building white nation could miss the sign that such a man carried in his own flesh, but for persons who were willing to see, more obvious signs were available. These were the years of black insurrections in Martinique, Cuba, Antigua, Tortola, Jamaica, and elsewhere in the Western Hemisphere, and black people in the States were not oblivious of them or of their promise. This was demonstrated in the fall of 1826, when 29 black people were being taken by sea from Maryland to Georgia on the *Decatur*, a vessel owned by one of the nation's largest slave traders. The black captives rebelled, killed two members of the crew, then ordered another crew member "to take them to Haiti" because they knew of the black struggle there. The boat was captured before they could reach their destination, but when the *Decatur* was taken to New York City, all but one of the captives escaped.[16]

Two years later a group of four black slave artisans were on a similar journey by ship from Charleston to New Orleans. Before leaving South Carolina, they vowed that they would never be slaves in New Orleans. By the time the boat docked, they all had committed suicide. At about the same time, fragmentary reports of rebellions and death on island plantations seeped out of other parts of Louisiana.[17]

There was no surcease. While Nat Turner saw visions and waited for signs, others continued to fight. In Mobile County, Alabama, a black man named Hal had led a group of outlyers for several years. By the spring of

1827 the fugitives were organized to the point where they were building a fort in the swamps. One day while the construction was still going on, they were surprised, attacked, and defeated by a large group of whites. Later one of the white men reported: "This much I can say that old Hal . . . and his men fought like spartans, not one gave an inch of ground, but stood, was shot dead or wounded fell on the spot."[18]

While Nat Turner waited for the sign, and black people fought on ships, in forests, and on plantations, there were still other options and other signs, especially for those who could no longer bide their time. David Walker was one such man. He had been born legally free in 1785 in Wilmington, North Carolina, the child of a free mother, but he knew that he was not free, that his status ultimately depended upon the good will of white men. By the 1820s, while Nat waited for signs and saw visions, Walker had traveled across the South and into the trans-Appalachian West, had seen what America was doing to black people in slavery, and had become concerned about what slavery might yet do to him. Later, two scenes from those journeys stood out especially in his mind. He claimed to have watched the degradation of two black men: a son who was forced to strip his mother naked and whip her until she died; and a black husband forced to lash his pregnant wife until she aborted her child. Walker knew that, if faced with such savage choices, he would kill white men—and most likely be killed. "If I remain in this bloody land," he told himself, "I will not live long." By 1826, led by his own signs and visions, David Walker had moved to Boston.[19]

By then he was 41 years old. A tall, slender, handsome man of dark complexion, Walker was a bachelor when he arrived. Perhaps he had thought it unwise to give too many hostages to white fortune while living and traveling in the South and West. Perhaps he wanted to be untrammeled in his passionate work on behalf of black freedom, a task he took up in very concrete ways soon after arriving in Boston. Almost immediately, the North Carolinian's house became a refuge for all black people in need of aid, especially the fugitives from slavery who came regularly into Boston. Walker was also an organizer and lecturer for the General Colored Association of Massachusetts, a black abolitionist organization, and when *Freedom's Journal*, the first black newspaper in America, began publication in 1827, Walker became an agent for the paper in Boston.[20]

The meeting of David Walker and *Freedom's Journal* in the Northern phase of the struggle raised a question of great moment: what is the role of the word—the spoken word, the preached word, the whispered-in-the-nighttime word, the written word, the published word—in the fight for black freedom?

In the slave castles and by the riversides of Africa, where our ancestors had gathered for the long journey into American captivity, the spoken word had many functions. It provided a bridge between and among them, to draw them together for the unity those first efforts demanded. On the ships the word was used to strengthen men and women and urge them toward the dangers of participation. It was often on the ships that the word, for the first sustained length of time, was directed toward the white captors. Early, in such a setting, the word was used in protest, in statements of black rights and white wrongs, of black people's determination to be men and women in spite of European attempts to dehumanize them. There, too, the word publicly spoken to white men often served as a rallying point for the Africans. For in many cases the word was openly uttered in spite of the rules and laws of the whites, spoken in the face of threats and punishment and even death. Such courageous speakers of the word understandably evoked strength and courage and hope in other captives.

Similar situations often prevailed when the black-white struggle moved from the prison ships into the fields and forests of the New World prison state. In the South, the word was used as an organizing tool for the flight into the outlyers' camps or toward the North. In many such situations it spoke the truth about white oppression, black suffering, and the potential power of organized black will. Such a word strengthened and encouraged friends to continue the struggle to survive, to bide their time toward the struggle to overcome. And on many occasions, the prison states exacted the same cruel penalties as the prison ships for the honest, defiant, encouraging black word. For such words were radical acts.[21]

No less dangerous to white power in the South were the words spoken honestly from the Bible, the Word, telling men and women of a humanity no one could deny them, reminding a people that God opposed injustice and the oppression of the weak, encouraging believers to seek for messianic signs in the heavens, for blood on the leaves. On the tongues of black people—and in their hands—the Word might indeed become a sword.

On the other hand, in the antebellum North the role of the word developed somewhat differently, progressing less starkly but in the same essential direction. There, in situations where black men and women brought that word to bear against their oppressors, they usually addressed two intersecting realities: the bondage forced upon their brothers and sisters in the South, and the racist discrimination practiced against their own immediate community in the North. When they spoke or wrote against slavery, the fate of their word often depended upon where it was spoken and to what audience it was directed. Put forth among black people or white sympathizers, words from black speakers and writers denouncing slavery and its defenders usually did not present the same outright, abrasive challenge as in the South. However, such words could never be confined to those circles. They carried their own resonance and therefore their own dangers. No black critics, whatever their audiences, were suffered gladly, and it was not unusual—especially as the nation's argument over slavery grew more heated—for white mobs to break in on abolitionist meetings and especially attack the black men and women who dared stand as public judges of white law and order.[22]

As the debate over slavery intensified, the black word from the North became more provocative, more slashing in its condemnation, more daring in its encouragement to resistance. Then, when attempts were made to publish and distribute those words among the Afro-American captives of the South, radical words and deeds were clearly joined, and the challenge was explosive. In the same way, as black men and women pressed their fierce arguments against the conditions of Northern racism, they found increasing hostility in that section, too. For the word often called upon their brothers and sisters to struggle for changes in their status there, to resist, to fight back. Ultimately, the words against slavery in the South and discrimination in the North were joined, for the black community of the North was finally called upon to resist the laws which endangered the fugitive slaves who came among them. From pulpit, platform, and press the black word would urge them to take up the struggle of the enslaved on free ground, thereby proclaiming all American soil to be contaminated, unfree, and in need of the rushing, cleansing movement of the river.

So the word had many roles and many places in the Northern struggle. In 1827 the almost simultaneous appearance of David Walker and *Freedom's Journal* represented one of the earliest institutional manifestations of what we have called the Great Tradition of Black Protest. As such, it was in the mainstream of the river, closer to the surface than the churning depths. In its first issue this pioneer black periodical announced: "The civil rights of a people being of the greatest value, it shall ever be our duty to vindicate our brethren when oppressed, and to lay the cure before the publick. We also urge upon our brethren (who are qualified by the laws of the different states) the expediency of using their elective franchise; and of making an independent use of the same. We wish them not to become the tools of party." For the *Journal*, the word meant quiet, sound advocacy of the black cause, an encouragement to acceptable black social and political development, and a source of information and advice for any whites who might be concerned about black needs. In 1827 the word of the Great Tradition was less strident than it had been on the slave ships, but it was the same tradition, and the time for its renewed stridency would come.[23]

By the following year, David Walker began his brief career as a goad to moderate voices like that of *Freedom's Journal*. For even as he moved within the Great Tradition, Walker's history, temperament, and commitments urged him toward deeper and more radical levels of struggle. In the fall of 1828 he delivered an address before the General Colored Association of his adopted state, calling on blacks to organize and act on their own behalf. In the address Walker first spoke of the need for political and social organization within the black community, identifying such structured, inner cohesion as a prerequisite to any effective struggle for freedom. "Ought we not to form ourselves into a general body to protect, aid, and assist each other to the utmost of our power?" Proceeding beyond this, he also said that "it is indispensably our duty to try every scheme we think will have a tendency to facilitate our salvation, and leave the final result to . . . God."

This last sentiment was not escapist. Rather, it suggested a certain affinity between Walker and the waiting Nat Turner. For David Walker was a staunch and faithful member of a black Methodist church in Boston, and he firmly believed that people—especially oppressed people—were called upon to act as well as pray, always placing their ultimate confidence in God. It was that context of active faith which illuminated the final words of Walker's speech to the Colored Association: "I verily believe that God has something in reserve for us, which when he shall have poured it out upon us, will repay us for all our suffering and misery."[24]

In February 1829, two months after the publication of Walker's December speech, a document which seemed to express certain elements of his thought more explicitly appeared in print. One Robert Young, a black New Yorker, published a pamphlet called *The Ethiopian Manifesto*, evidently intending to put forward a longer version later. It appears now that the larger statement never came, but the *Manifesto* picked up the themes from Walker's work and carried them forward. For Young, as for many Biblically oriented blacks of the time, the word Ethiopian was synonymous with African: where Walker had spoken generally of the need for political and social organization, Young seemed to advocate the establishment of a theocracy of Ethiopian people in America. Calling for the "convocation of ourselves into a body politic," Young said that "for the promotion of welfare of our order," it was necessary "to establish to ourselves a people framed into the likeness of that order, which from our mind's eye we do evidently discern governs the universal creation. Beholding but one sole power, supremacy, or head, we do of that head . . . look forward for succor in the accomplishment of the great design which he hath, in his wisdom, promoted us to its undertaking."[25]

Equally important, perhaps more so, was the *Manifesto*'s announcement to the black people of America and elsewhere that "the time is at hand, when, with but the power of words, and the divine will of our God, the vile shackles of slavery shall be broken asunder from you, and no man known shall dare to own or proclaim you as his bondsmen." This was a deliverance rather different from the kind Nat Turner pondered in Virginia, or that David Walker would soon propose. It depended solely on "the power of words" and the will of God. But according to Young, it would be manifested through a mulatto Messiah chosen by God from "Grenada's Island" in the West Indies. This Messiah would be the means whereby God would "call together the black people as a nation in themselves." Thus Young could say to white people: "Of the degraded of this earth, shall be exalted, one who shall draw from thee as though gifted of power divine, all attachment and regard of thy slave towards thee."[26]

Here was true messianic promise: divine intervention on behalf of the Ethiopian nation in America, to provide a savior to draw black people together as a nation, and somehow miraculously break the shackles of slavery. Its pan-Africanism, its sense of nationhood, its radical hope all marked this rather mysterious announcement as part of the stream of radical ideas in the struggle. But by then both David Walker and Nat Turner had heard other voices.

Not long after his arrival in Boston, David Walker had set up a new and used clothing shop on Brattle Street. That provided his living: but the freedom struggle of black people in America was his life. Not only did he regularly attend the abolitionist meetings and assist all the fugitives he could, but those who knew him noted that Walker was devoting very long, hard hours to reading and study. Driven by an urgency that he attributed to the spirit of God, his special role was taking shape, only faintly suggested by the speech near the end of 1828.

Sometime during this period Walker took time to get married, but there was no release of the internal pressure, no relaxation in the harsh schedule of reading and writing that he had set himself. Finally, having developed a series of notes and drafts, in September 1829 Walker supervised the printing of his explosive 76 page pamphlet, *Walker's Appeal . . . to the Colored Citizens of the World But in Particular and very Expressly to those of the United States of America*. It read as if all the passion and commitment of his life had been poured into the document. In its pages, filled with exclamations and pleas, with warnings and exhortations, one could almost hear the seething, roaring sounds of the black river, from the wailings of the African baracoons to the thundering declarations of Dessalines, and the quiet signals of the outlyers in Wilmington's swamps.[27]

Near the beginning of the work, Walker proclaimed it one of his major purposes "to awaken in the breasts of my afflicted, degraded and slumbering brethren, a spirit of inquiry and investigation respecting our miseries and wretchednesses in this REPUBLICAN LAND OF LIBERTY!!!!!" Essentially, he was demonstrating several of the major functions of radical teaching among dominated African peoples: to raise questions about the reasons for their oppression, to speak the truth concerning both oppressed and oppressor, to clarify as fully as possible the contradictions inherent in both communities, and to indicate the possible uses of these contradictions in the struggle for freedom. Actually, he accomplished even more than he set out to: for over a century, Walker's *Appeal* remained a touchstone for one crucial genre of black radical analysis and agitation. As such, its primary strength lay in the breadth and honesty of its analysis, in the all-consuming passion of its commitment to black liberation, and in the radical hope which lifted it beyond the familiar temptations to bitter despair. Understandably, then, David Walker's heirs, both conscious and unconscious, have been legion.[28]

In the pamphlet, which quickly went through three editions (with new material added to the later ones), ten major themes were addressed:

1. The profound degradation of African peoples, especially those in the United States, as a result of the racism and avarice which supported and shaped the system of slavery. (Walker was perhaps the first writer to combine an attack on white racism and white economic exploitation in a deliberate and critical way.)

2. The unavoidable judgment which a just God would bring upon the white American nation, unless it repented and gave up its evil ways of injustice and oppression.

3. The imperative for black people to face their own complicity in their oppression, and the need for them to end that complicity through resistance in every possible way, including the path of armed struggle.

4. The need for black people to develop a far greater sense of solidarity, especially between the "free" and captive populations within the United States, and between the children of Africa here and Africans in the rest of the world. (This was the first clear, widely publicized call for pan-African solidarity.)

5. The need to resist the attempts of the American Colonization Society to rid the country of its free black population.

6. The need to gain as much education as possible as a weapon in the struggle.

7. The possibility that a new society of peace and justice could come into being if white America were able to give up its malevolent ways, especially its racism and avarice.

8. The need for an essentially Protestant Christian religious undergirding for the black struggle for justice.

9. The likelihood that he, Walker, would be imprisoned or assassinated as a result of the *Appeal.*

10. The repeated statement of his own essential sense of solidarity with his brothers and sisters in slavery.

Actually, this last-mentioned sense of solidarity was the deepest source of Walker's radicalism. He was impelled not by a hatred of white America, but by a profound love and compassion for his people. It was this commitment to black people, and his unshakable belief in a God of justice, which led inevitably to an urgent statement of black radicalism, a call for uprooting and overturning of the system of life and death that was America.

Because of the nature and preoccupations of American society, the *Appeal,* in spite of its other urgent concerns, gained its greatest notoriety through advocacy of black messianic armed resistance to white oppression and slavery. Of course it was this advocacy which posed the most obvious, if not the most profound, threat to the American social order. Combining social, political, and economic religious messianism with the secular natural rights doctrine then current, Walker urged black people:

> Let your enemies go with their butcheries, and at once fill up their cup. Never make an attempt to gain our freedom or *natural right*, from under our cruel oppressors and murderers, until you see your way clear—when that hour arrives and you move, be not afraid or dismayed; for be you assured that Jesus Christ the king of heaven and of earth who is the God of justice and of armies, will surely go before you. And those enemies who have for hundreds of years stolen our *rights*, and kept us ignorant of him and his divine worship, he will remove.[29]

A black man had again taken products of white civilization and transmuted them for purposes of black freedom. In the *Appeal*, the two major systems of belief in early nineteenth-century America—Protestant evangelical Christianity and natural rights philosophy—were lifted up and bound in blood as a weapon in the struggle of black people toward justice. For Walker, the cause of freedom was the cause of God, and the cause of black justice was the cause of Jesus Christ; he readily promised the divine presence to all black people who would stand up and fight in that "glorious and heavenly cause" of black liberation.

Obviously such conclusions had never been dreamed of on the camp-grounds of the South, in the churches of the North, or in the town halls, universities, and legislatures of the white nation. But whatever those white assumptions, Walker knew his own purposes, and his urging of a divinely justified armed struggle against oppression was relentless. Calling upon black people to fight openly against all who sought to maintain them in slavery, he wrote: "If you commence, make sure work—do not trifle, for they will not trifle with you—they want us for their slaves, and think nothing of murdering us in order to subject us to that wretched condition—therefore, if there is an *attempt* made by us, kill or be killed." He also added: "It is no more harm for you to kill a man who is trying to kill you, than it is for you to take a drink of water when thirsty; in fact the man who will stand still and let another man murder him is worse than an infidel."[30]

As he saw it, the fight for black freedom was in reality a holy crusade. Black resistance to slavery was sacred obedience to God; continued submission was sinful and risked God's judgment. Nor was Walker reticent about his own views on the need for such judgment: "The man who would not fight under our Lord and Master Jesus Christ, in the glorious and heavenly cause of freedom and of God . . . ought to be kept with all of his children or family, in slavery, or in chains, to be butchered by his cruel enemies."[31]

(Had Walker read the words of Dessalines? A quarter of a century before, calling for the blood of the white oppressors, the Avenger had

asked: "Where is that Haytian so vile, Haytian so unworthy of his regen-
eration, who thinks he has not fulfilled the decrees of the Eternal by
exterminating these blood-thirsty tyggers? If there be one, let him fly;
indignant nature discards him from our bosom . . . the air we breathe is
not suited to his gross organs; it is the air of liberty, pure, august, and
triumphant.")[32]

For those who needed a different kind of encouragement, Walker offered the promised Messiah, a figure first raised up by Robert Young and
now militarized by Walker. Thus the passionate Boston radical promised
the black nation that "the Lord our God . . . will send you a Hannibal,"
and urged black people to fight valiantly under his leadership, since "God
will indeed deliver you through him from your deplorable and wretched
condition under the Christians of America." There was no doubt about
the warlike intentions of *this* Messiah, for under him, Walker said, "my
colour will root some of the whites out of the very face of the earth."
Indeed, David Walker was so certain of his God's judgment upon the evil
of white American society that he foresaw the possibility of another route
of judgment in case black people and their Hannibal-Messiah did not
prove adequate. Here, his prediction was eventually and vividly confirmed:
"Although the destruction of the oppressors God may not effect by the
oppressed, yet the Lord our God will surely bring other destructions upon
them—for not infrequently will he cause them to rise up against one
another, to be split and divided, and to oppress each other, and sometimes to open hostilities with sword in hand."[33]

Did David Walker see signs and visions, as the waiting Nat Turner had
seen them? Did such revelations explain the accuracy of his prophecies
regarding the nation? Although he did not claim this sort of inspiration
as explicitly as Nat Turner, Walker did reply to some of his critics by
saying: "Do they believe that I would be so foolish as to put out a book
of this kind without strict—ah! very strict commandments of the Lord?
. . . He will soon show you and the world, in due time, whether this book
is for his glory." So perhaps there really were visions; but there was something less esoteric as well. For it was obvious that Walker was driven to
many of his conclusions not by kaleidoscopic images and voices whirring
in the wind, but by a profound, unshakable belief in the justice of God,
an element of faith which remained consistently present in the radical
streams of black struggle. Confidence in that divine justice led to an assurance of divine retribution against America, which in turn encouraged
black struggle in the cause of that justice and retribution. At one point
in the *Appeal*, Walker asked: "Can the Americans escape God Almighty?
If they do, can he be to us a God of justice?" To Walker the central answer
was unmistakably clear: "God is just, and I know it—for he has convinced
me to my satisfaction—I cannot doubt him."[34]

But even more than this lay behind Walker's fiercely accurate conclusions. Not for nothing had he spent years of travel, reading, and research

examining white oppression in America, seeking to clarify his people's situation. For instance, his observations across the land led him to refer again and again to the economic motives behind white oppression. Early in the *Appeal* he said that, after years of observation and reading, "I have come to the immovable conclusion that [the Americans] have, and do continue to punish us for nothing else, but for enriching them and their country." This he called "avarice." Pursuing the theme of white avarice and greed, Walker moved to conclusions which would appear repeatedly in radical black analysis. Thus he continually referred to whites as "our *natural enemies*." He conceded that "from the beginning [of international contacts between blacks and whites], I do not think that we were natural enemies to each other." But he quickly added that since the opening of the slave trade, the whites by their avarice and cruel treatment had made themselves the natural enemies of blacks. It was therefore logical for him not only to call for relentless struggle, but also to explore the possibility of emigration: he suggested Canada or Haiti.[35]

The use of such a term as "natural enemies" raised questions that continued to arise: precisely who were the enemies of black freedom, of black humanity, natural or otherwise? Were they all white Americans, thereby positing a struggle of white against black? Were some white Americans not the enemy? What was the role of the federal government in this conflict? Was it also the enemy? These were crucial questions, profoundly affecting the ways in which black people looked at whites as well as themselves, and the ways in which they organized themselves for struggle toward freedom.

In the *Appeal* it was not always clear where Walker was focusing his attack and who was included among the "natural enemies." At times he mentioned "slave-holders and their advocates," but he also included Northern white racists, perhaps classifying them also as "advocates." On one occasion he pressed the issue to the critical point, saying, "Is this not the most tyrannical, unmerciful and cruel government under Heaven?" Generally, the primary enemies that he identified—with sometimes more, sometimes less clarity—were these: the system of slavery and its advocates in North and South alike; the American government, which supported that system and other aspects of white supremacy; and the white citizens of the country at large who co-operated in any way in the degradation of black people. To identify the government, the system of slavery, and most of the people of white America as the enemies of black freedom, was to put forward a radical analysis in keeping with the slave-ship experience.[36]

His sound and basic analysis of the American situation and of the human condition led Walker also to explore further the matter of black self-government that he had originally raised in 1828, and that Robert Young had put forward in a more spiritualized form in February 1829. Now, in the fall of 1829, Walker found no inconsistency in advocating implacable struggle on these shores, and at the same time preparing for self-government here or elsewhere. In the course of the *Appeal*'s powerful attack on the racism of Thomas Jefferson's *Notes on Virginia*, Walker wrote: "Our sufferings will come to an *end*, in spite of all the Americans this side of *eternity*. Then we will want all the learning and talents among ourselves, and perhaps more, to govern ourselves."[37]

Whatever the future of black people in America, by 1829 Walker had also developed a mature and fascinating sense of pan-African identity, tying together past, present, and future. He not only identified black people with the past greatness of Egypt and the rest of Africa, but went on to identify the bonds of future struggle. He spoke to all black people in America, especially those who "have the hardihood to say that you are free and happy." For him there was no true freedom or happiness apart from his brothers and sisters in slavery; moreover, he insisted to black people that it was "an unshakable and forever immovable *fact* that your full glory and happiness, as well as that of all other coloured people under Heaven, shall never be fully consummated [without] the entire emancipation of your enslaved brethren all over the world. . . . I believe it is the will of the Lord that our greatest happiness shall consist in working for the salvation of our whole body." For those who doubted and said such pan-African liberation could never be accomplished, Walker spoke out of his profound faith in the God of our ancestors: "I assure you that God will accomplish it—if nothing else will answer he will hurl tyrants and devils into *atoms* [!] and make way for his people. But O my brethren! I say unto you again, you must go to work and prepare the way of the Lord."[38]

Everything in Walker's mind led back to "the way of the Lord," the way of justice for the Lord's oppressed African peoples. This way demanded harsh judgment upon white America. Or did it? In spite of Walker's passionate commitment to black freedom and God's justice, the *Appeal* shows a certain ambivalence toward white America and its *future*, as in this ambiguous warning: "I tell you Americans! that unless you speedily alter your course, *you* and your *Country are gone*!!!! For God Almighty will tear up the very face of the earth!!!!" In his mind, then, there seemed to be some alternative: America might "speedily alter" its course. But was it really possible? He doubted it: "I hope that the Americans may hear, but I am afraid that they have done us so much injury, and are so firm in the belief that our Creator made us to be an inheritance to them for ever, that their hearts will be hardened, so that their destruction may be sure." Nevertheless, in a tradition soon to be firmly set, Walker continued to speak to the hopeless white "Americans," continued to call them to new possibilities. Perhaps there was no other choice, since black people jointly occupied with the "Americans" the territory which was to be torn up by God's judgment. Who could be eager for a judgment on America, when its land was filled with Africa's children?[39]

Thus he spoke as a kind of angry black pastor to white America: "I speak Americans for your good. We must and shall be free . . . in spite of you. You may do your best to keep us in wretchedness and misery, to enrich you and your children, but God will deliver us from under you. And wo, wo, will be to you if we have to obtain our freedom by fighting." And what if the miracle occurred, and America decided that it wanted to change its ways, to seek justice and love misery, to let the oppressed go free? What would repentance require where black men and women (to say nothing of the natives of the land) were concerned?[40]

Here, as in the case of many of his later heirs, Walker was vague: "Treat us like men, and . . . we will live in peace and happiness together." What did that mean? What did justice and manhood require? Ending slavery was, of course, one obvious requirement, and Walker cited it. But beyond that, his answer was less clear: "The Americans . . . have to raise us from the condition of brutes to that of respectable men, and to make a national acknowledgment to us for the wrongs they have inflicted upon us." Perhaps that statement implied compensation to the African captives for the generations of unpaid labor. Perhaps it meant reparations in other forms. Perhaps it suggested some special role of honor in the society for those who had been so long humiliated by its racism and greed.[41]

At this point, we cannot be certain what David Walker saw as the proper acts of white repentance and restitution. Whatever he meant, his "Americans" did not care. As the three editions of the *Appeal* came rushing off the presses between October 1829 and June 1830, white men were in no way drawn to Walker's pastoral/prophetic calls to penance for the oppression of black people. What they reacted to in the *Appeal* were the sanguinary calls to black men, the ringing summonses to armed struggle against the white keepers of the status quo. For the "Americans," *that* was Walker's *Appeal,* and it constituted sedition.

Of course it was precisely because they were not interested in Walker's invitations to repentance that white people were forced to be frantically concerned with his summonses to divinely ordained rebellion. They were right to be concerned. In the months following publication there is some evidence that David Walker, in addition to distributing it among Northern blacks, made distinct attempts to see that his *Appeal* reached black captives of the South, sometimes sewing copies into the inner linings of coats he traded to Southern-bound black seamen, sometimes using other clandestine methods—including at least one white courier—to circulate it. Word came back from Georgia and Louisiana, from the Carolinas and Virginia (did it reach Southampton County?) that the message was breaking through.[42]

Meanwhile white condemnation erupted from many sources. The governor of North Carolina, most likely mindful of the swamps around Walker's native Wilmington, denounced (and praised) the *Appeal.* He called it "an open appeal to [the black's] natural love of liberty . . . and . . . totally subversive of all subordination in our slaves." He was, of course, totally correct. More unusual was the response from Benjamin Lundy, the best-

known white antislavery publicist of the time: "A more bold, daring, inflammatory publication, perhaps, never issued from the press of any
country. . . . I can do no less than set the broadest seal of condemnation
on it." Thus conservatives who placed the preservation of their way of life
before black freedom, and liberals who placed the validity of their own
solutions before black-defined struggle, were equally dismayed.[43]

Some of Walker's "Americans" were more than dismayed. Shortly after
whites in the South first gained access to the *Appeal*, it is said that "a
company of Georgia men" not only vowed that they would kill David Walker, but offered a thousand-dollar reward for his death. When Walker's
wife and friends heard of this, they frantically urged him to go to Canada
at least for a time. It was useless advice to David Walker. He replied: "I
will stand my ground. *Somebody must die in this cause.* I may be doomed to
the stake and the fire, or to the scaffold tree, but it is not in me to falter
if I can promote the work of emancipation."[44]

Nor was he alone in this determination. Walker's message electrified
the black community of the North and provided new sources of courage
for those among them who saw no ultimate solution apart from the sword
of the Lord. Even more important, perhaps, scores of now anonymous
black people throughout the South risked their lives to distribute the *Appeal.* In Savannah an unidentified "negro preacher" distributed it after it
had reached the city by boat. In February 1830 four black men were
arrested in New Orleans on charges of circulating the *Appeal.* That same
winter, thirty copies of it were found on a free black man in Richmond,
Virginia. Meanwhile black seamen carried it along the coast at similar
peril.[45]

If he was able to follow the progress of the *Appeal* into the South, it is
possible that David Walker may have been most moved by its appearance
in his home town of Wilmington, North Carolina. As a result of it, much
"unrest and plotting" were noted in the black community. But there was
also a great cost to pay. Early in 1830, a report from Wilmington announced that "there has been much shooting of negroes in Wilmington
recently, in consequence of symptoms of liberty having been discovered
among them."[46]

Walker had said it: "I will stand my ground. *Somebody must die in this
cause.*" On the morning of June 28, 1830, in Boston's fair precincts of
liberty, David Walker became suddenly and mysteriously afflicted and fell
dead in a doorway near his shop. Almost all of black Boston was convinced
that the dauntless crusader had been poisoned.[47]

And what of Nat Turner? Did Walker's *Appeal* ever reach him as he
waited for the proper sign in Southampton County? No record exists of
that contact, if it ever occurred. But the contact was not necessary, for Nat
Turner had long been convinced that the God of Walker's *Appeal* had
always been in Southampton.

By the time of Walker's death, Turner had moved to a new home in the country, on the farm of Joseph Travis near Barrow Road. Legally, as such madness went, Nat was now owned by Putnam Moore, an infant. The child's father, Thomas Moore, Nat's last owner of record, had recently died, and in 1830 Moore's widow—Putnam's mother—married Joseph Travis. At that point she and the child moved with Nat to the Travis home and land. But wherever he was, working for whichever white person currently claimed to be his owner, Nat Turner knew that he had only one Master, who spoke in thunder and lightning and through the swaying, leafy trees. This was the Master who possessed his life, who had honed and harshened him in the wilderness, in the midst of the black community, in the movement of black struggle. This was the leader of the black angels who would scourge the white oppressors and pour judgment like a red bloodtide over the land. So Nat did his temporary work and bided his time, watching for the sign.[48]

> *Green trees a bending*
> *Poor sinner stands a tremblin'*
> *The trumpet sounds within-a my soul*
> *I ain't got long to stay here.*

The sign came in February 1831, with an eclipse of the sun. White men seeking a sign may have thought it marked an end to their bleak season of economic suffering in Virginia and North Carolina, but Nat found a different message: the movement of the last into their proper place had begun. And so, soon after the eclipse, he told his closest comrades that the time of battle and blood was approaching. With him in the initial leadership cadre were four men: Henry Porter, Hark Travis, Nelson Williams, and Samuel Francis. Evidently there was a group of some 25 who would form the core of the fighting force at first, convinced that others would be recruited as the struggle was openly joined.[49]

The Fourth of July, that prime symbol of white American contradictions, was chosen as the date for the uprising. But as the time approached, Nat became ill (were there fears or premonitions?) and the date was abandoned. Another sign had to be sought. On August 13, 1831, there was "a day-long atmospheric phenomenon, during which the sun appeared bluish green," and Nat knew that he had found the way again. One week later he met with Hark and Henry to agree on a final plan. The next night they met again, this time with several others; they agreed on their work, and ate a final meal together. In the dark hours of the morning of August 22, Nat Turner's God pressed him forward at the head of his band of black avenging angels, drove him in search of what seemed the ultimate justice: that "the first should be last and the last should be first." According to a black tradition, Nat's final words to his followers were: "Remember, we do not go forth for the sake of blood and carnage; but it is necessary that, in the commencement of this revolution, all the whites we meet should die, until we have an army strong enough to carry out the war on a Christian basis. Remember that ours is not a war for robbery, nor to satisfy our passions; it is a *struggle for freedom.*" Whatever the words, this was the goal, and the river now was churning.[50]

They began at the Travis household with hatchets and axes, and no life was spared. At that point, with very few exceptions, all whites were the enemy. It was not a matter of "good" and "bad" masters; all were involved in slavery. And the children—even Putnam Moore—were the heirs. Temporarily filled with such resolve, organized into rudimentary cavalry and infantry sections, Nat's men continued down the Barrow Road, storming house after house, destroying family after family: Francis, Reese, Turner, Peeples, Whitehead, each in its turn experienced the terrible slaughter, not alien to the children of Africa.

At the height of the advance, there were apparently some 60 men in Nat Turner's company, including several described as "free." Together, in a breathlessly brief period of solidarity, they were marching to Jerusalem, Virginia, and their leader was now "General Nat." Once again a captive black prophet, wresting the religion of white America out of its hands, had transformed it and had in turn been utterly changed. Now, as an insurrectionary commander carrying out the sanguinary vengeance of a just God, Nat Turner took up the spirit of David Walker's *Appeal* and burned its message into the dark and bloody ground of Virginia, streaking the black river with blood.[51]

Apparently, he had hoped to move so quickly and kill so thoroughly that no alarm would be given before his marchers reached Jerusalem, and had captured the cache of arms stored there. As in the case of Gabriel and Vesey, the steps beyond that action were not certain. Perhaps they would seek out a new word from Nat Turner's heavenly Master. Perhaps they planned to head toward the swamps. There were even rumors that they expected somehow to find their way to Africa. But in the brutal light of August, it was still Virginia, U.S.A. The skies had not broken open, the earth had not erupted in divine power and judgment—and they were not fully angels of light. Indeed, as time wore on that Monday there was a growing sense of confusion, disarray, and sometimes drunkenness among some of Nat's men. Often the prophet himself seemed distracted, and rode at the rear of his troops rather than at the front. Added to these internal problems was the tragic fact that General Nat's men "had few arms among them—and scarcely one, if one, that was fit for use." So it was still Virginia. They had not moved as rapidly, mobilized as effectively, transformed themselves as fully, nor destroyed as efficiently as Nat had expected. Before they reached the road to Jerusalem, the alarm had been spread, leaping like fire from one blanched and trembling set of lips to another, echoing in the clashing sound of church bells across the countryside. The alarm struck fear in the heart of some of Turner's band and they deserted. Others, still on plantations, decided that the struggle was now hopeless, and decided to remain with their masters, biding their time.[52]

Nevertheless, Nat had already challenged Virginia, the government of the United States, and all the fierce and chilling fears which raged within the depths of the white community everywhere. So vigilante groups, militia companies, and the ever-present military arm of the federal government were soon on their way to the battleground. By noon on Monday, in the blazing heat of a cornfield, Turner's insurrectionaries had their first encounter with the white militia and the volunteer companies which had rushed to organize. The blacks were heavily outgunned and, after suffering significant casualties among some of their best men, were forced to retreat. Still, with less than a third of his army remaining, General Nat maintained his resolve to reach Jerusalem. But the path was blocked each way he moved, fear was rising among his decimated command, and night was now upon them. So they hid and prayed and hoped, while isolated members of their company were being trapped, captured, and sometimes murdered in the woods.

By the next day, Tuesday, August 23, it was hard to see how hopes or prayers would prevail. The countryside was swarming with hundreds of armed white men from surrounding counties, cities, and military bases in Virginia and North Carolina, and Turner had fewer than 20 rebels remaining. Even in the face of these odds, Nat and his men were determined to fight on, if only they could draw more blacks to their side. Before daybreak they moved to attack a large plantation near their encampment, daring to hope they would attract fresh recruits out of the slave quarters there. Instead, Turner's fighters were repulsed by a defending force made up of the owners and their enslaved blacks. At least one of the rebels was killed there and several were severely wounded, including Nat's close friend, Hark. That may have been the decisive experience of defeat. Soon after, in one last skirmish with the militia, three more of Nat's little band were killed; others were wounded and captured, becoming offerings to a fearful spirit of vengeance which raged through the white community. Only Prophet Nat and four followers managed to escape. Finally, before Tuesday was over, as the beleaguered black remnant force separated in desperate search for other possibly surviving companions, all save Nat were killed or captured.

The march to Jerusalem was over. The band of black avenging angels was crushed. Still, Nat Turner was not captured and was not defeated. That night he hid and hoped. As hundreds of men and animals searched him out he dug a hole in the ground and lay there, daring to nurture the dream that he might yet regroup his forces, refusing to believe that the promised time of judgment for Virginia's slaveholders had not come (or had arrived in some form unrecognizable to him).[53]

In spite of Turner's desperate hope, there was no regrouping for his troops. Rather, while the residue of the black men hid or were rounded up, the outraged, terrified white forces struck back in overwhelming fury. Estimates range from scores to hundreds of black people slaughtered, most of whom evidently had no intimate connection with the uprising. Meanwhile, the prophet-turned-general was alone in the woods again, hiding, biding his time, most likely wondering if there would ever be another sign. He remained in hiding, avoiding capture for six weeks after the attempted revolution. But the signs were not propitious. His wife was found and lashed until she gave up those papers of his in her possession, papers "filled with hieroglyphical characters," characters which "appear to have been traced with blood."[54]

"The blood of Christ . . . was now returning to earth."

His friends were being captured and killed. Perhaps, though, there may have been some comfort afforded him if Turner learned that many of them manifested an amazing spirit of courage and commitment, even in the face of death. Of some it was said that "in the aggonies of Death [they] declared that they was going happy for that God had a hand in what they had been doing."[55]

While Nat was still hiding, another black preacher—this time one named David—attempted to enter the radical stream. In Duplin County, in southeastern North Carolina, far from Nat's place in the woods, David planned rebellion. With other enslaved Africans he plotted an insurrection for October 4, 1831, to culminate in a march on Wilmington. Were these some of David Walker's heirs, readers of the *Appeal*, marching on his native city in his honor? Or were they, as the authorities feared, part of Nat Turner's band of avengers? No one was certain, and the insurrection was blocked before it could demonstrate the direction of its flow. So even in Duplin County signs were not good, though the river was clearly in ferment.[56]

Out of that ferment, while Nat was still hiding, a fiery letter reached the town of Jerusalem, sounding almost as if the most stunning visions of Turner, Walker, and every other black insurrectionary leader had been put on paper and thrust into the Southern furnaces. Arriving from Boston, signed simply by "Nero," the missive proudly and provocatively announced to the white authorities that a paramilitary organization of black men was forming which would eventually lead hundreds of thousands of black people to take up arms in revenge for all the oppression of their people. According to Nero, their leader was even then traveling throughout the South, visiting "almost every Negro hut and quarters there." Key cadre members were training in Haiti, learning from the surviving leaders of that celebrated revolution. Everywhere in America they were recruiting, telling blacks "that if they are killed in this crusade that heaven will be their reward, and that every person they kill, who countenances slavery, shall procure for them an additional jewel in their heavenly crown." Had David Walker finally arrived in Southampton County, vindicating the hidden Turner and his scores of dead companions? Or was this simply another of those radical, bloody visions which must soar wildly out of the river of a people's freedom struggle, expressing all the yearnings buried in the spirits of the mute sufferers?[57]

The silence which followed the letter offered no answers for the future and no concrete hope in the present, least of all for the fugitive insurrectionary. Then on October 30, 1831, Nat Turner was captured. His sign had not come; Nero's army had not appeared. Charged with "conspiring to rebel and making insurrection," he told his counsel that he wished to plead not guilty, because he "did not feel" that he was a guilty person. Guilt was not a relevant category for an instrument of divine judgment— even if the last sign had not come.[58]

Perhaps he was sign in himself. Thomas Gray, a local slaveholding attorney who produced his own widely read version of Turner's confession, described Nat in prison as "clothed with rags and covered with chains, yet, daring to raise his manacled hand to heaven, with a spirit soaring above the attributes of man." Then Gray added, "I looked on him and my blood curdled in my veins." Turner's presence provoked similar terror and awe in other white observers, as well as deep levels of rage. Clearly some of that rage—and terror—had been spent in the postrebellion bloodletting, but lynching was still a possibility, so during the trial the court ordered the normal detachment of guards increased "to repel any attempt that may be made to remove Nat alias Nat Turner from the custody of the Sheriff." Nevertheless, when whites faced the reality of Nat Turner, other feelings and emotions seemed to overwhelm their rage. Indeed, there was something approaching fascination in the words of one contemporary: "During the examination, he evinced great intelligence and much shrewdness of intellect, answering every question clearly and distinctly, and without confusion or prevarication." Nat had no reason to be confused or to lie. Indeed, he did not hesitate to say that if he had another chance he would take the same bloody path to God again.[59]

It was on November 11, 1831, that Nat Turner went to the gallows, refusing to speak any final word to the crowd gathered to see him die, knowing that it was his living which had been his last, best testimony. Then, in its quiet, secret ways, the black community of Virginia and of the nation took his life into its own bosom and pondered it, just as some had done at the outset of his life. They continued to see signs, beginning with the day of his execution, for on that day, according to black tradition, "the sun was hidden behind angry clouds, the thunder rolled, the lightning flashed, and the most terrific storm visited that county ever known."[60]

My Lord He calls me, He calls me by the thunder
The trumpet sounds within-a my soul
I ain't got long to stay here.

Perhaps, though, in keeping with all the irony of the history of our struggle, it was the terrified and ruthlessly driven white community, which provided the ultimate sign of meaning for Nat Turner's movement. In the course of the massacre of blacks following the insurrection, the severed head of a black man had been impaled on a stake just where the Barrow Road, Nat's way of judgment, intersected the road to Jerusalem. The juncture became known as Blackhead Signpost and was meant, as usual, to be a warning against all future hope of black freedom.[61]

In spite of the white world's intentions, that macabre roadmark, with its recollections of similar slave-ship rituals and other bloody American roads, may have been the awaited black sign, fraught with many meanings: the suffering and death continually interwoven with the black march toward the freedom of Jerusalem; the white force of arms forever placed in the way of the life-affirming black movement. But even that terrible sign may have been transmuted to mean much more, just as Nat Turner meant more. Perhaps above all else it was a statement of the way in which all black people were a collective Blackhead Signpost for America. By the time of Nat Turner, that possibility was clearer than ever before. For white America's response to the black struggle for freedom might well determine the ultimate destination of its own people, moving them toward greater, truer human freedom, or eventually closing all pathways into a dead end of tragic, brutish varieties of death. So black struggle and black radicalism had no choice but to continue as an active, moving, relentless sign, forcing the issue of the nation's future, never allowing any of our God-driven, freedom-seeking, Jerusalem-marching fathers to have died in vain, pointing the way.

SIX

A Prophet in His Own Land

Support for Nat Turner and His Rebellion within Southampton's Black Community

PATRICK H. BREEN

In August of 1831 Nat Turner and a handful of men began a slave rebellion that left about 60 whites dead. Southern Virginia fell into chaos and terror spread throughout the South as whites wondered about the extent of the rebellion and the danger that their human property posed. Within six months, Virginia's house of delegates debated the propriety of slavery and considered emancipation schemes. Black people worried about their safety as bands of white men roved panic-stricken portions of the South seeking revenge, often with little concern for distinguishing the partisans of Nat Turner from bystanders whose only crime was their black skin. These responses to the rebellion have overshadowed any careful examination of the support that Nat Turner received in America's most famous slave rebellion.

Whites tried to reassure themselves that Nat Turner's rebellion was an anomaly with little latent black support. After all, the United States had a history remarkably devoid of slave rebellions of the sort that leveled parts of the Caribbean and Latin America. Indeed, many slaveholding Americans had viewed the apparent docility of their slaves as a sign of the virtue of their system. Concerns about black loyalty yielded to stories that white Southerners told themselves about their docile, loyal slaves. Kenneth S. Greenberg notes that many white reports of the day puzzled over why some Southampton blacks chose to rebel: "In several accounts of the episode, whites even seemed to have made the sun rather than any human agency responsible for the entire episode." Many whites who understood that the rebellion was not simply an act of nature focused their attention on those slaves who apparently provided no succor to the rebels. In a

Richmond paper, a correspondent from Southampton County commented upon the slaves of the county: "I must here pay a passing tribute
to our slaves, but one which they richly deserve—it is, that there was not
an instance of disaffection, in any section of our country; save on the
plantations which Capt. Nat visited, and to their credit, the recruits were
few and from the chief settlement among them, not a man was obtained."[1]

After 1831 such observations became the essential version that whites
told themselves about the event. Less than a year after the rebellion, the
devout colonizationist Mary Blackford traveled to Southampton County
and recorded in her diary the stories white survivors told of black loyalty
to masters and mistresses. In 1832 Thomas Roderick Dew, professor of
political economy at the College of William and Mary, reviewed the events
in Southampton: "[A] few slaves, led on by Nat Turner, rose in the night."
Later in the same paragraph, he repeated himself. "[T]his conspiracy embraced but a few slaves, all of whom . . . paid the penalty of their crimes."
This viewpoint persisted long after the Civil War. As incongruous as it may
appear, William Sidney Drewry, in the first formal history of the slave
rebellion, described the slaves as "the happiest laboring class in the world"
and praised the whites for their "gentle treatment" of their bound property: "The system of labor seems to have been an ideal one."[2]

That illusion deeply tainted the views of Nat Turner's relation to the
black community. According to this viewpoint, the rebellion only happened because Nat Turner wielded influence over a few other deluded
slaves, who were little more than pawns. John Hampden Pleasants, the
editor of the *Richmond Constitutional Whig*, wrote one of the earliest newspaper accounts of the rebellion from Jerusalem less than a week after the
rebellion began. Attached to the Richmond cavalry, Pleasants developed
a theory for the motives of Nat Turner's followers: "My own impression
is, that they acted under the influence of their leader Nat, a preacher and
a prophet among them." Thomas Gray, who recorded Nat Turner's confession, described the power that Turner's "gloomy fanaticism [had] acting upon materials but too well prepared for such impressions." Similarly,
Jeremiah Cobb, the judge who sentenced Turner to death, told him that
he was fully responsible for the deaths of those blacks killed during and
after the insurrection: "[A]s the author of their misfortune . . . [y]ou
forced them unprepared, from Time to Eternity." Newspapers, reporting
the details of the revolt, expressed contempt for Nat Turner's supporters.
In September, the *Richmond Enquirer* reported that Turner "used every
means in his power to acquire an ascendancy over the minds of slaves. . . .
[H]e used all the arts familiar to such pretenders to deceive, delude and
overawe their minds." In November the *Norfolk Herald* described the power
he had over his followers, "the few ignorant wretches whom he had se-
duced by his artifices to join him."[3]

More recent historians have tried to understand Nat Turner as an important leader of the black community. Herbert Aptheker makes clear

that Turner was "admired and respected by his fellow slaves" and "possessed the characteristic of great leaders." Stephen B. Oates describes how "slave friends spoke of Preacher Nat with a reverence," looked at him "in awe," and found him "spellbinding. He cried out what the slaves felt inside." For good reason, he was "the most prominent slave preacher in his neighborhood." In an introduction to a collection of primary documents, Kenneth S. Greenberg suggests that Nat Turner's "community acknowledged him as a religious leader" who "was a well-respected lay preacher among his people." Eric Foner also emphasizes the indubitable nature of Nat Turner's leadership: "[I]t is certain that Turner's position as a preacher made him a leader of the slave community. . . . Turner's role as the organizer of a slave rebellion cannot be understood unless his position of leadership among the slaves of Southampton is understood." Unfortunately for the image of Nat Turner as a great leader, the story that Turner told and Thomas Gray recorded in *The Confessions* described a more sophisticated, complicated, and ultimately interesting relationship between blacks in Southampton County and the instigator of America's most famous slave rebellion. To get at Turner's relationship with the black community before the rebellion, one must focus upon the main source of information about Turner's life before the rebellion, Gray's pamphlet of Nat Turner's *Confessions*.[4]

In the first part of *The Confessions*, Nat Turner told Thomas Gray the "history of the motives which induced me to undertake the late insurrection." In the story that Gray retold, one can capture a few glimpses of Nat Turner's world and his understanding of his relationship to the black community. Gray claimed that he wrote *The Confessions* "with little or no variation." He worked quickly, giving him little time to weave an entirely new story. But one must not overestimate the reliability of the stories Gray recorded. After all, Gray was not a disinterested bystander; a one-time slaveholder in Southampton County, he clearly sympathized with the whites who died. Moreover, as a failed planter and lawyer, he wrote with an eye steadfastly focused on the market, hoping to earn enough to pay off his mounting debts. Gray may have embellished *The Confessions* to make for more interesting reading. Human error is also likely in a document produced so quickly. Gray may have misheard Turner's tale or failed to copy down accurately what he heard. Even if Gray's work as an amanuensis were perfect, Turner had his own motives, which may have shaped how he told his story. For example, he omitted any reference to his wife, probably in an effort to protect her from further indignities or reprisals.[5] For all of these reasons, one must be careful when handling *The Confessions*, but historians would err by ignoring this seminal document that provides the best clues to Nat Turner's relationship to the black community before the rebellion. *The Confessions* captured a story fundamentally at odds with contemporary white reports and modern accounts, in both of which Nat Turner appears as a great leader of the black community.

In the first story that Turner told Gray, Turner described himself when he was "three or four years old." Apparently, the young child was telling his playmates a story that his mother recognized as a story about events that occurred before his birth. Curious, she questioned him. Not only did young Nat stick to his story, but he added details that apparently confirmed his knowledge of this event. At this point, Turner's mother called on others who were "greatly astonished." The others commented "in my hearing," as he told it, that "I would surely be a prophet, as the Lord had shewn me many things that had happened before my birth." His parents reinforced this, "saying in my presence, I was intended for some great purpose."[6]

One must be careful not to give too much weight to an incident that Turner related to Gray from his childhood. Surely, Turner might have erred about details from the 1804 incident, or Gray might have embellished this account. But as Nat Turner reviewed his life in anticipation of his quickly approaching death, he described this as "his first impression." In this central memory, he recounted how he had been anointed "a prophet" by "others," unnamed members of the black community.[7] Of all the stories he told, this was the one that he had the least reason to obscure. It took place long before the rebellion and did not involve accomplices in the rebellion who might pay for Turner's words with their lives. Furthermore, nothing in the story points to the insurrection. This story simply illustrates Turner's memory of a time when he held a special place in the black community.

Nat Turner related another story that also suggested he was a child prodigy. Teaching slaves to read had been outlawed in Virginia only months before the rebellion. While it had not been illegal for a slave to learn to read during Turner's childhood, it was unusual, and the literate Turner emphasized the peculiar way that he had learned. Most literate slaves were either taught by evangelical masters or mistresses concerned with the salvation of their slaves' souls, or else the slaves assiduously worked to acquire learning secretly. Frederick Douglass described both as part of his educational experience. Initially, Douglass's mistress taught him the alphabet, but after his master put a halt to such seditious sessions, young Frederick refused to accept his master's decision. "From that moment," as Douglass remembered, "I understood the direct pathway from slavery to freedom." In contrast, Turner testified that he had learned to read with "perfect ease." He continued, "I have no recollection whatever of learning the alphabet." According to his testimony, one day a book was given to him "to keep me from crying." Instead of simply playing with the pages of the book, "I began spelling the names of different objects." His learning with such facility elicited the "astonishment of the family" and, as Turner noted in *The Confessions*, "wonder to all in the neighborhood, particularly the blacks."[8]

Nat Turner recounted to Gray several stories that indicated the respect the black community had for the young Turner. In one, he described how the community's respect trickled down to his childhood playmates. Petty thievery was one of the slaves' most powerful tools to get back at those who owned their persons, and many slaves turned a blind eye to those who pilfered from their white owners. When some of Turner's playmates began to appropriate their masters' goods, Nat expressed little interest in these activities. Nevertheless, he found himself roped into these expeditions. Why? "[S]uch was the confidence of the negroes in the neighborhood, even at this early period of my life, in my superior judgment, that they would often carry me with them when they were going on any roguery, to plan for them."[9]

Repeatedly then, Turner described himself in *The Confessions* as a prodigy, one considered "a prophet" whose talents filled the black community with "wonder." This image fit perfectly with the whites' assumption that Turner had overawed the minds of his followers in order to get them to follow him on a suicidal mission. *The Confessions*, however, reveals a more textured story with nuances unlikely to have been fabricated by a racist amanuensis simply to sell more books. To Gray, Nat Turner recounted how, as a youth, he questioned his position as a prophet. Far from a fanatic, the young Nat Turner did not have the same confidence in himself that the black community apparently had in him: "Having soon discovered to be great, I must appear so, and therefore studiously avoided mixing in society, and wrapped myself in mystery." While he diligently cultivated a persona in Southampton, he worked even harder to figure out God's plan for himself. He prayed daily, fasted regularly, and sought confirmation of his special calling. Then, in about 1820, his faithful perseverance paid off. The Lord spoke to him. "As I was praying one day at my plough, the spirit spoke to me, saying 'Seek ye the kingdom of Heaven and all things shall be added unto you.'" Curious, Gray asked Turner what he meant by "the Spirit." Turner replied unambiguously: "The Spirit that spoke to the prophets in former days."[10]

Turner answered Gray with the confidence of a prophet or a fanatic who believed he had a conduit to divine providence, but he did not describe himself as having this confidence when he first heard the voice as he stood by the plow. He thought that he might have witnessed the true voice of God—not least because he remembered this biblical passage commented upon at church—but he knew how dangerous it was to say he spoke for God. Jesus' opponents arranged his execution because they believed him guilty of such blasphemy. Turner admitted to spending two years praying feverishly, wanting to make sure that the voice he heard was authentic, not simply a delusion. Two years later, he had the same revelation. He said that this repeated message "fully confirmed me in the impression that I was ordained for some great purpose in the hands of the Almighty."[11] The confidence of the black community and "many events," which either Gray did not trouble to write or Turner did not bother to detail, assured Turner of his holy calling.

Confirmed in his own mind and that of the community as a prophet, Turner worked to divine his sacred mission. He had to serve the Lord, but what he was called to do remained unclear. Turner redoubled his spiritual effort to learn what the God of the Israelites had in mind for a modern prophet of a different enslaved people. At the same time, he prepared other slaves to hear God's revelations from his lips. Communicating to his fellow slaves the revelations he witnessed, Turner noted, "[T]hey believed and said my wisdom came from God." He told them more and more of his visions and related that "something was about to happen that would terminate in fulfilling the great promise that had been made to me."[12] At this point, the narrative—as Gray recorded it—stops abruptly. Apparently, Turner had readied his fellow slaves for some chiliastic event, but the realities of slavery got in the way of an immediate fulfillment of God's "great promise" to him. Turner had a new overseer. Contemporaries and later historians have generally viewed hired overseers as more brutal than the owners. At least owners' violence was tempered by an understanding that each scar a slave bore would lessen his market value. Overseers usually had little incentive to protect slave property and much reason to try to increase short-term production. The unnamed overseer in Nat Turner's *Confessions* probably used the whip and other tested methods of motivation, while he increased both the production and the resentment of the slaves. Turner responded as many young men did to similar oppression: he ran away.

Running away was one of a slave's most effective weapons of resistance. Unlike insurrectionaries—who faced the longest odds—the flight to freedom was a measured way to get back at a system that tried to deny their humanity. By stealing himself, the slave punished the slaveholder by taking away a valuable asset. At the same time, the slave asserted his volition and denied the founding principle of slavery: that his will could be compelled to conform to that of his master. There were considerable risks involved in escape, and many who tried failed. Tracked by dogs and subject to capture by any free person, the runaway needed a little luck and much determination. Those who failed faced the possibility of brutal punishments: barbarous whippings, confinement, and possibly sale to a distant and less hospitable place. Even the successful runaway had to accept the likelihood that he would never again see family or friends. Understandably, many slaves did not try to escape. But those who did, including Nat Turner, became important symbols for the entire black community, reminding everyone that slavery was an imposed condition and keeping alive the hope for freedom for all who were enslaved.[13]

Following in the footsteps of his father, who had escaped from the shackles of slavery, Nat Turner fulfilled the great promise that the black community had seen in the child prodigy, the untutored literate child, and the youthful exhorter. For 30 days sometime in the early 1820s, Nat Turner reminded the black community in Southampton County of the limits of bondage. Even as the black community believed that Turner may have made it to freedom—in *The Confessions* he testified that "the negroes on the plantation . . . thought I had made my escape to some other country"—they surely understood that the odds against escape were long, even for the most intelligent, literate slave. No slave would have faulted Turner if he had been captured. The hounds, the patrollers, the reward notices, any of these could have foiled the best-laid plans of a runaway slave far from freedom's shore. His best effort was all that anyone expected, and after 30 days without communication with his fellow slaves, even the most pessimistic slaves must have thought that Nat Turner's best might have been enough to escape slavery's long reach.[14]

After 30 days away from slavery, Nat Turner returned to his plantation. He described the other slaves as responding to his reappearance with "astonishment." To muddle matters further, he did not return for any of the most understandable reasons. He had not been captured or injured. Neither pangs of hunger nor loneliness forced him back to the plantation. Instead he told the other slaves something that they found absolutely amazing: God himself had ordered Turner back. According to *The Confessions*, "[T]he Spirit appeared to me and said . . . that I should return to the service of my earthly master."[15] The voice that Nat Turner heard, that same voice that had convinced him that he was a prophet and that the other slaves had previously accepted as "wisdom come from God" commanded him to return to bondage. This was a critical moment in Nat Turner's relationship to the black community at large. All the effort that he had expended to convince the other slaves of his divine commission depended upon his convincing the other slaves that he spoke for the Lord, even when the message was the same as the message of obedience that slaves heard from their masters and white ministers.

At this point, those in the black community had two choices: they could accept Turner as a true prophet and bow to inscrutable Providence, or they could reject what he revealed. As a group, the slaves balked. Fidelity to one's master was beyond their sense of what God required of a slave. Turner recalled, "[T]he negroes found fault, and murmured [*sic*] against me, saying that if they had my sense they would not serve any master in the world."[16] From this point, Nat Turner had lost his privileged place within the black community. He would always be exceptional—a literate mystic slave—but only as an eccentric or a crank. The prophet returned to his own land to find that friends and neighbors rejected the authenticity of the voices he heard. No longer was he an unquestioned prophet. No more would he act as an intermediary through which the black community would learn God's plans.

The black community's rejection of Nat Turner's visions was not only a rejection of his claim of the authenticity of the voices that he heard. The black community implicitly rebuked him for being overly submissive to the power of slavery. If the voice that told him to return to slavery were not the voice of God, then Turner must have returned on his own account. Worse, when he returned, he told the others that the voice that commanded him to return had echoed the Gospel of Luke: "For he who knoweth his master's will and doeth it not, shall be beaten with many stripes, and thus have I chastened you."[17] He understood his real master to be God, but one can not avoid the distasteful implication that Turner believed that the slaveholders and overseers were tools of the Lord. Even the most ardent proslavery writers would have been chary in making this claim, especially by focusing on the practice of whipping slaves. That another slave would justify floggings as a part of God's plan brought to Nat Turner the scorn of those friends and neighbors who understood the arbitrary nature of southern punishment. Future generations would describe such an apologist as an Uncle Tom, and Nat Turner almost certainly suffered a similar rebuke from the black community.

Nat Turner's *Confessions* describe two ways in which he responded to the sharp criticism of the black community. First, he became much more radical. Rather than becoming an apologist, he became a revolutionary. The first vision that prefigured the insurrection in the narrative occurred immediately after he described how the other blacks had rejected him for apparently being too accommodating. After he recounted being mocked by the other slaves, Turner related his most dramatic, violent vision: "And about this time I had a vision—and I saw white spirits and black spirits engaged in battle, and the sun was darkened—the thunder rolled in the Heavens, and blood flowed in streams." The religious devotion that he had evidenced throughout his life suddenly became endowed with a political component, one that suggested nothing less than an impending race war. Second, he worked even more to withdraw from communion with the other slaves. Earlier he told Gray that he had "studiously avoided mixing in society," but in that case his goal was to wrap himself "in mystery" and to help cultivate his public persona as a prophet. After he returned to slavery, his reputation was in shambles, and he became an outcast: "I now withdrew myself as much as my situation would permit, from the intercourse of my fellow servants."[18] At the time he first had inklings that he might start a race war, he kept himself apart from his foot soldiers, those who would fight and die in the battles he envisioned.

In this separation from the other slaves, Nat Turner's rebellion contrasted sharply with other famous slave plots. Gabriel, who planned Virginia's most famous near-rebellion in 1800, "tap[ped] into the illicit network of communication that free blacks and slaves used" to spread the word and recruit allies. He enlisted friends and family in his plans, and he recruited other slaves at religious services. Denmark Vesey, author of Charleston's great insurrectionary plot of 1822, cultivated a group of loyal followers through the classes that he led at the city's African Methodist Episcopal Church. As early as 1818, Vesey identified Peter Poyas as a lieutenant and told him about his hope to free Charleston's slaves. As the day originally selected to begin the rebellion, 14 July 1822, approached, Vesey's recruiting efforts broadened in scope. According to the confession of Monday Gell, by March 1822, Vesey "ceased working at His trade and employed himself exclusively in enlisting men, and continued to do so until he was apprehended." His concerted efforts, both within and beyond the limits of Charleston, produced many recruits, and it seems likely that a tremendous part of Charleston's black community had heard that plans for a rebellion were afoot.[19] Compared to these recruitment efforts, Nat Turner's outreach appears anemic. Indeed, Turner steadfastly refused to inform others of his plans.

For six years, from 12 May 1825 to February 1831, the outcast prophet remained silent about his insurrectionary visions. He prayed and fasted, but he did not tell the blacks of Southampton about his premonitions of war. According to *The Confessions*, he told no one of his visions until an eclipse of the sun in February 1831: "[T]he first sign appeared. . . . And immediately on the sign appearing in the heavens, the seal was removed from my lips, and I communicated the great work laid out for me to do, to four in whom I had the greatest confidence." No direct evidence proves that Turner refused to disclose his visions of a racial Armageddon to other blacks, but this testimony was consistent with the records about the years before the insurrection. Moreover, the earliest reference to the revolt that found its way to the white community did not take place until after the unusual appearance of the sun, less than one week before the revolt began.[20]

The black community at large, then, had little reason to change its mind about the prophet's message. Turner remained aloof, withdrawn "as much as my situation would permit" from his fellow slaves, and he did little to counter the perception that he was an apologist for the slave system. He stayed silent about his visions of a racial war, and, instead, he emphasized to everyone that the great day of eternal judgment was fast approaching. He received more signs about the impending Armageddon and related these to others in the neighborhood, "both white and black." Interpreting leaves marked with blood, Turner understood that "the Saviour was about to lay down the yoke he had borne for the sins of men, and the great day of judgment was at hand."[21]

As a result of—and one of the most intriguing pieces of evidence of—his steadfastly focusing upon Judgment Day instead of upon the problems of slavery, a white man, Etheldred T. Brantley, became Turner's only religious disciple named in *The Confessions*. One could argue that because of his white skin, Brantley might have been the only follower that either Turner or Gray believed worthy of including in the story. But this does not seem to be the case. According to the story, Brantley was not just a notable follower. He was the only person in Southampton County willing to get baptized with Nat Turner.

According to *The Confessions*, Etheldred Brantley heard Turner's story of the approaching end of history and reformed his ways. He "ceased from his wickedness." At the same time, his skin became inflamed with pustules that oozed blood. After nine days of prayer and fasting, the festering sores were healed. Both Brantley and Turner apparently accepted these as signs from God, and they decided that they should both be baptized. As Turner remembered it, "[T]he white people would not let us be baptised [*sic*] by the church."[22] *The Confessions* are silent about the reasons that the whites denied Turner and Brantley's request for baptism. Most historians assume that the denial stemmed from the impropriety of having a slave baptize a white man. In the most recent monograph on the insurrection, Stephen Oates describes the affair: "When the word was out, it created a sensation in the neighborhood. A white man baptized by a Negro! Well, it was unheard of, even in tidewater Virginia, and white Christians absolutely refused to let Nat perform the ceremony at their altars." Oates is wrong. By agreeing to baptize Turner and Brantley, the church would have dictated the terms of the baptism, including making sure that the baptism fit within its ideas of racial propriety. By rejecting Turner and Brantley's request, the white church made it possible that a black man "in the company of a white man, did actually baptize himself." There is no evidence for Oates's assertion that Turner asked to baptize Brantley. Indeed, Turner testified that both he and Brantley asked to be baptized "by the church."[23]

One does not have to look hard to find a more plausible explanation for the church's denial. It is likely that any church would have had serious reservations about the message that Turner boldly proclaimed. He steadfastly insisted on his position as a prophet, asserting that "the Holy Ghost was with me." In addition to his unique access to the Holy Spirit, he saw himself plodding along a path to perfection: "And from the first steps of righteousness to the last, I was made perfect." More than a prophet or a saint, he began to believe himself to be a messianic figure. By the time of the rebellion, Turner explained more completely his special role in the coming end of the world: "Christ had laid down the yoke he had borne for the sins of men, and that I should take it on."[24] Most Christians—black and white—would have had serious reservations about such messianic proclamations. To those who rejected the petition for baptism, Nat Turner was not a prophet; he likely seemed a heretic.

Turner hoped to use the baptism as an important symbolic moment when he could win back the support of the black community and regain the status that he claimed as his birthright. According to a newspaper account of the baptism, written shortly after the rebellion, Nat Turner "announced to the Blacks, that he should baptize himself on a particular day, and that whilst in the water, a dove would be seen to descend from Heaven and perch on his head." He had hoped to "collect a great crowd"

to witness this unambiguous sign from God that Turner was not a charlatan but one upon whom the Lord's favor rested. Turner's bid to recapture the respect of the black community failed. No dove perched on his
head. One should not make too much of this story. It came secondhand
from a white man who sought to investigate the causes of the rebellion
years after the baptism took place. As with Turner's own recollections of
his youth, some of the details might be wrong, and this account of the
baptism differed in some respects from that given by Turner to Gray. In
The Confessions, Turner made no mention of predicting that a dove would
land on his head.[25] Whatever actually happened at the baptism a few years
before the rebellion, one thing is perfectly clear: when an interested white
writer looked for stories about Nat Turner—the then still-at-large leader
of the cataclysmic rebellion—he found disparaging stories in circulation.
Whatever happened during the baptism, the oral tradition in Nat Turner's
neighborhood described the event as another time when Turner's attempt
to stake out a position of leadership failed.

Historians have accepted the baptism as an occasion on which Nat
Turner suffered the derision of the community, although they have seen
the contempt coming from the whites. Kenneth S. Greenberg writes that
when Turner and Brantley asked to be baptized in the church, "whites
refused to allow them to use the church, and 'reviled' them during the
ceremony." At the same time, blacks were understood to have been
Turner's silent supporters. According to Oates, "the slaves [gathered] to
see their holy man save a white sinner."[26] Given the separation that Nat
Turner described between himself and the black community, and his conspicuous lack of black disciples, it seems unlikely that most black witnesses
saw Turner as a "holy man." In fact, once one puts together the two different accounts—Turner's own confession and the oral tradition saved on
the pages of the *Richmond Enquirer*—the most likely scenario suggests that
blacks mocked both Brantley and Turner. When Turner testified that "in
the sight of many who reviled us," he and Brantley were baptized, Turner
acknowledged his position not only as a failed prophet, but also as an
outcast, a man "reviled" by both blacks and whites alike.

Nat Turner's relationship to the black community changed dramatically
once he began to speak out against the wrongs of slavery. A story collected
after the rebellion about a whipping he received suggested that some in
the community might have noticed Turner's increasing radicalization
even before an eclipse in February 1831 removed "the seal . . . from my
lips." Once he began to speak against slavery, his religious pronouncements tapped into a deep discontent felt by many in the black community.
For a variety of reasons unrelated to Nat Turner's religion, men rallied
to Turner's side to fight slavery. A modern David needed yeoman soldiers
to fight Goliath, and Nat Turner found among the slaves of St. Luke's
Parish, Southampton, men willing to fight and die with him.[27]

Southampton County provided fertile soil for someone recruiting an army against the powerful forces of slavery. Southampton was long home to many white opponents of slavery, even if they never approached majority status. The Society of Friends had two different meeting houses in Southampton, although it appears that both of the meetings had ceased to function before the rebellion. Evangelical Christians were often sharply divided on the question of slavery. Nothing reveals this fault line in Southampton's white society better than the history of the Baptist Black Creek Church and its tempestuous relationship with its most outspoken ministers. One, David Barrow, was born in 1753 in Brunswick County, Virginia, west of Southampton County. He became a minister just before the American Revolution and spent over two decades in Southside Virginia preaching the Good News. He thought that Virginia suffered from its commitment to slavery, and in 1784 he manumitted his slaves. When he published an antislavery circular—in 1798—he was dismissed from the service of Black Creek Church. That year, Barrow left Southampton for the greener pastures of Kentucky, where he continued to speak out forcefully against the system of human bondage.[28]

No doubt, Southampton included many strong supporters of slavery. Black Creek Church itself contained more members who disagreed with its outspoken minister than agreed with him, but the degree to which opponents of slavery persisted in Southampton can be seen in the tradition of manumissions. Well before Nat Turner's rebellion terrified many Southampton whites, manumissions created a large free black population in the county. Although more than 70 of the county's free blacks left for Liberia between 1824 and the 1831 rebellion, the free black population in the county continued to grow, both by birth and manumission.[29]

While the vast majority of Southampton whites supported slavery, the continued presence of white opponents of slavery reminded those in the black community that they were not alone. On the fourth weekend in December 1825—just months after Turner had his first premonition about a war for freedom—Jonathan Lankford, the minister at Black Creek Church, told the congregation that he would no longer perform his duties as minister. To the same congregation that David Barrow had left 30 years earlier, he announced that he could not serve them "because Part of the church were slaveholders." The congregation had no tolerance for such words from the pulpit. Lankford was expelled from the church that he had belonged to for a quarter of a century and had led for seven years. A church committee reviewing the incident two years later upheld the action of the congregation, finding that Lankford had "yielded too much to the delusion of Satan."[30]

Without a doubt, slaves found as much wrong with the system of human bondage as their most sympathetic white allies. Most black Christians certainly believed that racial slavery was not part of the message of Jesus. Because of the impediments of slavery, however, the historical record is silent to the great "amen" that Lankford's and Barrow's words would have elicited in the slave quarters throughout Southampton, let alone the powerful words proclaimed by black witnesses against the institution of slavery to their fellow slaves. Only one piece of evidence tenuously links the Christian tradition to the supporters whom Turner was able to assemble. In one of the trials of the participants in the insurrection, Levi Waller testified that his slave Davey was called "brother Clements" by another member of Turner's band.[31] While it remains unclear whether Christianity led Davey and his friend to join the rebellion, this shred of evidence indicates that at least two of the soldiers seem to have been members of Christian communities. One suspects that of the 60 or more supporters who joined Nat Turner, more than these two men were Christians. Whatever the final number, the black Christians in Turner's army believed that they had God on their side as they fought against a sinful institution.

While some of Nat Turner's allies may have supported the rebellion because of their religious beliefs, other slaves joined to escape the discipline of slavery. Breaking free from the discipline of slavery—even if only for a short time—was tempting to many slaves. In October 1831, in Fincastle, Virginia, 250 miles from Southampton, local whites examined Billy, a slave. They were looking for Nat Turner, the at-large leader of the rebellion, when they heard testimony against Billy. The evidence against him was limited, and one of the whites remarked in a letter that Billy "only wanted an opportunity to do mischief."[32] Slaves in Fincastle had little chance to flout the social conventions of the day, and Nat Turner's rebellion offered the Southampton slaves who joined the rebellion a unique opportunity to act as they pleased.

Before the first blow was struck, the first six recruits took advantage of the liberties that came with their decision to rebel. On Sunday afternoon, they enjoyed a dinner to which Hark brought a pig and Henry brought brandy. Alcohol, to which slaves' access was usually restricted, was available to the rebels in almost unlimited quantities. Henry's brandy was followed by fellowship and free-flowing applejack from Joseph Travis's still. Levi Waller testified at the trials that he saw the rebels drinking after they had killed ten schoolchildren and his wife. John Turner captured two rebels, Curtis and Stephen, and told the court that they appeared drunk at the time. Nelson, too, was witnessed drinking, and his trip to the gallows was assured when a witness testified that Nelson had "had his tickler filled by his own request."[33]

Alcohol was not the only luxury that may have lured some slaves into the rebellion. Nat Turner reported that as soon as the killing was done at any household, there was a search for money and ammunition. The importance of arms is obvious, but it is revealing that money, which had little practical use during the insurrection, was a priority for the rebels. Some may have believed that if the rebellion failed they would escape detection and keep the booty they acquired, as apparently happened. A newspaper report of the rebellion suggested that the rebels had probably taken between 800 and 1,000 dollars, only "part of which [was] recovered." Several weeks after the rebellion, some of that money was found in the room of Lucy and Moses and was part of the evidence that led Lucy to the gallows. Hark, one of Nat Turner's first recruits, was also caught with silver in his pocket and with a victim's pocketbook.[34] Other recruits may have hoped that if the rebellion were successful, they would be able to use the money.

Money was as important for what it symbolized as for what it could buy, for it conferred status upon blacks just as it did whites. The rebels had an understanding that their leaders would get a higher salary than the foot soldiers. While each private was supposed to get a dollar for each day, defeated rebels explained to their inquisitors that the paymaster, Henry, would get five dollars per day and Nat Turner would get ten. Even on the bottom of the pay scale, the lowliest foot soldier could dream of wealth and status far surpassing what was possible for a typical slave to accumulate. When Isaac thought about joining the rebellion, he was extraordinarily excited: if the revolt succeeded "he would have as much money as his master."[35] For him, money was not simply a way of getting goods; rather it was a yardstick that could be used to make clear the equality of himself and the man who had been his owner.

Nothing was a more potent recruiting tool for Nat Turner's army than some slaves' desire for revenge. For a brief moment—when Southampton's social order was turned upside down by the rebellion—blacks had a chance to redress some of the wrongs they had endured. For some, the notion of revenge was directed against all whites. According to one witness, Hardy commented that "the negroes had been punished long enough" and that the deaths of many white people "was nothing and ought to have been done long ago." While some, such as Hardy, looked to avenge the wrongs committed by whites upon blacks in general, for others revenge was something directed at specific people against whom the rebels had specific grievances. Barry Newsom wanted revenge on Benjamin Edwards, who Newsom described as a "damned Rascal." The descriptions of some deaths also suggest that some of those who were killed had filled their attackers with particular venom. Mrs. William Williams seems to have been particularly disliked by the rebels. Instead of summarily executing her, one of the insurgents brought her back: "[A]fter showing her the mangled body of her lifeless husband, she was told to get down and lay by his side, where she was shot dead." While no reason was given for Mrs. Williams's gruesome fate, one can readily understand Thomas Barrow's death. Before the rebellion, Barrow refused to let an unnamed slave marry one of his slave women. During the rebellion, the slave took revenge by impaling Barrow upon a spit.[36]

Other slaves drew their inspiration to join the rebellion from the rhetoric of the Declaration of Independence. The first decision that Nelson, Henry, Hark, Sam, and Nat Turner—the first five participants of the rebellion—made together was to begin the war for African-American independence on the Fourth of July.[37] On the same day that Americans across the country gathered to hear readings of "self-evident" truths—notably, "That all men are created equal, that they are endowed by their Creator with certain unalienable rights"—these men were going to hazard their lives to make the Declaration's rights real. Nat Turner never testified as to which of the five collaborators first hit on the idea to begin their revolution on that day. Possibly, Turner himself was the moving force behind the decision, although the passive voice, "It was intended by us to begin the work of death on the 4th July last," makes certain attribution impossible.

There are several reasons to think that Turner was not responsible for the initial decision to begin on the Fourth of July. First, throughout *The Confessions,* Turner described his actions clearly and specifically. Since he was sure to hang at the gallows, he did little to hide his role in the plans. If he single-handedly decided to begin the rebellion on the Fourth of July, he would not have said that the decision was made "by us." Second, Turner had thought about the rebellion for years before he enlisted his first supporters. If he had it in mind to begin on the Fourth of July before he revealed his plans to anyone, why would he describe this decision as taking place after he had recruited Henry, Hark, Nelson, and Sam? Finally, Turner lacked a personal commitment to this anniversary that would have seemed unlikely had he been the one who selected it. When the Fourth of July came, Turner worried so much that he "fell sick, and the time passed." A prophet, not a patriot, Turner looked for a sign from God, not a national holiday, to spur him to action. In contrast to his queasiness at the thought of beginning the rebellion on the Fourth of July, Turner was intrepid once he received his sign. One week after receiving that supernatural sign, an unusual appearance of the sun, Turner and his small contingent began their historic rebellion. Given these three clues, one surmises that it was Henry, Hark, Nelson, or Sam who understood and wanted to highlight the similarities between themselves and the founding fathers and so first suggested beginning the war to end slavery on Independence Day.[38]

This implicit contrast in motivation between Nat Turner and others who joined the rebellion became clearer as the circle of insurrectionaries grew. On Sunday afternoon, after their last supper together, Nat Turner joined his recruits: Jack, Will, and the first four men whom he had invited to join the rebellion. For the first time in the six months since he had told anyone in the black community about his rebellion, Turner faced recruits whom he had not personally selected. "I saluted them on coming up, and asked Will how came he there?" Will answered that "his life was worth no more than others, and his liberty [was] as dear to him." With those two reasons, Will explained that he was ready to die in the war for freedom. Asked by Nat if he thought that in this rebellion he would win his freedom, Will responded, "He said he would, or loose [*sic*] his life."[39] Will's testimony is interesting for what he did not say. He expressed no fealty to Nat Turner, his religion, or his vision. The promise of liberty— not salvation—led Will to join the rebellion.

In not becoming a disciple of Turner, Will likely represented the majority of recruits. No hint exists that any of the warriors in Nat Turner's war were his disciples. There is no indication that he baptized any blacks, even as we know he baptized himself and a white man. Once the rebellion had begun, those who followed Turner appeared amazingly different from their leader. While he abstained from alcohol, even his earliest, most trusted recruits indulged. At the first home, "all went to the cider press and drank, except myself." As the revolt grew, new recruits showed little concern for the prophet's religious message even as many enlisted in his army. Nothing testifies to Turner's own isolation from the black community as clearly as the scene at the Parker farm. Three miles from Jerusalem, the slave army was as close as it would get to the county seat. Turner urged his men to continue their progress, but "some of the men having relations at Mr. Parker's[,] it was agreed that they might call and get his people."[40] While most of the rebels went forward to recruit more rebels, Turner remained conspicuously behind at Parker's front gate. The rebels reasonably thought that the entreaties of relatives would be more compelling than the visions of the peculiar prophet and, by not accompanying the recruiting party, it appears that Turner agreed.

Despite the best efforts of whites to portray Nat Turner's soldiers as pawns in the hands of a fanatic, or of historians to portray his allies as supporters of an important leader of the black community, the record is clear: the slaves of Southampton did not follow Nat Turner because they believed that he was a prophet. While Turner never disowned his religious vision, his rebellion was not limited to disciples. In fact, it may not have included any disciples. Slaves and free blacks joined his rebellion because they wanted to fight against slavery. Some black Christians may have seen rebellion as their religious duty. Other slaves and free blacks saw the revolt as a unique chance to get guns, money, and alcohol. Still others acted when they saw a unique opportunity to take revenge. Some slaves may have believed that they would win their liberty, while the more realistic were willing to die in a bid for freedom. For all of these reasons, and likely others shielded from the historical record, slaves in Southampton rebelled. Inspired by his religious visions, Nat Turner tapped into the latent hope and discontent of slaves and free blacks in Southampton. The prophet became a general and led his men in a desperate battle against slavery.[41]

SEVEN

Reading, Revelation, and Rebellion

The Textual Communities of Gabriel, Denmark Vesey, and Nat Turner

———

JAMES SIDBURY

One Sunday late in the summer of 1800, a group of slaves gathered at a spring near their Richmond, Virginia, Baptist Church to discuss a planned rebellion. A conspirator named Ben Woolfolk had second thoughts about the pending insurrection and warned that he "had heard that in the days of old, when the Israelites were in Servitude to King Pharoah [*sic*], they were taken from him by the Power of God,—and were carried away by Moses—God had blessed them with an Angel to go with him, But that I could see nothing of that kind in these days." Martin, the brother of Gabriel, who was the conspiracy's leader, answered Woolfolk with a citation to Leviticus: "I read in my Bible where God says, if we will worship him, we should have peace in all our Lands, five of you shall conquer an hundred and a hundred, a thousand of our enemies." Two decades later, in Charleston, Denmark Vesey sought to inspire enslaved South Carolinians to rise in rebellion by reading to them "from the Bible, how the children of Israel were delivered out of Egypt from bondage." Slightly less than ten years after that, in Southampton County, Virginia, Nat Turner found similar inspiration by interpreting the world through a Christian lens: "And now the Holy Ghost had revealed itself to me, and made plain the miracles it had shown me—For as the blood of Christ had been shed on this earth, and had ascended to heaven for the salvation of sinners, and was now returning to earth again in the form of dew—and as the leaves on the trees bore the impression of the figures I had seen in the heavens, it was plain to me that the Saviour was about to lay down the yoke he had borne for the sins of men, and the great day of judgment was at hand."[1]

That the Bible and biblical citation played an important role in each of these three major acts of slave resistance comes as no surprise. The Bible had, after all, inspired the poor and dispossessed throughout much of the world to struggle for justice before chattel slavery came to America, and it has continued to do so. And the church has long been recognized as an important locus of black political activism in the United States both before and after Emancipation. There has been, in fact, a tendency among those writing about slave Christianity to reify "the slave church" into a single overarching, if "invisible," institution.[2] This tendency is largely rooted in the primary sources scholars have used to examine the spiritual lives of the enslaved—especially spirituals—many of which homogenize slaves' religious beliefs. The resulting scholarship on slave Christianity has been both influential and valuable in providing a general interpretation of slaves' spiritual lives. But, given white efforts to control slave literacy and religion as well as the deeply localistic nature of antebellum southern society, the image that emerges from the literature, that of a unified slave church, seems too simple. Surely the neighborhood arbor churches with their unordained and often self-educated preachers developed idiosyncratic local variants of Christianity. But how can we approach and seek to reconstruct, even partially, these secret local worlds of the sacred?

Slave conspiracies and insurrections offer surprisingly useful snapshots of these varied and creative sacred worlds. By paying close attention to the ways in which participants in Gabriel's conspiracy, the Denmark Vesey conspiracy, and Nat Turner's rebellion used the Bible and understood themselves biblically, we can gain glimpses of the different communities of biblical interpretation that had emerged in these three places. This approach, in turn, sheds useful light on the meanings of literacy among enslaved Americans, and especially on the forms of authority that literacy conferred on the limited number of slaves who could read. These three examples of collective resistance indicate that literate slaves who were recognized by their peers to have spiritual insight could and did use the Bible to find a place for themselves and for their people in a sacred universe. In doing so, they built "textual communities" integrated through a shared interpretation of sacred script.[3] This process could, and in these three cases did, inspire radical activism, but the mechanisms through which local religious communities coalesced must have been germane to the daily religious practices of enslaved Americans throughout the antebellum era.

Gabriel's conspiracy was the first of these insurrectionary movements, and it is also the one for which the least evidence exists showing conspirators invoking religious rhetoric. In fact, the quotations reproduced at the beginning of this essay constitute the only direct appeal to the Bible in all of the recorded testimony produced during the trials and investigations of Gabriel and his alleged followers, a fact that has led some to discount the role of religion in the conspiracy.[4] There are, however, reasons to believe that religion did play a central role in the conspiracy. Many recruiting meetings took place at the Hungary Baptist Meeting House that Gabriel and his two brothers (and coconspirators) appear to have attended, and several—though by no means all—white Virginians who commented on Gabriel's conspiracy cited religion as central to the planned insurrection. In addition, there is substantial evidence of growing black allegiance to the Baptist Church in the region around Richmond during the late 1790s.

The best evidence of the role of religion in the conspiracy, however, and the best window into the sacred world of the conspirators, is the brief exchange in which the Bible was actually cited. Before turning to it, it might be worth remembering that very few of the discussions held by conspirators in and around Richmond during the summer of 1800 ever found their way on to paper. For that to happen, two conditions had to be met—one of the participants in the conversation (or someone who had heard a conversation or speech) had to relate the words to white Virginians, *and* those white Virginians had to write down what was reported to them. Given the rather sparse documentary record produced by the trials associated with Gabriel's conspiracy, it is certain that most of what the conspirators said to one another has not survived for historical analysis. The argument between Ben Woolfolk and Martin referenced above is the only one of those *recorded* conversations that mentions the Bible, but that does not mean that it was the only conversation in which the Bible played a role.[5]

Close attention to the dispute between Woolfolk and Martin lends credence to the assumption that biblically inflected discussions were common among Gabriel and his followers. The discussion between Martin and Ben Woolfolk found its way into the record only because, at least according to Woolfolk, it occurred at a pivotal moment. Though the surviving record will not allow a reliable reconstruction of each stage of the conspiracy during the summer of 1800, it appears that several groups of Richmond-area blacks spent part of that summer recruiting followers willing to commit to an insurrection. Once August—the appointed month for the rebellion—had arrived, the core of leaders had to decide whether to proceed to action. A conspirator named George Smith presided over the key meeting when it opened and called for the insurrection "to be deferred some time longer." Gabriel responded by calling on his brother Martin to speak, and Martin took the floor claiming that the Bible warned that "Delays bring Danger." It was then that Woolfolk responded, and his words are worth repeating: "I told them that I had heard that in the days of old, when the Israelites were in Servitude to King Pharoah [*sic*], they were taken from him by the Power of God,—and were carried away by Moses—God had blessed them with an Angel to go with him, But that I could see nothing of that kind in these days."

Strikingly, Woolfolk said nothing explicitly about Virginia or the conspiracy, though his reference to them is unmistakable. Instead, he argued through an analogy that he assumed all his listeners would understand, questioning Gabriel's leadership by insisting that he saw no angel of the Lord at the insurrection's head. Martin's response shows that Woolfolk was right to assume that his listeners would understand him: Martin accepted the analogy between enslaved Virginians and their God's first Chosen People, but insisted that Woolfolk's interpretation of that analogy was faulty. Martin asserted his ability to "read in [his] Bible," and then proved he could do so by quoting a specific passage from Leviticus—"five of you shall conquer an hundred and a hundred, a thousand of our enemies." Martin, in short, laid claim to greater interpretive authority than Woolfolk, and the other leaders of the conspiracy appear to have accepted his claim: after Martin's speech, Woolfolk reported, the leaders "went into a Consultation" and Martin set the day for the revolt.[6] This exchange makes little sense unless the conspirators—at least the leaders—saw themselves, their place in the cosmos, and the proper course that they should follow in Virginia through a lens shaped by the Bible and Christian belief.

However interesting or important the question of religion's role in Gabriel's conspiracy, these passages raise a more fundamental issue. If, as I have argued, the Bible was central to the conspirators' sense of themselves, do these cryptic surviving fragments of their debate provide enough pieces to reconstruct a more specific picture of the way that these black Virginians came together as a "textual community"—a community of believers united by an understanding of sacred text? The very limited documentary record presents formidable problems. Without knowing what texts conspirators used in different conversations (if and when they used Biblical citations at other times), there is no way to know whether the focus in this discussion on the Exodus reflected the dominant role that the story of secular deliverance in the Pentateuch played for this group of enslaved Virginians, or if, to the contrary, it simply reflects the judgment of Martin and Woolfolk that such passages were especially relevant to the issue then at hand.[7] What does seem clear, however, is that the leadership of the conspiracy shared several things: a familiarity with the Bible, a strong conviction that the stories in the Bible spoke directly to their situation on earth, and respect bordering on deference for those who could read and be trusted to interpret God's word reliably. For it was Martin's greater facility with the Bible, and especially his ability to relate it convincingly and specifically to the matter at hand, that, at least according to Woolfolk's account, won him so much influence at this critical meeting.

A shared knowledge and interpretive position regarding the Bible—presumably including the ability to invoke isolated passages from the Bible like Leviticus 26—must have played a crucial role in building the conspirators' sense of unity and destiny. This does not, of course, mean that the conspirators were "simply" religious "fanatics" inspired to bring about the end of days. Like many Christian rebels stretching from participants in the German Peasants' War to members of the Kongolese Antonian Movement and beyond, Gabriel's followers used the Bible to interpret the injustices in the world in which they lived and to make sense of their own responsibilities in light of those injustices.[8] The argument between Woolfolk and Martin can be understood, at least in part, as yet one more example of one of the ancient controversies among believers: should man, as Woolfolk suggested, wait for God to bring justice to the world, or, as Martin insisted, could they just rely on God to make them victorious against their oppressors if they would only seek to further his cause? Answering this question relied in part on forging a shared interpretation of the text that the conspirators believed to be the repository of God's word.

White South Carolinians created a much fuller record of the later Denmark Vesey conspiracy, which permits us to penetrate further into those conspirators' different world of textual interpretation. The differences were rooted first and foremost in the different histories of Richmond in 1800 and Charleston in 1821. Gabriel's Richmond was a rapidly growing town of about 6,000 people, but it had been Virginia's capital for only two decades, and it remained in many ways a provincial backwater. Liberalized manumission laws in the wake of the American Revolution had helped produce a growing population of free black people in the town, and economic development had drawn many skilled artisanal slaves to Richmond. Almost all black Richmonders, however, were either enslaved or had only recently acquired their freedom. While the blacks in and around town were building informal institutions through which they could pursue their interests, they, even more than white Richmonders, remained less cosmopolitan than their counterparts in Charleston.[9]

Charleston in 1821, it should be noted, offered a tough standard of comparison. In retrospect the city had, by then, begun to descend from its perch as one of the premier cities in eighteenth-century British North America. But Charlestonians continued to conceive of themselves as living in an important cultural center, and the city retained a thick layer of cultural institutions because of its former prominence. More important for understanding Denmark Vesey's conspiracy, black Charlestonians—or, to be truer to their conceptions of difference, Charlestonians of color— had developed their own cultural institutions, from the racially discriminatory Brown Fellowship Society to the then-southernmost congregation of the African Methodist Episcopal Church. Reliable literacy figures are unavailable, but it is certainly true that more black and colored Charlestonians could read than could black Richmonders, and knowledge of the world beyond Charleston and South Carolina ran much deeper in black Charleston than did analogous knowledge in any other North American slave town except New Orleans.[10]

Unsurprisingly, access to written texts appears to have been much more widespread among Vesey's conspirators than among Gabriel's. While several leaders of Gabriel's conspiracy kept lists of participants, and one letter from a conspirator has survived, there is little additional evidence of conspirators handling or producing written material. The contrast with Vesey is striking. A white Charleston woman reported in passing that authorities had found "voluminous papers" among Vesey and his followers; she found the "gain in knowledge" among the slaves who surrounded her "astonishing." The trials of the alleged conspirators bear out this observation. Denmark Vesey himself was literate, and several witnesses testified that he had firsthand knowledge of Haiti and could understand French—he had spent some time in revolutionary Saint Domingue before being sold into South Carolina and had traveled extensively as a mariner after arriving. They also testified to his ownership of copies of legislative debates concerning slavery.[11] Nor was Vesey alone in this regard: Monday Gell, one of his chief lieutenants, reportedly "read daily the papers" and also kept acquaintances informed about events occurring outside of Charleston.[12] There is no way to measure how many of the conspirators could read and write, but all lived within a world shaped by written texts, and the leaders of the conspiracy sought to build their liberation movement through their access to books and their skill in interpreting them.

The most important text was the Bible. Vesey's conspiracy centered on a church—the Charleston congregation of the African Methodist Episcopal Church—and Vesey and other leaders laid repeated and specific claim to a special ability to interpret God's word.[13] In part these assertions grew out of the leaders' institutional responsibilities in the city's various evangelical churches: a resident of nearby Savannah, Georgia, reported that the "ring leaders" were all "[Methodist] class leaders or [Baptist] Deacons."[14] Vesey and his followers enhanced the authority of their church offices by actively contesting white interpretations of the Scripture. The insurrectionary leaders denied that the Bible sanctioned slavery or that it required obedience. Vesey reinforced his allegation that whites offered slaves an adulterated interpretation of God's word by pointing out to his followers that a white clergyman had "made a Catechism *different* for the negroes"—an observation whites had to concede.[15] The Charleston magistrates who reported on the Vesey conspiracy implicitly conceded the importance of his biblical interpretations by effectively attempting to refute his theology of resistance in their public proclamation of Vesey's guilt.[16] Denmark Vesey's conspiracy, then, offers an unusually richly documented example of slaves and some free people of color coming together through the evangelical efforts of a small charismatic group to forge a textual community. What were the interpretive contours of that community?

Vesey chose not to speak to authorities after being apprehended, so we must rely entirely on secondhand reports to reconstruct the biblical vision that he offered his followers.[17] Fortunately, there are several such accounts and they generally corroborate one another. A South Carolinian writing in the *Carolina Gazette* accurately summarized the trial testimony on this issue as follows, with, of course, expected biases:

> The designing leaders in the scheme of villainy availed themselves of these occasions to instill sentiments of ferocity by *falsifying the Bible*. All the several penal laws of the Israelites were quoted to mislead them, and the denunciations in the prophecies, which were intended to deter men from evil, were declared to be divine commands that they were meant to execute. To confirm this doctrine, they were told that Heshbon, that Bash with its 60 cities, had been destroyed men, women and children; that in the destruction of Midian, only the males were destroyed, at which Moses was displeased and deliberately ordered the death of the boys and their mothers. That Joshua levelled the walls of Jericho and regarded neither age or sex; that David vanquished empires and left not one man, woman or infant alive.[18]

This white Charlestonian focused on Vesey's "misinterpretation" of the Bible and was especially interested in the bloody quality of Vesey's theology. In his focus he revealed the potency that he feared in Vesey's readings. Of more interest for this analysis, however, is the centrality of the Old Testament, and of specific portions of the Old Testament, to Vesey's message.

That slave conspirators would foreground the Old Testament comes as no surprise. The story of God's Chosen People being delivered from slavery has long been recognized as an important and inspirational narrative foundation for slave Christianity. But given the mediated nature of the sources with which historians of slavery must work, it is, perhaps, too easy to meld the different stories of Jewish captivity and to fail to pay careful enough attention to the specific passages that different interpreters chose. It is, for example, striking that all of the stories that the South Carolinian found so troubling in Vesey's interpretive hands are drawn from periods during which Israel enjoyed successful charismatic military leadership— either from Moses during the trek through the wilderness, from Joshua as the Chosen People arrived at the Promised Land, or from David.[19] It is hardly necessary to belabor the obvious utility of these specific texts in building a movement for freedom among enslaved people. Vesey's use of them underscores two conventional interpretations of slave Christianity— that it was deeply influenced by the story of the Exodus and that enslaved people of African descent developed a vision of themselves as God's new Chosen People.[20] White Carolinians' need to assert that Vesey was "falsifying," like the magistrates' public refutation of his theology of liberation during sentencing, emphasized that they perceived how much was at stake if Vesey's interpretive authority were accepted.

Perhaps because the stakes were so high, whites recorded much testimony regarding Vesey's interpretation of the Bible, testimony that permits unusually precise analysis of the conspirators' textual community. Various reports made clear that Vesey knew his Bible well and could range broadly through the Old Testament in making his case. The confessions of two conspirators—Bacchus Hammet and a young boy named John—described his preaching even more specifically. They cited a specific chapter of Exodus as central to Vesey's exhortation. At a meeting of his followers, Vesey read from "different chapters from the Old Testament, but most generally read the whole of 21st Chap. Exodus," and he "exhorted from 16th verse the words 'and He that stealeth a man.' "[21] The full text of the verse reads: "And he that stealeth a man, and selleth him, or if he be found in his hand, he shall surely be put to death." A more apposite text to inspire enslaved rebels would be difficult to imagine. Vesey's unsurprising decision to exhort upon that verse should not, however, draw too much attention from the fact that he "read the whole of" chapter 21. In that chapter, sometimes called a part of the "Book of the Covenant" within the Book of Exodus, the Lord restated to Moses and to the children of Israel the laws they must obey to uphold their end of the covenant and thus retain his blessing. In the previous chapter the Lord had restated many of the sacred laws of the covenant, but in chapter 21 his focus is on more secular matters involving the treatment of servants, assault, and attempted murder, as well as man stealing. The retributive sense of justice suggested in the punishment for man stealing runs consistently through the chapter. It prevails in both specific punishments for listed crimes and in the Lord's more general instruction in dealing with "any mischief" resulting from a man mistreating a woman or child: "thou shalt give life for life, Eye for eye, tooth for tooth, hand for hand, foot for foot." Vesey rallied his followers by turning to the Bible to resurrect for them a vengeful God of secular deliverance, and he no doubt suggested, as had Gabriel's brother Martin 20 years earlier, that this God would guide his Chosen People to liberty if they would take the first step by rising against their sinful masters.[22]

Some of those masters revealed through their responses that they understood, at least implicitly, the interpretive acts that Vesey committed and the need to answer them with alternative interpretations. The South Carolinian wrote in the *Carolina Gazette* charging Vesey with committing an "execrable perversion" of the Bible by quoting the "penal laws of the Israelites," which were "intended to deter men from evil," but presenting them as "divine commands" to be carried into practice. In this way, Vesey sought to turn the "God of Mercy" into a "Juggernaught." The magistrates who reported Vesey's sentence shared the South Carolinian's opinion and sought to redirect enslaved Carolinians' attention away from the Old Testament and back to the New. They addressed the by-then-deceased Vesey directly: "If you had searched . . . [the Scriptures] with sincerity, you would have discovered instructions, immediately applicable to the deluded victims of your artful wiles—" '*Servants (says St. Paul) obey in all things your masters, according to the flesh, not with eye service, as men pleasers, but in singleness of heart, fearing God.'"* And again, *"'Servants (St. Peter) be subject to your masters with all fear, not only to the good and gentle, but also to the forward.'"* "On such texts," the magistrates insisted, "comment is unnecessary."[23]

But comment on those texts was precisely what Vesey had done. The record does not reveal the specific critique that he offered of these scriptural staples of proslavery thought, but it does show that he pointed out to his followers that white evangelicals were writing special catechisms for blacks. And several witnesses at trial testified to the effect that Vesey "studie[d] the Bible a great deal" and tried to "prove from it that Slavery and bondage" violated God's law, and thus that slaves were divinely justified in rising against their earthly masters.[24] He must have argued that the God of the New Testament would approve of the same harsh punishments for false Christians as the God of the Pentateuch had authorized for children of Israel who failed to keep the Covenant. Vesey worked through the institutional infrastructure of the local African Methodist Episcopal Church—class leaders played key recruiting roles, and the trial transcripts sometimes read as if church membership alone was evidence of participation in the conspiracy—but, as many have pointed out, the African Methodist Episcopal Church did not, at that time, condone revolutionary activity like that which Vesey had planned. Rather than forging an oppositional movement out of the reformist theology of that church, Vesey offered members of that church a theological alternative grounded in his interpretation of Exodus and its meaning within the context of a putatively Christian slaveholding society. According to both the testimony of black Charlestonians convicted of joining Vesey's conspiracy, and the commentary of white Carolinians on the trials and the behavior of the alleged conspirators, Vesey built among his followers a community of men who shared his understanding of God's promise to them. This understanding was based upon Vesey's selection and interpretation of God's word. It would be misleading to think of this interpretive community as being an integral part of some pan-southern construct called "the slave church." Vesey and his lieutenants had been forced to work hard to convert black Charlestonians who were already members of Christian churches to their revolutionary theology. It makes better sense to think of this textual community as local, inspired to action by its members' shared interpretation of a common text.

The Denmark Vesey conspiracy produced more and richer evidence than did Gabriel's conspiracy, and that evidence permits a fuller exploration of the relationship of the conspirators to each other and to the Bible. But like Gabriel's conspiracy, analysis of Vesey's textual community is hampered by a gaping absence at the center of the record: like Gabriel, Vesey himself never spoke to authorities after his intended revolution was thwarted. Nat Turner's 1831 rebellion in Southampton County, Virginia, did not produce a record of court testimony as rich as that of the Vesey conspiracy, but it did produce the most important extended testimony that we have from a leader of a North American slave rebellion. Unlike the other two cases, then, Turner's confessions offer the chance to examine the building of a textual community from the perspective of the charismatic interpreter of the text.

There are, inevitably, drawbacks that accompany this opportunity. Notwithstanding complications involving transcription, Turner's confessions offer an almost unparalleled view of a leader's perspective, but the transcripts from the trials of Turner's followers are remarkably silent regarding Turner's belief in and use of the Bible. While that might seem surprising on first consideration, it makes perfect sense. Those tried for participating in Turner's rebellion were being tried either for murder or for being accessories to murder. There was little reason for the courts to delve into alleged rebels' motives for joining and even less reason for court clerks to record those reasons when they were mentioned in court.[25]

A letter published in a Virginia newspaper while Turner himself remained at large indicates that Turner's religious beliefs were discussed at greater length during his followers' trials than the transcripts suggest. Turner escaped capture during the initial military repression of the rebellion and managed to elude authorities for two months. During that time the Southampton County court completed its trials of his followers.[26] Meanwhile, a letter appeared in the *Richmond Constitutional Whig* that anticipated much (but not all) that Turner would reveal in his *Confessions*.[27] This letter told of Turner's religious visions, of his assertions that he had special skills, and of claims that he made to his followers during the insurrection that recent natural events should be interpreted as divine encouragement. This letter does not provide specific textual citations like those of which followers of Denmark Vesey spoke, but it makes clear that Turner based his assertions of military authority on his ability to interpret metaphysical script. He can be understood, at least in part, as having sought to build a textual community in opposition to slavery, and his *Confessions* reveal much about the interpretive acts through which he did that.

Turner himself saw the roots of his revolutionary leadership in his ability to interpret God's word. Early in adulthood he grew obsessed with a biblical passage—"Seek ye the kingdom of Heaven and all things shall be added unto you"—and, after much prayer regarding that passage, "the spirit spoke" to him.[28] As the literary critic Eric Sundquist has shown, Turner was an accomplished interpreter of the Bible who used his gifts to command profound spiritual authority. Like Vesey he explicitly refuted proslavery interpretations of the Bible—in Turner's case, by reinterpreting Luke 12:47 ("For he who knoweth his Master's will, and doeth it not, shall be beaten with many stripes"), a staple of the masters' version of Christianity that he turned into a call for rebellion. Turner, however, went beyond claiming ministerial authority as an interpreter of the Scripture.

He laid claim to the authority of revelation. His claims were both explicit—he said that "the spirit" spoke to him and then said that he later "had the same revelation"—and implicit, but they were strongest when implicit. In the way that he cited biblical passages, he represented himself to be either a new prophet of the Lord, and thus the harbinger of a new prophetic age, or he went even further—to present himself as the second coming of Christ.[29]

Thus, while Turner based his authority on his special ability to understand the Bible, his interpretive gift allowed him to turn nature into a new divine text and to read God's intentions there. Turner reported having had visions of a "darkened sun" and of "white spirits and black spirits" fighting in the heavens. He withdrew into himself in order to make sense of these visions, and "the Spirit" reappeared to him to promise that it would "reveal . . . the knowledge of the elements, the revolution of the planets, the operation of the tides, and the changes of the seasons." This process of revelation continued until Turner was "made perfect" and the "Holy Ghost" stood before him speaking "in the Heavens." The Holy Ghost did not initially *tell* Turner the meaning of these visions. Instead, it initiated him into true knowledge by communicating through a mystical written text: Turner "discovered drops of blood on the corn as though it were dew from heaven," and then found "on the leaves in the woods hieroglyphic characters, and numbers, with the forms of men in different attitudes, portrayed in blood." In this way the Holy Ghost "revealed itself," indicating that "the Saviour was about to lay down the yoke he had borne for the sins of men, and the great day of judgment was at hand." After that the Spirit spoke directly, telling Turner to take up the yoke that Christ had "laid down" and to "fight against the Serpent, for the time was fast approaching when the first should be last and last should be first."[30] In this case, of course, the Spirit was speaking from Scripture to Turner, but it had endowed its listener with a new ability to understand the true and immediate meaning of that Scripture, an ability directly comparable to that of Christ.

There is little in Turner's telling up to this point that helps explain the building of a community based upon his interpretive precocity. He had been marked since childhood as possessed of special perception, and he reported having told others of at least one of his discoveries—the blood on the corn, but he described an almost-monastic withdrawal into contemplation as his main response to these visits from the Spirit. He had shared a broader sense of his visions with Etheldred Brantley, a white man with whom he had entered a river to be "baptised by the Spirit" within the "sight of many who reviled us." But shortly after this, the Spirit told Turner to "conceal" his understanding from the "knowledge of men" until given a "sign" from heaven that he should "slay" his "enemies with their own weapons." After receiving the sign—a solar eclipse—he "communicated" to four select lieutenants "the great work" that God had appointed him to do, and they began to plan the rebellion. That plan called on the rebels to travel down the "road leading to Jerusalem"—Southampton County's seat—and, presumably, to bring God's justice to this new-world Jerusalem. How did Turner's local reputation as an interpreter of the Bible and of God's writing in nature contribute to his followers' willingness to accept his leadership?[31]

The main evidence we can bring to bear on this question comes from white Virginians' informal (as opposed to official) descriptions of the interrogations of rebels and their descriptions of the rebellion itself. To some extent these reports are too superficial and condescending to be of much help. It is difficult, for example, to muster the confidence to analyze an allegation that Turner used "tricks to acquire and preserve influence." Several things do seem clear, however, from contemporary whites' attempts to understand Turner's appeal and from Turner's own *Confessions*. His authority was rooted in stories of his lifelong ability to see things others could not and in his extraordinary access to the written word— Turner said that he acquired literacy without being taught to read. That authority had, however, been transformed during the period leading up to the conspiracy as he had, in the words of a newspaper correspondent, "acquired the character of a prophet." His religious authority was not based in any church, at least according to Virginia Baptists who sought to distance themselves from Turner. Instead he had "assumed ... [a preacher's authority] of his own accord" while claiming that he was "divinely inspired." He and whites who heard other conspirators' testimony agreed that he shared his plan with only a small cadre of followers prior to the beginning of the rebellion, but the willingness of others to join and obey suggests that other Southampton slaves had been prepared for him to assume the role of holy avenger. According to the *Norfolk Herald*, it was by "comparing his pretended prophecies with passages in the Holy Scriptures" that "he obtained the complete control of his followers."[32]

Turner's personal history as a communally acknowledged spiritual prodigy combined with the visions that he began to have toward the end of his life to create among slaves in the Southampton region a belief that he could, indeed, interpret signs from God. Such a belief was tied in his own mind and in those of his followers to his knowledge of and skill in interpreting the Bible. But the interpretive community that arose around Turner, to the extent that he himself understood and accurately represented it in his *Confessions*, was one that granted to its charismatic leader much greater authority than had the community that rallied to Gabriel's or Vesey's plans. Turner did not stop at interpreting the Bible as a promise by God to aid his people. Turner claimed to be the legitimate heir of Christ—he healed the sick and explicitly compared himself to Christ— and of the prophets. And his vision of the conflagration that he was starting was, as Eric Sundquist has pointed out, based more immediately on

New Testament passages promising Christ's return than on Old Testament stories about the deliverance of a Chosen People.

It is, in fact, the differences among the religious visions that inspired these three examples of slave resistance that are most important for furthering the analysis of the place of spirituality in the cultures of enslaved people. This is not to say that there were no similarities. In all three cases the insurrectionary movements were inspired, in important part, by Christianity, and in all three cases the participants drew on a common belief that enslaved Americans of African descent constituted God's new Chosen People and the instruments of his will on earth. In this way the three movements support conclusions reached by previous interpreters of slave Christianity. The variations among the movements do not so much call those interpretations into question as permit useful complications to be introduced.

They show, for instance, the local interpretive vitality that formed the base for the broad "slave church" that modern scholarship has uncovered. The rich spiritual traditions that have been the subject of so much scholarship have often seemed to emerge as a "folk religion" in some organic process from "the slave community." It should be emphasized that the scholars examining the slave church have neither intended nor made such an argument, but their focus on "folk" sources—spirituals, folk tales, the reminiscences of very elderly former slaves—effectively effaced the intellectual work that enslaved spiritual leaders devoted to interpreting the Bible, as well as the active decisions that these leaders' followers made about when and whether to accept various interpretations.[33] The specific but different biblical citations of Martin, Vesey, and Turner, and the explicit efforts of Vesey and Turner to counter white Southerners' proslavery interpretations of Scripture provide specific instances of the work of textual interpretation that unordained black preachers must have engaged in throughout the slave South. While the folk sources that have shed so much light on the sacred lives of the enslaved reveal the biblical stories that resonated within slave communities throughout the South—the stories of the Exodus and Daniel for example—the evidence from Martin, Vesey, and Turner show that even shared stories could be and were interpreted differently by different communities.

We will never be able to uncover very many of these local worlds of textual interpretation among southern slaves. Uncovering the dynamics of a few of them, however, does reveal the way in which a largely illiterate people became, in the course of considerably less than a century, very self-consciously a people of a book. Accepting Christianity entailed real dangers for slaves, because white Southerners sought openly and vigorously to shape Christianity into a tool they could use to control bondsmen. That such dangers were avoided is a tribute to the interpretive work of the relatively small group of literate religious leaders who studied the Bible, compared its text to the messages that they and their followers heard from white ministers, and formulated alternative interpretations. Those interpretations could, in rare cases, fuel revolutionary action; more commonly, they nourished innumerable local variants of a general belief that God would not allow his Chosen People to languish forever in a new Egypt.

It would be misleading, however, to close on a note that treated revolutionary moments in the history of Christianity among the slaves as the norm. As many historians have pointed out, the simple demographics of the slave South militated against frequent rebellions, and the movement toward a textual community united behind violent resistance to slavery was very much the exception within the South. Nonetheless, as shown by an incident that occurred a few counties to the west of Southampton at roughly the same time that the Spirit was visiting Nat Turner, potential black leaders' efforts to make sense of the Bible and of their people's place in the spiritual and sacred worlds, and their struggles to win a following among the enslaved were a part of the more "normal" spiritual life of slave communities.

During the 1820s in southeastern Virginia two black preachers engaged in a contest for the allegiance of blacks within that neighborhood.[34] Their debate emerged in response to the rise to prominence of a black preacher named Campbell, who offered a biblical vision similar in some ways to Turner's. Campbell, like Turner, could read, but because "few of the blacks" were literate, he argued that spiritual leaders of the enslaved should turn away from the "written word of God" and depend "entirely upon the teachings of the Holy Spirit." In response to a dream, he threw his Bible into the fire to keep himself from consulting it and thereby putting himself "above the people." The surviving account of Campbell gives no indication that he argued for a social transformation, but it does note that this egalitarian doctrine brought Campbell great success and caused concern among "the owners of slaves in that section of the country."

Campbell's reputation spread up into Southside, Virginia where it reached another prominent black preacher known, at least to whites in the region, as "Uncle Jack." Jack traveled down to confront Campbell publicly, and, upon arriving in the neighborhood, he got area slaveowners to arrange a meeting at which he could challenge "these new and strange doctrines." According to Jack's biographer, the debate was no contest. Campbell opened with his typical "torrents of 'great swelling words of vanity,'" but then Jack silenced him through his personal authority and by challenging Campbell to "prove" his doctrine. When Campbell quoted the Bible in support of his views, Jack "objected on the ground that he had burned his Bible, and accordingly had no right to the use of any thing it contained." This telling blow supposedly carried the day, and "*coloured Campbellism* died entirely."[35]

Skepticism about the death of "coloured Campbellism" is certainly in order, not only because of the biases of the source, but because of the telling congruence between Campbell's reliance on communication with the Holy Spirit and the way in which Turner developed his theology of revolution. Interesting as any possible lost connections between this little-known black preacher and Nat Turner might be, however, the story of Campbell's dispute with Jack is more important for the way it redirects attention from the charismatic leaders—whether Jack and Campbell, Turner, Vesey, or Gabriel's brother Martin—and back toward their listeners. It underscores the fact that the largely nonliterate people listening to these leaders were not passive receptacles; they were, instead, active listeners discriminating among different interpretations of the relationship between the sacred and the world. While they had, as Campbell appears to have emphasized, very limited access to God's written word, that did not lessen their respect for the Bible or their belief that plausible interpretation must place the enslaved within a biblically based—if not biblical—narrative. They were a people of the book.

But as has been true throughout the history of Christianity in Europe, Africa, and the Americas, a shared conviction that the Bible contained God's word and the key to his plan left ample space for different communities' understandings of that plan. The Christianity of enslaved African Americans must have emerged as a varied set of local interpretations that could be combined and read as a mosaic.[36] There is much of value in conventional readings of that mosaic as a single unified picture, a single "folk" religion that found expression in the rich musical and oral traditions that have come down to us in homogenized form from the days of slavery. Understanding the ways that enslaved Christians understood themselves through the Bible, however, requires closer attention than has sometimes been paid to the differences among the stones that make up that mosaic. Such attention allows us to make better sense of the occasional emergence of Christian movements that sought the radical restructuring of this world, and it redirects attention toward the all-but-irretrievably-lost intellectual history of the enslaved. That history is one of people insisting on some control over the interpretation of texts that they may not have been able to read, but which they believed to hold the key to secular and sacred salvation.

EIGHT

Nat Turner in a Hemispheric Context

DOUGLAS R. EGERTON

"I . . . wrapped myself in mystery," Nat Turner once admitted, and ever since, historical fact has remained the captive of his myth. With the possible exception of Abraham Lincoln, Turner, more than any other anti-slavery activist of the nineteenth century, resides largely in legend and popular imagination. Long before the publication of William Styron's 1967 Pulitzer Prize–winning fiction, novelists from G. P. R. James to Harriet Beecher Stowe to Mary Spear Tiernan tried their hand at fabricating the lost world of old Southampton, and over the years few historians have proven immune to the infection of popular culture. Indeed, Styron's well-known characterization of Turner as a mentally unstable "nut" is only one of many attempts to depict the slave general as a dangerously irrational rebel; three decades earlier, Arna Bontemps, one of the leading voices of the Harlem Renaissance, begged off writing about Turner. There was the problem of Nat's "visions and dreams," Bontemps lamented, as he explained why he chose instead to pen a fictional history of Gabriel's far more secular conspiracy of 1800.[1]

But *did* Turner stand outside the mainstream of black resistance in the Americas? This essay seeks not merely to answer that question but to separate fact from legend by comparing Turner to other enslaved rebels who orchestrated conspiracies in the western hemisphere during (or shortly after) his lifetime. By measuring his revolt against those led by Gabriel, Denmark Vesey, and the slaves in British Jamaica and Demerara, as well as with the rebels in La Escalera, Cuba, Turner's enormous strengths and profound weaknesses, his organizational strategies, and his leadership capacity come into sharp focus. In so doing, one finds far more similarities than differences. If modern writers are correct in suggesting that Turner was "not very heroic looking at all," that opinion must stand as an indictment of a long line of slave generals who ultimately were far more alike than they were distinctive.[2]

Neither Styron nor Bontemps, of course, created the popular imagery of Turner as mercurial. In fact, allegations of insanity, or at least rhetorical hints of instability, first appeared only days after his revolt collapsed. On Thursday, 30 August 1831—eight days after his uprising began, and two months prior to his capture by Benjamin Phipps—the influential *Richmond Enquirer* printed an extract of a letter from Southampton. "A fanatic preacher by the name of Nat Turner," reported the correspondent, "was at the bottom of this infernal brigandage." Then, as now, "fanatic" was synonymous with "maniac" or "zealot," and it bears noting that earlier white polemicists failed to apply similar epithets to earlier black rebels. In the fall of 1800, the *Norfolk Herald* crowed that the "villon" Gabriel had at last been captured, and 22 years later, Anna Haynes Johnson of Charleston used the same expression in branding Denmark Vesey "a villain." Johnson's language implied that the old carpenter was a criminal and a dastard, but nothing in her terrified missive hints at the thought that he was mentally imbalanced.[3]

The conventional wisdom—among southern whites, at least—that Nat was a very different sort of slave only grew in the months after his death. According to some accounts, just before his execution Turner sold his body to local surgeons and used his earnings to purchase ginger cakes as a last meal. Whatever the truth of that legend—and the fear most Africans had of physical dismemberment as impeding entrance into the spirit world would seem to cast doubt upon it—Southampton whites evidently kept portions of his remains as macabre souvenirs. Toward the end of the nineteenth century, pioneering historian William S. Drewry interviewed a number of elderly whites who had "seen Nat's skull." Most described it as abnormal. "It was very peculiarly shaped," Drewry insisted, "resembling the head of a sheep, and at least three-quarters of an inch thick."[4]

Skulls and bones aside, for Turner's white contemporaries, as well as for more than a few modern writers and scholars, his profound religiosity was the most obvious manifestation of madness. The men who sat in judgment of Turner, naturally, were disinclined to dignify black theology with the term "religion." Turner's desire to be free was instead "instigated by the wildest superstition and fanaticism," editorialized the *Norfolk Herald,* and served as "proof of his insanity." Writing at the dawn of the twentieth century, influential scholar James Curtis Ballagh agreed. "Fanaticism followed the mental aberration of Nat," he alleged, "which was brought to a climax by an eclipse and the consequent peculiar appearance of the sun."[5]

Many scholars, even those sympathetic to Turner's cause, are uncomfortable with the sort of visions and voices that Turner described to white attorney Thomas R. Gray; the profane, twenty-first-century mind resists the notion that sane men might see "white spirits and black spirits engaged in battle" when they gaze up at the sky. But rural Americans in the antebellum years would have had an equally difficult time understanding the rationalist tone of modern life. As theologian and sociologist Vincent Harding observes, writers who would isolate Turner's visions from the antebellum mainstream strip his revolt of historical context. The apocalyptical Christianity so common in the Jacksonian era, he notes, "promised that justice would cost the perpetrators in very real and very concrete ways." Many Americans, white and black, devoutly believed that the end of time was near, and that Christ would soon return to rule his earthly kingdom. To that extent, Harding writes, Turner was simply "living within the popular nineteenth-century Euro-American millenarian religious tradition."[6]

There was a time when most whites shared Turner's apocalyptic fervor, even to the extent that overseer Etheldred T. Brantley once invited Turner to baptize him. It was only, as Merton L. Dillon has noted, when slaves refused to interpret the Bible "correctly," that is, according to conventional proslavery standards, that whites leveled charges of "fanaticism." But as Herbert Aptheker observes, early American Christianity was infused with "superstition and mysticism," and perhaps Ballagh might have been reluctant to brand as "fanatical" those white farmers who planted their crops according to the signs of the zodiac. Admittedly, there is a qualitative difference between planting wheat and launching a revolution. Yet white scholars who found it absurd that Turner relied on God's guidance probably saw nothing terribly unusual in the prayers that followed the collapse of Vesey's conspiracy. "Oh heavenly Father," prayed Eliza Ball, who had been raised on the same Windsor plantation with conspirator Peter Poyas, "how great has been thy mercy to us, [in] protecting and saving us & our city from fire & murder which threatened us."[7]

By the time Eliza Ball fell to her knees in supplication, the skeptical deism of the Revolutionary generation had given way to the evangelical fervor of the Second Great Awakening. The religiously based reform movements of the Burned Over District are best remembered today, but the flame of Christian perfectionism scorched the rural South as well. Hundreds of blacks, and more than a few working-class whites like Etheldred Brantley, turned out each Sunday to hear stump preachers interpret God's will. At one camp meeting near the Virginia border in mid-August 1831, blacks from as far away as Winton, North Carolina, traveled to hear Preacher Turner exhort from the Book of Revelation. If Turner's sermon on the apocalyptical four horsemen struck his congregation as anything out of the ordinary, they failed to note it at the time.[8]

More to the point, enslaved rebels in other parts of the western hemisphere relied on very similar messages to animate their followers or to justify their demands for freedom. In the year that Nat turned 16, slaves in the Brazilian towns of Santo Amaro and Sao Francisco do Conde went on a killing spree following a Catholic celebration; Christian theories of equality and universal brotherhood, it appears, motivated black converts to purify several grand estates with fire. Two decades later in 1835, Males (African-born Muslims) briefly captured Salvador, the capital of the Brazilian province of Bahai, when denied time to study Islamic doctrine. The final insult was the seizure of Pacifico Licutan, a scholar and Male elder, who was confiscated as property to pay off his Christian master's debt.[9]

Whether the creed was Baptist or Catholic, Muslim or a pre-Islamic West African derivation, a devout sense of faith inspired numerous leaders from Southampton to Bahai to believe that the heavens were on the side of the oppressed. In 1844 in La Escalera, Cuba—just as in 1791 in Saint Domingue—slave recruiters inspired their followers through the use of protective *brujeria*, enchanted objects that could ward off the white man's power.[10] One need not, of course, embrace the proposition that rituals or supernatural objects might deflect bullets, or, indeed, that the skies opened up above the Turner plantation, to understand that each religious culture functions within its own specific cosmology and behaves according to the logic inherent in those teachings. If belief in *brujeria* or the imminent return of Christ were widespread among early national people of both African and European descent, does that make all such adherents "nuts," to employ Styron's term?

When it comes to overt comparisons to Southampton, the Jamaican slave revolt of 1831 presents the most obvious parallel, not merely in time, but also in theology. Due to the labors of Baptist missionaries, western Jamaica was every bit as aflame with revivalism as was southern Virginia in that contentious year. Christmas Day fell on a Sunday, a traditional day of rest for bondpeople, but local authorities announced that the holiday would not extend to Monday. For stump preachers like Sam Sharpe, a literate and charismatic slave who lived near Montego Bay, that meant the less-Christianized of his enslaved brethren would slumber when they should be at chapel. Sharpe had already concluded that unfree labor was antithetical to Christian brotherhood, and this studied insult to his flock convinced him that God demanded that he not turn the other cheek.[11]

If Sharpe and Turner adopted the New Testament as their essential text, other leaders turned to the Hebrew Bible. Following a brief membership in Charleston's Second Presbyterian Church, former slave Denmark Vesey found solace in "the stern and Nemesis-like God of the Old Testament." Embittered by the continuing bondage of his children and his first wife, and disgusted with the proslavery ministers of South Carolina, Vesey turned his back on a messiah who would have him forgive his enemies. He became the master, as white magistrates later conceded, of "all those parts of the Scriptures" that dealt with servitude, and he could "readily quote them, to prove that slavery was contrary to the laws of God." Vesey's favorite text became Joshua 6:21: "Then they utterly destroyed all in the city, both men and women, young and old [with] the edge of the sword."[12]

Like Turner, Vesey taught his disciples not only that God would consent to their freedom, but also that holy Scripture actually enjoined them to rise for their liberty. "Denmark read at the meeting different Chapters from the Old Testament," recalled a slave named John, "and exhorted from the 16th Verse [of Exodus 21] the words 'and He that Stealeth a man' [shall] be put to death." Vesey's tendency to preach to all comers grew so overpowering that even "his general conversation" at carpentry sites and taverns, reported Benjamin Ford, a 16-year-old white boy, "was about religion, which he would apply to slavery."[13]

None of this is to imply that there were no significant distinctions between Turner and other rebel leaders. Turner obviously differed, even on matters of faith, from his enslaved brethren in other parts of the Americas. Black Charlestonian William Paul confessed that Vesey "studies the Bible a good deal and tries to prove from it Slavery and bondage is against" God's will. But where the old carpenter looked to the Old Testament for divine sanction and historical precedent, Turner's Christian God actually told him what to do. As a young man, Nat ran away and remained in hiding for almost a month. But "the Spirit appeared to me and said I had my wishes directed to the things of this world," Turner later confided to Thomas Gray, "and that I should return to the service of my earthly master."[14]

There can be little doubt that apocalyptic Christianity was not only more prevalent in Turner's revolt than in any other hemispheric conspiracy, but that Nat's reading of Revelation actually guided events that August. The slave general "seems quite communicative," reported the *Richmond Enquirer* shortly after his capture, adding that Turner "says he was commanded by the Almighty to do what he did." Aptheker has gone so far as to suggest that Turner's abortive attack on the hamlet of Jerusalem was directly inspired by his desire to walk in the figurative footsteps of Jesus. According to the apostle Matthew, Jesus warned his followers "that he must go unto Jerusalem, and suffer many things [and] be killed," a premonition that appeared especially relevant following Nat's retort to attorney Gray regarding the failure of his revolt: "Was not Christ crucified[?]"[15]

Nat's quick answer mystified Gray, as did so many things about the slave prophet. Indeed, even as most whites denounced Turner as a fanatic with a messianic complex, some Virginians suspected he was more of a pragmatic charlatan than a zealot. A correspondent of the *Enquirer* charged not that he was a false messiah, but rather that Turner was little more than a trickster who "used all the arts familiar to such pretenders, to deceive, delude, and overawe [the] minds" of his disciples. In short, even Turner's greatest enemies failed to achieve a meeting of minds as to the relative balance of his.[16]

Contradicting the pervasive myth that Turner was mentally unsound is the ample evidence that there was a crafty method to his madness. Slave conspiracies in the Americas, as Eugene D. Genovese once observed, "took root amidst bitter antagonisms among the whites," and events in Southampton were no different. Two years before, in 1829, Virginia politicians assembled in Richmond to draft a new state constitution. Delegates from the slave-poor western counties, where plantation agriculture had yet to take root, called for greater representation. Tidewater aristocrats like Abel P. Upshur feared that the "principal object" of the reformers was "to induce a gradual abolition of slavery." Not without good cause, rumors that Virginia bondpeople might be liberated hummed along the slave grapevine. The convention ended in bitter recriminations on both sides; given such fiery rhetoric, it was hardly illogical for Turner to believe that western yeomen might prove a bit tardy in riding to the aid of their planter brethren.[17]

An ugly division of the master class was indeed common to literally all New World slave conspiracies, and if Turner did regard the Virginia constitutional debate as his moment, that fact renders him a most unremarkable rebel. Five years before his birth, in 1795, rebellious slaves near Pointe Coupee, Louisiana, picked up similar rumors from the revolution-torn continent. One held that the king of Spain had proclaimed black liberation, but that the colonial governor, fearing the local planter elite, refused to implement the decree. Five years after that, urban bondmen in and around Richmond planned to rise amidst the bitter partisan divisions inspired by the Quasi War and the election of 1800. As Federalist newspapers predicted an "ultimate appeal to arms by the two great parties," slaves like Jack Ditcher prepared to pick up a sword. "We have as much right to fight for our liberty as any men," he told one recruit.[18]

In May of 1822, at about the same time that Turner was sold to Thomas Moore, nearly 300 slaves on the Boa Vista plantation in Brazil threw down their tools in protest over the new overseer chosen by their master. As word of the coming war of independence spread along the coast, slaves hoped that relations between white Brazilians and Portugal would deteriorate enough to allow for a massive servile insurrection, in the same way that tensions between the *grands blancs* and the *gens de couleur* paved the way for Haitian liberty. In the same month, published accounts of the rancorous Missouri debates and New York Senator Rufus King's eloquent denunciation of unfree labor taught South Carolina bondmen that the United States was two countries—slave and free. Denmark Vesey, who modern novelists have yet to characterize as a "nut," regarded "Mr. King [as] the black man's friend," for he pronounced slavery "a great disgrace to the country."[19]

Carolina planters who feared King's egalitarian rhetoric were right to be concerned. During the course of the following year, Africans living along the Demerara River on the Guyana plantation of John Gladstone—

the father of the reform-minded prime minister—took heart from demands by British abolitionists to "ameliorate" the material condition of
slave life in preparation for their eventual emancipation. As in Southampton eight years later, the Demerara rebellion was born in part of sectional
tensions, in this case a triangular struggle for power between resident
masters, absentee landlords, and London abolitionists.[20]

Due to a curious coincidence of timing, only months after Turner tried
to take advantage of the political disharmony in his state to bring on the
day of Jubilee, slaves in Jamaica followed much the same path. Under
pressure from the Anti-Slavery Society, the Colonial Office demanded a
number of improvements in slave housing and treatment. Resident planters responded with a series of angry protest meetings, which only served
to alert Jamaican bondpeople to the rising tide of antislavery sentiment
in Parliament. The governor, the Earl of Belmore, echoed Abel P. Upshur
in worrying that the meetings might "disturb the minds of the slaves," but
the demonstrations only ceased when the slaves finally rose for their freedom during the week of Christmas.[21]

An angry, crippling division among the heavily armed master class, however, was only half of any conspiratorial equation. Black generals like
Turner also had to count heads and gauge the potential numbers available
to them. Here too, despite obvious demographic differences, Nat appears
more like his Caribbean and South American counterparts than he appears distinctive. In British Guyana, as in French Saint Domingue, likely
rebels enjoyed the benefits of a black majority; not only were there as
many slaves along the Demerara and Essequibo Rivers as there were on
the entire island of Jamaica, blacks in the colony outnumbered whites by
as many as 20 to one. Along the 25 mile coast from Georgetown to Ma-
haica, rebel leaders like Jack Gladstone might easily rally 12,000 black
soldiers to their standard. Around the Travis farm, Turner lacked those
sorts of inviting odds. Yet if Virginia as a whole boasted a white majority,
Southampton was 60 percent black. Equally important was the fact that
the county was home to an unusually large number of "free persons of
color," many of whom had familial ties to the slave community. Although
Turner could only have guessed at these statistics, only three Tidewater
counties had more free blacks than Southampton.[22]

Scholars skeptical of Turner's plan point to the dispersed nature of
white settlement across the vast, sprawling county. This area of isolated
farms and scattered cotton plantations, William W. Freehling suggests, was
hardly the "crowded stage" of Vesey's Charleston, "where thousands of
throats were present to be sliced." In the end, less than one percent of
Southampton fell under the control of Nat's army. Genovese agrees that
the North American backcountry was unlikely to give birth to the sort of
successful revolution found in Saint Domingue. With a hinterland filled
with armed yeomen, a plantation world of resident landlords, and a
nearby federal government prepared to back up white hegemony, few

secular radicals, with the notable exception of Gabriel, risked their lives in the name of black liberation. "What judgments should be rendered on a society," Genovese wonders, "the evils of which reach such proportions that only madmen are sane enough to challenge them?"[23]

But if the inhospitable Southampton geography militated against armed insurrection, why did so many bondmen rise when he called? Indeed, perhaps a somewhat more pressing question is what the black general intended to do with his soldiers. Even assuming that Turner could persuade numbers enough to rise with him, the objective of his army remains a mystery. Genovese concedes that Turner's goals "remain obscure" but suspects that he planned to establish "a large maroon colony in the Dismal Swamp." More recently, Donald R. Wright suggests that Turner, after successfully capturing the hamlet of Jerusalem, planned to remain in Southampton and to try to "hold out against whatever forces were sent against him." But whereas Genovese rebukes Turner for failing to adopt "careful planning, preparation, and foresight," Wright hints instead that the evangelical mind had little interest in such temporal matters: "Turner may have preferred to leave the aftermath in Jehovah's hands."[24]

Turner's lack of specificity did not, of course, prevent his hurriedly planned plot from turning into an actual uprising. By ironic comparison, that most precise and well-planned of conspiracies, the far-flung intrigue conceived of by Gabriel in the spring of 1800, collapsed even before a single white life was taken. According to the meticulous slave blacksmith, Henrico County slaves planned to march toward the capital, "after which he [Gabriel] would fortify Richmond and proceed to discipline his men." Gabriel proposed to take hostages, including Governor James Monroe, whose lives could be bartered for black liberty. The young revolutionary expected "that every Frenchman would join them, every free negro and mulatto, and many of the most redoubtable democrats in the state." If Monroe agreed to their demands, Gabriel planned to "hoist a white flag, and he would dine and drink with the merchants of the city." Although a sudden downpour washed away Gabriel's prospects, most white observers believed his plan perfectly feasible. James Thomson Callender, who shared the Richmond jail with the conspirators, thought the plot "could hardly have failed of success."[25]

Imprecise planning in the face of dangerous odds, which might testify to a lack of mental stability, was also far from the case in Denmark Vesey's equally abortive plan. Yet if any of the men who rose for their liberty during Turner's brief life appears to stand outside the mainstream, it is Vesey rather than Nat. Whereas Toussaint L'Ouverture hoped to lead his French colony to republican independence, and Gabriel sought a more democratic society in Virginia, and Turner obviously proposed to remain in the land of his birth, only Vesey plotted a slave exodus, a mass escape from the Carolina low country. When some of his disciples "asked if they were to stay in Charleston" after the 14 July revolt, Vesey "said no, as soon as they could get the money from the Banks, and the goods from the stores, they should hoist sail for Saint Doming[ue]."[26]

In the end, of course, both Gabriel and Vesey swung from the gibbet without liberating a single bondman. Perhaps Turner's failure to recruit hundreds of followers over the course of several months—as Gabriel had—was as strategically wise as was his refusal to reveal his plan to even his closest lieutenants until the last possible moment. If this was madness, then there was a sensible and rational method to it. Turner planned to rise quickly and present area bondpeople with a *fait accompli;* slaves would only hear of the revolt as mounted soldiers thundered into the plantation quarters. According to one unnamed correspondent of the *Richmond Constitutional Whig,* the "seizure of Jerusalem, and the massacre of its inhabitants, was with [Turner], a chief purpose, & seemed to be his ultimatum; for farther, he gave no clue to his design."[27]

Hindsight is often the enemy of understanding. Secure in the knowledge that Turner failed in his mission, scholars are tempted to assume that no other outcome was possible. But once Jerusalem was within the grasp of his army, Turner could either have fortified the village and waited for word of the rising to spread across the countryside or, if white counterassaults became too potent, could have galloped the 25 miles east into the Dismal Swamp. Here then lay the basis, not of a fanatical plan doomed to failure, but of a maroon island of black liberty deep within the slaveholding South. Although Turner did *not* succeed in drawing thousands of recruits into the town, he yet "might have," admits Eugene Genovese, "had he sustained his pilot effort even for a few weeks or escaped to forge a guerrilla base in the interior." According to a correspondent of the *Norfolk Herald,* Turner freely confessed that he planned to conquer *"the county of Southampton . . .* [just] as the white people did in the revolution."[28]

A final point of comparison thus follows. Assuming that Turner's plan did stand a chance of victory—and this essay makes just that assumption—how successful was he as a recruiter, and how effective was he as a leader once the uprising had begun? For some scholars, it is not even clear that the black preacher *was* the leader of the 1831 revolt. "Nat Turner has remained trapped in the narrative of 'great man' history," observes Scot French, who theorizes not only that Turner was part of a much broader two-state conspiracy, but that bondmen other than Nat were far more crucial to the plot. Perhaps so; it is certainly true that no one man, however forceful or charismatic, can single-handedly create a revolution. Yet every popular revolt requires a leader, a Georges Danton or Boukman Dutty or Tom Paine, to give shape and form to widespread anger and discontent. As E. P. Thompson observed years ago, popular revolutions arise precisely when "the politically-conscious minority" verbalizes the "grievances of the majority."[29]

Few men were more respected in Southampton than Turner. The baptism of white overseer Etheldred T. Brantley indicates that this esteem cut across lines of race and authority, and even Thomas R. Gray praised Turner's (atypically southern) habits of sobriety and munificence. Turner "was never known to have a dollar in his life," he conceded, or "to swear an oath, or drink a drop of spirits." Like Virginia leaders white and black, Turner cultivated a posture of aloof sagacity. "Having soon discovered to be great," Turner mused, "I must appear so, and therefore studiously avoided mixing in society." For "a natural intelligence and quickness of apprehension," Gray agreed, Turner was "surpassed by few men I have ever seen." Historians critical of Herbert Aptheker's pioneering study of slave resistance much doubt that bondmen, "faced with a huge expanse of territory, controlled by a white majority, [willingly] engaged in [a] large number of extensive slave revolts." But Turner shrewdly understood that all it would require to ignite decades of buried frustration was one determined leader. Jim and Isaac, two embittered Southampton slaves, put it best. Should Turner's insurgents ride their way, they assured one startled bondwoman, "they would join and help kill the white people." Jim's "master had crossed him and [now] he would be crossed before the end of the year."[30]

Turner's actual revolt may have exhibited little organization, yet the slave preacher carefully laid the groundwork for insurrection months in advance. On Sunday, 14 August, near the border Southampton shared with Nansemond County and North Carolina, blacks and whites congregated near Barnes's Methodist Church for a grand revival. Slaves arrived from as far away as Winton, North Carolina, to hear a series of stump preachers, one of whom was later identified as Turner. According to one account, Turner spent the afternoon preaching and recruiting; he urged those sympathetic to his cause to show their solidarity by wearing red bandannas around their necks. Charity Bower, an elderly black woman who lived near Wilmington, was quite familiar with "Prophet Nat." Samuel Warner, a white Virginian, concurred that Turner was "promised the aid of many of their enslaved brethren in North Carolina."[31]

By preaching nothing more than vague generalities and incendiary sermons, Turner was practicing the same pragmatic strategy as rebel leaders in British Guyana, who restricted word of the plot to what the modern world would identify as revolutionary cells. Most slaves along the Demerara River heard nothing of the plan until the moment on Monday night when planners burst into the quarters with news that an uprising was under way. In Southampton, just after the collapse of Turner's revolt, one wounded lieutenant—who may have been Hark—confessed that "the insurrection commenced with *six* only under an impression that all would join if their masters were murdered." Given Turner's weekly sermons over the previous months, there was sound logic in this assumption. Aged residents of Southampton told William S. Drewry that local bondmen adorned themselves with "blood-red" bandannas and "long red sashes around their waists and over their shoulders," not knowing that for some time Turner had beseeched his disciples to identify themselves in just this fashion.[32]

If anything, it was the sane, secular Gabriel who committed the blunder of allowing his lieutenants actively to recruit followers at Sunday services and barbecues during the summer of 1800. Gabriel hoped to induct several hundred young men into his army in this fashion, but in the process he also enlisted several turncoats. Yet, in this instance, Turner's behavior stands not alone but is indistinguishable from that of North Carolina rebels in 1802. "[W]e shall most certainly Suceed without difficulty if our Schem is not betrayed," wrote an obviously literate black Carolinian, "as thee is but one in a Family to know of it Untill the time is but Actually arrived." Denmark Vesey, organizing his exodus in cramped Charleston, also required more officers than soldiers. Only after Vesey's close followers had slain their "own master[s] and males about the house" and overpowered the city guard would urban bondmen be awakened with frantic orders to "fire the city in various places, seize upon certain ships" and move toward the docks with their families for a hurried departure "to Hayti."[33]

When it came to his choice of officers, Turner was as cautious and practical as any slave general in the western hemisphere. All successful military leaders, black or white, tend to be shrewd judges of men's characters, and in this respect Turner was the equal of Gabriel. When Charles, a Richmond-area bondman, overheard whispers about a rising in July of 1800, he told the charismatic blacksmith that he "wanted to be a Cap't." Gabriel laughed that "he might be a Sergeant—he was too trifling a fellow." Similarly, as Turner sized up his confidants, he instinctively understood which were leaders and which were followers: "Jack, I knew, was only a tool in the hands of Hark."[34]

Soldiers were critical, but timing was everything. Stephen Oates chides Turner for his dangerous indecision regarding on which day to begin the revolt, and not without reason: a number of false alarms in Jamaica in 1831 served to put white administrators on their guard. Yet both dates suggested by Turner were chosen with great care, for each was highly symbolic. The first was Independence Day. "It was intended by us to have begun the work of death on the 4th July," Turner admitted to Gray. But the preacher "fell sick, and the time passed." The cadre finally decided upon the early hours of 22 August, which, as Peter H. Wood observes, was, "perhaps through sheer coincidence," the 40th anniversary of Haiti's Night of Fire. But coincidence in history, as opposed to Victorian fiction, will simply not do, and recently Stanley Harrold and John McKivigan have suggested that the timing was no accident.[35]

Not surprisingly, Turner's nervous companions inevitably inquired as to how many soldiers they could count on. Turner "assured them of [his plan's] practicability—saying that their numbers would increase as they went along." Like Denmark Vesey before him, Turner did not require hundreds of soldiers prior to the night of 4 July; indeed, it was foolhardy to spread the word too widely. Perhaps thinking of Gabriel, whose legend was well-known in the southern counties of the state, Turner warned that Virginia bondmen "had frequently attempted, similar things, [and] confided their purpose to several, and that it always leaked out." As they marched from plantation to farm, he insisted, they would find men enough.[36]

Nor was there anything absurd about Turner's stated expectation that his army could obtain weapons as they marched. In 1802 Virginia slaves in Nottoway County anticipated Turner's strategy, for they "expect[ed] to be furnished with Arms and Ammunition" as they advanced on Petersburg. In imitation of the 1739 Stono revolt, one of the rebels, Sancho—a veteran of Gabriel's conspiracy—also hoped to plunder two general stores for "weapons to fight with." Admittedly, Nat's army lacked easy access to the sort of cane hatchets that slaves in Saint Domingue or Guyana wielded on a daily basis, but given the tendency for most white Southerners to keep rifles in their homes, Turner was right in assuming that weapons would fall into rebel hands as their original owners perished in the revolt. By the afternoon of Monday, 22 August, Turner's forces numbered "50 or 60 [men], all mounted and armed with guns, axes, swords and clubs." The village of Jerusalem promised even more. "I had a great desire to get there," Turner confided to Gray, "to procure arms and ammunition."[37]

The fact that Turner's soldiers employed those weapons in the murder of women and children horrified antebellum journalists as it does modern audiences. But vicious slave societies rarely give birth to passive martyrs who behave as did the fictional Uncle Tom. In understanding that black liberty necessitated the death of slaveholding whites, Turner stood in a long line of antislavery activists that stretched from Toussaint L'Ouverture to Abraham Lincoln. In the months prior to Turner's birth, Gabriel told one young recruiter that "none were to be spared of the Whites except Quakers, Methodists, and the French people." Two years later, Isaac Turner instructed his North Carolina followers "to kill all the White People [and] to Burn Houses & blow them up." During the first moments of Haiti's Night of Fire, one terrified witness saw dead planters spiked to the ground with wooden stakes. Perhaps the most ruthless in his determination to buy black freedom at any cost was the aged Denmark Vesey, who as a child had briefly chopped sugarcane in Saint Domingue's killing fields. More than a few slaves heard the old carpenter remark that all of the master class, young and old, had to perish: "[I]f you kill the *Lice*, you must kill the *Nits*."[38]

Magnanimity was rarely to be found in such a world, yet it is curious that those who point to Turner's murder of Margaret Whitehead as evidence of mental instability have so little to say about subsequent white brutality. Vengeful whites not only retained Turner's skull until well after the Civil War, they sliced up his black followers with a cruelty rarely found outside of London's Whitechapel district. Henry's "head is expected momentarily," gloated one mounted volunteer from Norfolk. "The skull of Nelson [was also] taken by us." The intersection of Barrow and Jerusalem-Cross Keys Roads for years afterward was called the Black Head Sign Post, a grim reminder of a disembodied head impaled there in the revolt's aftermath.[39]

Evidence indicates that Turner did not expect the most brutal parts of his war to continue indefinitely. "[I]ndiscriminate massacre was not their [Turner and his followers] intention," he assured his inquisitors, but was merely the method by which he hoped to spread "terror and alarm." As frightened whites abandoned Southampton to the rebels, and as blacks from adjoining counties flocked toward his Jerusalem stronghold, "[w]omen and children would afterwards have been spared, and men too who ceased to resist." Like Gabriel before him, Turner did not desire a war of extermination; he planned only to kill enough to force terrified whites to grudgingly accept black liberty.[40]

Conventional wisdom aside, perhaps the best evidence that Turner *did* engage in precise planning and forethought was his decision to bypass Giles Reese's farm in favor of the home of Joseph Travis. Cabin Pond, where Turner and his lieutenants dined on stolen pig and made their final plans, was on Reese land. Yet the rebels gave the house wide berth. Wood suspects that Turner wished to avoid the powerfully built Reese and his two large bulldogs, and that may well have been the case; the insurgents needed to attack in silence for as long as possible. But according to pamphleteer Samuel Warner, Turner's "wife was a slave, belonging to Mr. Reese." Turner either feared that an attack on the Reese household would endanger Cherry and their children or that their survival would cast suspicion on them. (As it was, white authorities later obtained "some papers given up by his wife, under the lash.") But whatever his motivation, Turner made the calculated decision to march south toward the Travis family rather than west toward the Reese estate.[41]

More to the point, the fact remains that the supposedly irrational Turner accomplished what other black revolutionaries failed to achieve. He not only transformed angry talk into an actual revolt, he came extremely close to attaining his initial objectives. Abolitionist-turned-soldier Thomas Wentworth Higginson, whose involvement with the Massachusetts Kansas Aid Committee and a black regiment during the Civil War gave him an appreciation for tactics both guerrilla and regular, believed that Turner's goals were quite nearly attained. "[E]verything was as he predicted: the slaves had come readily at his call, [and] the masters had proved perfectly defenceless." Had the insurgents not committed the fatal error of lingering at the Parker plantation, which gave local militiamen the opportunity to launch a counterassault, Turner might have captured "the arms and ammunition at Jerusalem," Higginson believed, "and with these to aid, and the Dismal Swamp for a refuge, he might have sustained himself indefinitely against his pursuers."[42]

Despite this near success, the pervasive myth of an imprudent, even aberrant, Nat Turner lives on, advanced by well-intentioned novelists and academics who habitually train the next generation of young scholars *not* to think in broad, comparative terms. To suggest, as this essay has, that Turner was more like rebel leaders across the Americas than not, of course, hardly implies that there were *no* differences among these individuals; Nat Turner differed from Gabriel just as much as evangelical reformer Charles Grandison Finney differed from secular revolutionary Thomas Jefferson. But placed in the proper hemispheric context, these dissimilarities appear of little consequence. Those character traits that writers have used to illustrate his singular irrationality—his apparent lack of a precise goal, his refusal to recruit widely in advance of the rising, and most of all, his profound religiosity—can be found in slave conspiracies from the Carolinas to Cuba, and from Barbados to Brazil. If Turner was indeed an unsound, messianic crusader, he found ample company in his madness among hundreds of potential liberators throughout the western hemisphere.

Nat Turner and Sectional Crisis

LOUIS P. MASUR

T he heavens darkened and Nat Turner prepared to strike. "And on the appearance of the sign, (the eclipse of the sun last February) I should arise and prepare myself, and slay my enemies with their own weapons," he proclaimed. The sign that signaled the beginning of the rebellion was no figment of his imagination. "THE GREAT ECLIPSE OF 1831," alerted *Ash's Pocket Almanac*, "will be one of the most remarkable that will again be witnessed in the United States for a long course of years."[1]

On that day, 12 February 1831, Americans from New England through the South looked to the heavens. One diarist saw "men, women and children . . . in all directions, with a piece of smoked glass, and eyes turn'd upward." The *Boston Evening Gazette* reported that "this part of the world has been all anxiety . . . to witness the solar eclipse. . . . Business was suspended and thousands of persons were looking at the phenomena with intense curiosity." The *Richmond Enquirer* noted, "Every person in the city was star gazing, from bleary-eyed old age to the most bright-eyed infancy."[2]

In his *Confessions*, Turner explained that, following the eclipse, he initiated plans to strike on 4 July, but he fell ill and postponed the revolt until, in August, "the sign appeared again, which determined me not to wait longer." That reappearing sign was every bit as real as the first one. Down the east coast, noted an observer in Philadelphia, the "western heavens seemed as one vast sea of crimson flame, lit up by some invisible agent. Thousands of our citizens gazed at the spectacle—some with wonder, oth-

This essay is adapted from Louis P. Masur, *1831: Year of Eclipse* (New York: Hill & Wang, 2001).

ers with admiration, and others fearful that it was a sad augury of coming evil."[3]

Turner's insurrection marked a seismic shift in sectional tensions between South and North. The work of liberation and retribution begun by Turner in Virginia opened a national debate that fueled regional rivalries and triggered a wide-ranging discussion over what to do about slavery in Virginia. In assessing the multiple causes of the rebellion, southern writers placed northern interference high on their list. Even in praising Northerners for their sympathy, southern editors displayed acute sensitivity to sectional tensions. One writer expressed relief that, in most northern newspapers, "we have seen no taunts, no cant, no complacent dwelling upon the superior advantages of the non-slave holding states. . . . We have no doubt, that should it ever be necessary, the citizens of the Northern states would promptly fly to the assistance of their Southern brethren." The *Alexandria Gazette* quoted New York papers that expressed support and offered "arms, money, men . . . for the defense of our Southern brethren." The *New York Telegraph* opined, "The spirit of the times rebukes discord, disorder, and disunion."[4]

The problem, thought most Southerners and Northerners, was a small but influential group of reformist demagogues and religious fanatics who nurtured disaffection and fomented servile insurrection. "Ranting cant about equality," a Southerner argued, heated the imagination of the enslaved and could create the only force that might lead to a general insurrection across the South—"the march of intellect." One writer cautioned "all missionaries, who are bettering the condition of the world, and all philanthropists, who have our interest so much at stake, not to plague themselves about our slaves but leave them exclusively to our management." Particularly obnoxious, and dangerous, from the Southern perspective, was the circulation of northern abolitionist newspapers that "have tended, in some degree, to promote that rebellious spirit which of late has manifested itself in different parts" of the South. Refusing to believe slaves capable of plotting an insurrection on their own, and disavowing any precedents or provocations for rebellion among the enslaved, Southerners blamed the timing and ferocity of Turner's revolt not on the darkening of the heavens, but on the actions of outside agitators. And of all the missionaries, philanthropists, politicians, and abolitionists who challenged slavery, one alone seemed culpable for the events at Southampton: William Lloyd Garrison and his newspaper the *Liberator*.[5]

Addressing the public in the first issue of the *Liberator* on 1 January 1831, Garrison explained his position on slavery. Invoking the principles of the Declaration of Independence, Garrison demanded the immediate, unconditional abolition of slavery and vowed to use extreme measures to effect a "revolution in public sentiment." He proclaimed that he would abjure politics and refuse to ally himself with any denomination. Instead, he desired a brotherhood of reformers willing to raise their voices to defend "the great cause of human rights." He warned that he would not compromise nor would he rein in his words: "I *will be* as harsh as truth, and as uncompromising as justice. On this subject, I do not wish to think, or speak, or write with moderation. No! No! Tell a man whose house is on fire, to give a moderate alarm; tell him to moderately rescue his wife from the hands of a ravisher; tell the mother to gradually extricate her babe from the fire into which it has fallen;—but urge me not to use moderation in a cause like the present. I am in earnest—I will not equivocate—I will not excuse—I will not retreat a single inch—AND I WILL BE HEARD."[6]

Garrison not only agitated for the immediate abolition of slavery in the South, he also struggled for the equal rights of free blacks in the North. At a convention of free people of color in Philadelphia, he confessed, "I never rise to address a colored audience without being ashamed of my own color." With Independence Day celebrations a few weeks away, Garrison admitted that "if any colored man can feel happy on the Fourth of July, it is more than I can do. . . . I cannot be happy when I look at the burdens under which the free people of color labor." "*You are not free,*" he lamented, "you are not sufficiently protected in your persons and rights." Garrison saw hope in the Constitution of the United States that "knows nothing of white or black men; it makes no invidious distinctions with regard to color or condition of free inhabitants; it is broad enough to cover your persons; it has power enough to vindicate your rights. Thanks be to God that we have such a Constitution." But just as Garrison came to see through gradual schemes of emancipation, so too did he lose faith in the Constitution when he recognized that through such provisions as the three-fifths and fugitive slave clauses it defended slavery. Setting the document on fire, the flames lapping at his fingertips, he condemned the Constitution as a proslavery compact, "a covenant with death, an agreement with hell."[7]

Among the many subjects broached in the pages of the *Liberator* in its first months of publication, slave insurrections received special attention. The focus of discussion was a brief work first published by David Walker in the fall of 1829 and then in its third printing: *Appeal to the Colored Citizens of the World.* Born free in North Carolina, Walker traveled throughout the South and North lecturing against slavery before settling in Boston in the 1820s. The *Appeal* began by declaring that "we (colored people of these United States) are the most degraded, wretched, and abject set of beings that ever lived since the world began." Rejecting all gradual, ameliorative approaches to slavery, he appealed directly to his race: "Brethren, arise, arise! Strike for your lives and liberties. Now is the day and the hour." Walker implored all people of color to challenge Thomas Jefferson's racial judgment as expressed in *Notes on the State of Virginia,* urging them to show that they were men, not brutes, and to demonstrate that "man, in all ages and all nations of the earth, is the same." The way to accomplish this, he argued, was for them to escape the state of ignorance in which they were kept, to overturn the tenets of slaveholding religion for a gospel of equality, and to adhere to the words of the Declaration of Independence, even if white Americans would not. Sounding both millennial and revolutionary chords, Walker alerted Americans that "your DESTRUCTION is at hand."[8]

Southerners sought immediately to suppress the publication and circulation of the *Appeal*, which nonetheless made its way to southern ports, carried by black sailors and ships' stewards who had been approached by antislavery agents in Boston harbor. One bemused writer in North Carolina found it odd that "when an old negro from Boston writes a book and sends it amongst us, the whole country is thrown into commotion." State legislatures met in closed sessions and passed laws against seditious writings and slave literacy. Across the South, prohibitions on slaves' reading, writing, and preaching were augmented. The mayor of Savannah asked the mayor of Boston to arrest Walker, and newspapers reported prices as high as ten thousand dollars on the author's head. Walker perished in 1830 under mysterious circumstances. One writer, "a colored Bostonian," had no doubt that Walker was murdered, a casualty of "Prejudice—Pride—Avarice—Bigotry," a "victim to the vengeance of the public."[9]

In the second issue of the *Liberator*, Garrison condemned Walker's call for violence. Garrison believed in the Christian doctrine of nonresistance, that evil should not be resisted by force; moral, not violent, means would transform public opinion and bring an end to slavery. "We deprecate the spirit and tendency of this *Appeal*," he wrote. "We do not preach rebellion—no but submission and peace." And yet, while proclaiming that "the possibility of a bloody insurrection in the South fills us with dismay," he averred that "if any people were ever justified in throwing off the yoke of their tyrants, the slaves are that people." Garrison also observed that "our enemies may accuse us of striving to stir up the slaves to revenge," but their false accusations are intended only "to destroy our influence."[10]

In the spring of 1831, Garrison published an extensive three-part review of the *Appeal* by an unidentified correspondent. The writer acknowledged that Walker was an extremist but denied reports that the pamphlet was "the incoherent rhapsody of a blood-thirsty, but vulgar and ignorant fanatic." Quoting at length from the text and approving Walker's analysis, the correspondent proclaimed that insurrection was inevitable, justifiable, even commendable. He recalled that "a slave owner once said to me, 'Grant your opinions to be just, if you talk so to the slaves they will fall to cutting their master's throats.' 'And in God's name,' I replied, 'why should they not cut their master's throats? . . . If the blacks can come to a sense of their wrongs, and a resolution to redress them, through their own instrumentality or that of others, I shall rejoice.' "[11]

When word of Turner's revolt came, Garrison did not rejoice, but neither did he denounce: "I do not justify the slaves in their rebellion: yet I do not condemn *them*. . . . [O]ur slaves have the best reason to assert their rights by violent measures, inasmuch as they are more oppressed than others." Noting that the "crime of oppression is national," he directed his comments at New Englanders as well as Virginians. Indeed, it astonished him that northern editors opposed to slavery would express support for the South. *Badger's Weekly Messenger* offered the "tenderest sympathy for the distresses" of the slaveholders. And the *New York Journal of Commerce* thought it understandable that "under the circumstances the whites should be wrought up to a high pitch of excitement, and shoot down without mercy, not only the perpetrators, but all who are *suspected* of participation in the diabolical transaction."[12]

Among those "suspected" of inciting the slaves to revolt was Garrison himself. Within several weeks of the insurrection, southern editors were seeking information about the dissemination of abolitionist literature. The *Richmond Enquirer* asked its readers to "inform us whether Garrison's Boston *Liberator* (or Walker's *Appeal*) is circulated in any part of this State." The Vigilance Association of Columbia, South Carolina, offered a $1,500 reward for the arrest and conviction of any white person circulating "publications of a seditious tendency." In Georgia, the Senate passed a resolution offering a reward of $5,000 for Garrison's arrest and conviction. The *National Intelligencer* reprinted a letter claiming that the *Liberator* is published "by a white man with the avowed purpose of inciting rebellion in the South" and is carried by "secret agents" who, if caught, should be barbecued. Northern editors also evinced hostility and pledged "to suppress the misguided efforts of . . . short-sighted and fanatical persons." Garrison began receiving "anonymous letters, filled with abominable and bloody sentiments," some of which he published in the *Liberator*. One slaveholder, writing from the nation's capital, warned Garrison "to desist your infamous endeavors to instill into the minds of the negroes the idea that 'men must be free.' " The prospect of martyrdom only deepened the activist's resolve: "[I]f the sacrifice of my life be required in this great cause, I shall be willing to make it."[13]

As to the charge of inciting the slaves to murder, Garrison proclaimed that the *Liberator* "courts the light, and not darkness." He reminded readers that he was a pacifist whose creed held that violence of any kind for whatever reason was contrary to Christian precepts. With typical sarcasm, he retorted that if Southerners wanted to prohibit incendiary publications, they should ban their own statute books and issue a warrant for Thomas Gray whose pamphlet on Nat Turner "will only serve to rouse up other leaders and cause other insurrections." The blow for freedom, he explained, originated in experiences, not words on the page: "The slaves need no incentives at our hands. They will find them in their stripes—in their emaciated bodies—in their ceaseless toil—in their ignorant minds— in every field, in every valley, on every hill-top and mountain, wherever you and your fathers have fought for liberty." Garrison likened Turner to other revolutionary leaders: "[A]lthough he deserves a portion of the applause which has been so prodigally heaped upon Washington, Bolivar, and other *heroes,* for the same rebellious though more successful conduct, yet he will be torn to pieces and his memory cursed."[14]

Garrison was not alone in viewing Turner's revolt as part of a transatlantic revolutionary movement. "The whole firmament," he believed, "is tremulous with an excess of light." In 1830 and 1831, across the Western world, blows for freedom were being struck. The Belgians obtained independence. In France, the King fled. The British Parliament debated the Reform Bill. In Poland, the Diet declared independence. David Child, the editor of the *Massachusetts Journal,* proclaimed that "the oppressed and enslaved of every country, Hayti and Virginia as well as France and Poland, have a right to assert their 'natural and unalienable rights' whenever and wherever they can." A New York editor declared, "These are the days of revolutions, insurrections, and rebellions, throughout the world." And yet "do we hear any portion of the American press rejoice at the success of the efforts of the *enslaved* AMERICAN to obtain *their* liberty—mourn over *their* defeats—or shed a solitary tear of sympathy and pity for *their* misery, unhappiness, and misfortune?" The writer denounced the hypocrisy of those who "rejoice at the success of liberty, equality, justice, and freedom, or mourn and sympathize at its defeat abroad" yet say nothing of its course at "home." By their actions, "some of the enslaved population of free America . . . have declared their independence." Had the writer known that Turner originally planned to strike on the Fourth of July, he would have had even more evidence for his analysis.[15]

The *Free Inquirer,* published in New York by Robert Dale Owen, the son of the famous utopian planner Robert Owen, also viewed the insurrection as part of the spirit of the times and warned slaveholders not to resist it. Southerners may "suppress partial insurrections; by shooting and hanging, they may for a time intimidate and check that reforming and revolutionizing spirit which has always been extolled when successful; but a knowledge of the world's history, and man's nature should teach them that there is a point beyond which oppression cannot be endured, and they ought to anticipate the horrors of the oppressor when that day shall come."[16]

Southerners could not tolerate such talk by Northerners. "Has it come at last to this," lamented Thomas Dew of the College of William and Mary, "that the hellish plots and massacres of Dessalines, Gabriel, and Nat Turner, are to be compared to the noble deeds and devoted patriotism of Lafayette, Kosciusko, and Schrynecki?" Dew and others placed the blame for the Southampton tragedy on the mischievous effects of Garrison's *Liberator* and Walker's *Appeal,* not on a transatlantic revolutionary ideology of rights and liberties. Southerners sought a simple explanation for a tragedy that they could not comprehend in any other way because to do so would challenge the basis of southern society. If slavery was wrong, if slaves were human, and if liberty belonged to all and at some level every enslaved person knew it, then widespread rebellion and death would mark the future of the slaveholding states.[17]

The publication of incendiary writings raised another issue as well: the relationship of the North and the South under the federal government. Garrison often noted that "the bond of our Union is becoming more and more brittle" and thought "a separation between the free and slave States" to be "unavoidable" unless slavery was speedily abolished. Governor John Floyd of Virginia reached similar conclusions for different reasons. In his diary on 27 September, 1831, he wondered how it was possible that no law could punish the editor of the *Liberator* and other "Northern conspirators" who displayed "the express intention of inciting the slaves and free negroes in this and the other States to rebellion and to murder the men, women and children of those states." He concluded, "A man in our States may plot treason in one state against another without fear of punishment, whilst the suffering state has no right to resist by the provisions of the Federal Constitution. If this is not checked it must lead to the separation of these states."[18]

In the immediate aftermath of the rebellion, sectional tensions ran not only North/South through the nation, but east/west across the state of Virginia. As a result of Turner's rebellion, the unsettling question of how, if at all, to end slavery filled everyday discussion. In political circles, private talk of the need to do something dated from the moment Turner struck. Jane Randolph, the wife of Jefferson's grandson, Thomas Jefferson Randolph, spoke for many of the women of the gentry class when she exclaimed that the horrors at Southampton "aroused all my fears which had nearly become dormant, and indeed have increased them to the most agonizing degree." She even asked her husband to consider moving west to Ohio.[19]

Governor Floyd was also contemplating Virginia's future. On 19 November 1831, he wrote to the governor of South Carolina and explained his belief that "the spirit of insubordination . . . had its origin . . . from the Yankee population." He confided that he planned in his annual message to the legislature to recommend laws "to confine the Slaves to the estates of their masters—prohibit negroes from preaching—absolutely to drive from the State all free negroes—and to substitute the surplus revenue in our Treasury annually for slaves, to work for a time upon our Rail Roads etc etc and these sent out of the country, preparatory, or rather as the first step toward emancipation." Two days later, in his diary, the slaveholder confessed: "[B]efore I leave this government, I will have contrived to have a law passed gradually abolishing slavery in this State." And on the day after Christmas: "I will not rest until slavery is abolished in Virginia."[20]

Meanwhile other legislators thought it improper to discuss the issue at all. They believed it fell beyond the scope of the select committee created in response to the governor's annual message that called for an examination of "the subject of slaves, free negroes and the melancholy occurrences growing out of the tragical massacre in Southampton." William Osborne Goode moved that a Quaker antislavery petition calling for legislative action on emancipation should not be referred to the committee. Agreeing with another member that the only appropriate question was "how we should get rid of our free black population," he warned that "agitation" on the question of abolition was "worse than useless."

The chair of the select committee, William Henry Brodnax, who led the militia during the insurrection, disagreed. The committee's mandate, he thought, was wide in scope, and a respect for the opinions of constituents necessitated their being heard. Shocked that the august body feared a petition, Brodnax wondered if the legislature wanted the world to believe that Virginia "was not even willing to think of an ultimate delivery from the greatest curse that God in his wrath ever inflicted upon a people." In asking that the petition be admitted, Brodnax confessed that he did not think the legislature "would take any direct steps toward the emancipation of the slaves." Another legislator agreed that the appearance of open discussion was necessary to put the public mind at rest. As for slavery, it was an evil, but one "so interwoven with our habits and interests . . . it was too late to correct it."[21]

By a vote of 93–27, the House accepted the Quaker petition, which had been introduced by William Henry Roane, Patrick Henry's grandson, and for several weeks the select committee sifted through additional petitions, memorials, and resolutions. William Goode could not tolerate it any longer, and on 11 January 1832, he moved that the committee be discharged and that the body rule that "it is not expedient to legislate on the subject" of emancipation. He argued that "a misguided and pernicious course of legislation" had to be arrested because the legislature was treading dangerously close to considering whether "they would confiscate the property of the citizens" of Virginia. Talk of emancipation, moreover, only increased the likelihood of future rebellions: "[T]he slaves themselves were not unconscious of what was going forward here. . . . They are an active and intelligent class, watching and weighing every movement of the Legislature. . . . By considering the subject [of emancipation], their expectations were raised; expectations that were doomed to disappointment, the effect of which might be the destruction of the country." Why, Goode wondered, continue the charade of consideration?

Goode miscalculated. In response to his motion, other legislators expressed their views on the abolition of slavery. Thomas Jefferson Randolph presented a substitute motion that provided a specific plan of gradual emancipation. No slave currently in bondage would be freed, but "the children of all female slaves, who may be born in this state, on or after the 4th day of July, 1840 shall become the property of the Commonwealth" and either would be sold further south at adulthood or would work off the costs of their transportation to Africa. Such was the "plan"

that generated passionate discussion and induced the governor to describe the legislature as divided into slave and abolition parties. The slave
party delegates hailed from the Tidewater and Piedmont districts in the
east and collectively owned over 1,000 slaves. The abolition party, including Governor Floyd, drew its strength from the Valley and trans-Allegheny
in the west; its supporters owned fewer than 100 slaves. Sectional tensions
in Virginia mimicked the split over reapportionment just two years earlier,
when the western regions had lost in their attempt to have representation
based solely on the white population and, as a result, the slaveholders of
eastern Virginia received an additional seven seats.

But the ideological differences between the slave and abolition parties were not nearly as severe as the names might signify. Merely being
willing to consider some form of future gradual emancipation made one
a member of Floyd's abolition party; it did not make one an abolitionist
by any definition of the word that a northern activist might recognize.
When the *Richmond Enquirer* proclaimed that "the seals are broken,
which have been put for fifty years upon the most delicate and difficult
subject," the editors were not commenting on Goode's or Randolph's
motions, but on the astonishing and disturbing opinions being voiced,
opinions that had always been whispered in private but almost never
shouted in public. Almost no one in 1831–32 believed that the legislature would actually enact a plan that might lead one day to the disappearance of slavery from Virginia. Plans did not pose the danger;
speech did. Every Virginian knew that David Walker and William Lloyd
Garrison and Nat Turner breathed fire, and every resident of Southampton knew someone enveloped by the flames. But now a white Virginian rose in the house of delegates and declared through open doors
that "slavery as it exists among us may be regarded as the heaviest calamity which has ever befallen any portion of the human race.... The
time will come, at no distant day, when we shall be involved in all the
horrors of a servile war which will not end until ... the slaves or the
whites are totally exterminated." A Virginian rose and declared that,
based on the principle that all men are by nature free and equal, "it is
an act of injustice, tyranny, and oppression to hold any part of the human race in bondage against their consent."[22]

The comments shocked James Gholson, who owned 20 slaves. He spoke
for the slave party of the Tidewater and the Piedmont. Deprecating a
discussion that "from its very nature should never be openly" conducted,
he denounced Randolph's proposal as "monstrous and unconstitutional."
Slaves, he reminded his colleagues, were property and the source of
wealth. "Private property is sacred" and could not be appropriated by the
state for public use without just compensation. Only under extreme necessity might the legislature consider such an action, and such conditions
did not currently apply. Gholson offered his own history of Turner's revolt: "[A]n ignorant, religious fanatic, conceived the idea of insurrection.

He succeeded in involving four or five others, of his *immediate neighborhood,* in his designs: they commence the massacre—they traverse a region of country containing hundreds of slaves; but neither threats, promises, nor intoxication, could secure more than 40 to 50 adherents—they remain embodied something more than 24 hours—they disperse without being forced—are taken without resistance—and are at last hung on evidence of persons of their own class and color." With safety and order quickly restored, Gholson contended that "the people of our country again sleep quietly on their pillows, and would, in all probability, have enjoyed uninterrupted repose, had it not been for this false legislative cry of 'Wolf!' 'Wolf!' "

The slaves of Virginia, Gholson asserted, "are as happy a laboring class as exists upon the habitable globe . . . contented, peaceful, and harmless." But if the legislature adopted Randolph's plan, the slaves would become dangerous. A law that only freed a future generation would create untold resentments: "[I]t argues but little knowledge of human nature to suppose that we reconcile one generation to servitude and bondage by telling it that [the one] to follow shall be free." Such a scheme not only failed to meet the demands of the putative emergency created by Turner, it threatened to offer the lesson that "if *one insurrection* has been sufficient to secure the liberty of *succeeding* generations, might it not be inferred that *another* would achieve the freedom of the present?"

Gholson did not wish to argue "the abstract question of slavery, or its morality or immorality." He chided the legislators from the west, "Will you believe," that the "great men of the revolution *owned slaves?* Yes, actually owned slaves, and worked them too—even died in possession of them, and bequeathed them to their children." There were no "lights of the age" dating from the Revolution, no beacons of freedom for all. "I have heard of these lights before," Gholson averred, "but I have looked for them in vain." Turner thought "*he* saw them . . . and now, all his lights and all his inspirations are shrouded in the darkness of the grave." Northern lights had indeed appeared in the form of incendiary publications, but "these are not lights of the age, or lights from heaven" but "a darkness visible." Rather than spreading illumination, this "unjust, partial, tyrannical, and monstrous measure," meant to commence on the Fourth of July, a day made sacred by Randolph's grandfather, would forever extinguish the "lights of liberty and justice."[23]

John Thompson Brown, from Petersburg, also denounced any scheme of abolition. He warned that for the government to generate sufficient surplus revenue to purchase and remove the black population, it would have to impose "high duties on imports." "It is a well known fact," he added in the midst of South Carolina's threat to nullify the tariff, that "the burden would rest chiefly on the Southern states. It would be nothing more or less than drawing from the pockets of the slaveholders, by indirect taxation, the money with which their slaves were eventually to be purchased." "It would be better economy to abandon them at once," he snorted, "without compensation, than to go through the troublesome and expensive ceremony of furnishing the means to have them bought."

An even greater danger lurked beneath the reliance on government surplus revenue. By allowing the federal government a direct role in the disposition of slavery, southern states would yield their autonomy. "When the general government shall have obtained the control of this subject," predicted Brown, "and the slave holding states lie defenceless at her feet, you will hear no more of the purchase and removal of slaves. You will be told that they are persons and not things. . . . The bill of rights will be quoted to prove that they are men and entitled to their freedom. They will be removed and slavery extinguished, but it will be without compensation, and at your expense." Brown dismissed those who averred that because of slavery "the body politic is languishing under disease." Slavery, he concluded, "is our lot, our destiny—and whether, in truth, it be right or wrong—whether it be a blessing or a curse, the moment has never yet been, when it was possible to free ourselves from it."[24]

William Brodnax, who owned 26 slaves and chaired the special committee, spoke next. He regretted that matters had come to this because he believed that the committee's final report would have recommended against any action on the subject. Brodnax, a representative from Dinwiddie County in the eastern Piedmont district, disagreed with Gholson over whether the subject should be discussed: "[T]he people all over the world are thinking about it, speaking about it, and writing about it. And can *we* arrest it, and place a seal on the subject? We might as well attempt to put out the light of the sun." He also disagreed with Gholson and Brown on the perniciousness of slavery: "That slavery in Virginia is an evil, and a transcendent evil, it would be idle, and more than idle, for any human being to doubt or deny." Calling slavery an "incubus" that sapped the energies of the state and retarded its advancement, he argued that, "*something* should be done to alleviate it or exterminate it . . . *if any thing can be done*, by means less injurious or dangerous than the evil itself." Brodnax, an ardent colonizationist, was willing to support emancipation, not under the terms of Randolph's proposal, but provided that the state expelled all the slaves and that the slaveholders did not suffer financially.

In reality, there was not much difference between Gholson, a slaveholder who defended the institution, and Brodnax, one who questioned it. It was easy to call slavery an evil and then refuse to pay a price to eliminate that evil. Brodnax suggested that legislators forget about the enslaved until they first demonstrated that they could do something about the free black population. Before the state could deal with over 450,000 slaves, it must first show that it could remove nearly 50,000 free blacks. Brodnax argued that free blacks had an injurious influence on the slave population and played an indirect role in "fomenting conspiracies and insurrections." He recommended targeting 6,000 per year for colonization in Liberia. Acquiring Texas and making it an independent black state ("a sable nation") had been discussed, but such a plan would prove unpalatable to the bordering slaveholding states to the east. Rather, Brodnax thought it imperative to restore "these people to the region in which nature had planted them, and to whose climates she had fitted their constitution." The colonization of all the free blacks would be accomplished in less than a decade, paid for by state taxation and by monies rightfully received from the federal government "without the slightest violation of those strict State Right principles which distinguish our Virginia political school."[25]

Thomas Jefferson Randolph knew all about that school. In 1798 his grandfather authored the resolutions adopted by the Kentucky legislature in protest against the Alien and Sedition Acts. Those resolutions declared that "the several States composing the United States of America are not united on the principle of unlimited submission to their General Government." Randolph was close to his grandfather. He lived nearby, managed Monticello for the last ten years of Jefferson's life, and served as executor of his estate. It was Randolph who sold Jefferson's slaves in order to pay off debts of $40,000.

Thomas Jefferson never figured out what to do about slavery. In 1787 he proposed a plan of gradual emancipation in which the children of slaves would be raised and educated at public expense until a certain age and then declared "a free and independent people." Throughout his life, he thought it a sound and practicable solution. Any abolition scheme, he believed, had to be accompanied by colonization. To the question "why not retain and incorporate the blacks into the state?" he answered that "deep rooted prejudices entertained by the whites; ten thousand recollections, by the blacks, of the injuries they have sustained; new provocations; the real differences which nature has made; and many other circumstances, will divide us into parties, and produce convulsions which will probably never end but in the extermination of the one or the other race."[26]

In retirement, Jefferson watched, and at times worried, as slavery became an increasingly divisive national issue. But it was left to his relations to take any action. In 1820 his son-in-law, Governor Thomas Mann Randolph, suggested using tax monies to remove slaves to Saint Domingue. The legislature did not pursue the recommendation. And in 1831, 39-year-old Thomas Jefferson Randolph was elected for the first time to the House of Delegates. Without question, Randolph burned with beliefs and ambitions fueled by bloodlines as well as book lines. He felt the need to demonstrate his worthiness by proving himself in the public arena. As the House began to discuss the various petitions submitted in the aftermath of Turner's insurrection, Randolph received a message from Edward Coles, who had left Virginia in 1819, freed his slaves, and gone on to become governor of Illinois.

Coles informed Randolph that "now is the time to bring forward & press on the consideration of the people & their representatives, not only the propriety but absolute necessity of commencing a course of measures for the riddance of . . . the colored population of Va." Appealing to the grandson's place in history, Coles told Randolph that he had "inherited the feelings & principles" of his "illustrious Grand Father" and that "no one of the young generation could be more suitable to lead or could bring more moral and political weight of character to aid the good work than his grandson."

Coles suggested a plan that would commence in 1840 and free children at the age of 21. If they then had to work for two years to pay costs of transportation to Africa, "it would bring the year 1863 before the first Negro under this act would be sent out of the country." Coles lived through the Civil War, and if he stayed true to his conscience, on 1 January 1863, the day the Emancipation Proclamation took effect, he squirmed remembering what he had proposed three decades earlier.[27]

On that frigid January day when Thomas Jefferson Randolph rose in the Virginia House of Delegates to move for a plan of gradual emancipation, he did so because Turner's insurrection horrified his wife, because he was a Jefferson and a Randolph, and because a letter had arrived that he, unlike his grandfather, took to heart. But as he rose to speak, his words evaporated. The thoughts that flowed so easily when conceived in his closet vanished "as mist before the sun" when presented in public. His lineage summoned the oracle of Virginia's past, dead not even five years. The "weight" of his grandfather's name, Randolph complained, "was thrown into the scale to press me down farther." Randolph did not want to debate whether Thomas Jefferson would have supported this specific proposal, but he quoted from Jefferson's letter to Coles to show that throughout his life the sage of Monticello thought it "expedient" to do something about slavery.

Expedient. That was the word over which so many words issued forth in the Virginia debate over slavery. Randolph proclaimed that he never intended for his resolution to be debated so vociferously. It was not a bill, only a resolution of inquiry designed to probe the possibility of some future plan. Brodnax's committee reported that it "is inexpedient for the present legislature to make any legislative enactment for the abolition of slavery." A trans-Allegheny representative, William Preston, moved to strike the word "inexpedient" and substitute "expedient." Randolph was one of only six Piedmont representatives to vote for it; the motion lost 73–58. Ultimately, "inexpedience" won. A preamble to the report of the special committee, moved by Archibald Bryce, a slaveowner from Piedmont, offered that "further action for the removal of the slaves should await a more definite development of public opinion." No one knew what that meant. Bryce said he only wanted to submit the question to the people. Preston said he would vote for it if it were intended as a declaration that the House would one day act. One representative observed that if he voted for the preamble and afterward was asked what he had voted for, he would be unable to answer.[28]

Bryce's preamble to the special committee report passed by a vote of 67–60, and the Virginia debate came to an end. Unable to act against slavery, the legislature acted against what it believed to be the sources of insurrectionary spirit. Within weeks, a colonization bill to provide for the removal of free blacks moved swiftly through the legislature. A "police bill" further eroded the rights of free blacks, denying them trial by jury and allowing for their sale and transportation if convicted of a crime. The legislature also revised the black codes, barring slaves and free blacks from preaching or attending religious meetings unaccompanied by whites. In the aftermath of Nat Turner, Virginians sought to reassure themselves that in the future "successful insurrection would be impossible."

Thomas Jefferson Randolph was not so certain. Perhaps in the event of a full-scale revolt, if Virginia's resources proved inadequate, the federal government would send troops and "reclaim a country smoking with the blood of its population." Far more likely, he thought, "there is one circumstance to which we are to look as inevitable in the fullness of time; a dissolution of the Union. God grant it may not happen in our time, or that of our children; but . . . it must come, sooner or later; and when it does come, border war follows it, as certain as the night follows the day." Randolph imagined an invasion by Virginia's enemy "in part with black troops, speaking the same language, of the same nation, burning with enthusiasm for the liberation of their race; if they are not crushed the moment they put foot upon your soil, they roll forward, an hourly swelling mass; your energies are paralyzed, your power is gone; the morass of the lowlands, the vastness of the mountains, cannot save your wives and your children from destruction."[29]

With the eclipse of the sun, Nat Turner's prophecy came to pass. In time, Randolph's would as well.

TEN

"What Happened in This Place?"

In Search of the Female Slave in the Nat Turner Slave Insurrection

MARY KEMP DAVIS

As she [Mrs. Barrow] fled[,] a negro girl, named Lucy, seized her with the determination of holding her for the rebels, but "Aunt" Easter came to the aid of her mistress and fled with her to the woods.

Martha Waller was concealed by the nurse under the large apron, but the child would not endure the reckless destruction of furniture, so [she] arose and threatened to tell her father. One of the negroes seized her and dashed her to death against the ground.

William Sidney Drewry, *The Southampton Insurrection*[1]

The trial records compiled by Henry Irving Tragle in *The Southampton Slave Revolt of 1831: A Compilation of Source Material* do not mention a single female slave who rode with Nat Turner and his men as they swept through lower Southampton County, Virginia, 22–23 August 1831. They do hint that the wife of a free black was perhaps a coconspirator since she was seen with the insurgents at one site. This unnamed woman was with her husband, Billy Artist, when he and other insurgents stopped by a slaveholder's home on Tuesday, 23 August. Like other rebels, Artist was probably on horseback, and his wife, whether free or enslaved, may have been riding a horse as well. No further information is given about this shadowy woman, such as what she said or did at the scene—if anything. Artist was jailed for conspiracy and seems to have committed suicide while incarcerated; his wife's fate is unrecorded.[2]

The mystery surrounding Billy Artist's wife is emblematic of the mystery surrounding all of the female slaves who lived in lower Southampton

County, the site of the revolt. Where were they on 22–23 August, 1831? What role did they play in the planning or execution of the insurrection? To date, no one has presented a coherent and comprehensive analysis of the roles of female slaves in the Nat Turner insurrection. True, the surviving evidence is scattered and meager, and some of it belongs to the realm of folklore. However, half of a loaf is better than none, as the old saying goes. This article attempts to fill a gap in Turner scholarship by surveying the images of female slaves found in an array of documentary, historical, and pseudo-historical sources, including Thomas R. Gray's *The Confessions of Nat Turner* (1831) and a biographical essay about Turner published in 1955 by his granddaughter, Lucy Mae Turner. Even though the information in these sources is quite sketchy, individualized portraits of a number of female slaves can be retrieved. Often, these images tell us more about their creators than about the actual women of the rebellion. However, if used carefully, the sources do cast some light on a topic that has so far remained completely obscure.

The official trial record is the best place to begin because it brings so many slave women to center stage. Forty-four slave men and one woman stood trial for conspiracy and insurrection between 31 August 1831, and 27 November 1831. Thus, the participation of female slaves—at least the type of participation that led to an indictment—was almost nonexistent. This situation was true even though, according to the 1830 federal census, 46 percent of the slaves in Southampton County, Virginia, were female. Indeed, a mere year before the Turner revolt, slave women significantly outnumbered white women in the county.[3]

Nonetheless, such a massive presence of female slaves did not result in a mixed army of men and women for Nat Turner. The slave Lucy, who was between 18 and 20 years old, was the lone female to stand trial for conspiracy and insurrection. According to the trial records, her mistress, Mrs. Mary T. (or Mrs. John) Barrow, accused her of seizing and holding her on the day that Nat Turner's men were overrunning her property—presumably so the men could kill her. Another female slave, named Bird, aligned herself against Lucy and with Mrs. Barrow. She testified that an unnamed person, "several weeks after the murder of Mr. [John T.] Barrow[,] [found] four pieces of money in a bag of feathers [,] . . . covered with a handkerchief—that the room was occupied by the prisoner and another (Moses since hung)." The testimony of these two, along with that of a white man and a male slave, was enough to secure a guilty verdict for Lucy. Lucy was hanged, thereby joining the ranks of 20 slave men who met this fate. Her trial and execution are anomalous. According to James Sidbury, "of 236 slaves tried for insurrection in Virginia between 1785 and 1865," only two were female.[4]

Bird, the woman who testified against Lucy, was a member of an insidious and surprisingly numerous sisterhood—female slaves who appeared in the trial records were most often witnesses for the prosecution. An examination of these records reveals that eight female slaves testified in the trials of eight men and one woman: seven testified for the prosecution and one for the defense. All of the accused were found guilty, although only six of these were executed. The sentences of the remaining three slaves were commuted, probably to transportation out of the state. Whereas Bird testified against only one slave, two female slaves testified against more than one slave: Venus against two males (Jack and Andrew) and Beck or Becky against three males (Jim, Isaac, and Frank). Ben, the last slave to stand trial, holds the dubious honor of having been the *only* slave against whom two slave women (Charlotte and Cherry) testified. In contrast, Delsey was the only female slave who testified for the defense, although the defendant (Moses) was found guilty anyway. How she managed to break ranks with the slave women who were prosecution witnesses is an intriguing but unanswerable question.[5]

As a defense witness, Delsey tried to mitigate Moses's guilt for this capital crime even though she somehow managed to offer damaging evidence as well. Delsey testified that the insurgents forced Moses to join them by threatening his life. They also gave him weapons over his objections. Unaccountably, Delsey added that she thought "the prisoner could have escaped while the insurgents were coming up" since he was already on horseback when the insurgents arrived. The failure of Moses to gallop away immediately may have struck the justices as evidence of guilt. On the other side, additional evidence by others assigned Moses an active role in the insurrection. This additional testimony, might have been an important factor in the guilty verdict for Moses.[6]

No internal clues reveal conclusively whether Delsey was a house slave or a field slave. The action she described occurred on the evening of the first day of the revolt and could have taken place either in the slave quarters or the "Big House." Since by her own admission she merely "lived" at Mrs. Vaughn's, Delsey was probably a hired slave, perhaps a domestic one.

The remaining female slave witnesses—Beck (or Becky), Cynthia, Mary, Venus, Charlotte, and Cherry—were almost certainly domestic slaves. Beck (or Becky) stated outright that she was a house slave. In fact, she made a point of saying that she was seldom in the slave quarters or "the outhouses." In her testimony, she seemed to have wanted to create as much distance between herself and the slaves "out there in the outhouses" as she could. Cynthia *may* have been a house slave as well, for she was in the kitchen, perhaps cooking, when a slave named Nelson sauntered into the kitchen and swiped meat from a pot. Mary was probably a nurse, since Mrs. Blunt instructed her "to take her child and make escape with her." Likewise, Venus's domestic status can be inferred from several clues. For one, she said she was at "her master's house," not in the fields, when the insurgents swooped down on the first day of the revolt. They arrived "on Monday around 9:00 A.M.," several hours after field work would have begun. Finally, when they testified against Ben and implicated his brother Nathan, both Charlotte and Cherry said that they had been in the house.[7]

Almost to a person, then, the testimony of these female slaves reveals them to have been more loyal to the state than to their fellow slaves. William Sidney Drewry, a Southampton historian who wrote and published his dissertation on the Turner insurrection, uses evidence like this to support his view that "slavery in Virginia was not such as to arouse rebellion, but was an institution which nourished the strongest affection and piety in slave and owner." His view is worth examining in some detail. Although Drewry believes Nat Turner's followers were merely deluded by a "wild fanatical Baptist preacher," a simpler explanation may account for the behavior of the female slaves who were prosecution witnesses. They were domestic workers, unlike the great majority of slaves in Southampton County who, like Nat Turner, were agricultural or field slaves. The revolt actually occurred in the slave-rich, wealthier half of Southampton County. House slaves, of necessity, had more intimate (and conflicted) relationships with their owners and other whites in the master's household. Their social position made it less likely that they would cast their lot with the field slaves who constituted virtually all of the rebel force.[8]

It is easy to ignore Drewry's work because of his proslavery bias. However, this much can be said for him: he makes visible the acts of female slaves during the Turner insurrection that others have ignored, minimized, or even erased. Relying on oral history—with all the attendant problems—Drewry revisits the horrific scene of mass death at Levi Waller's, where he somehow manages to find an exemplary slave woman amid the carnage. He also discusses three additional women: Mary (Blunt), "Aunt" Edie, and "Aunt" Easter. Drewry is indefatigable in his search for faithful slaves. However, as he reconstructs the stories of "Aunt" Edie and "Aunt" Easter, a repressed, oppositional discourse bursts free and challenges his trademark proslavery rhetoric, thus unintentionally restoring a little balance to his one-dimensional images.

Drewry includes the story of a heroic house slave when he recounts what happened at Levi Waller's—a description that must be supplemented by other sources. Levi Waller was one of the two witnesses against Nat Turner. He was the owner of 18 slaves and a fairly self-sufficient farm, with a blacksmith shop, wheelwright shops, and a distillery. His children attended the boarding school nearby. On the first morning of the revolt (Monday, 22 August), Waller received word that the slaves had risen. Taking care to send a son to alert the schoolmaster and to retrieve his own children from the schoolhouse, he quietly concealed himself in several places as the insurgents overran his farm. In the words of Stephen B. Oates, Waller's wife was "slashed . . . to death" and his two daughters "beheaded." Oates reports, "Inconsolable with grief, [Waller] fled into the woods and swamps." Meanwhile, at the schoolhouse, the insurgents decapitated ten children and mortally wounded another child.[9]

Apparently, Levi Waller was not a man to play hero that Monday morning; that role was left to an unnamed female slave and her white charge. A male slave named Davy had already helped Waller escape to the plum orchard, where he "heard the screams of his family and friends as they were murdered." Meanwhile, a slave nurse tried but failed to save one of Waller's children by concealing her "under her large apron." The nurse could not save the child because the child, distraught, ran out to stop the slaves from wantonly destroying her parents' furniture. This brave but impetuous act cost the child her life.[10]

Another slave whose acts drew Drewry's praise was Mary (Blunt), who testified against Moses (Barrow). Mary was owned by Simon and Mary Blunt, masters who seemed to command the loyalty of their slaves. Blunt was a wealthy planter, possessing some 64 slaves. According to Drewry, he was "a positive but indulgent master." After he heard of the revolt, Blunt supposedly offered his slaves a choice: "remain and defend him and his family or join the insurgents." Armed "with grubbing hoes, pitchforks, and other farm implements, the slaves stationed themselves in the kitchen at the side of the house, while the whites [armed with guns] protected the dwelling." As added protection, Blunt's wife ordered the slave Mary to escape with her child. Mary fled and was joined by other slave women. The rebel Moses pursued them all, but before he could catch them, a battle erupted, ending with the defeat of Turner's men.[11]

It is instructive that at the Blunt house two white men and three boys or young men were armed with guns, while the blacks were not. Did Blunt, deep down, not trust his slaves after all? More important, all of the slaves, both male and female, fought from the kitchen—a separate, domestic space. The kitchen is typically the domain of women; however, in Drewry's account, the dividing line between slave men and women is removed. In the minds of readers of Drewry's book, this gender parity may either degrade the black men or elevate the black women, or it may degrade both groups, since all were fighting against other slaves who were fighting for their freedom.[12]

Gender parity again appears in Drewry's book when he praises Ben and Aaron in his tribute to "Aunt" Edie. Ben, Aaron, and "Aunt" Edie were devoted to their respective masters and mistresses when the slave system was under assault. Edie was the wife of Aaron and the sister of Ben; the two brothers were the "Negro overseers" of Captain Newit Harris. After Ben heard about the trouble in the county, he insisted that his invalid master go into hiding. When his master balked, Ben, Aeneas-like, hoisted him upon his shoulders and bore him to the swamps. "Aunt" Edie performed a similar service for Harris's daughter, Mrs. Robert Musgrave, who had a one-year-old child. Mrs. Musgrave fled to her father's home at the height of the insurrection, then promptly fainted when she saw the disorder there. Quick-thinking "Aunt" Edie revived Mrs. Musgrave and spirited her to the woods. F. Roy Johnson continues this Drewry story about

Edie. He, too, seems to draw on the same folk tradition. Johnson says that when Mrs. Musgrave's baby threatened to reveal their hiding place, Edie "stuffed a handkerchief" into the baby's mouth, then "set out in search for water. It was a dry August, but eventually water was found in a cow's track. She fashioned a cup of oak leaves and returned to quench the child's thirst."[13]

After sharing a wealth of stories about loyal slaves, Drewry sometimes becomes entangled in his own proslavery discourse. This time, in his zeal to memorialize other faithful slaves like "Red" Nelson and Easter, he casts light on Easter's shadow: "wicked Charlotte." All three slaves belonged to Nathaniel and Lavinia Francis. After nearly all of the couple's slaves had joined the insurgents, "Red" Nelson concealed Mrs. Francis in a cuddy to shield her from the rebels. Once the danger had passed, Mrs. Francis "emerged from her cuddy and descended the stairs." She had "heard some of her servants quarreling"; now, she saw them "dividing her wedding dresses." In a convoluted passage that pulls in contrary directions, Drewry sketches what ensued:

> They [the slave women] were very much surprised to see her, and one of them said: "I thought you were dead," and, making for her with a dirk, continued, "If you are not dead you shall soon be." But the other negro, Easter, who had belonged to her before her marriage to Mr. Francis, rushed up and said: "You shall not kill my mistress, who has been so kind to me. Touch her if you dare and I will kill you." Mrs. Francis then asked where the negroes were, and the wicked Charlotte replied that they had gone, but would be back to dinner, as they had killed several chickens for the purpose. Without further delay, except to hang up her keys and to take from the rack a homemade cheese, she went in search of her husband with Nelson, the slave who had saved her.[14]

The images of the slaves are contradictory: two slaves, Easter and "Red" Nelson, are faithful; "wicked Charlotte" and other unnamed—and even unnumbered—slaves are assertive, opportunistic, grasping, and perhaps impertinent. One female slave wields a dirk and says that she thought (or hoped?) that Mrs. Francis was already dead then assured her that she certainly would be dead soon. "[W]icked Charlotte" must have been one of the women fighting over the dresses, although Drewry does not say this explicitly. In any event, Charlotte unaccountably expects the insurgents to return for chicken dinner as if it would be perfectly natural for murderous slaves to pull a chair up to her master's table. In spite of all of these mixed signals, Drewry is enchanted with Easter and "Red" Nelson because they give meritorious service to the slavocracy. Conversely, Stephen B. Oates supplies a somber ending to Charlotte's story. Oates says that when Nathaniel Francis saw Easter and Charlotte among the captured slaves, he "hugged Easter and secured her release." Francis's reaction to

Charlotte was quite different: "Seized by an uncontrollable rage, he dragged her outside, strapped her to an oak tree, and shot her to death."[15]

Another writer, L. Minor Blackford memorializes two slave women and a slave girl who gave selfless service to the master class during Turner's insurrection. Two years before Drewry published his book, Blackford published a biography of his recently deceased grandmother, Mary Berkeley Minor Blackford, an ardent colonizationist whose life spanned most of the nineteenth century (1802–96). Blackford's book was entitled *Mine Eyes Have Seen the Glory* (1898). In chapter two, he copies several entries from his grandmother's journal that relate to the Turner insurrection. Mrs. Blackford wrote that, in the summer of 1832, she talked with several surviving members of the family of Catherine Whitehead, a victim of the insurrection. Whitehead was a wealthy planter-widow of Southampton County. She owned around 40 slaves (according to Henry Irving Tragle) or 27 or 28 slaves (according to Stephen B. Oates). Three of her slaves (Tom, Jack, and Andrew) defected and were convicted of conspiracy and insurrection, although the sentences of Jack and Andrew were commuted. All told, seven members of the Whitehead family were killed: Mrs. Whitehead, four grown daughters, her minister-son Richard, and a grandson. Mrs. Whitehead has achieved a rather dubious fame in our own time as the mother of Margaret Whitehead, the linchpin of William Styron's controversial novel, *The Confessions of Nat Turner* (1967). Surprisingly, in contrast to William Styron, who is obsessed with Margaret Whitehead's murder, Mrs. Blackford neither mentions Margaret Whitehead nor names Nat Turner as her murderer. Harriet Whitehead is a more congenial subject for Blackford's focus because she was saved by a family slave.[16]

L. Minor Blackford's narrative is an especially distanced account, interweaving multiple points of view. Mrs. Blackford says that she talked with Mrs. Whitehead's son and his wife, who did not live with Mrs. Whitehead. Presumably, young Whitehead's unnamed wife told Mrs. Blackford several stories about what transpired at her mother-in-law's home—stories which Mrs. Blackford recorded in her journal and which her grandson partly copied. The grandson quotes Mrs. Blackford as saying, in reference to her daugther-in-law, "I took down *from her words* the following incidents to show that justice had not been done them [the slaves] generally in the recital of the crimes committed by a comparatively small number." She also cites slave informants without giving their names. The slaves' voices are filtered through the voices of "an odd couple": a well-meaning, anti-slavery colonizationist (Mrs. Blackford herself) and a close relative of the victims (Mrs. Whitehead's daughter-in-law).[17]

Despite the carnage at the Whiteheads', Mrs. Blackford celebrates the slaves who tried to protect the whites—three females—but also celebrates slaves like Hubbard, Wallace, and Tom. In a particularly conflicted passage, Mrs. Blackford gives her reasons for recording these stories: "Such instances of faithfulness 'twere pity should be lost. I record them hoping that some day they may appear in better garb for the honour of the poor negro, and to prove how much of goodness and kindness there is in his nature." She says she agrees with a bishop who said that the slaves "are the most amiable people in the earth." Then, she adds, "For though I have recorded fearful wickedness in this insurrection, we must remember how few those have been, and *how ignorant and deluded the Negroes who joined it were.* I only know of one insurrection before that of Nat Turner's, and none since. And I am sure that with an hundredth part of the wrongs they suffer, we white people would have risen in arms 50 times."[18]

Male slaves receive most of the attention in Mrs. Blackford's journal. However, for our purposes, the slave girl Aggy deserves special mention. Mrs. Whitehead's youngest daughter (unnamed) had concealed herself in high corn. Aggy, who was with her, implored her to be quiet, but "losing all presence of mind," the daughter betrayed their whereabouts by her loud screams. Undaunted, Aggy attempted "to shield her mistress at the risk of her own life" after "the murderers rushed upon her." Her mistress "was torn from her with such force as to tear the strong Virginia cloth dress she had on her shoulders"; then, she was "thrown to the ground where she expected to be killed herself, but they contented themselves with the murder of her young mistress." A female slave child is singled out in this account, too. Mrs. Blackford praises this little slave girl who "clung to her Mistress and begged for her life until her own life was threatened." Then, she "fled and hid under the bed."[19]

A final Blackford story implicitly contrasts yet another loyal female slave with the infamous Lucy (who detained her mistress and was executed for it). This unnamed slave woman saved the lives of Mrs. Porter and her husband, a couple who probably lived near Mrs. Whitehead. First, Mrs. Blackford says that "A negro woman ran from a distance to warn them just in time for them to escape to the woods." Meanwhile, other slaves turned their attention to the insurgents and sent them off on a fruitless chase. Of these loyal slaves, Mrs. Blackford comments: "By a point of the finger of any of the slaves there, the family might all have been murdered, but so far from betraying them they contrived to direct the steps of the murderers in another direction."[20]

The next female slave—and the last one in this large group of "loyal" women—served the slavocracy by voicing its deepest fears and anxieties. This unnamed female slave was immortalized by John Hampden Pleasants, the editor of the *Richmond Constitutional Whig.* On 4 September 1831, Pleasants recounted the tragedy at Mrs. Rebecca Vaughn's, where the slave Cynthia lived. Four people were murdered at this site: Mrs. Vaughn, her 15-year-old son Arthur, her 18-year-old niece Ann Eliza, and her unnamed overseer. Seizing the story from the mouth of a slave eyewitness, Pleasants weaves objective reporting and harrowing narrative. In doing so, he makes this "venerable negro woman" simultaneously a subject (she tells her own story) and an object (her point of view merges with Pleasants's and, by implication, with the victims' perspectives, could they speak). Pleasants writes:

> A venerable negro woman described the scene *which she had witnessed* with great emphasis: it was near noon and her mistress was making some preparations in the porch for dinner, when happening to look towards the road she discerned a dust and wondered what it could mean. In a second, the negroes mounted and armed, rushed into view, and making an exclamation indicative of her horror and agony, Mrs. Vaughan ran into the house.—The negroes dismounted and ran around the house, pointing their guns at the doors and windows. Mrs. Vaughan, appeared at a window, and begged for her life, inviting them to take everything she had. The prayer was answered by one of them firing at her, which was followed by another, and a fatal shot. In the meantime, Miss Vaughan, who was upstairs, . . . rushed down, and begging for her life, was shot as she ran a few steps from the door. A son of Mrs. Vaughan, about 15, was at the still . . . and was shot as he got over the fence. (emphasis added)[21]

As the scene unfolds before the reader's eyes, Pleasants provides generous cues to guide the reader's response. For instance, he says that, without warning, these "defenceless ladies" fell into "the power of a band of ruffians." *And again, "It is difficult for the imagination to conceive a situation so truly and horribly awful"* (emphasis added). At most, "instant death" was all the terrified women could expect from the insurgents. Warming to his task, Pleasants continues:

> *In a most lively and picturesque manner did the old negress describe the horrors of the scene;* the blacks riding up with imprecations, the looks of her mistress, white as a sheet, her prayers for her life, and the actions of the scoundrels environing the house and pointing their guns at the doors and windows, ready to fire as occasion offered. When the work was done they called for drink, and food, and becoming nice, damned the brandy as vile stuff. (emphasis added)[22]

This lengthy depiction of a female slave witness—circulated in one of the newspapers in the state's capital—is noteworthy on two accounts. It underscores the peril in which white women were placed, and it underscores the way white dominance extended to all aspects of slavery—even to the slave's language. Pleasants is an observer twice removed; he is, in fact, an observer of an observer. When Pleasants usurps the slave woman's voice, he transforms her into an obliging servant like so many others discussed thus far.

It would be easy to say that the "old negress" in Pleasants's account seems loyal to the slave regime because she is overawed by Pleasants. However, the same excuse cannot be offered for Allen Crawford's grandmother. Crawford was a 102-year-old ex-slave whose reminiscences are contained in the Works Project Administration (WPA) slave narrative collection. Because he lived in North Emporia, Virginia, when he was interviewed in 1937, Crawford's interviewer was black like all WPA interviewers in the state.[23]

Crawford was born four years after the Turner revolt. He says that one day Nat Turner was brought to Peter Edwards's farm, where his (Crawford's) grandmother lived and where Crawford himself "was born and bred." This was about three miles from Turner's old home (Travis's), where the revolt began. According to Crawford, after Turner was brought to Edwards's farm, something unexpected happened: "Grandma ran out and struck Nat in the mouth, knocking the blood out and asked him, 'Why did you take my son away?' " Unfazed, Turner replied, " 'Your son was as willing to go as I was.' " The grandmother's fearless act is counterrevolutionary.[24]

Crawford's account of two additional female slaves echoes and revises the story Drewry told about Charlotte and Easter. Once again, two slave women fight over Lavinia Francis's clothes. However, Easter is not in this version: a slave named Lucy is inserted. Crawford seems amused by his story, with its incongruous gender and racial codes. The slave women behave like typical *women*, not *slave women*. Furthermore, as the two slaves argue over who should have what, the mistress literally "stands in fear," an inversion of the usual discourse of slavery. And well she should. Nat Turner had just murdered a schoolteacher, reifying the breakdown in social order. His act likely emboldened the two slave women who seized their mistress's clothes. This multifaceted, vernacular account is worth quoting in its entirety:

> *Ole Nat* den went on out to Miss Venie Frances, a lady's house close to whar I was born and he asked ef ole man Nelson was dar—a colored man. She said, 'No.' Den he went through [the] orchard, going to the house—*met a school mistress—killed her.* Miss Frances ran in de house skeer'd after he left and hid herself in a closet between the lathes and plastering. *Dar was two house gals, Lucy and Charlotte.* They thought this woman teacher was their missus kilt after nobody cound find her [i.e., that their mistress, not the teacher, had been killed since nobody could find her]. Ha, ha, ha, so dem gals was standing dar 'viding her clothes and things—argueing [*sic*] who should have dis and dat like you 'omen folks do. *Miss Frances dar in the closet couldn'd say a word—fear'd to speak.* Way in the evening she—Miss Venie—came down out house [i.e., came out of the house] met her husband and she tole [*sic*] him what had happened. She left everything and went back to North Carolina with him. (emphasis added)[25]

This last story is different from most analyzed thus far. As a group, the female slaves in these accounts tend to blend into each other with only the occasional contrary type. The slave woman's domesticity, specifically her love and devotion to her white "family" even in the middle of the insurrection, marks her as a type. She is rather like the archetypal "mammy" in pre- and post-Emancipation texts. According to M. M. Manring in *Slave in a Box: The Strange Career of Aunt Jemima* (1998), the "mammy" "was depicted as genuinely loving her masters and mistresses, thus providing a justification for slavery." Historians disagree about the authenticity of the "mammy" type; nonetheless, according to Manring, this mythic figure—who "supervised other house slaves, cooked, and watched children"—was "fondly" remembered by "children and housewives of postbellum America."[26]

The women who fiercely resisted the master class, like the various versions of Lucy and Charlotte already described—also include a trio of heroic women who are important to the story of the insurrection. They are Nat Turner's mother, his grandmother, and his wife. Their "motto" was resistance, to adapt Henry Highland Garnet's famous line from "An Address to the Slaves of the United States of America" (1848). They had indeterminate roles in the insurrection yet loom very large in several Nat Turner stories.[27]

Certain basic "facts" about Turner's life, specifically the seminal influence of his mother and grandmother, are well known, for they appear in Thomas R. Gray's oft-cited "as-told-to" narrative, *The Confessions of Nat Turner*, published three weeks after Turner's capture on Sunday, 30 October 1831. Gray's details about Turner's female ancestors are vague and sketchy. Interestingly, Gray does not mention Turner's wife, if he had one.[28] Other writers believe not only that this wife existed but that she intensified Turner's sense of urgency about the revolt. After all, she was the mother of his children.

In Gray's *Confessions*, Nat Turner singles out his unnamed mother as the first person to witness his extraordinary prescience. When she communicated her observations to others—also unidentified—they, too, were "greatly astonished," saying within Nat's hearing that "surely" he "would be a prophet," for the Lord had shown him things that had happened before he was born. Somehow, Turner's unnamed father and unnamed grandmother also became aware of his uncanny powers, and, as Turner notes, "strengthened" him in his "first impression" and agreed in his presence that he "was intended for some great purpose, which they had always thought from certain marks on [his] breast." This early section of *The Confessions* is very ambiguous and conflicted. The grandmother is "very religious"—her Christian religious denomination is unspecified—but she and Turner's father also seem conversant in an alternative non-Christian sign system—they "read" his body for evidence that he had certain supernatural powers. Far from counseling submission, Turner's mother, grandmother, and other unnamed persons encouraged him to see himself as divinely unfit for slavery. If his mother was a house slave, as Stephen B. Oates theorizes, she was not the self-effacing, loyal house slave who is the dominant type in most of the texts surveyed thus far.[29]

In 1955 Lucy Mae Turner, Nat Turner's granddaughter, published a two-part narrative essay in the *Negro History Bulletin* about Nat Turner, his parents, his wife, and some of his descendants. She uses fictional and expository techniques, causing the essay to read like fiction even though it presents itself as "factual." Using an omniscient narrator, she follows the life of Nat Turner's son, Gilbert Turner, from his life in slavery to his life in freedom. From a beginning more inauspicious than Benjamin Franklin's, Gilbert rises in the world to become a successful freeman, an upstanding, productive citizen, a model father and husband, and, above all, an untiring, Christian soldier.

This Lucy Mae Turner essay is part autobiography and part family history. Lucy Mae Turner wants to show that her father and his children are worthy descendants of Nat Turner and his noble wife, Fanny. They, in turn, are worthy heirs of their African parents. Nat Turner's mother is overshadowed by her husband, but that does not mean that she is relegated to a bit part. She says and does little in the course of the essay, but she is still a haunting presence in Gilbert's life and thus in Lucy Mae Turner's. Like Nat Turner, she has spiritual power, in her own way.

When we meet Gilbert, he is at an auction, about to be torn from his 20-something mother and his two-year-old sister, Melissa. They were put up for sale after the insurrection. According to Lucy Mae Turner, Nat was responding to "the urge" that God had "put into him" and so "fought for and demanded his freedom, and the right to stand and walk upright, as befitted one made in the image of God." The penalty for this "presumptious [*sic*] thought and action" was that "everyone with a drop of Nat Turner's blood must be shackled and sold into the far South" to be worked to death. Of course, "blood" will tell. Gilbert's ultimate success—not to minimize his hard work—is traceable to the Turner blood that runs in his veins: his father's and his mother's.

In the auction scene, Fanny is the typical victim at first. She cringes timidly in a corner as a "tall, gaunt, red-faced, cruel" auctioneer brings his whip down on her shoulders. Not herself but her young daughter and her son Gilbert are her primary concerns. She does what she can to protect her tender daughter from physical harm. Nevertheless, the time comes when she and her daughter are sold to an Alabama planter for $125, and Gilbert is sold to his father's young mistress. From the auction block, Fanny whispers words that Gilbert hears in his heart only. He had heard them sung in his father's slave cabin the night before the insurrection; Lucy Mae Turner will use them also as the closing words of her essay:

"Trust in the Lord, And you'll overcome, Somehow, Somewhere, Someday!"[30]

In the way they are repeated in this essay, these words signify links among Nat Turner, his followers, Fanny, Gilbert, Lucy Mae Turner, and other Turner descendants. Lucy Mae Turner extends these links even more deeply into the past elsewhere in her article as she emphasizes her grandparents' African heritage. Gilbert specifically remembers his grandmother—or Nat Turner's "aged and high-spirited mother"—who was reputedly "of royal African blood." She was a bearer of ancestral traditions: Gilbert "vaguely remembered stories his queenly-looking black grandmother had told of the happiness of the family in Africa, before they were captured, and before the dark days of slavery." Nat Turner replicated this happy family when he married Fanny and had three children by her. Gilbert remembered "a happy home, in spite of slavery, for there was love, and Christian fellowship in the home." He also recalled "the hours of daily family prayers" and his father's proscriptions against alcohol and blasphemy. That Nat Turner and Fanny created a (Christian) home—that they created a home because that was what their African ancestors had done before them—is an important theme in this essay. It is instructive as well that Fanny, a slave woman, is central to this construct.

Stephen B. Oates does not doubt that Nat Turner had an African mother—and perhaps an African father—but he does not believe that Turner's parents created an enduring, nuclear family structure. Oates makes several interlocking assertions: that Nat's mother, an African, was purchased in 1799 by Benjamin Turner, a Methodist Southampton County slaveholder; that he renamed her "Nancy"; that she gave birth to Nathaniel the following year on 2 October 1800; that the newly named "Nancy" reportedly tried to kill her son rather than have him live as a slave; that Nat's unnamed father was the son of another slave named "Old Bridget"; and that Nat's father was rumored to have been African.[31]

According to Oates, circumstantial evidence suggests that Nat's father ran away before 1810. In that year, his first owner, Benjamin Turner, died and willed the ten-year-old Nat, his mother Nancy, and his paternal grandmother, Old Bridget, to his son, Samuel Turner. The family remained together for some years, but in 1822 Samuel Turner, who now owned 20 slaves, died at age 32 and left Nat's mother to his wife Elizabeth. Oates speculates that Nat, following the example of his father, ran away sometime after late 1821. Whether he ran away before or after Samuel Turner died is unclear. It is certain that Nat Turner was sold to Thomas Moore in 1822. Once this happened, he was separated from his mother, and his family structure, already weakened by an absent father, suffered a mortal blow.[32]

As if all this were not stressful enough, Oates theorizes that Nat Turner married one of Samuel Turner's slaves sometime before his master's death. Her name was Cherry, not the Fanny described by Lucy Mae Turner. Their lives were disrupted when Samuel Turner's property had to be divided to settle his estate. Turner was then sold to Thomas Moore and Cherry to Giles Reese. At some point, "Cherry bore two children by Nat—a daughter and one or two sons," writes Oates. The family lines grow rather faint after this. Most astounding, Oates's version of Nat Turner's family and Lucy Mae Turner's version are quite different. Lucy Mae Turner traces her descendants in absolute ignorance of other Nat Turner relations like Redic Turner, Herbert Turner, and Asphy Turner—all of whom say they also descend from Nat Turner.[33]

Lucy Mae Turner casts all of her ancestors, male and female, in a heroic mold. However, she does not mention Cherry Turner as her grandmother. In other writings, Cherry is sometimes portrayed as a coconspirator. Stephen Oates, for example, notes that "Nat discussed his work with Cherry, too, telling her that he had been plotting insurrection in his mind since 1828 and that God had not given him a sign to begin." A corroborating statement appeared in the *Richmond Constitutional Whig* of 26 September 1831, in which an anonymous writer said emphatically: " 'Tis true, that Nat has for some time thought closely on this subject—for I have in my possession, some papers given up by his wife, under the lash—they are filled with hieroglyphical characters, conveying no definite meaning." Almost as an afterthought, the writer added the following: "There is likewise a piece of paper, of late date, which all agree, is a list of his men; if so, they were short of twenty." Regrettably, Cherry's papers, if they ever existed, are not extant. Perhaps, they were lost along with other documents allegedly forwarded to Governor Floyd, a bundle of papers Henry Irving Tragle says "has never been found." To trouble the water even more, Thomas Parramore cautions that Nat Turner's wife *may* have been the slave Mariah, who, along with her child, belonged to Thomas Moore. To borrow a phrase from Thomas Gray, Turner's wife—Cherry or Fanny or Mariah or whoever she was—remains "wrapt in mystery."[34]

Clearly, Nat Turner's wife is hard to track—like the rest of her slave sisterhood. The information in trial records, newspapers, historical and pseudo-historical texts, Thomas R. Gray's *Confessions*, and Lucy Mae Turner's biography of Nat Turner is tantalizingly brief and frequently elliptical. Most of the women portrayed in these sources fall in the faithful-slave category. Exceptions—such as the two Lucys, the two Charlottes, and Nat Turner's mother, grandmother, and wife—hint at a buried, and perhaps irretrievable, history.

It is unlikely, though, that this buried history was excavated by Daniel Panger in his 1967 novel *Ol' Prophet Nat*. As I demonstrated in a recent study of six Nat Turner novels published between 1856 and 1967, Panger's novel was the sole novel to depict female slaves who rode with Nat Turner. Were there slave women who simply never made it into the historical record? Or can their absence be explained by West African cultural practices, as suggested by James Sidbury and Douglas Egerton in their studies of the conspiracies led by Gabriel (1800) and Denmark Vesey (1822)? According to Sidbury and Egerton, female participation in both of these conspiracies was virtually nonexistent. They believe the exclusion of women is partly traceable to West African cultural practices. Male-only secret societies and armies were common in West Africa, and these practices seem to have influenced the makeup of male groups that spearheaded and carried out the massive conspiracies in Richmond, Virginia, and in Charleston, South Carolina.[35]

Such theories *may* explain the absence of active female insurrectionists during the Nat Turner rebellion. In the documents surveyed in this article, women engaged in violent forms of resistance are barely evident. Yet the trail of blood that snaked through sections of lower Southampton County was incontrovertible proof that an intractable spirit of resistance, hitherto invisible, was nevertheless there. This spirit was certainly alive in the male insurrectionists whom everyone saw; it was also doubtless alive in many female slaves whom no one saw. This is the central irony of the Nat Turner insurrection—its enduring mystery. The event invites and resists interpretations at every turn.

PART FOUR

MEMORY

ELEVEN

Styron's Choice

A Meditation on History, Literature, and Moral Imperatives

CHARLES JOYNER

And the people of Israel groaned under their bondage, and cried out for help, and their cry came up to God. And God heard their groaning.

—*Exodus 2:23–24*

The spoils taken from you will be divided among you. . . . The city will be taken, the houses plundered, the women ravished.

—*Zechariah 14:1–4*

Then they utterly destroyed all the city, both men and women, young and old, oxen, sheep, and asses, with the edge of the sword.

—*Joshua 6:21*

The day dawned bleak and chill that Friday in the Virginia tidewater, and an enveloping gray light seemed to come out of the northeast. The dry leaves whispered a little in the windless November. Around noon the jailer unlocked the condemned hole of the Southampton County Jail. It was cold and musty in the hole, and the rank smell fouled the air.

For nearly two weeks Nat Turner had been lying there in darkness, secured with manacles and chains to make certain he could not escape. For nearly two weeks he had been lying there on a pine board, neither asleep nor awake, as though his very being were itself a part of darkness

This essay was originally published in *Southern Writers and Their Worlds*, ed. Christopher Morris and Steven G. Reinhardt (College Station: Published for the University of Texas at Arlington by Texas A & M Press, 1996).

and silence. All he had done, all he had felt and suffered, had passed before his mind there as he had tried to explain his actions to an uncomprehending white man named Thomas Gray. It was strange to him that whites could comprehend neither motivation nor explanation for his actions. To whites he seemed to have appeared abruptly with a dark band of avenging angels to cut a red swath through Southampton County in the summer of 1831. But as Nat Turner lay upon his hard pine board in his ragged garments, he saw again how the actual and urgent need to accomplish his purpose had been revealed to him in the heavens. There had been no choice, just one right thing without alternatives, just one right thing without either falling short or overshooting. It had been as though the opposed forces of his destiny and his will had drawn swiftly together toward a foreordained mission.

Now armed guards took Nat Turner from his cell and struggled through a morass of hostile white faces. The prisoner was clothed in rags but held his head erect. The procession did not seem to progress at all but just seemed to march in place while the earth moved as they made their journey through the streets of Jerusalem, a journey that seemed to have neither definite beginning nor ending. At length the party approached a field northeast of the town. A large crowd, sullenly inert and immobile, had gathered around a gnarled old live oak.

The sheriff asked the prisoner if he had anything to say. Turning slowly, quietly, holding his body erect, Nat Turner answered in an unexpectedly pleasant voice. "I'm ready" was all he said. Then, waiting under the tree without impatience or even emotion, he stared out beyond the mob of hostile white faces into the distant skies. They threw one end of the rope over a limb of the tree and pulled him up with a jerk. Eyewitnesses said Nat Turner did not move a muscle, he hung there as still as a rock.

So they hanged Nat Turner from a live oak tree in 1831. They skinned his body and rendered his flesh into grease. They sliced a souvenir purse from his skin and divided his bones into trophies, to be handed down as family heirlooms.[1] If all this was supposed to have killed Nat Turner, it would seem to have failed miserably. Nat Turner still lives in history, for he led the greatest slave revolt ever to take place in the greatest slave republic in the New World. No one has yet been able to explain satisfactorily the tragic enigma of Nat Turner, the spiritual and charismatic young carpenter with visions of apocalypse who at the age of 31 was taken to Jerusalem to hang upon a tree.[2]

William Styron left his native Virginia in the 1940s, but in his novel, *The Confessions of Nat Turner*, he goes home again. "It took place not far from where I was born," he told his friend James Jones as early as 1963, adding that the idea of writing a book on the rebellion was "something that I've been thinking about for fifteen years." He believed that the Nat Turner rebellion was "the most important thing that happened in the history of Southampton County." He eventually decided to write the book

in the early 1960s. "As with everything I've ever written, I took long re-
cesses from it. Several times I was baffled by the way the book was going.
Once, I abandoned it for six or seven months. But then I knuckled down
and the structure came as I wrote." His *Confessions of Nat Turner* "wasn't
something that I conceived in some great Jovian way in the beginning."[3]

The form of Styron's *Confessions* is pervaded by frames, by memories of
memories, by stories within stories, centering his protagonist within a
novel that brings him out of the opaque darkness of the past through his
contact with a white lawyer named Thomas Gray.[4] Part I opens with the
rebel caged, awaiting his trial and telling his story of the uprising to lawyer
Gray. "I knew with this book that the place I had to start was with Nat in
his cell," Styron told an interviewer. "Since the last scene had to do with
his death, the first one had to partake of that, too."[5] In this section Styron
explores the enigma of Nat Turner in his conversations with Gray, in his
selective recollections as he tries to come to terms with his memories, in
his snatches of conversation whispered through the jail wall to a fellow
conspirator, and in the trial itself. In Styron's *Confessions* Nat is as fascinated by the paradox of Thomas Gray as Gray is by the riddle of Nat
Turner. Nat has "an impression, dim and fleeting, of hallucination, of talk
buried deep in dreams." He stares at this strange white man, concluding
that he is "little different from any of the others." Still he found it "a
matter of wonder" where "this my last white man (save the one with the
rope) had come from." He sometimes felt that he had "made him up."
Since it was hard "to talk to an invention," Nat Turner resolved to remain
"all the more determinedly silent."[6]

The core of Styron's *Confessions* is the story of Nat's early life, portrayed
in a flashback constituting most of the novel, framed by his execution. It
takes the form of a pastiche of the slave narrative genre. "My mother's
mother was a girl of the Coromantee tribe from the Gold Coast," Styron's
Nat reports, "thirteen years old when she was brought in chains to York-
town aboard a schooner sailing out of Newport, Rhode Island, and only
a few months older when she was sold at auction beneath a huge live oak
tree in the harborside town of Hampton, to Alpheus Turner." She died
in childbirth the same year, survived only by Nat's mother.[7]

If Styron's Nat is born in bondage and remains conscious of his invisible
chains, he is nevertheless spoiled by benevolent paternalism. As the son
of a scullery maid and cook, he grows up in the Big House, scornful of
the field hands he considers to be "creatures beneath contempt." If a
"wretched cornfield hand, sweating and stinking," approached the front
veranda of the Big House in need of medical assistance after gashing his
bare foot with a hoe," Styron has his fictional Nat Turner recall, "I would
direct him to the proper rear door in a voice edged with icy scorn." To
Styron's Nat, the mass of the plantation slaves were "so devoid of the
attributes I had come to connect with the sheltered and respectable life
that they were not even worth my derision."[8]

Styron's Nat, his disdain for blackness balanced by a reverence for whiteness, dreams of being white. Waiting on a deserted plantation, he fantasizes about possessing the plantation: "In a twinkling I became white—white as clabber cheese, white, stark white, white as a Marble Episcopalian. . . . Now, looking down at the shops and barns and cabins and distant fields, I was no longer the grinning black boy in velvet pantaloons, for a fleeting moment instead I owned all, and so exercised the privilege of ownership by unlacing my fly and pissing loudly on the same worn stone where dainty tiptoeing feet had gained the veranda steps a short three years before. What a strange, demented ecstasy! How white I was! What wicked joy!"[9]

Styron's young slave is greatly affected by a "good master," Samuel Turner, whose surname he assumes and who introduces him to the idea of hope. When Nat steals a book, his master sees proof that slaves are, after all, "capable of intellectual enlightenment and enrichment of the spirit." So he and his wife begin an educational experiment, giving Nat a Bible and teaching him to read. The brilliant young pupil memorizes many scriptural passages and comes to know the Bible better than some of the local white preachers. Aware of his own charm and intelligence, aware that he has been spared the harshness and brutality that most slaves have to endure, Styron's Nat grows accustomed to affection from everyone. "I became in short a pet," he says, "the darling, the little black jewel of Turner's Mill. Pampered, fondled, nudged, pinched, I was the household's spoiled child." The young slave feels a regard toward his master, Samuel Turner, "very close to the feeling one should bear only toward the Divinity." Between them are not only "strong ties of emotion," but "a kind of love."[10]

Samuel Turner gives his precocious young slave training, encouragement, and responsibilities. Eventually, three years before Nat comes of age, Samuel Turner promises to set him free. The young slave is initially appalled by the prospect. After all, servitude and a kindly master are all that he has known. He wonders what would have become of him if his life had continued without the promise of freedom. His meditation is an eloquent account of what "slavery at its best" might mean. Without the hope of freedom, he might have become "an ordinary, run-of-the-mill house nigger, mildly efficient at some stupid task like wringing chickens' necks or smoking hams or polishing silver." He probably would have become "a malingerer whenever possible," although he would have been "too jealous of my security to risk real censure or trouble," would have been "cautious in my tiny thefts, circumspect in the secrecy of my afternoon naps, furtive in my anxious lecheries with the plump yellow-skinned cleaning maids upstairs in the dark attic." He muses that he probably would have grown "ever more servile and unctuous as I became older," would have become a "crafty flatterer on the lookout for some bonus of flannel or stew beef or tobacco," all the while developing "a kind of purse-

lipped dignity" behind his "stately paunch and fancy bib and waistcoat."
He would have become a "well loved" and "palsied stroker of the silken
pates of little white grandchildren," although "rheumatic, illiterate, and
filled with sleepiness, half yearning for that lonely death which at long
last would lead me to rest in some tumbledown graveyard tangled with
chokeberry and jimson weed." He would be known, of course, as Uncle
Nat. As things turn out, Nat becomes instead a carpenter, a skilled crafts-
man, an asset to his white masters. At the same time he becomes a
preacher to his own people. Yet the foretaste of freedom only excites
growing hunger. His life takes on new direction. In one morning, in one
glimpse of the possibilities of the future, Samuel Turner converts his little
slave Nat into a human being burning to be free.[11]

Then the tidewater land goes sterile and Samuel Turner goes bankrupt.
Forced to sell out and move to Alabama, he abandons his plan to free his
pet slave. At the age of 20 Styron's Nat is on the threshold of freedom
when he suddenly realizes that slavery is "the *true* world in which a Negro
moves and breathes." To learn that even his beloved Marse Samuel could
treat slaves so inhumanly is "like being plunged into freezing water." Samuel Turner hands Nat over to a fanatical Baptist minister, the epitome of
ecclesiastical evil. Although the preacher is legally obliged to free the
young slave in a stated time, Nat gets a year's taste of just how bad slavery
can be before he is sold for $460. He is then forced to submit to a suc-
cession of stupid, brutal, and swinish slaveholders. They beat him and half-
starve him. They subject him to every kind of humiliation. For Styron's
Nat, the dream of freedom is shattered; he knows that the slaveholders
are his moral inferiors.[12]

From such experiences Styron's Nat learns "how greatly various were
the moral attributes of white men who possessed slaves, how different each
owner might be by way of severity or benevolence." Slaveholders range
"from the saintly (Samuel Turner) to the all right (Moore) to the barely
tolerable (Reverend Eppes) to a few who were unconditionally monstrous." But "the more tolerable and human white people became in their
dealings with me," Styron's Nat observes, "the keener was my passion to
destroy them." Nat Turner's revolt is not represented in the novel as the
irrepressible rage of the intolerably oppressed. Instead, Styron's Nat directs his deepest anger against Samuel Turner, the man who first held
out to him the prospect of freedom.[13]

Turning more and more to the Bible for consolation, Nat Turner recognizes the bitter truth of Ecclesiastes: "The preacher was right. He that
increaseth knowledge increaseth sorrow." He nourishes his newfound hatred of whites on the harsh words of the prophets, on the promise of
vengeance to be visited upon the enemies of righteousness, upon the
enemies of God's chosen people.[14]

Nat's years with one cruel master last nearly a decade and seem twice
as long. Thomas Moore "hated all Negroes with a blind, obsessive hatred

which verged upon a kind of minor daily ecstasy." For nearly a decade
Nat feeds on Old Testament prophets and nurtures a hatred so bitter it
verges on madness. Styron's Nat is strictly an Old Testament figure; he
thinks and speaks in the blood-stained rhetoric of his Hebrew heroes Eze-
kiel, Daniel, Isaiah, and Jeremiah. For nearly a decade scriptural poetry
weaves in and out of his ruminations. He fasts and prays in the wilderness
and waits for a sign that eventually comes: in the "midst of the rent in the
clouds" he sees "a black angel clothed in black armor with black wings
outspread from east to west; gigantic, hovering, he spoke in a thunderous
voice louder than anything I had ever heard: 'Fear God and give glory to
Him for the hour of His judgment is come.' " After such visions Nat has
little doubt of his mission. And the sins of the white fathers visited upon
their black slaves leave him little doubt of his method. With great care
and with great intelligence he begins to plan his strategy of
extermination.[15]

For nearly a decade Nat's camouflage is to become "a paragon of rectitude, of alacrity, of lively industriousness, of sweet equanimity and un-
complaining obedience." He becomes a keen observer of slave personality
types, not only of those given to "wallowing in the dust at the slightest
provocation, midriffs clutched in idiot laughter," those who "endear themselves to all, white and black, through droll interminable tales about ha'nts
and witches and conjures," but also of those who "reverse this procedure
entirely and in *their* niggerness are able to outdo many white people in
presenting to the world a grotesque swagger," a posture suited to the black
driver or the tyrannical kitchen mammy and butler, who were skilled in
keeping "safely this side of insolence."[16]

Styron's Nat chooses to cast himself in the role of a promising young
slave given to "humility, a soft voice, and houndlike obedience." He learns
how to affect that "respect and deference it is wise for any Negro to assume" in the presence of a strange white man. He learns to shuffle and
scrape and to adopt obsequious field hand accents and postures. He
learns how to "merge faceless and nameless with the common swarm,"
how "to interpret the *tone* of what is being said," and how to sense danger.
But Styron's Nat Turner is always conscious of "the weird unnaturalness
of this adopted role," always counseling himself "to patience, patience,
patience to the end," always biding his time.[17]

But the wait is not aimless; Nat spends much of it enlisting potential
recruits for his divine mission of vengeance and liberation. He often loses
heart as he observes his fellow slaves "half drowned from birth in a kind
of murky mindlessness," their mouths agape in "sloppy uncomprehending
smiles, shuffling their feet." They seem to him "as meaningless and as
stupid as a barnful of mules," and he "hate[s] them one and all." But he
also feels "a kind of wild, desperate love for them." He is ambivalent toward Hark, whom he hopes to make one of his commanders. Hark, he
muses, has "the face of an African chieftain," a godlike frame and

strength, and a mortal grievance against his master for selling his wife and child. "Yet the very sight of white skin cowed him, humbled him to the most servile abasement." Nat is enraged by Hark's "dull, malleable docility." When in the presence of any white, Hark unconsciously becomes "the unspeakable bootlicking Sambo, all giggles and smirks and oily, sniveling servility." Hark's only excuse is that he is overwhelmed by "dat black-assed feelin'." The expression, Nat concedes, perfectly expresses what he calls "the numbness and dread which dwells in every Negro's heart."[18]

Styron's narrative flows relentlessly toward Nat's appointment with apocalypse. Preparing for the hour of the bloodbath, Nat seeks out those slaves "in whom hatred was already ablaze" and cultivates "hatred in the few remaining and vulnerable." He tests and probes, "warily discarding those in whom pure hatred could not be nurtured and whom therefore I could not trust." Tirelessly he strains to instill in his followers confidence in themselves and faith in their leader. Tirelessly he strains to overcome their fears. After all, he asks, what have slaves to lose but their chains?[19]

When the time comes for their long march through the Virginia countryside, Nat's rebels hack off heads as if their aim were vengeance rather than freedom. In the predawn darkness of August 22, 1831, they wander from house to house severing limbs, crushing skulls, and slaughtering every white man, woman, and child in their path. But when Nat raises his axe over his master's head, his hand shakes so much his blow misses. Over and over, between violent seizures of vomiting, Nat tries to kill. Over and over he fails. Among the scores slain by the rebels, Nat takes but one life: that of the sympathetic young girl Margaret Whitehead, "her dimpled chin tilted up as . . . she carols heavenward, a radiance like daybreak on her serene young face," the one white person he still loves, the one white person whose "closeness stifled me . . . wafting toward me her odor—a disturbing smell of young-girl sweat mingled with the faint sting of lavender."[20]

Once the slaughter of the whites is over, the slaughter of the blacks begins. Virginia's defense of slavery is even bloodier than Nat Turner's revolt against it. Nat and his black followers are hunted down, tried, and executed. They have killed 60 whites. White Virginians in reprisal kill more than two hundred blacks, only a few of them involved in the rebellion at all. At Nat's trial, Thomas Gray tells the court that "save in the inexplicably successful murder of Margaret Whitehead—inexplicably motivated, likewise obscurely executed—the defendant, this purported bold, intrepid, and resourceful leader, was unable to carry out a *single feat of arms!* Not only this, but at the end his quality of leadership, such as it was, utterly deserted him!" He tells the court that "pure Negro cowardice" explains "this base crime—the slaying not of a virile and stalwart man but of a fragile, weak, and helpless young maiden but a few years out of childhood." He tells the court that "all such rebellions are not only exceedingly rare in occurrence but are ultimately doomed to failure, and this as a result of the basic weakness and inferiority, the moral deficiency of the Negro's character."[21]

Awaiting his execution, Styron's Nat has an erotic fantasy about Margaret Whitehead, a kind of symbolic sacrament of extreme unction. "And as I think of her, the desire swells within me and I am stirred by a longing so great," he muses, "it seems more than my heart can abide. *Beloved, let us love one another: for love is of God; and everyone that loveth is born of God, and knoweth God.*" In the darkness of his cell, "I feel the warmth flow into my loins and my legs tingle with desire. I tremble and I search for her face in my mind, seek her young body, yearning for her suddenly with a rage that racks me with a craving beyond pain; with tender stroking motions I pour out my love within her; pulsing flood; she arches against me, cries out, and the twain—black and white—are one."[22] As he is led to his execution, Styron's Nat reflects, "I would have done it all again. I would have destroyed them all. Yet I would have spared one. I would have spared her that showed me Him whose presence I had not fathomed or maybe never even known."[23]

But Nat Turner would not die. He set the House of Bondage on fire. He made history, and he lives in history. "I think this may be a valuable book in a certain way," Styron told an interviewer in 1967. "Very few people know anything about slavery and Negro history, and I don't know of any modern work of fiction that has touched on the problem. Writers probably have been intimidated by the sheer, awesome fact of what it must have been to be a slave. I just had to seize the bull by the horns and become one."[24]

The boldest choice William Styron made was to "become one," to assume the persona of Nat Turner. White authors, whether looking up an avenue of live oaks leading to a plantation Big House or up a red clay road leading to a sharecropper's shack, had customarily viewed the South through the eyes of white Southerners. Preoccupied with the moral problems of white people and guilt-stricken at white brutality toward blacks, modern white writers had often been guided by impulses of contrition and expiation. And modern black critics had often come to take for granted such contrition and expiation on the part of guilt-stricken white writers. But in *The Confessions of Nat Turner* Styron chose as his point of view to look through a black lens, chose to try to see Nat's world from behind the black mask. His decision to write the book in the first person, to let Nat tell his own story, was a crucial decision.

With no participants leaving behind firsthand accounts and no white victims living to tell the tale, evidence is inevitably scanty. Styron felt he had little to go on beyond his own imagination. The best-known source is a 20-page pamphlet, "The Confessions of Nat Turner," written by Thomas Gray, a Virginia lawyer who interviewed Turner in the Southampton County jail. Beyond that, Styron "invented almost everything except what was directly connected with the revolt."[25]

Before 1968 William Styron was relatively obscure, at least to the general public; thereafter he was notorious. His *Confessions* became for a time the moral storm center of American history. Perhaps it could not have been otherwise. As C. Vann Woodward observes, "Slavery was, after all, the basic moral paradox of American history." Styron's novel was not without honor. It won the Pulitzer Prize for fiction and indelibly inscribed his representation of Nat Turner on America's consciousness.[26] But Styron's *Confessions* also stimulated alarmed reactions and infuriated complaints in some quarters. The novel was widely condemned for all sorts of sins, and his critics were not reluctant to be blunt. Some of the scandalized permitted their reviews to degenerate into polemic. Nat Turner lives in history, they argued, but not in the pages of Styron's novel.[27]

If Styron found the initial responses dismaying, worse was to come. A group of black intellectuals who, as Albert Murray put it, took it upon themselves to "keep check on such things," wrote a book-length response under the collective sobriquet "Ten Black Writers." Their objections were primarily that, beneath a facade of Southern liberalism, Styron's *Confessions* paraded such racist stereotypes as black cowardice, incompetence, and immorality; the decline of black family values; and black sexual preoccupation with white women. Styron, they charged, had corrupted the historical record by inadequate research and misuse of documents and had constructed a novel entirely lacking in historical substance and literary merit (his Pulitzer Prize notwithstanding).[28]

The Ten did not find credible what they called the "vacillating introspection" of Styron's protagonist. He was a Nat Turner that whites could accept, they said, but he was emphatically not the Nat of "the living traditions of black America." He was not the "hero with whom Negroes identify." According to them, the real Nat Turner was "a virile, commanding, courageous figure" who "killed or ordered killed real white people for real historical reasons." They faulted Styron for his abhorrent attribution of ambivalence, complexity, and mixed motives to the man they called "our black rebel." Styron's *Confessions*, they charged, were "part of the whitened appropriation of our history by those who have neither eaten nor mourned." The novelist, "unable to eat and digest the blackness, the fierce religious conviction, the power of the man," had substituted "an impotent, cowardly, irresolute creature of his own imagination." Styron's Nat, they complained, is not powerful but pathetic, not Othello but Hamlet, not a folk hero but a groveling, grinning Uncle Tom, prancing about the piazza while kindly ole Cunnel Massa benevolently sips his julep. To be sure, Styron's Nat is only intermittently groveling (and deceptively so, at that); but he is hardly the single-minded black nationalist revolutionary constructed by the Ten Black Writers.[29]

Nor was their attitude toward what they called "Styron's assault on Nat Turner's family" any more favorable. The Ten contrasted the female-headed family of Styron's Nat with that of the historical Nat Turner. Growing up in a "strong family unit," they said, "buttressed his sense of identity and mission." They pointed out that the historical Nat told Thomas Gray his early religious inspiration and teaching came from his parents and his grandmother. Styron, however, minimizes their influence. In his hands Nat's main religious influence comes from a white family, especially from the young daughters of the family. The Ten charged that Styron's change wrenches Nat Turner out of the unique context of African-American religion.[30]

Styron, the Ten contended, devalues the historical presence and influence of the black family. They pointed out that in Gray's *Confessions*, Turner fondly recalled his beloved grandmother whom he describes as "very religious, and to whom I was much attached." Styron's Nat, however, tells Gray that "I never laid eyes on my grandmother." She "is immediately banished" from Styron's book. Also in Gray's *Confessions* Nat remembered his father and mother, who had taught him to read and write, with special fondness. When he was three or four, he recalled, he was told that "I surely would be a prophet, as the Lord had shewn me things that had happened before my birth. And my father and mother strengthened me in this my first impression, saying in my presence, I was intended for some great purpose, which they had always thought from certain marks on my breast." In his *Confessions*, Styron alters the line to read, "And my mother strengthened me in this my first impression. . . ." It is not surprising that, to the Ten, that appeared "a remarkably revealing translation"; the white Virginian had not only eliminated the African grandmother, but also the troublesome father.[31]

The Ten were vexed by Styron's "psychoanalytical emphasis upon Nat's so-called tormented relationship with his father following psychoanalyst Erik Erikson's book *Young Man Luther*." The historical Nat Turner, they noted, had told Thomas Gray that he had become convinced by "my father and mother" that he was "intended for some great purpose." The Ten believed Nat's discontent with slavery may very well have been inspired by his father, who had escaped from the plantation. Nat himself escaped when placed under a new overseer, but he returned to the plantation after a month out in the woods. His fellow slaves, dismayed at his return, told him that if they had his intelligence, "they would not serve any master in the world."[32]

Styron's representation of Nat Turner as a house slave also troubled the Ten. They complained that Styron "detaches mother and son from black people" by making his mother a "house nigger," when "according to tradition" (unspecified) she was an African who hated slavery so much she had to be tied at Nat's birth to keep her from murdering him. By giving his fictional Nat a white upbringing and white values, by separating him from the slave community and making him contemptuous of his fellow blacks, they claimed, Styron reduces the significance of the historical insurrection to little more than fear and self-loathing in Tidewater Virginia. The insurrection of the historical Nat Turner, they insisted, was driven by love, not hatred, for his fellow slaves.[33]

What the Ten called "the apologist theme" running through Styron's

Confessions came in for special condemnation. Styron, the grandson of slaveholders, portrays a gallery of his ancestors ranging across a spectrum from "saintly" to "all right" to "barely tolerable" to "monstrous." In their opinion "a master was a master was a master." Styron fails, they declared, to portray "American slavery as the cruelest, most inhuman, slavery system in the entire recorded history of man's bestiality to man." They found the obvious explanation for his "failure" to see what was so clear to them in Styron's "preconceptions of black inferiority." They did not attempt to explain the paradox of a cruel and dehumanizing system that failed to dehumanize its victims.[34]

The most conspicuous complaints clustered around Styron's representation of Nat Turner as a celibate who sublimates his sexual drives into fantasies and into a religious fanaticism that inspires his revolt. The homosexual and asexual tendencies Styron invents for Nat proved especially controversial. The Ten accused him of denying Nat Turner's manhood. According to them Styron roots Nat's apocalyptic religious vision in sexual perversion, downplaying his religious fervor. The closest Styron's version of Nat Turner comes to a realized sexual experience is homosexual experiments with another young black slave, from which he comes to his baptism burdened with guilt. According to them it was an attack on the manhood of "our black rebel," implying that he was "not a man at all" and suggesting Nat was "really feminine." According to them there was nothing in the historical record to suggest that "Nat had no love whatever for black women, which is how Styron depicts him. As a matter of fact, he was married to one, but you wouldn't know it from the novel." Nor is there anything to suggest "Nat's great lust and passion for white women, but this is the way he is presented throughout Styron's novel." According to them Styron ignores evidence that the historical Nat Turner had a black wife in order to fabricate an ambivalent (and wholly fictional) romance between Nat and Margaret Whitehead, a white girl whom Styron's Nat loves and toward whom he deflects his sexual drives platonically. But she is also the only white person he kills with his own hands during the uprising. According to them this relationship exemplifies the racist stereotype of black men lusting after white women. Clearly, they believed, "Styron feels that Nat Turner's emotional attachment to this white 'forbidden fruit' was a key factor in his psychological motivation." The Ten found Styron's book tainted by his talent as a novelist. The artist had used his art "to reconcile Nat Turner to an unacceptable reality by making him confess that he would have spared at least one white person. ("Go ye into the city and find one . . . just one.") Thus, they said, "the child-woman, Margaret, who was a victim of history, becomes the central image by which Styron rejects history." The interracial love affair with Margaret had nothing to do with Nat Turner and the slave experience, they maintained. It had everything to do with Styron's own fantasies and Styron's own racism.[35]

Nor did the Ten find other black men in the novel faring any better at Styron's hands. They were particularly infuriated at his portrait of Will—the slave rebel who kills more voraciously than any other—as "a lunatic hell-bent on raping white women." In what they call "Styron's fantasy," Will joins the revolution because he wants to "get me some of dat white stuff." The fictional Nat Turner is put off by the "foaming and frenzied nature of his madness," but the Ten absolved the historical Will of any guilt during the insurrection except that of "dispatching" a number of whites with a single-minded efficiency. Their verdict is that "like Joshua, he is simply engaged in the destruction of the Lord's enemies." In the novel Nat warns his followers, "Do not unto their women what they have done to thine." Despite his injunction, however, soon "this scarred, tortured little black man was consummating at last ten thousand old swollen moments of frantic and unappeasable desire" between "Miss Sarah's thrashing, naked thighs." Styron's purpose appeared transparent to the Ten. "It looks," they proclaimed, "as if nigger-beast has struck again." Could a black man be motivated to such a large-scale assault on white lives, they asked rhetorically, only by sex and insanity?[36]

"Styron's fantasy," the Ten declared, attempts to undercut the black rebel's "credentials as a leader" by presenting him as "a panicky, fearful, impotent man," unable to strike a death blow. They saw Nat Turner as a heroic military commander, who "initiated the rebellion by striking his master with a hatchet." In the dark the hatchet glanced from his master's head and Nat was unable to kill him. Will "laid him dead." "General Nat," as they explained it, was "the *leader* of the Southampton insurrection, and generals seldom kill." They pointed out that General Nat sent "fifteen or twenty of the best armed and most to be relied on" to approach "the houses as fast as their horses could run." This was intended to strike terror among the inhabitants and prevent them from escaping. As a result he "never got to the houses" until after "the murders were committed," although he occasionally arrived in time to see "the work of death completed, viewed the mangled bodies as they lay, in silent satisfaction, and immediately started in quest of other victims."[37]

The Ten also objected to Styron's portraying Nat Turner after the murders as "remorseful" and "contrite," as "alone and forsaken," and as feeling "a terrible emptiness." Styron, they claimed, "has coerced poor Nat Turner into a full confession, proving—beyond a shadow of doubt—the vengeful ingratitude of a literate, pampered slave for his benevolent masters, an ingratitude which turns unprovoked into hatred and murder!" Nat Turner, they insisted, was calm and cool to the end.[38]

Nat Turner's insurrection, as the Ten Black Writers saw it, had yet to be fully appreciated and understood. It was the most profound historical experience of African Americans. What was needed (and what Styron did not supply) was attention to an African-American oral tradition of Nat Turner as an "epic hero, a special, dedicated breed of man who had given his last full measure of devotion to liberation and dignity." The tradition asserted by the Ten is very much at odds with Styron's fictional creation. His Nat Turner "is one whom many white people will accept at a safe distance," but he "is not the hero with whom Negroes identify." Styron's protagonist, they noted with irritation, is "a Nat Turner who is simply not to be found in the astringent report of Lawyer Gray, or in the living traditions of black America."[39]

"The voice in this confession," the Ten charged, is not the voice of Nat Turner but "the voice of William Styron." And the images are not the images of Nat Turner but "the images of William Styron. The confession is the confession of William Styron." According to them the fictional Nat Turner embodies "a lot of Styron's own personality." According to them his "selection of 'factual' and psychological material speaks for itself."[40]

Styron was stung by the criticisms of the Ten. Confronted with the furious reception of his *Confessions*, already dubious about critics, shy and uncomfortable as a public speaker, he was rarely very effective in his own defense. I was present in 1968 at a discussion of fiction and history among Styron, Robert Penn Warren, Ralph Ellison, and C. Vann Woodward. Eugene Genovese had organized the panel for the annual meeting of the Southern Historical Association. There Ellison defended Styron against the charges of racism and bigotry, and Woodward defended Styron against the charges that he had falsified history. But one of the Ten relentlessly taunted Styron from the audience: "I can remember that the last time I called you a liar, it became very bitter," he heckled. "It seems as though we confront each other from the North to the South. I met you in Massachusetts this summer, and now all the way down in New Orleans I'm here to call you a liar again." Inexperienced in such skilled polemics, Styron fell into his antagonist's trap, responding irritably that "indeed you have haunted me. You're my *bête noir*."[41]

At times Styron insisted ineptly on his fidelity to the evidence, despite considerable evidence to the contrary. At other times he responded to charges that he ignored historical scholarship by demanding "When were writers of historical novels obligated in any way to acknowledge the work of historians?" On such occasions he claimed impatiently that it is the "right and privilege" of the novelist "to substitute imagination for facts," that "if perfect accuracy had been my aim, I would have written a work of history rather than a novel." On another occasion he told an interviewer that "an obsession with absolute accuracy is impossible if you are writing a novel dealing with history. It becomes ridiculous, simply because you are writing a novel." Such a defense might have been more impressive had he not explicitly denied in his author's note to *The Confessions of Nat Turner* that it was a historical novel (a genre he considered "disreputable"). He called his book rather a "meditation on history" and boasted that he had not made up anything that ran counter to the evidence. "I have rarely departed from the *known* facts about Nat Turner and the revolt of which he was the leader," he wrote, and he said he had allowed himself to use "freedom of imagination in reconstructing events" only "in those areas where there is little knowledge in regard to Nat."[42]

Precisely what Styron meant by the term "meditation on history" is unclear. In a 1968 interview he conceded that "I've found that the phrase 'meditation on history' has buffaloed quite a few people, and I've never really been able to figure out just what I meant by it." If a "meditation on history" would be expected to bear a greater resemblance to historical reality than would an historical novel, Styron would seem to have flunked badly. In fact, he seems to have assumed that a "meditation on history" required lesser, rather than a greater, obligation of fidelity to the historical record. What he considered "known facts," for example, seems to have meant facts known to *him*; and "areas where there is little knowledge" seems to have referred merely to areas in which *he* had little knowledge. As he was writing the book, he bragged to interviewers of his having mastered the sources. The evidence consisted of Gray's *Confessions*, "a few little newspaper clippings of the time, all of them seemingly sort of halfway informed and hysterical and probably not very reliable," and a "biased book" published "seventy years after the event" by "a very proslavery" Virginia historian, one William S. Drewry. "Basically," he said, "these few are the only documents on the insurrection." It is true that evidence regarding Nat Turner is relatively scanty, but it is not quite so scanty as Styron assumed. It is true that the evidence is incomplete, but incomplete as it is, there is sufficient surviving historical evidence to suggest a rather different Nat Turner from the one depicted in his pages. Styron sought the historian's authority without the historian's discipline. As historian Bertram Wyatt-Brown put it, he "showed contempt for what historians must always demand—an attentiveness to accuracy and substantiation."[43]

Back and forth the controversy went, occasionally in civilized low key, more often at shrill pitch, depending on the temperaments of attackers and defenders. The most vigorous defense came not from the author himself, but from historian Eugene D. Genovese, who responded to the attacks with ample polemical skills of his own.[44] The Ten had insisted that "the historical data reveal the real Nat as commanding, virile, and courageous." Genovese retorted, "The historical data reveal no such thing. In fact, they do not reveal much at all about Nat Turner's qualities." Nor did Styron acknowledge that "the historical data" revealed any such virility, courage, and commanding qualities. "The facts tell us this," he said, "that if you examine the testimony, the original *Confessions*, any intelligent person is going to be appalled by this vision of a heroic figure, because he's not very heroic looking at all. He looks like a *nut* who gathers together several followers, plows through a county one evening, admittedly without even having devised a plan, and kills fifty-some white people, most of whom are helpless children. *Big Deal!* Fine hero." If Nat Turner's revolt was unable to kill the domestic institution, it killed something more vulnerable than its white victims. As historian William Freehling has observed, Turner's rebels murdered the "slaveholders' domestic illusions," and white Virginians "turned the Domestic Institution into an anti-domestic prison." The Virginia debate over slavery the following year resulted not in emancipation but in slavery being clamped even more tightly on the Old Dominion. The insurrection had resulted in catastrophe, not only for Nat Turner and of course for the white victims, but especially for the slaves. Genovese denied that Styron convicted Nat Turner of cowardice. "The inner conflict and pain can be interpreted as cowardice and irresolution by those who wish to do so," he wrote, "but this interpretation seems to me more revealing of its authors than of either Styron or the historical Turner." On the other hand, Genovese pronounced Gray's *Confessions* suspect. Gray was a disinherited and downwardly mobile white slaveholder who was hardly free of the passions stirred up by the rebellion. Turner's testimony to Gray was ambiguous evidence that could be read as "the reflections of one of those religious fanatics whose single-minded madness carried him to the leadership of a popular cause." Of course Nat Turner tried to make himself appear to Gray "as if he always knew what he was doing," Genovese noted, but under the circumstances could his testimony really be taken for anything more than the words of a man with "no wish to bare his innermost thoughts to the enemy?"[45]

Styron's critics had maintained that, far from being contemptuous of his fellow slaves, the historical Nat Turner was driven by love, not hatred, for his people. But Genovese insisted that Styron's Nat *had* expressed such love in the novel. Had he not loved his people, he "would not have protested so much against their weakness in the face of oppression; he could not even have perceived them as victims of oppression." His condemnation of them, Genovese believed, was "essentially a hatred for the oppression rather than for the oppressed." It was the kind hatred from which no revolutionary could ever be entirely free. Not even the fiery orator David Walker, whose "magnificent call for slave insurrection" in 1829 may have inspired Nat Turner's action, ever "feared to mix the professions of love for his people with the harshest condemnation," according to Genovese. "Why is it," Walker demanded, "that those few, weak, good for nothing whites are able to keep so many able men, one of whom can put to flight a dozen whites, in wretchedness and misery?" It was, he said, because blacks were "ignorant, abject, servile and mean—and the whites know it, they know that we are too servile to assert our rights as men—or they would not fool with us as they do." And "why do they not bring the inhabitants of Asia to be body servants to them?" he asked. "They know they would get their bodies rent and torn asunder from head to foot." That humanity, Genovese declared, the humanity of such a genuine revolutionary as David Walker, the "humanity of men capable of doubt and anguish," was what Styron gave to his Nat Turner.[46]

The Ten faulted Styron for ignoring Walker's *Appeal*, insisting that Nat must have "read and been inspired, yes inflamed" by the pamphlet they

regarded as "the most inflammatory indictment of slavery ever written."
For them, the question was why Styron did not motivate Nat Turner with
Walker's *Appeal.* "Was he unaware of it?" they asked. "Or was he trying to
give the impression that there was little evidence of unrest amongst the
black folk? And that Nat Turner was some kind of freak among his brethren?" Certainly at the time Virginia's Governor John Floyd, was "fully convinced" that Walker's "incendiary" pamphlet had been read from the
pulpits by "every black preacher, in the whole country east of the Blue
Ridge."[47]

It is true that many of the slaves in Styron's novel personify the kind
of stereotypical personality type that historian Stanley M. Elkins had described nearly a decade earlier as Sambo. Elkins, in his controversial 1959
book *Slavery,* drew a dramatic parallel between the experiences of slaves
on southern plantations and prisoners in Nazi concentration camps. He
concluded that the personality patterns of both slaves and prisoners had
been reshaped under the influence of powerful arbiters of life and death
who functioned as "perverse father figures." Accepting Bruno Bettelheim's
controversial interpretation of the behavior of concentration camp victims, Elkins portrayed the putative "dehumanization" of the Jewish prisoners   as   analogous   to   the   putative   "dehumanization"   of   the
African-American slaves. More concerned than any previous scholar with
the slave personality structure, he assumed that the "sanctions of the system were in themselves sufficient to produce a recognizable personality
type"—the Sambo type. After a generation of slavery, he believed the
conditioning process was simply a matter of raising children within the
new framework of enforced infantilism. So horrendous were the psychological effects of slavery, according to Elkins, that slaves lost their sense of
identity, became childlike, and adopted the values of their white masters.
Slaves not only *played* Sambo, he concluded, they actually *became* Sambos.
In time the *role* became the *self.*[48]

But it is not true that Styron's Nat Turner lives in Elkins's slave South.
Styron borrows only Elkins's Sambo characterization, not his harsh portrayal of the slave plantations as "concentration camps." Styron places his
Virginia slaves in a very different plantation setting, one more nearly
drawn from the work of an earlier historian, Ulrich B. Phillips. Elkins had
described slavery in the American South as "uniquely dehumanizing in its
effects on the enslaved" and had asserted that "no other form of slavery
so thoroughly deprived a slave of all the rights and responsibilities of
humanity." In his introduction to the second edition of *Slavery,* Elkins's
friend Nathan Glazer writes that American slavery was "the most awful the
world has ever known." But Phillips's slave regime had been "a curious
blend of force and concession, of arbitrary disposal by the master and self-
direction by the slave, of tyranny and benevolence, of antipathy and affection." Phillips's slave regime had been "a school for civilizing savages,"

a beneficent institution for both master and slave. Phillips had set the classic pattern for the scholarly defense of slavery in an interpretation that dominated the subject until the 1950s. Styron, promiscuously mixing Phillips's stereotyped stage settings with Elkins's stock characters, depicts his Nat living in a far more complex and varied slave South than the one depicted by either Elkins or Phillips.[49]

The Ten had lumped Phillips with Elkins into what they term "the Elkins-Phillips-Styron dream," with little apparent understanding that Phillips's and Elkins's depictions of slavery are diametrically opposed to each other. To them Phillips was "the classic apologist for slavery," and Elkins was "the sophisticated modern apologist." Styron might claim to be "meditating on history," they wrote, "but we are not fooled. We know that he is really trying to escape history." To the Ten, Nat Turner's insurrection was the culmination of a long and continuing black drive for freedom, a tradition of both active and passive resistance to slavery. And so to them Styron's omission of that drive and that tradition amounted to a denial of the central theme of black history.[50]

Styron reacted to the charge that he ignored evidence of the historical Nat Turner's black wife with a forthright denial: "There is not a shred of contemporary evidence—not a hint, not a single statement either in the original 'Confessions' or in the few newspaper accounts—to show that Nat Turner had a wife." With characteristic verve, historian Eugene Genovese came to Styron's defense by attacking the Ten Black Writers. He noted that they had attached great importance to Nat Turner's references in Gray's "Confessions" to his parents and to his grandmother. "How incredible, then," he declared, "that he failed to mention his wife. Perhaps she existed, perhaps not; perhaps she had some importance in his life, perhaps not. We do not know." He said that "the slim thread of evidence—or gossip" for "Turner's alleged black wife" dated from a secondary account "written thirty years after his death." William Styron had therefore "not falsified history by ignoring her." Styron agreed: "Gene Genovese is absolutely right when he puts down this myth about Nat's wife—that's one of the most idiotic of the criticisms."[51]

The secondary source Genovese referred to was an 1861 essay in the *Atlantic Monthly* by Thomas Wentworth Higginson, a radical abolitionist from Massachusetts, who claimed to have obtained his information from "contemporary newspapers." According to Higginson, the historical Nat Turner had a wife Cherry Turner, a daughter, and one or two sons. All were sold off after the revolt. We know, Higginson said, "that Nat Turner's young wife was a slave; we know that she belonged to a different master from himself." And, Higginson said, there was "one thing more which we do know of this young woman: the Virginia newspapers state that she was tortured under the lash, after her husband's execution, to make her produce his papers." Styron, who had apparently not read Higginson, blamed the uproar on "a fanatic named Howard Myer," who had written a biography of Higginson. "Myer quotes Higginson as saying—this is in 1860— that Nat Turner had a wife. Total hearsay."[52]

Another secondary source that Styron was familiar with, however, was *The Southampton Slave Insurrection*, by William S. Drewry, who reported that "Nat's son, Redic, survived him." Despite its having been written by an "unreconstructed Virginian" nearly three-quarters of a century after the rebellion, Styron had explicitly considered *The Southampton Slave Insurrection* a "valuable" source of "considerable information and detail." Why he doubted Drewry in this instance but not others he did not attempt to explain.[53]

Genovese and Styron were mistaken that there was "not a shred of contemporary evidence" for the existence of Nat Turner's wife, nor was her existence merely a matter of "gossip" or "total hearsay." There was in fact a letter, apparently from Governor John Floyd, published in the Richmond *Whig*, September 17, 1831, stating that "I have in my possession some papers given up by his wife under the lash."[54]

On the question of Margaret Whitehead, Styron responded to his critics in *The Nation* that "Nat Turner *was* hung up on Margaret Whitehead, bashing her brains out because of the same hatred and love and despair that make Americans today as then all hopelessly hung up—black and white—one with the other, wedded inseparably by the error and madness of history." In an interview he declared that Nat Turner "desired her; he wanted her. She represented to him all sorts of unnameable things." He conceded that he could not prove it, but he insisted that the "psychological truth" of his portrayal "lies in the fact that one often wishes to destroy what one most earnestly desires." If Styron's Nat lusts after the flesh, he is hardly the only preacher to have done so, either in fiction or in fact.[55]

The Ten had been especially angered by Styron's calling up the stereotype of the black beast by emphasizing rape in the rebellion. Styron had portrayed the rebel Will as a madman. The Will of William Styron's *Confessions* is not the Will of Thomas Gray's *Confessions*. According to Gray, Nat testified that Will had insisted to him that he would obtain his liberty or "lose his life." He said "his life was worth no more than others, and his liberty as dear to him." "That was enough," Nat said to Gray, "to put him in full confidence."[56]

Certainly, as historian Winthrop Jordan notes, "if ever insurrectionary slaves in the United States had good opportunity for ravishing white women, it was during the Nat Turner rebellion in 1831." Yet no sexual incidents are mentioned in the record of the trial. In all the anguished outpouring of public horror called forth by the bloody rebellion, no newspaper at the time seems even to have hinted at rape or attempted rape on the part of the rebels. In the midst of all the shocked denunciations of the violence, a report in the Richmond *Constitutional Whig* went to the trouble of pointing out that "it is not believed that any outrages were offered to the females."[57]

Thirty years after the Southampton County rebellion, the erstwhile abolitionist Thomas Wentworth Higginson published a brief history of the insurrection in the *Atlantic Monthly*. He declared that during the rebellion one fear, though it must have racked "many a husband and father," had been groundless. He reminded his readers that the rebels "had been systematically brutalized from childhood; they had been allowed no legalized or permanent marriage; they had beheld around them an habitual licentiousness, such as can scarcely exist except in a Slave State; some of them had seen their wives and sisters habitually polluted by the husbands and the brothers of these fair white women." Yet, he wrote, he had searched "through the Virginia newspapers of that time in vain for one charge of an indecent outrage on a woman against these triumphant and terrible slaves." When white women were "absolutely in their power," these brutalized men did not seize the opportunity to retaliate in kind. They committed "no gratuitous outrage beyond the death-blow itself, no insult, no mutilation." Wherever they went they killed men, women, and children impartially, sparing "nothing that had a white skin." As Higginson put it, "Wherever they went, there went death, and that was all."[58]

Sixty-nine years after the Nat Turner revolt, William S. Drewry, a historian Styron would later describe as an "unreconstructed Virginian," discussed his own interviews with people who claimed to remember the days of terror. "Some say that victims were murdered and no further outrages committed," he wrote, "but this is in error." Shrouding his words in the polite euphemisms of the time, he declared that "women were insulted." He said he had been told that "Nat offered protection to one beautiful girl if she would consent to be his wife, but death was to this noble woman a blessing in comparison with such a prospect."[59]

The Ten had resented what they considered Styron's attempts to undercut Nat Turner's credentials as a heroic military commander. In Styron's *Confessions* Nat is made to say, "all strength had left me, my arms were like jelly"; and when he tries to kill he "missed by half a foot." According to Turner's own testimony to Gray, one of the rebels observed that the leader "must spill the first blood." Thus, "armed with a hatchet, and accompanied by Will, I entered my master's chamber." But, "it being dark, I could not give a death blow." Nat's hatchet glanced off Travis's head. "He sprang from the bed and called his wife," Nat told Gray; but "it was his last word," for "Will laid him dead, with a blow of his axe." At another house Nat chose a woman to be his victim. "I struck her several blows over the head, but not being able to kill her, as the sword was dull. Will turning around and discovering it, dispatched her also." Styron maintained that "it was quite clear to me that he was unable to kill. In his confession, he says more than once that the sword glanced off a head or that the sword was dull and he could not kill. Now this seems to me a patent evasion." As Genovese reads Turner's testimony, the rebel leader "hit a defenseless man on the head with a hatchet and could not kill him; he hit a woman on the head with a sword and could not kill her." According to the Ten, however, Nat failed to kill his master because it was dark and his hatchet glanced, and he failed to kill the woman because his sword was dull and light. Genovese notes wryly that "neither darkness nor inferior weapons kept his associates from doing better."[60]

The Ten had objected to Styron's portraying the caged Nat Turner as being rueful and penitent, contending that he went to his grave without remorse for what he had done. The Governor of Virginia had noted that all the insurrectionists "died bravely indicating no reluctance to lose their lives in such a cause." But Higginson, on whom the Ten had relied for other data, portrayed Nat after the murders in a manner remarkably similar to Styron's depiction:

> Now the blood was shed, the risk was incurred, his friends were killed or captured, and all for what? Lasting memories of terror, to be sure, for his oppressors; but, on the other hand, hopeless failure for the insurrection, and certain death for him. What a watch he must have kept that night! To that excited imagination, which had always seen spirits in the sky and blooddrops on the corn and hieroglyphic marks on the dry leaves, how full the lonely forest must have been of signs and solemn warnings! Alone with the fox's bark, the rabbit's rustle, and the screech-owl's scream, the self-appointed prophet brooded over his despair.

But according to Thomas Gray, who had asked Nat in prison, "Do you not find yourself mistaken now?" Nat had answered, "Was not Christ crucified?" Upon his arraignment, Nat refused to plead guilty, "saying to his counsel, that he did not feel so." Virginia authorities regarded the prisoner's appearance to be "not remarkable, his nose is flat, his stature rather small, and hair very thin, without any peculiarity of expression." Gray, on the other hand, said he looked upon Nat Turner's "calm, deliberate composure, and my blood curdled in my veins."[61]

The Ten did not find credible the last-minute confession of Styron's Nat that he would have spared at least one white person. According to them, the rebels had determined that "neither age nor sex was to be spared," and they had not made any exceptions. But in fact, as the governor of Virginia wrote to the governor of South Carolina, Nat Turner did spare a family of poor whites: "They spared but one family and that one was *so* wretched as to be in all respects upon a par with them."[62]

The Ten did not write as temperate scholars seeking to set the record straight with patient citations to verifiable evidence, but as political activists, as clever polemicists who made their way through Styron's novel with scathing distaste. Their discourse was marked by an unnecessary tone of personal invective that embarrassed even some of their allies. Their indictment of William Styron as a perpetrator of fraud and deception was quite overt; they imputed to the author not only a lack of historical or literary merit but also moral turpitude. They professed to "catch him red-handed manipulating evidence," and they accused him of deliberately deceiving the public about the true nature of slavery in general and Nat Turner in particular. According to the censorious Ten, Styron had created a character filled with his own white neuroses and the degrading character traits of his own white bigotry. According to them, his selection of "the types of psychological material which appear to emasculate and degrade Nat Turner and his people" betrayed both "obvious" and "subtle" exhibitions of white racist attitudes. According to them, Styron, as a white Virginian raised in a racist society, "is not free from the impact of its teachings." According to them, he "has not been able to transcend his southern peckerwood background." In their opinion, Styron's *Confessions* was "a throwback to the racist writing of the 1930s and 1940s."[63]

According to Styron, Genovese's "counterattack" in the *New York Review of Books* had "effectively demolished my critics." Not only that, but he had done it "with such lofty outrage that the effect was like that of a catharsis." Genovese, he believed, had "disposed of the case once and for all." He had done no such thing. Despite the strident, almost hysterical tone of their criticism, the Ten Black Writers had made a strong case against Styron's representation of Nat Turner. Much of their indictment was on target in that Styron's book rested upon a weak historical foundation. Reading Styron's *Confessions*, one was uncomfortably aware of his having borrowed characters, events, and language from history without quite giving them vitality. Stripped of its layers of invented detail, much of the factual substance of Styron's *Confessions* stood rather painfully reduced.[64]

If Styron had failed at the challenge of creating a historically accurate Turner, what about the Ten Black Writers? Were they not also guilty of creating a Nat Turner for a specific audience? Were they not also guilty of projecting their own psychic needs upon their construction as surely as did William Styron? They had certainly corrected some of Styron's numerous errors of fact. And in cases in which Gray's *Confessions* lent itself to more than one interpretation, they certainly interpreted the evidence differently. But their version of history, like Styron's, was painfully ill-informed. They apparently entertained the delusion that historical research consisted of no more than reading *American Negro Slave Revolts*, Herbert Aptheker's 1937 master's thesis, ultimately published in 1966. In fact, their construction of Nat Turner did not even purport to rest upon historical sources so much as upon folkloric ones, upon an image they claimed to exist in "the living traditions of black America." This image is an invented tradition. It is certainly not supported by any evidence in the scores of collections or analyses of authentic field-recorded African-American oral tradition. Indeed, their construction of a powerful, commanding Nat Turner is far more nearly in the image of the Paul Bunyans and the frontier boasters of white folklore than in that of the great tricksters—Anansi, Buh Rabbit, and High John de conquer—that have been so characteristic of African and African-American folklore. The tricksters, whether animal or human, overcome larger and more powerful critters not by using their physical force but by using their intellect.[65]

There is, to be sure, evidence about Nat Turner in both forms of the so-called slave narratives: the memoirs of escaped slaves and the interviews with ex-slaves conducted in the 1930s by the Federal Writers Project. But this evidence does not seem to have been used by either Styron or the Ten Black Writers, or indeed, by anyone else. It certainly does not provide much support for the constructions of either Styron or the Ten. In fact, if it could be verified, some of the evidence of the WPA interviews would seem to contradict both Styron and the Ten, and most other sources as well.

According to self-emancipated slave Henry Clay Bruce, the rebellion caused "no little sensation amongst the slaveholders." Allen Crawford, a former slave interviewed in 1937 in North Emporia, Virginia, described the rebellion vividly. "It started out on a Sunday night," he said. "Fust place he got to was his mistress' house. Said God 'dained him to start the fust war with forty men. When he got to his mistress' house he commence to grab him missus baby and he took hit up, slung hit back and fo'h three times. Said hit was so hard for him to kill dis baby 'cause hit had bin so playful setting on his knee and dat chile sho did love him. So third sling he went quick 'bout hit—killing baby at dis rap." The rebels then went to another house, according to Crawford, and "went through orchard, going to the house—met a school mistress—killed her."[66] Crawford's testimony—based on family memories of his Uncle Henry, who was hanged as one of the insurrectionists—differs from Gray's purported "Confessions of Nat Turner" and other sources that contend Nat Turner only killed Margaret Whitehead, a detail that plays a pivotal role in Styron's novel.

Another Virginia slave remembered well the fear of the white folks. According to Fannie Berry, "I can remember my mistress, Miss Sara Ann, coming to de window an' hollering, 'De niggers is arisin', De niggers is arisin', De niggers is killin' all de white folks—killin' all de babies in de cradle!' " Harriet Jacobs wrote in her memoirs, *Incidents in the Life of a Slave Girl,* that she thought it strange that the whites should be so frightened "when their slaves were so 'contented and happy'!"[67]

As news of Nat Turner's murderous foray spread, the slaveholders forbade their slaves to hold meetings among themselves. Charity Bowery, a former slave born in 1774 near Pembroke, North Carolina, recalled in an interview with abolitionist Lydia Maria Child published during the 1830s that "all the colored folks were afraid to pray in the time of old Prophet Nat. There was no law about it; but the whites reported it round among themselves that, if a note was heard, we should have some dreadful punishment; and after that, the low whites would fall upon any slaves they heard praying, or singing a hymn, and often killed them before their masters or mistresses could get to them." Nevertheless, as former slave James Lindsay Smith recalled, "notwithstanding our difficulties, we used to steal away to some of the quarters to have our meetings." Charity Bowery recalled a hymn from that period from the white hymnbooks:

> A few more beatings of the wind and rain,
> Ere the winter will be over—
> Glory, Hallelujah!

> Some friends has gone before me,—
> I must try to go and meet them
> Glory, Hallelujah!

> A few more risings and settings of the sun,
> Ere the winter will be over—
> Glory, Hallelujah!

> There's a better day a coming—
> There's a better day a coming—
> Glory, Hallelujah!

"They would't let us sing that," Bowery testified. "They would't let us sing that. They thought we was going to *rise*, because we sung 'better days are coming.' "[68]

The day following the insurrection, the Virginia militia was mustered to search the quarters of all slaves and free blacks. Harriet Jacobs said the militia planted false evidence to implicate some slaves in the rebellion. She claimed, "The searchers scattered powder and shot among their clothes, and then sent other parties to find them, and bring them forward as proof that they were plotting insurrection." Allen Crawford recalled that "Blues and Reds—name of soldiers—met at a place called Cross Keys, right down here at Newsome's Depot. Dat's whar they had log fires made and every one dat was Nat's man was taken bodily by two men who catch you and hold yer bare feet to dis blazing fire 'til you tole all you know'd 'bout dis killing." In the wake of the Turner insurrection, Henry Box Brown wrote in his memoirs, many slaves were "half-hung, as it was termed—that is, they were suspended from some tree with a rope about their necks, so adjusted as not quite to strangle them—and then they were pelted by men and boys with rotten eggs." The air was filled with shrieks and shouts. Harriet Jacobs said she "saw a mob dragging along a number of colored people, each white man, with his musket upraised, threatening instant death if they did not stop their shrieks." Jacobs could not contain her indignation. "What a spectacle was that for a civilized country!" she exclaimed. "A rabble, staggering under intoxication, assuming to be the administrators of justice!"[69]

According to Crawford, "Ole Nat was captured at Black Head Sign Post, near Cortland, Virginia—Indian town. He got away. So after a little Nat found dem on his trail so he went back near to the Travis place whar he fust started killing and he built a cave and made shoes in this cave. He came out night fur food dat slaves would give him from his own missus plantation." After about a month Nat Turner's hiding place was discovered, and he was taken into custody. Turner's captors, Crawford said, "brought him to Peter Edward's farm. 'Twas at this farm whar I was born. Grandma ran out and struck Nat in the mouth, knocking the blood out and asked him, 'Why did you take my son away?' In reply Nat said, 'Your son was as willing to go as I was.' It was my Uncle Henry dat they was talking about." Then, Crawford said, Virginia "passed a law to give the rest of the niggers a fair trial and Nat, my Uncle Henry, and others dat was caught was hanged."[70]

Charity Bowery recalled that "the brightest and best men were killed in Nat's time. Such ones are always suspected." After Nat Turner's revolt, slaveholders became much exercised over the question of what privileges—if any—they should grant to their slaves. Jamie Parker, a self-emancipated former slave, reported that the slaveholders finally decided that fewer privileges for slaves would afford "less cause for insurrections."[71]

Granting that Styron's Nat Turner is not the historical Nat Turner, and acknowledging that his exercise in blurring genres may have been misguided, even conceding that the author brought some of his troubles on himself by trying to wriggle out from under the "historical novel" label,[72] it would seem willful blindness not to reconsider the shallowness of evaluating a novel as though it were a historical monograph. With some misgivings about attempting literary pronouncements, one might at least say that the question of the book's ultimate standing is more likely to rest upon its literary qualities than upon its historical ones.

No one who has read Styron's earlier books will be surprised to find in *The Confessions of Nat Turner* persistent themes that have been at the center of his consciousness throughout his career. His novels are almost obsessively preoccupied with the polarities of power and submission, of authority and subservience, of being and nothingness; with conflicts between fundamentalism and skepticism; with the destruction of innocence by time and experience, with the loss of childhood's naive faith in an ordered and benevolent world; and, perhaps, above all, with the power of guilt and the possibility of redemption. His novels are all narrated in an almost biblical rhetoric of storytelling. His novels all reveal an intense and deeply religious sensibility. For Styron's protagonists to be saved, their existence demands justification by faith, whether faith in themselves or in something beyond self.[73]

Not only are Styron's persistent themes reiterated in his *Confessions*, but his Nat Turner is created in the image of the generic Styron hero-victim of the earlier novels, doomed to wrestle with the most profound existential questions. One can hardly miss the resemblance of Styron's Nat Turner to his Captain Mannix in *The Long March*, another awkward and unwilling rebel who defies the tyranny of another authoritarian institution, in his case the United States Marine Corps. "Even Mannix," Styron writes, "was aware that his gestures were not symbolic, but individual, therefore hopeless, maybe even absurd." One can hardly miss the resemblance of Styron's Nat Turner to his Cass Kinsolving in *Set This House on Fire*, who, like Nat, chooses being rather than nothingness. A would-be painter enslaved to alcoholism rather than to the Peculiar Institution, he is subjected to all sorts of public indignities by his boorish patron Mason Flagg in exchange for the liquor that helps him hang on. Feeling "sick as a dog inside my soul," but unable to figure out "where that sickness came from," he stumbles through a cycle of drunken depravity followed by spiritual retching in Styron's complex narrative of the terror of guilt and the horror of freedom. Ultimately, however, when Flagg rapes a young Italian girl, Cass kills him. "To choose between them," he says, "is simply to choose being, not for the sake of being, or even for the love of being, much less the desire to be forever—but in the hope of being what I could be for a time."[74]

In his first novel, *Lie Down in Darkness*, Styron evokes a world of complex, half-conscious feelings and perceptions of being and non-being. In a stunning Joycean interior monologue, his heroine-victim Peyton Loftis looks back over her life before she ends it. Locked in a stream of memories from which the sole escape is drowning in the airless void of time, she strips herself to what she calls "this lovely shell" of her naked body, and plunges out the window to her death on the street below. "Perhaps I shall rise at another time, though I lie down in darkness and have my light in ashes." Birds, symbolizing her sexual guilt and her yearning for freedom, haunt Peyton throughout the novel; and their wings rustle over her death.[75]

The predominant image of Peyton's last moments is drowning, but Styron also uses water as a symbol of rebirth. The strange epilogue of *Lie Down in Darkness* is dominated by the baptismal rites of Daddy Faith, an African-American evangelist. Styron represents black Christians immersed and purified in the waters of life with a power and glory in dramatic contrast to the pity and terror of Peyton's plunge into death. Styron depicts the joy and faith of the black Christians (qualities conspicuously absent from the lives of his white characters) with great respect, even as he evokes the image of "a crazy colored preacher howling those tremendously moving verses from Isaiah 40."[76] It is an image, at least on the surface, not altogether unlike his "crazy colored preacher" revolutionary in *The Confessions of Nat Turner*.

The Ten Black Writers accused Styron of constructing a Nat Turner more autobiographical than historical, a Nat Turner representing his own character traits. According to them, the fictional Nat Turner embodied "a lot of Styron's own personality." According to them, "the voice in this confession is the voice of William Styron. The images are the images of William Styron. The confession is the confession of William Styron." They are not, of course, entirely mistaken. To some extent all fiction is autobiographical in that the created characters necessarily must come from the author's own experience and imagination. How could it be otherwise? The actions, attitudes, and emotions of any fictional character are first created within the consciousness of the writer. As Eudora Welty notes, "any writer is in part all of his characters. How otherwise would they be known to him, occur to him, become what they are?" Styron did not deny that he endowed his created Nat Turner with a personality very much like his own: "I wrote part of Nat as a projection of my own character, of course, like any creation of a writer, but he had to differ from the historical figure as we know him." The novel is written in what Styron calls "first person filtered through my own consciousness and my own thought processes. Actually, Nat is *me* in many of his responses to his life and environment."[77]

If Styron's Nat is autobiographical in his inward and most deeply felt responses, in his outward identity he is more nearly patterned after James Baldwin. Styron and Baldwin—the grandson of a slaveholder and the grandson of a slave—were close friends. From late fall of 1960 until early summer of 1961 Baldwin had lived in Styron's Connecticut studio. Although Baldwin's first novel, *Go Tell It On the Mountain*, was admired in literary circles, he was not yet a celebrity. A mutual friend had asked the Styrons to give Baldwin a place to stay, as he was having financial problems at the time. The "frightfully cold winter" of 1960 was "a good time for the Southern writer, who had never known a black man on intimate terms, and the Harlem-born writer, who had known few Southerners (black or white), to learn something, to learn something about each other." Baldwin inherited vivid images of slavery times passed down from his grandfather to his father. "Because he was wise," Styron wrote of his friend, "Jimmy understood the necessity of dealing with the preposterous paradoxes that had dwelled at the heart of the racial tragedy—the unrequited loves as well as the murderous furies." Styron, by his own testimony struggling to emancipate himself from "the prejudices and suspicions that a Southern upbringing engenders," considered himself "by far the greater beneficiary."[78]

Styron's Nat, at least in his outward experiences, would seem to be modeled as much on Baldwin's fictional heroes as on Baldwin himself. Baldwin represents rejection as the very essence of the black experience in America. But he approaches that essence by means of an extended metaphor of African Americans as the bastard children of American civilization. Johnny Grimes in Baldwin's *Go Tell It On the Mountain* is an archetypal image of the bastard black child. Rejected by whites for reasons he cannot understand, he is afflicted by an overwhelming sense of shame, the most destructive consequence of rejection. There must be something mysteriously wrong with him, Johnny reasons, to account for his rejection. Like Styron's Nat, Baldwin's Johnny undergoes an ecstatic and trance-like conversion experience. But not even African-American religious ritual is free of the corrosive effects of racial rejection. As Baldwin notes, it is saturated in color symbolism. "Wash me, cried the slave to his Maker, and I shall be whiter, whiter than snow! For black is the color of evil; only the robes of the saved are white."[79]

Even the surreal spiritual visions of Styron's Nat have their counterparts in the religious fantasies of Baldwin's Johnny. As he lies before the altar in the depths of despair, Johnny's "ears were opened to this sound that came from the darkness. . . . It was a sound of rage and weeping . . . rage that had no language, weeping with no voice—which yet spoke now . . . of boundless melancholy, of the bitterest patience, and the longest night; of the deepest water, the strongest chains, the most cruel lash; of humility most wretched, the dungeon most absolute, of love's bed defiled, and birth dishonored, and most bloody, unspeakable, sudden death. Yes, the darkness hummed with murder . . . ?"[80] The victim of prolonged emotional rejection cannot escape its effects. The normal human personality will defend himself with hatred and dreams of vengeance. It may lose forever the capacity for love. Certainly Styron's Nat Turner would have had no difficulty understanding Baldwin's bitter and violent jazz drummer, Rufus Scott, the hero of book I of his *Another Country*, who sublimates his hatred by beating on the white skin of his drums.[81]

Styron may well have modeled Nat's relationship to an absent father on Baldwin's relationship to his own father and, perhaps even more, to his spiritual father, Richard Wright. According to Styron, "Jimmy once told me that he often thought the degradation of his grandfather's life was the animating force behind his father's apocalyptic, often incoherent rage." Baldwin's father, a Harlem preacher whom he described as "fanatical," left "a terrifying imprint on his son's life." He had died in 1943, and within a year Baldwin had met Wright for the first time. It is clear from his essays that the 20-year-old Baldwin adopted the older man as a father figure. He also transferred his habit of defining himself in opposition to his father to the new relationship. Wright had elevated protest fiction to a new level, thus Baldwin would launch his own career with a rebellious essay called "Everybody's Protest Novel." Baldwin suppressed his own prophetic strain while Wright lived, but upon Wright's death in 1960, he could *become* his father. Baldwin soon ventured out on the lecture circuit, where "with his ferocious oratory," Styron notes, "he began to scare his predominantly well-to-do, well-meaning audiences out of their pants."[82]

Styron's Nat has other sources in African-American literary tradition. With no disposition to downplay significant differences between Richard

Wright's Bigger Thomas and William Styron's Nat Turner, striking parallels are inescapable. Wright in *Native Son* creates in Bigger a protagonist who, like Nat, broods over the dissonance between subservience and freedom: "We black and they white. They got things and we ain't. They do things and we can't. It's just like living in jail. Half the time I feel like I'm on the outside of the world peeping in through a knot-hole in the fence." Like Nat, Bigger finds fulfillment in violently defying the legal and moral codes of the society that oppresses him. Like Nat, his victim is a kindhearted young girl who is "friendly to Negroes." Wright represents Bigger's sickness as beyond the reach of mere kindness. His employers, the Daltons, are "good" people who hire him because they "want to give Negroes a chance." They are as innocent and as guilty as Styron's Samuel Turner. Styron's Nat and Wright's Bigger would seem to be violent twins, turning upon themselves in tautological fury, driven by what Baldwin called a "complementary faith among the damned," a faith that leads them at last to impel "into the arena of the actual those fantastic crimes of which they have been accused, achieving their vengeance and their own destruction through making the nightmare real."[83]

The most controversial component of Styron's *Confessions*, the component that infuriated his critics more than anything else, the component that called forth their most unmeasured epithets of contempt, was his representation of Nat's imagined sexual attraction to white women. "It was always a nameless white girl," he muses, "between whose legs I envisioned myself—a young girl with golden curls." He is particularly attracted to Margaret Whitehead, the only person he will actually kill personally. As Styron depicts it, Nat desires to fill his future victim with "warm milky spurts of desecration" or, in another instance, to repay the "pity" and "compassion" of a weak white woman with "outrageous spurts of defilement" and produce in her "the swift and violent immediacy of a pain of which I was complete overseer."[84]

If Nat's sexual attraction manifests white racist attitudes, however, what is one to make of Rufus Scott's love-hate desire for white women in Baldwin's *Another Country*? As he has sex with a white woman, Rufus fumes to himself that "nothing could have stopped him, not the white God himself nor a lynch mob arriving on wings. Under his breath he cursed the milk-white bitch and groaned and rode his weapon between her thighs." If Nat's sexual attraction manifests white racist attitudes, what is one to make of Bigger Thomas's rape and murder of Mary Dalton in Wright's *Native Son*? Even as he felt "a sense of physical elation" for this young woman who "did not hate him with the hate of other white people," even as he "watched her with a mingled feeling of helplessness, admiration, and hate," he thought to himself, "This little bitch!" He reflected that "she was white and he hated her." And after he had killed her, "he did not feel sorry for Mary; she was not real to him, not a human being." However unhistorical his construction of Nat Turner may have been, William Styron invested his protagonist with considerably more humanity and sensitivity than James Baldwin and Richard Wright bestowed upon Nat's counterparts. And if Nat's sexual attraction manifests white racist attitudes, what is one to make of the real life experiences of Eldridge Cleaver, for whom raping white women became a deliberate expression, both symptom and symbol of his dehumanization? "I became a rapist," he writes in *Soul on Ice*, published the year after Styron's *Confessions*. He raped, he said, "deliberately, willfully, methodically." He raped as a way of "getting revenge." He raped as "an insurrectionary act. It delighted me that I was defying and trampling upon the white man's law."[85]

Baldwin's Rufus Scott and Wright's Bigger Thomas are endowed with no such articulate self-understanding as Styron's Nat Turner. Wright stresses his protagonist's ignorance and his self-centered inability to perceive the humanity of whites: "To Bigger and his kind white people were not really people; they were a sort of gray natural force, like the stormy sky looming overhead." Killing Mary Dalton fills Bigger not with shame but with elation, with a sense of exhilaration, with a sense of purpose that transcends the meaninglessness of his former existence. "He had murdered and had created a new life for himself. It was something that was all his own. It was the first time in his life he had had anything that others could not take from him."[86]

A character in African-American fiction who *does* possess the kind of articulate self-understanding with which Styron endows his Nat Turner is the unnamed protagonist of Ralph Ellison's *Invisible Man*. But even he strikes out in a "frenzy" in response to an insult on a dark street, knocking his white tormenter to the ground. "In my outrage I got out my knife and prepared to slit his throat." Even Ellison's hero feels a generalized hatred of whites, believing in his soul that all black tragedies come from the same source. "You ache with the need to convince yourself that you do exist in the real world, that you're a part of all the sound and anguish, and you strike out with your fists, you curse and you swear to make them recognize you."[87] But Styron makes his Nat Turner a man capable of willed choice, and, therefore, he achieves a transcendence over the degradation of his enslavement. He shows that even in the worst circumstances a degraded state may be transcended. Does he really embody a stereotype more negative than the characters created by such African-American writers as Wright and Ellison?

However imperfectly Styron may have portrayed the Nat Turner revolt, few other American writers have made any effort to treat a slave insurrection at all. One who tried was Herman Melville. In some minor ways, Styron's novel echoes Melville's "Benito Cereno," the story of a shipboard slave rebellion, published in 1856. Like Melville, Styron is fascinated by the evil of slavery and what he sees as its inevitable connection with violence and corruption. But in Melville's slave rebellion there is still a memory of innocence. For Styron's Nat there is neither innocence nor redemption. From the corruptions of childhood, he acts out his damnation, moving hesitantly but relentlessly toward his revolutionary bloodbath. And Styron is different from Melville in another and more significant way. "Benito Cereno" is viewed entirely from a white perspective—that of the Yankee skipper Captain Amasa Delano. Styron at least tries to see Nat Turner's rebellion through Nat Turner's eyes. In the tragic encounter between sentimental and comic stereotypes, Melville seems as baffled by the behavior of his black rebels as is his protagonist. Delano is prepared to believe almost any evil of such a spiritually wasted European aristocrat as the slaveholder Benito Cereno. But the New Englander refuses to credit "the imputation of malign evil in man" to such simple and jolly primitives as he believes blacks to be. The fact that barbarous sadists lurk behind their masquerades makes the problem of slavery and slave revolts an exotic one for Melville, and makes "Benito Cereno" into a gothic horror tale.[88]

In the same year Harriet Beecher Stowe published her own fictional treatment of a slave revolt. *Dred* never had as much impact as her *Uncle Tom's Cabin*, with its melodramatic scenes of Eliza crossing the ice, the death of Little Eva, or Uncle Tom's brutal beating at the hands of Simon Legree. In *Dred* her rebellious slave protagonist is based in part on Nat Turner. But unlike Styron's Nat, Stowe's Dred is represented as a brutish madman, and his anticipated insurrection is prompted by a twisted perversion of biblical prophecy. Stowe is betrayed by her inability to construct believable black characters who are neither servile nor insane. She manipulates her plot so that Dred dies before receiving the heavenly sign that would precipitate the bloody insurrection. Thus, unlike Styron, she avoids having to consider either the deeper motivations or the deeper results of the revolution. And, unlike Styron, she opts for a sentimental ending in which her slaves and their white sympathizers go north to freedom.[89]

A more impressive novel about a slave conspiracy was Arna Bontemps's *Black Thunder*, published in 1936. Like Styron's Nat, Bontemps's protagonist is based on an actual historical figure, Gabriel Prosser, who led an abortive slave rebellion near Richmond in the summer of 1800, the year Nat Turner was born. In *Black Thunder* he constructed a narrative of men and women desperate enough to seek a revolution. "Anything that's equal to a gray squirrel," they believe, "want to be free. A wild bird what's in a cage will die anyhow, sooner or later," they conclude. "He'll pine hisself to death. He just as well break his neck trying to get out." Bontemps's Gabriel is "too old for joy, too young for despair." He is ready to write history with his life. One may or may not lose one's life striking out for freedom; but since slavery is inevitably a living death, what have slaves to lose? Thus, like Nat Turner, Gabriel leads an uprising against the slaveholders. His insurrection, however, is sparked not by a longstanding hatred of enslavement carefully nurtured over the years (as in the case of Nat Turner), but by an immediate cause, by an unusually cruel punishment visited upon a mischievous slave. Also unlike Styron's Nat, Bontemps's Gabriel finds supporters not only within the slave community but also among free persons of color and even among some white sympathizers. And Gabriel's uprising comes much closer to success than did Nat Turner's. Only the intervention of a torrential rainstorm and a last-minute betrayal prevent the rebels from seizing Richmond. As in the case of Nat Turner, the rebellion is suppressed, the leaders are captured, and white Virginians visit blind and bloody retribution on the slaves. And the courageous but defeated hero Gabriel, like Nat Turner, pays for his love of freedom with his life. Unlike Styron's choice to write in the persona of Nat Turner, however, Bontemps chooses to tell Gabriel's story from a constantly shifting point of view, focusing in progressive chapters on the various participants, in the manner of John Dos Passos, forcing readers to collate the various perspectives themselves.[90]

William Styron might have spared himself considerable pain and humiliation had he fictionalized more rather than less. The inevitable accompaniment of Styron's choice was black fury. Without question the most offensive of Styron's faults to the Ten was his assuming the persona of Nat Turner, his writing about Nat Turner in the first person. From a literary standpoint no less than from an historical standpoint, Styron's choice was selfdefeating, fatally undermining the tragic potential of his novel.

It need not have been so. Styron has been (perhaps inevitably) compared to William Faulkner. But it was not one of Faulkner's books but Robert Penn Warren's *All the King's Men* that was the turning point in Styron's efforts to realize himself as a novelist: Styron had before him Warren, a distinguished example of how to avoid corrupting the construction of an historical figure with one's own personality. The book made an extraordinary, unforgettable impact on Styron when he first read it. "The book itself was a revelation and gave me a shock to brain and spine like a freshet of icy water," he wrote. "I had of course read many novels before, including many of the greatest, but this powerful and complex story embedded in prose of such fire and masterful imagery—this, I thought with growing wonder, this was what a novel was all about, this was *it*, the bright book of life, what writing was supposed to be." He completed the book, he said, "in a trance, knowing once and for all that I, too, however falteringly and incompletely, must try to work such magic."[91]

It is obvious that Warren's protagonist, Willie Stark, is modeled in some respects on the colorful Louisiana politician Huey Long. But as a novelist, Warren, while following the general outlines of Long's career, is free to create a Willie Stark who does not resemble Huey Long in every particular. Furthermore, in *All the King's Men* Warren assumes the persona not of Willie but of a failed history graduate student named Jack Burden. Some critics—noting that Warren never finished his Ph.D. either and that his first book was a pedestrian attempt at historical biography—find in Jack

Burden more than a trace of Red Warren himself. In many of his vacillating responses to his life and his environment, Jack Burden is Robert
Penn Warren. At least, so the argument goes. Whatever the source of Jack
Burden's personality—and it should be remembered that Warren, after
all, created the personalities of *all* his characters in the novel—the enhanced perspective of Burden's introspective consciousness strengthens
rather than weakens *All the King's Men.*[92]

Not only did Styron have an obvious authorial model in Warren, he
had an obvious candidate for the author's persona in the character of
Thomas Gray, the lawyer to whom the historical Nat Turner dictated his
jail cell "Confessions." Although he had once lived on an eight-hundred-
acre estate worked by twenty-one slaves, young Thomas Gray by 1831 was
disinherited and down to three hundred acres and one slave. He risked
social ostracism to defend four of the insurrectionary slaves. Here was an
inviting figure for Styron to endow with his own hesitations and vacilla-
tions, with his own ambivalence between an abstract commitment to justice and a very personal and concrete love for Virginia and its people.
Here was an ambiguous but fascinating figure in whom to embody historical and literary anachronisms and contradictions.[93]

But ultimately neither historical nor literary considerations dictated Styron's choice to write of Nat Turner from within. One of the states of mind
from which art may spring is an urgent sense of moral crisis. In "This
Quiet Dust," an article he wrote for *Harper's* in 1965, two years before *The
Confessions,* Styron reflected on what he thought and felt upon returning
to the Virginia tidewater. The returning native saw much that he had
missed before. "My boyhood experience," he wrote, "was the typically ambivalent one of most native Southerners, for whom the Negro is simultaneously taken for granted and as an object of unending concern." He had
come to realize that "the Southern white's boast that he 'knows' the Negro" is not true. "An unremarked paradox of Southern life is that its racial
animosity is really grounded not upon friction and propinquity but upon
an almost complete lack of contact." But that lack of understanding would
no longer suffice for a man of conscience in 1965. "To come to *know* the
Negro," Styron concluded, "has become the moral imperative of every
white Southerner." Thus his search for Nat Turner, his attempt "to recreate and bring alive that dim and prodigious black man," was his effort
to respond to that moral imperative.[94]

How can the strange career of Nat Turner as man and as symbol be
summarized? Styron's dilemma was the ambiguity of Nat Turner, and the
dilemma is doubly ironic in Turner's appearing to be what he must but
cannot become—a symbol rather than a human being. Styron's choice,
to assume the persona of his protagonist, was a choice to treat his protagonist as a human being rather than as a symbol. If Styron's Nat is at times
uncertain, he is hardly alone; many of the greatest leaders have hesitated.
It is not difficult to think of either fictional or historical counterparts.

Much of the controversy over Styron's *Confessions* was characterized by rival sets of clichés. One set of them tiresomely reiterated Styron's failures of historical accuracy. The other tiresomely reiterated Styron's right as a novelist to make up his own characters and plots any way he wanted to. Each position was, in its own way, equally correct and equally irrelevant. Whatever the therapeutic value of such pronouncements, the issues were considerably more complex than either Styron, his attackers, or his defenders were willing to concede. Styron's imagination desired the novelist's freedom to create recalcitrant details rather than the historian's responsibility to uncover them. It is sometimes a source of great insight, sometimes of egregious error. Robert Penn Warren phrases it memorably, "the autonomy of the art is always subject to the recalcitrance of the materials," to which Ralph Ellison responds: "Yes. And I'm all for the autonomy of fiction; that's why I say that novelists should leave history alone." Efforts to recreate historical figures, Ellison says, "are *poison* to the novelist; he shouldn't bother them. Don't appropriate the names. Don't move into the historian's arena, because you can only be slaughtered there." Readers bring certain perspectives to their response to any book. Those informed by knowledge of the historical Nat Turner bring to Styron's *Confessions* a different cultural competence from those uninformed by any such knowledge, and thus a different reading position that allows them to activate the meaning of the book in ways beyond the reach of those whose cultural competence allows them to read the book only as fiction. As C. Vann Woodward noted in another connection, "Omniscience and mind reading are part of the novelist's license and are regularly used in writing of fictional characters without special cause for wonder." It is only "when the same license is used about real people, historical people we know a great deal about" that the "constant juxtaposition and confusion of the real and the imagined gives the historian chills and fever, whether or not he shares the entertainment enjoyed by the laity."[95]

Styron, like William Faulkner before him, endows his protagonist with contradictory characteristics. According to Ralph Ellison, Faulkner built upon "the Southern mentality" in which blacks were "dissociated" into "malignant" and "benign" stereotypes. Although Faulkner was "more willing perhaps than any other artist" to "seek out the human truth" hidden behind such stereotypes, his usual method was to create "characters embodying both." Similarly, Styron endows his protagonist with both benign and malignant characteristics, with elements from both prevailing stereotypes. But in some interesting ways his Nat Turner derives less from the stereotypes than from the wise old grandfather in Ellison's *The Invisible Man*, who counsels his grandson: "I want you to overcome 'em with yesses, undermine 'em with grins, agree 'em to death and destruction, let 'em swoller you till they vomit or bust wide open." Until the time is ripe, the very servility of Styron's Nat is the perfect pose for a revolutionary living with his head in the lion's mouth. As historian Willie Lee Rose attested, "at rock bottom" Styron's *Confessions* was "a sympathetic fictional exploration of the complex mind and heart of a revolutionary."[96]

Perhaps black intellectuals were justified in taking offense at Styron's choice as presumptive. It was not the task of white writers "to define Negro humanity," Ralph Ellison had observed earlier, "but to recognize the broader aspects of their own." Ellison's words were clear, and perhaps Styron should have heeded them. Granting the contributions of white historians to the field of black history, the Ten may still have had understandable cause for dissatisfaction. But surely the Ten's denunciation of what they called Styron's "unspeakable arrogance" for "daring to set down his own personal view of Nat's life" is an overreaction. Styron's "first mistake," the Ten declared, was "to attempt the novel." His "second mistake" was "to pretend to tell the story from the point of view of Turner." The second mistake, they said, "was a colossal error, one that required tremendous arrogance." But the fault of the author lay not in his arrogance. When his novel is viewed in the light of his persistent thematic concerns, Styron appears far less arrogant and far more admirable than when he was attempting ineptly to defend himself against unfair attacks. If he fails to create an historically accurate Turner, he constructs as a novelist a sympathetic revolutionary, a hero of "humanity and sensitivity" who balances a "resolve to liberate his people" with "doubt and foreboding about the means." Far from demeaning Nat Turner, by endowing his fictional creation with "a more impressive character," Eugene D. Genovese suggests, Styron "may well exaggerate Turner's virtues." Styron may be a faulty historian; but he is a novelist of high seriousness. And his willingness to take risks for moral purposes is worth any number of petty perfectionists.[97]

For Styron his choice to try to create Nat Turner from what he called "a sense of withinness," from an "intensely 'inner' vantage point," his choice to try to see slavery through the eyes of Nat Turner in order to assume the "moral imperative" of every white Southerner to make good his claim to "understand the Negro"—was absolutely central. Conceding that he might very well have been trying to redress an imbalance in his own life, it is important to remember that in his first novel, *Lie Down in Darkness*, he represented a woman's depression partly through her own consciousness, and in his 1979 novel, *Sophie's Choice*, he represented the Holocaust partly through the consciousness of a Polish Catholic. Styron's struggle to achieve racial understanding was more characteristic and more admirable, and his measure of success was more precarious than has been generally recognized. In *Confessions* Styron's choice was an act of willed empathy not only with Nat Turner but also with such writers as Ralph Ellison and Richard Wright, who had regarded African-American history as existing not in a vacuum but within the overall pattern of American history. Styron himself had indicated of Nat Turner, "The natural working out of his life was symbolic—a metaphor for most of Negro life, I guess." But Wright had gone further. "The history of the Negro in America is the history of America written in vivid and bloody terms," he had insisted. "The Negro is *America's* metaphor."[98]

Toni Morrison in her *Playing in the Dark* stresses the importance of efforts to look into "the mind, imagination, and behavior of the slaves." But the "sense of how Negroes live and how they have so long endured," according to James Baldwin, has long been "hidden" from white Americans. The barriers to achieving that sense are formidable, Baldwin wrote in 1951, declaring that for white writers to comprehend the qualities of black life, white psychology "must undergo a metamorphosis so profound as to be literally unthinkable." At about the same time William Faulkner expressed a strikingly similar reservation: "It is easy enough," he wrote, "to say glibly, 'If I were a Negro, I would do this or that.' But a white man can only imagine himself for the moment a Negro; he cannot be that man of another race and griefs and problems." If, in *The Confessions of Nat Turner*, Styron was unable to "be that man of another race," if he fell short of achieving that "sense of how Negroes live and how they have so long endured," it was not enough merely to deplore his difficulties. That he made the effort, and that he made it in his characteristically ambitious fashion, was a deeply moral and deeply heroic choice. If, in *The Confessions of Nat Turner*, Styron fails in painful ways, who can be grateful that white writers—nor do black writers turn their talents to white subjects—make no further effort at fictional realization of African-American life? Have we not rung down a curtain of literary segregation more absolute than any political one?[99]

Sitting chained in his cell, Styron's Nat Turner ponders all he has done, all he has felt and suffered before his life is taken from him on the gallows, as Peyton Loftis in his *Lie Down in Darkness* ponders her life before taking it herself by plunging out the window to the street below. They speak to the deepest perceptions of the human condition, to a vision of tragic ambiguities and ironic necessities, to ecstatic moments of *being*, all the while surrounded by the terror of the timeless void. To have understood Nat Turner's tragedy in somewhat the same terms that Richard Wright, Ralph Ellison, and James Baldwin have understood the African-American experience is a considerable achievement. Despite Styron's difficulties, *The Confessions of Nat Turner* is a contribution of lasting literary value.[100]

"Ultimately," historian Joel Williamson has shown, "there is no race problem in the South, or in America, that we, both black and white, do not make in our minds."[101] Thus, whatever his novel's historical and literary shortcomings, William Styron may have achieved a usable historical image of Nat Turner after all, an image not of the powerful and peerless leader but of the potential for hate—and the potential for love—in everyone. Perhaps, as Edward Gibbon understated of another convulsion, "this awful revolution may be usefully applied to the instruction of the present age." And perhaps—in some strange, undefinable way, some way unfathomable by any ideology presently known, but in some way simply bestowed by the compassion of art—Nat Turner's symbolic ashes may yet give forth light.

TWELVE

Interview with William Styron

Q: The best way to begin this conversation is to talk about your early childhood growing up in the South.

William Styron: I guess I was a little unusual as a kid growing up in the Virginia Tidewater, in a segregated society in the 1930s, in that I was a bit more sensitive than most of my young contemporaries to the ironies and paradoxes of this thing they called Jim Crow segregation. I was sensitive to it because it seemed to me a situation that had no real reason for being. I couldn't understand why an entire race of people in an area which was 40 percent black should be treated as second-class citizens. I don't claim any special enlightenment, but I do think I had the influence of both my mother and father who were, by the standards of that day, advanced in their thinking, liberal, enlightened, and who I think at an early age taught me that this whole system was something profoundly wrong, profoundly evil.

I also think I was influenced by the fact that I had a direct connection with slavery. My father's mother, my grandmother, as an old lady in her eighties when I was probably 10 or 11 or 12, was able to tell me about the fact of her own ownership of slaves. She was a little girl on a plantation in North Carolina, and she had two little slave girls that were her own property. During the Civil War, the plantation where she lived was ran-

Edited from an interview conducted for the documentary film entitled *Nat Turner ~ A Troublesome Property*, produced and written by Frank Christopher and Kenneth S. Greenberg, directed by Charles Burnett.

sacked by the Yankees, and the little girls disappeared. This was a story she told me over and over and over again—Drusilla and Lucinda. This old lady, sitting in her living room in North Carolina telling me this story when I was 11 or 12, made an enormous impression upon me.

Q: What did the disappearance of the girls mean to you and to her?

William Styron: I think her problem was that she had become bonded with these two little girls. They were like sisters to her. And when the Union troops made off with everything on the plantation, including many of the slaves and these little girls, it was a wrenching loss to her.

Q: So her feeling wasn't that they chose to leave slavery voluntarily, but that they were taken?

William Styron: Her misery and her sadness lay in the fact that these slave children were like sisters to her. And that was a wound she had all of her life. But, the most amazing thing to me was that as I grew older I realized that I had been in touch with a human being, namely my grandmother, who had actually owned slaves. I remark on that amazing fact even now— that I have a remembrance of a woman, my grandmother, who actually owned two other human beings. So I think that matters like this wound of slavery were very much a part of my childhood and my remembrance. It impelled me later to just have an enormous interest in slavery and its meaning.

Q: What about the institution of segregation you experienced?

William Styron: Early on I learned that segregation was something that was leaving another wound on me. It's often unremarked that segregation, in addition to the injustice it worked upon black people, had a concomitant effect on white people. To be an upright Christian, as I was as a young boy, growing up in a society full of rectitude and Christian morals, to see existing in this society this extraordinary injustice; to see the fact that the shipyard, at four o'clock in the afternoon, this enormous shipyard where my father worked and which employed literally thousands of black people, when they left the shipyard at four in the afternoon, they all disappeared. Where did they go? They went to a ghetto. I never saw black people in any real, understandable environment. They disappeared. And I was always mystified over the fact that these vast numbers of black people who were shipyard workers were consigned to a separate part of the town of Newport News, Virginia. Early on this bothered me. I couldn't figure this out—why we lived side by side but separate. That caused me a lot of consternation as a young boy growing up.

Q: Did you discuss your feelings with anyone?

William Styron: I cared about blacks in a curious, covert way. I think if I had let myself tell people what I really felt, I would have been castigated by that awful phrase "nigger lover." But I had a feeling that I still can't quite describe or put my finger on, a feeling that somehow black people had this soul, which I had to try to understand. And much of that soul was evoked in the music. I was a passionate devourer of and listener to Negro spirituals. There was a program every Sunday that came on the radio called "Wings Over Jordan." "Wings Over Jordan" was a program that recorded spirituals, usually going to the black colleges throughout the South—Fisk, Howard, Hampton Institute, Morehouse, Tuskegee. Each of these colleges had a chorus or a quartet. I was passionately in love with this music and I remember gluing my ears to the radio every Sunday, to this program called "Wings Over Jordan," because I was so moved by these spirituals. It meant an enormous amount to me, and somehow just got in my soul.

Q: When did you first encounter Nat Turner?

William Styron: I remember when I was about 13 or 14 years old I was the assistant manager of the high-school football team, in Morrison, Virginia, a rural town outside of Newport News. The football team played throughout the Tidewater part of the state. One fall, we went over to play Southampton High School, and on our way I remember stopping to see this highway marker. And the highway marker said something like this: "twelve miles South of here in the year 1831, a Negro slave, Nat Turner, perpetrated an insurrection, in which 55 white people were killed. And the fomenter of the insurrection, Nat Turner, was tried and hanged." That made an enormous impact upon me.

I was just mystified by this. It struck me with enormous force because here I was living in a segregated society in which the black face, en masse, was that of compliance, subservience, docility—which is true for Jim Crow times. Beneath all of this, of course, there was enormous discontent. But the face of black society seemed, on the surface at least, content with its lot. When, in reality, there had to be the same impulse toward revolt as had been evidenced in this sign about Nat Turner. A hundred years before, there had been an extraordinary revolution, this insurrection, and I wanted to find out about it. I wanted to discover what this insurrection was. So that planted the seed in my mind of my interest in Nat Turner.

Q: During the 1930s were you aware of the beginnings of an attack on segregation?

William Styron: In the 1930s there was almost no sense of any restlessness, or rebellion, or anything. The 1930s was a period of absolute stasis in terms of any sense of movement toward civil rights. Plainly, during the Roosevelt years there was a stirring in that direction, but in the Virginia Tidewater of my youth you didn't see anything. If you had told me when I was 13 or 14 that within my lifetime there would be a black governor of Virginia, I would have said you were insane. The idea of any black achieving anything more than a low-level position in maybe a small business was about as far as you expected a black person to go in those days. The idea of black achievement itself was simply not a possibility to most white Southerners.

Q: You had a general sense of the unfairness of segregation. Were there any particular incidents that you remember other than just the general background of segregation, incidents that outraged you?

William Styron: The Virginia of my childhood had a different code of behavior than the deep South. For instance, in the 1930s there were still lynchings in the deep South—in Mississippi and Georgia. Virginians would have looked with horror upon anything so violent as a lynching. In fact, there were very few lynchings in Virginia compared to the deep South. The injustice perpetrated was of an entirely different kind. It was low-keyed. It had to do with manners and morals. It had to do with such a simple thing as this: I recall on the school bus that I took every day from the little village I lived in to go to my high school we would pass by a Negro school. Now our school was state-of-the-art in those days. It had a rather marvelous public-address system, which was advanced even for the 1930s. We had a beautiful brick building, with immaculate hallways. The black school was, by contrast, an absolute disgrace. It was a tumbledown building with nondescript construction—so obviously inferior that even when I was a kid I wanted to turn my eyes away from it. That, to me, represented the inequity of black and white life more than anything I know, or could remember.

Q: After having your interest in Nat Turner sparked by that sign, when did you begin to think of writing a book about him?

William Styron: I had Nat Turner in the back of my mind for many years. Ever since I saw that sign, Nat was lodged in my mind as a symbol of something, a paradigm. I was probably in my twenties. I'd finished writing my first novel, *Lie Down in Darkness*. Soon after that I began to think of writing a novel about Nat Turner. I had made the acquaintance, an acquaintance that had ripened into a friendship, of a distinguished black scholar named J. Saunders Redding. He was at that time a friend of my editor, Hiram Haydn. Saunders Redding taught English at Cornell. He was a distinguished black teacher. During these early years he had been teaching at Hampton Institute. I told him about my interest in Nat Turner, and it was he who supplied me with a remarkable book, *The South-*

ampton Insurrection by Drewry, which, of course, is the seminal work for anyone who wants to know anything about Nat Turner. He also gave me a lot of other documents from the Hampton Institute Library. And I began to amass a considerable little dossier of information about Nat Turner as early as the 1950s, at least 20 years before the book was written.

Q: These were also the years of the beginnings of the civil rights movement. Did that enter your consciousness in some way?

William Styron: I don't think I really began to be intensely aware of the civil rights movement until the 1960s. Of course, I remember the *Brown v. Board of Education* decision. But I was busy at that time, engaged in other work, and I didn't quite connect the civil rights movement with my study of slavery. I was by that time reading a great deal about slavery. I was amassing a considerable small private library about slavery, reading Ulrich Phillips, and many of the other works on slavery. I was reading Olmsted's *Journey to the Seaboard States,* and quite a few early books on slavery. But I don't think it was until that famous speech of Martin Luther King, in Washington in the early sixties, that I began to realize that the civil rights movement was gaining momentum.

I might add to that, along about that time, James Baldwin—Jimmy Baldwin—became a house guest of mine for eight or nine months. It was my acquaintance with him, my friendship with Jimmy, that caused me to learn more about the black experience than I had ever known before that time.

Q: What was your reaction to the Martin Luther King speech?

William Styron: Martin Luther King's great speech, the "I Have a Dream" speech, was a watershed moment in American history. But it marked a conciliation rather than a revolt. Six years later, when my Nat Turner book was published, all hell had broken loose. The Martin Luther King prescription was no longer there.

Q: You were speaking about James Baldwin and your relationship with him.

William Styron: Jimmy Baldwin moved into my house here in Connecticut in the winter of 1960. He was needy. He needed a place to live and to write, and he was having financial problems. I had an extra place for him, so I invited him, willingly and happily, to come and join the family, so to speak. This was a very illuminating thing for me. I had never really, as a southern-born white man, ever had intimate contact with a black person, except, of course, the nannies and maids one has, but I'm talking about an intellectual connection. He, at the same time, had never really known any southern whites at any intimate remove. So, this was a kind of an interesting pairing. I think he learned a lot from me and I learned a lot from him. We were both grandchildren of people involved in slavery. My grandmother was a slave owner, and his grandparents were slaves. We were that close to the institution of slavery. Knowing Jimmy was a great illumination because I, for the first time, saw firsthand how enraged a black person could be in American life. We had a lot of things in common. We both liked many of the same writers. We liked to listen to the same music. We liked to drink. We sort of cross-pollinated each other in emotional and intellectual matters. I learned a great deal from him about what it was like to be spat upon, scorned, sneered at. This was an enormous bonus for me, when it came to writing *The Confessions of Nat Turner.*

Q: In what specific way did this experience relate to the Nat Turner book?

William Styron: One of the fascinating things about Jimmy's connection with Nat Turner is almost a technical matter. We were both writing. He was writing a novel, *Another Country,* which involved getting into the minds of white people as a black man. I was a little hesitant in my own work. I had not really begun to write Nat Turner, but I was making notes for the book. I was very hesitant about plunging into the persona of Nat Turner, about becoming Nat Turner, writing in the first person. Jimmy and I would discuss this. He felt that it was a necessity for a writer to try to plunge into alien worlds. He sort of grabbed the bit, so to speak and, jumping into the consciousness of white people, he encouraged me at the same time to try to become a black man. He said, "I've done this as a black writer trying to become white people." He said, "What you should do, as a white writer, is to be bold, and take on the persona of a black man, Nat Turner."

Q: What about the things you were reading? Perhaps you can make a comment or two about books that were influential in the preparation of writing the novel?

William Styron: I think the most influential book for me, in putting together *Nat Turner,* was Stanley Elkins's book *Slavery.* It's a work that's been a subject of great dispute and of course has had much criticism descend upon it. But for me it was a seminal book because it discussed the whole historiography of slavery in a way that I had never understood before. He showed how the argument about slavery had fluctuated from apology to its opposite. He showed how slavery was portrayed on the one hand by Ulrich B. Phillips as a benevolent system, and how another historian such as Kenneth Stampp tried to portray it as an unremittingly vicious institution. The great virtue of Elkins's book was to try to calm the waters and to examine slavery far more objectively. And so it was an important book to me.

Q: Perhaps you could describe your trip to Southampton County while you were writing *The Confessions of Nat Turner*.

William Styron: It occurred to me when I was only a chapter or so into *Nat Turner* that I had to really go back and retrace some of the insurrection itself. I had to rediscover the atmosphere of Southampton County. So I did go down there and spent some time, back in the early 1960s. I had a family friend who took me and my wife on a wonderful day-long journey through the county. We retraced the path of part of the insurrection and finally ended at the house where Margaret Whitehead met her fate at the hands of Nat Turner. It was an emotional day for me, having this long-ago event recreated for me in the way it was.

Q: What was your intention in writing the book? What do you think you were hoping to accomplish?

William Styron: Interestingly enough, after I finished *Lie Down in Darkness*, I had a friend and advisor, the man who had been the editor for *Lie Down in Darkness*, Hiram Haydn, who was a wise and a thoughtful man. I was only 26 years old. I told him I was going to write about Nat Turner. I told him about it and he said, I think, wisely, "You know, your instinct at the moment is for melodrama. And I think you'd be making a big mistake if you plunged into this bloody story without giving it a lot more seasoning and thought." I took his advice and I'm glad I did because, ten or 12 more years passed before I seized the day, so to speak, and wrote about Nat Turner. Because during that period I was able to do all the necessary reading that I felt I had to do. I had to read the chronicles of the slave period. I had to read Frederick Law Olmsted's *Journey in the Seaboard States*. I had to read Frederick Douglass and a lot of the oral history of slavery. This was essential. If I had plunged in early to write about Nat Turner I think I would have come a cropper. This period allowed me to create a background for the book.

Q: Could you describe the initial reception of the book?

William Styron: I was quite happy in the latter part of 1967, when the book was on the verge of being published, to realize that it was going to be a big success. It had been excerpted, 45,000 words, in *Harper's* magazine. There had been a lot of fanfare about the book. It had received an enormous amount of favorable advance publicity, and when the book came out it was a stunning success. Generally speaking, it was reviewed with enormous praise. It was an exhilarating time. It plainly was a book which had found its moment.

Overall, the reception was what every writer looks forward to. It was a number one best-seller week after week. The reviews were, by and large, favorable—more than favorable; some were ecstatic.

What pleased me most in the intellectual reception of the book, as opposed to the popular reception, was the fact that quite a few distinguished white historians endorsed the book wholeheartedly, including not just second-rank historians, but people like C. Vann Woodward and Arthur Schlesinger, Jr. This gave me a great deal of encouragement to feel that somehow the book had been endorsed and approved by such qualified scholars. But it was this very endorsement that helped lead to dismay in other quarters—namely, that of black intellectuals, who, within a few months after the book was published, began to see this reception as something they didn't want, although there were one or two black scholars who supported the book, not the least, John Hope Franklin. But, in general, I think there was a sense of dismay on the part of black intellectuals. I think they said once again to themselves, "We are now confronting a white interpretation of our history. A white man has written a book about a black historical figure, and his work has been underwritten, so to speak, by historians. Where is our collective voice?" And that was one of the things that stampeded them into this violent reaction against my work.

Q: What was the first hint you had of the negative reaction?

William Styron: The first hint I got about a negative reaction was from a *New York Times* article which I read just by chance, saying that a book was planned on the part of a group of black writers to display the essential shoddiness and weakness and historical inaccuracy of my work, a book that at that moment was untitled, but which did appear later on that year in the summer. It was called *William Styron's Nat Turner: Ten Black Writers Respond.*

Q: And do you have any idea how that book came into existence?

William Styron: I was never able to substantiate it, but I'm almost certain that one of the people behind the *Ten Black Writers* book was Herbert Aptheker, the historical theorist of the American Communist Party. It's an odd connection, but I'm convinced it's true. Aptheker, I think, was upset over my interpretation of Nat Turner. Aptheker himself had written a book about Nat Turner, one that more or less took the conventional view that the South was filled with such revolts. He was upset over my interpretation of Nat Turner and was determined to do what he could to make it clear that my view, my interpretation, wouldn't stand. I'm almost certain that it was he, together with John Henrik Clarke, also a Communist, who was responsible. All this sounds like red-baiting. I don't mean to make it sound like that at all, but, nonetheless, these are the facts. And it was John Henrik Clarke who got together the ten black writers and published the book.

Q: Could you make a general comment about your thoughts on the relationship between writing a novel and doing a history?

William Styron: I think that what became the basic bone of contention and provided the central misunderstanding from the very beginning was a failure on the part of the people who attacked the book to read it as a novel. They read it as an attempted literal transcription of the historical record, which it wasn't. It was a work of the imagination, in which I, as the writer, availed myself of a writer's prerogative to transform Nat Turner into any kind of creature I wanted to transform him into. One of the beauties of the whole situation, from a novelist's point of view, was the fact that almost nothing was known about this man. The historical record is so incredibly skimpy. We have virtually no understanding of what kind of person he was, so this allowed me to make him into what I, as a novelist, wanted to make him into. Since he did not correspond, on the crudest level, to a kind of stereotypical cardboard black hero, but instead a person with enormous frailties, wounds, miseries, and indecisions—that is what disturbed the black critics of the book more than anything else.

Q: Let's get specific. One of the charges made by the black writers against the book was your invention of Nat Turner's lust for a white woman as a kind of driving force in his decision to revolt.

William Styron: When I read the original *Confessions* I was struck by the one salient fact that Nat Turner was unable himself to kill anyone during this murderous rampage, with one exception—and that was this young girl of 18 or 19 named Margaret Whitehead, who was reputed to be very beautiful and was also known as the belle of the county, by the account of one historian. When I read this fact, my instincts as a novelist just flowered because I considered that there had to be some kind of relationship between these two. It was inconceivable to me that there wasn't a connection between Nat and this young girl. So I wrote a story in which there was a connection. The connection imputed to me has been, I think, stretched all out of its relationship to reality because the allegation is that I made Nat Turner a victim of runaway lust for this young girl. In reality, a careful reading of the book will show that the relationship, which takes about 18 pages in a 400-page book, was really very tentative. It was basically a relationship in which she was the little southern tease, playing the role of the little southern vamp; that he was, himself, more a victim of her than the other way around. This idea of the connection between the two has been completely distorted and twisted out of all reality.

Q: What about the absence of his wife?

William Styron: The absence of his wife was another charge which I disregarded from the very beginning and still disregard. I don't think there is any conclusive evidence of the existence of a wife.

Q: How do you respond to the criticism that your novel failed to convey the power of black religion and black language?

William Styron: There were some very legitimate criticisms leveled against *Nat Turner,* which I took seriously. I may have failed in plumbing the depths of the religious element of the book. Not being black, I think I missed certain nuances that were part and parcel of black life, even back then. I always did feel that I was able to penetrate the past in a way that I could not possibly have done had I tried to penetrate the present. I want to explain by saying that I would never for a moment have attempted to write a book about Harlem, because I don't know the vernacular. I don't know the speech. I don't know the social patterns. I don't know the rhythms. But I did feel it was legitimate for me, as well as any black person, or any black writer, to try to grapple with slave times because this was a vernacular we both shared. Historical understanding is the common property of a white writer and a black writer.

Q: Another criticism of your novel was that it depicted a Nat Turner who hated other black people.

William Styron: The alleged hatred of Nat Turner for his own people was a criticism leveled against the book by several writers, including Toni Morrison. But I find that this is preposterous. All one has to do is to read David Walker's *Appeal.* David Walker, the great antebellum spokesman for his people, was constantly harping on the theme of the degradation of black people. He expressed his contempt for a race that would allow itself to be thrust into such a condition as slavery. If Nat Turner also spoke like this, he did it out of the same motive, the desire to be a cheerleader for his race, to goad them out of their own degradation and to make them a better people. Nat Turner did just what David Walker did. So I claim innocence on that charge.

Q: Could you reflect a bit on the nature of the changed racial climate during the time between when you started the novel and when it was published?

William Styron: It always struck me as a great irony that I began to write *Nat Turner* the summer of Martin Luther King's great speech in Washington. It was a time of reconciliation, of nonviolence and peacefulness. There was a sense that blacks and whites could work this thing out together. The intervening years between that date and the time the book was published was the "fire next time." It was when Detroit burned down and Watts burned down. America was in flames and there was no reconciliation. The book itself was published on the verge of the most bitter confrontation in the history of the United States since the years of slavery. I think that was one of the reasons the book received both such extraordinary attention and such amazing negative criticism from black intellectuals.

Q: Can you comment on the reception your novel received at some American universities?

William Styron: I began to see I was in deep trouble when I went to universities back in 1968. I ran into a stone wall. What disturbed me the most about the confrontations I had in public was that early on I had an almost sickening awareness that I was being attacked by people who had not bothered to read the book. And I had proof of that from some of the comments that came from the audience. When I would pin them down, they revealed that they had not read the book. As a result, I began to see that I was really becoming less a target for literary criticism than a kind of political whipping boy, that I was being used for political reasons, and at that moment I signed off. I decided I would not appear any further in public and I didn't.

Q: Maybe you could give us one specific description of one of these confrontations at a university.

William Styron: The confrontations often took this profile: I would be standing there and a member of the audience, usually a young black, would rise up and say, "Why did you not give our hero a wife?" And I would struggle with that question by saying if the original confessions of Nat Turner had provided Nat with a wife I would have given him a wife; but I tried to hew to what you consider the facts. And we would get into a kind of argument like that. It would go back and forth. I would finally realize that the edge of the attack was getting ugly and I would then just sign off and change the subject.

Q: Could you comment on the attempt to make a movie about your book around the time of its initial publication?

William Styron: I'm glad the film was not made. Movie rights were acquired very early in 1967. I participated, to some degree. I helped write the treatment. But by this time a storm of protest had begun. The Black Screenwriters Guild had lodged a large and vociferous protest against Twentieth Century Fox, who were producing the movie. And I began to see that the original shape of my book, if transferred to the screen, would have been horribly diluted and aborted. They were going to turn Nat Turner from a revolutionary hero into a fine little bourgeois citizen of Beverly Hills. An amazing transformation was afoot. They were going to give him a wife and a family. I was delighted to have my hands washed clean of the whole thing. I got out of that and I never looked back. Fortunately, that year was the year that Twentieth Century Fox had financial difficulties. They dumped the whole project and it's never been resurrected. So I had the best of all possible worlds in the sense that I took the money and the movie went down the drain.

Q: As you look back over this whole episode, how have you come to understand the whole thing? How do you frame it for yourself? Are there lessons that you've learned from this?

William Styron: I've often asked myself, and I've been asked, would I do it over again. Would I have written the book again? Part of me has been tempted to say, "No, I wouldn't do it because of the extraordinary bitterness it created." I'm appalled by the idea, for instance, that the book was so despised that in black history courses, I happen to know, the *Ten Black Writers* book was taught and my book was not, that women writers as well-known as Paule Marshall would describe it as racist, that Alice Walker would describe it as racist. In other words, that I created a book which would be greeted with such scorn and contempt by the very people I was attempting to reach out to has caused me a lot of second thoughts. But that is just one part of the agenda. The truth is that of course I would have written it again because I think the book does say some important things about slavery. I think I confronted, head-on, a man who had to be made into a historical figure whether by a white writer or a black writer. Even if I had created a book less valuable as literature, I think it would have been important that the book appeared, if only to rescue this man from obscurity and to give him public recognition.

Q: Where do you place your book in the larger tradition of writing about Nat Turner?

William Styron: It was often overlooked by the black critics that I was actually writing in a tradition in which black writers themselves had participated; that Nat Turner had been dealt with many times before, often by black writers, who interpreted Nat in a way that they felt was necessary for their place in time, and that I was merely doing the same thing—

turning Nat Turner into a figment of my own imagination and making
him a product of what I felt he had to be for our time.

Q: What has been the reception to the recent 30th anniversary republi-
cation of *The Confessions of Nat Turner*?

William Styron: I believe that the book, although it still has its detractors,
mainly in the black community, has been regarded with considerably
greater equanimity by black intellectuals. The times have changed, and
sophisticated black readers have been able to see that the book, whatever
its defects, is an honest attempt to interpret an important historical figure.
I think that many of the cranky animosities that energized the ten black
writers have been dissipated. The careful reader, black and white, will
really see the book as a valid interpretation on the part of an honest writer
of a very important historical figure.

Q: Would you feel comfortable giving us a brief summary of your attitude
toward Nat Turner? Do you regard him as a figure worthy of admiration?

William Styron: There's a lot of ambiguity about the real Nat Turner. One
could, on the one hand, regard him as a religious maniac, a psychopath
of almost fearful dimensions, while, if nothing else, the Nat Turner that
I created was a humanized creature, a man who probably had far more
decent and human attributes than the historical figure himself. I softened
the man without, in any sense, sentimentalizing him, and made him into
a human being instead of a rather stark and fearsome black, religious
maniac.

Q: Do you think that the 1960s controversy over Nat Turner resonates in
the current climate and culture? Is it connected to a modern conversation
about race?

William Styron: The activism and violence of the sixties is no longer a
central fact in American life. I think that there is, for many black intellectuals, a need to retreat from a sense of brotherhood. For example,
August Wilson's program to set himself apart as a playwright to write from
only a black perspective is an attitude which is unfortunate because it
encourages the races to become more isolated from each other than they
once were.

Q: Do you think the further study and interpretation of Nat Turner is a
useful activity at this particular cultural moment?

William Styron: Anything that allows us to understand the nature of slavery in America is of enormous value. I think that we suffer from historical

amnesia, historical ignorance, and that very few people really realize the unbelievable dehumanization wrought by slavery.

Americans have a penchant for historical amnesia. Very few Americans are aware of the continuity that exists between slavery and the racial dilemma we still live with in this country. Without an understanding of slavery I don't think there can be any true perception of the complexity of the racial agony in the nation. And any legitimate story, such as the one that involves Nat Turner, or any other aspect of slavery, could be an illumination for our society. Most people don't understand the extent of the utter dehumanization created by American slavery, the almost uniquely monolithic, emasculating quality that slavery possessed. If a story like Nat Turner could be made part of the general consciousness of Americans at this time, I think it would be of enormous value.

THIRTEEN

Interview with Alvin F. Poussaint, M.D.

Q: When did you first encounter Nat Turner as a figure in history?

Dr. Alvin F. Poussaint: I knew about Nat Turner when I was a teenager because I used to attend left-wing summer camps in New York and New Jersey. They were interracial camps and very concerned about segregation and the oppression of black Americans. One of the historical figures they discussed, rightly, was Nat Turner and how he had been a leader of a rebellion against slavery in the nineteenth century.

The most important camp that taught me a great deal about black history in the United States was called Wochica, located in New Jersey about two and a half hours from New York City. Wochica stood for "workers' children's camp." It was supported by left-of-center labor unions. A few organizers were people who were probably associated in one way or another with the Communist party. One of the causes they took on was the cause of black Americans and the fact that they were oppressed and that they were segregated in the United States. As part of that mission, they taught all the campers something about black history and about important people in the evolution and movement toward black freedom and liberation.

My father was in the American Federation of Labor Party. He was a printer. He was also chairman of the boys department at the YMCA in

Edited from an interview conducted for the documentary film entitled *Nat Turner ~ A Troublesome Property*, produced and written by Frank Christopher and Kenneth S. Greenberg, directed by Charles Burnett.

Harlem, on 135th Street. The people who ran camps like Wochica came in pursuit of black kids who they thought should have an opportunity to go to camp. They would give scholarships to the YMCA for families to give to their children. My father brought back one of these scholarships for me and my sister to attend Camp Wochica. I don't know that he saw it as a political camp. I think he saw it as an opportunity for us to get away for two weeks or a month from East Harlem during the summer.

A bus would take all the kids from Manhattan. The camp would have many activities usually associated with summer camps such as swimming and sports. However, we wouldn't have "color wars" between campers because the camp was opposed to war and they didn't want to encourage us to engage in that kind of competition. We sang songs, especially labor-union songs, and we discussed many issues. We had a lot of political discussions with the counselors. There were also many social events mixed with politics. Paul Robeson would visit the camp and would sing to the campers and talk to the campers. The kids were very intellectual. I know it was very eye-opening for me. Black kids were there in token numbers; perhaps five percent to ten percent of the campers. The rest of the campers were white, primarily Jewish, but there were also non-Jewish white kids there.

Q: What was the context in which Nat Turner might come up for discussion?

Dr. Alvin F. Poussaint: Nat Turner might come up in a discussion when we were talking about black history, about slavery, about the Civil War, about liberation and liberation movements, or about revolutionaries. That is also the way I first learned about Paul Robeson.

Sometimes these discussions would take place on the grass outside, or inside one of the cabins, or in one of the recreational halls where we met to sing. There were also, frequently, skits put on about different kinds of historical issues or social issues. The camp also had access to a lot of dramatic material, music, and songs that had to do with the left-wing movement. Another person I met up there, who used to come to sing every summer, was Pete Seeger, the folk singer.

Some of the discussions were about what was happening in China and the Soviet Union. Some were very involved with World War II and the defeat of the Nazis. The camp had an international flavor and outlook. It wasn't that they were just looking at the United States. I think for most of the campers and the staff one of the countries high on their list of "good" countries at that time was the Soviet Union. I remember during World War II we had rallies in the camp for the United States to open the second front in Germany, because the Russians were getting wiped out by the Germans in the east. They felt that the United States was purposely holding back to let the Russians get a whipping by the Germans.

We had readings as part of the camp experience. I remember reading several books by Howard Fast, especially his book about slavery called *Freedom Road.* I remember reading books by Herbert Aptheker, who tried to present the true history of black Americans—a story that he believed was repressed and omitted from regular history books. It was in Herbert Aptheker's writings that I first came across a lot of information about Nat Turner.

Q: The camp, you said, was about 5 percent to 10 percent black. Were there any racial tensions?

Dr. Alvin F. Poussaint: There were occasional racial tensions, but not too many. When racial tensions did come up, we had discussions about them. They were very, very into talking about white supremacy. I think the biggest disappointment for the campers was when they left the camp and went back to New York City reality. At camp, black kids actually became very good friends with some of the white kids. But when you got back to New York City, some of the white kids, even though they came from progressive families, didn't want to hang out with you, or their parents didn't want them to hang out with you. That happened to me a few times, which was very upsetting.

But in most cases, kids carried on the social relationships after you left camp and came back to the city. We maintained a lot of contact and we continued to do things together. I think that is how I saw a dramatic production that told the story of Nat Turner—through my relationship with this same group of kids. It was a small community of young people who were a bit ahead of their time in trying to tackle such issues as interracial dating and interracial marriage. The experience shaped my whole life. It opened up a new world to me. I was associating with kids who were smart and intellectual. That helped me. At first, I didn't have any visions of going to college or doing anything. But as a result of my association with those kids, I got more interested in school. I started to do very well and then went on to college and to medical school.

Q: Did you ever encounter Nat Turner during your public-school education?

Dr. Alvin F. Poussaint: Never. I never heard anything about Nat Turner in public school; nor did I hear anything about black history. They would pass over slavery with a brief mention. Usually they'd tell you that Abraham Lincoln freed the slaves. You heard a little bit about Reconstruction, but you didn't know whether it was good or bad. In high-school history class I learned nothing about Nat Turner and I didn't in college either.

Q: Were you politically active during the 1950s and 1960s?

Dr. Alvin F. Poussaint: I went to college in the late 1950s and then went on to medical school. During those years I was pretty tied up with medical school, but I always remained involved in organizations such as the NAACP when I could find the time. I also was still in touch with a lot of the young people I had met in camp who were now also in colleges. The old camp was shut down because local people said Communists were there, and they would threaten to raid the grounds. The counselors actually sat guard around the camp with rifles because the local people would threaten to send truckloads of white men up to the camp saying they were going to burn it down. The FBI was around constantly looking for fugitive Communists. The camp directors felt it was just too dangerous to have the camp there. So they shut it down and moved it to upstate New York and changed the name. I became a counselor at this new camp.

Q: What kinds of political activities engaged you during the years just before 1967?

Dr. Alvin F. Poussaint: I went to psychiatric training at UCLA after medical school. I became involved in some community activities, helping open a psychiatric clinic for black people in a church over in the Watts area. We were over at UCLA and few black patients came to UCLA. I was also involved with some physicians—Physicians for Social Responsibility—and occasionally would participate in demonstrations of various types in downtown Los Angeles. Then when I was finishing my training, I became a bit disenchanted with psychiatry for a variety of reasons. About that time, early 1965, one of my friends from New York and high school was Bob Moses, who had headed the Mississippi Freedom Summer in 1964. That was the year the three civil rights workers were murdered. Bob Moses called me and said there was really a lot of stress and trauma down there in Mississippi and other places. They needed medical help for the civil rights workers. At the same time my sister, who was head of the Student Non-Violent Coordinating Committee office in New York, called and also urged me to go down to Mississippi. A group of doctors known as the Medical Committee for Human Rights had been organizing doctors to go to Mississippi for a week or two at a time. They called me and asked me if I would come down, not as a volunteer, but to stay. I had to think about it long and hard. Finally I decided on political and emotional grounds that it would be a good thing for me to do. I believed that the most important thing I could do to affect the mental-health status of black Americans was to fight to eliminate segregation and discrimination.

So I decided that I should go down and help them as much as I could. In early March of 1965, they invited me down just to look over the territory and for me to meet everyone. I went back to L.A., and then they called me down for the beginning of the final Selma march. They wanted me to participate with other doctors in handling the medical problems on the march from Selma to Montgomery. I think I was the only physician that actually walked the whole 50 miles. I treated the civil rights workers for all kinds of things—from blisters on their feet to colds or headaches—until we got to Montgomery. Then I went back to L.A. but returned to Mississippi in June in order to set up an office in Jackson.

Q: What was your work?

Dr. Alvin F. Poussaint: I set up a general medical practice. Many of the white civil rights workers and the black civil rights workers would not go to white doctors because they had segregated offices. We set up a clinic; we had medication; we had a pharmacy made up of samples contributed by doctors; and we had a rotating group of volunteer doctors and nurses. I had a staff of four nurses that the Medical Committee for Human Rights supported. Civil rights workers would come there for treatment. I would treat them, give them their medicine, and give them their physical exams. We worked closely with local black physicians who supported the movement.

The medical staff had to be present on all demonstrations, both to treat people who were injured and also to be a deterrent to police brutality. When the police saw Red Cross vans or knew a health worker was around who could document injuries, it tended to deter them from attacking people. From our Jackson office we tried to staff every demonstration. I was dealing with volunteers coming through from all over the country. We would give them assignments as they came through—nurses, doctors, social workers, and psychologists. We also systematically went around to document all the hospitals that were still segregated. Then we would write complaint letters to Washington, D.C. Washington would send down investigators after the complaints and go to the hospitals and tell them they were in violation of the law, and their money was going to be withdrawn if they didn't desegregate. We didn't just stick to Mississippi. Sometimes we went to Louisiana to participate in a march. We used to cover a lot of the South.

One of the culminating points was the Meredith March through Mississippi. We started in Hernando, Mississippi, near Memphis, and we went all the way down to Jackson. That march was led by Martin Luther King, Jr., and by Stokely Carmichael.

Then, in '67, I felt my term was up and I moved to Boston. I was given an offer of a faculty position at Tufts Medical School, but I really came because they wanted me to work in a neighborhood health center. By that time I was very interested in the community. That neighborhood health center was out at Columbia Point, a low-income housing project. It was the first one in the country that was actually created by some of the doctors who were my colleagues in the Medical Committee for Human Rights. They were on the faculty at Tufts so I came up to Boston to work there.

Q: Did you regard your experience in Mississippi as continuous with your earlier camp experience?

Dr. Alvin F. Poussaint: I felt that the camp experience gave me the underpinnings for my commitment, my idealism, my sense of wanting to fight for justice. I think that had something to do with it, certainly. I don't think I would have been of the mind-set or quite understood it all if I hadn't had those earlier experiences.

Q: Did Nat Turner ever come up as a figure during your years in the civil rights movement?

Dr. Alvin F. Poussaint: There were various times that Nat Turner came up. Frequently, we would get into discussions about why there weren't more slave rebellions. Some people would say there were actually thousands of them, but we just don't know about them because they were not recorded. Always in that context, Nat Turner would come up. Denmark Vesey would come up and we would also talk about him. Then, occasionally, some other relatively unknown name would come up—someone who had been hanged or lynched because they had participated in slave rebellions. But Nat Turner was the one who seemed to cause the greatest fear among slaveholders. He also inspired black people. It seemed as if it was a real beginning of a revolutionary movement that was squelched. In our mind, Nat Turner was a hero, a hero of the antislavery forces among black people.

Also, there was the image of black people being passive in slavery. All of the propaganda from the South portrayed slavery as benign and that slaves actually liked to be in slavery. They had that same kind of talk about segregation—that blacks really didn't mind it. In fact, some actually said it was protective of blacks. They said blacks didn't commit suicide if they were segregated. They believed all kinds of nonsense. So Nat Turner stood out as a different image, in opposition to the docile black slave, singing on a plantation and picking cotton. He picked up arms and fought and gave his life.

Another thing we noticed was that Nat Turner was young. He died when he was 31. He was a young man, just like the young people in the civil rights movement—young men in their twenties like Bob Moses, Stokely Carmichael, John Lewis, and Martin Luther King, Jr. Also, many of the foot soldiers were young people. When I had to drive to areas of the Delta where it might be dangerous, the person assigned to me by the Student Non-Violent Coordinating Committee was a 16-year-old

Mississippi high-school student who was totally involved with the civil rights movement. She took me around and made sure that I was safe. The whole black consciousness movement was put into motion by young people.

Q: Did you experience violence or the threat of violence during your years in the civil rights movement?

Dr. Alvin F. Poussaint: Yes, a number of times. During the teargassing by Mississippi state troopers in Canton, Mississippi, in June 1966, a lot of the medical workers were injured. Sometimes I felt that they were after the medical workers. Also, there was one occasion when some white men chased me and my nurse down the highway after we had left a demonstration near Greenville. We had to make a U-turn and tear out to get away. There were many occasions when police were tailing me, right on my bumper in Alabama and Mississippi and other places. I was also frightened every time something tragic happened. For a month after an NAACP official died in a car bomb attack in Hattiesburg, Mississippi, I couldn't get in and start my car without opening up the hood and looking around for bombs. I would do this and I would feel a little bit crazy that I was doing it, but it would relieve my sense of fear.

Q: Do you have a memory of the moment when Stokely Carmichael first began to use the phrase "black power"?

Dr. Alvin F. Poussaint: The incident with Stokely Carmichael and the black-power movement occurred in June 1966, during the Meredith March. There had been a debate going on among young people in different civil rights organizations about black consciousness versus integration and in what direction they should move in order to keep the movement going and to keep liberating black folks. In 1966 Stokely Carmichael was the head of SNCC. On the Meredith March, after police on a school ground teargassed all the marchers and kicked people and hit people with rifles and put people in the hospital, Stokely Carmichael and his friend Willy Ricks were enraged. Everybody was enraged. It was just pandemonium right through the night, with kids who thought they were blind from the tear gas. It was really nasty. So, the next day, Carmichael was still seething from this. There was national coverage of this teargassing. All the national reporters were there, all the major networks. They went to interview Stokely Carmichael and Willy Ricks to ask them about their reaction to the gassing and beating by the police. Stokely Carmichael was still very angry. He looked into the camera and raised his fist and said "black power, black power, black power." Then, it spread throughout the United States. Suddenly it just swept the country.

Q: How did you personally react to the black-consciousness movement?

Dr. Alvin F. Poussaint: I was learning a lot down there, enormously, constantly. Sometimes I would get corrected by a 16-year-old black worker. I would ask the young high-school student, "Do you think you are going to be accepted by the white people at the high school you are going to in a few months?" And she would turn and say, "What do you mean by 'accepted?' Why do I have to be accepted? What about me accepting them? They are the ones with problems." I also saw how demoralized the black males were, in Mississippi and in the South. People didn't think much of themselves. We were dealing with people with a history of 250 years of slavery and a hundred years of segregation. We could not suddenly expect them to rally and feel good. I felt something really needed to be done so that they could feel a greater sense of worth and pride as black people. That was very, very critical for them taking part in the mainstream of America. I knew it had some negative ramifications. I even knew how it would be perceived, but I felt it was important to do that. The communities needed that. They needed to feel some sense of pride in who they were. Out of that whole movement came the association with Africa, dashikis, and afros. Blacks began to assert their cultural identity. It was also important in getting black kids not to think of themselves as ugly because they were black. It was important to get rid of the color conflicts within the black community that were a problem—the hierarchy of color, the light skinned versus the dark skinned. We had to come together around a black-consciousness platform. It was that movement that eliminated a lot of that color prejudice among black people themselves toward each other. It made them less ashamed. They couldn't go around and talk about so-called good hair and bad hair.

Racism was so much a part of American culture that the blacks themselves had internalized a lot of this racism. They had to be purged of white racism. How were you going to do that? You couldn't do it just through integration on the terms of the white people in control in Mississippi, because they were going to be the dominating group. What had to happen was that the black kids themselves and the black families had to begin to feel a sense of worth and empowerment. They had been slaves and sharecroppers and didn't have a dime after enriching the entire country and had to start from scratch. Then you had a bunch of laws that didn't mean anything to them. Even though they said there is going to no longer be discrimination, the black population was still intimidated. We would take down the signs in a waiting room in the hospital where it said white and colored, and you would go back in six months and black people were still sitting on the colored side. You would ask, "Why are you still sitting on the colored side?" They would say, "Well, these white people haven't changed attitudes. You sit on the white side and the doctors and nurses may let you die and not give you proper treatment, and I'm not going to do it." It was very hard to overcome patterns of behavior in their relationships to whites. There was a lot of work to be done in mobilizing blacks to feel a sense of participation. Even though they could vote, they had a history of not voting. They hadn't been part of it and they had no faith in it.

Now if you go to Mississippi a whole lot has changed, but at that time it took pressure. The police didn't run out and suddenly hire black police officers unless someone did something. That is how affirmative action started. There wasn't supposed to be any discrimination or segregation, but you would go down two years later and there were no blacks on a police force. You would go to them and say, "Why, if you're not discriminating, why aren't any blacks on the police force?" They would say, "Well, we can't find any that are qualified." What was the government to say? They would say, "This doesn't make sense. You have to begin to hire blacks for this police force." I think people have lost sight of that as a reason why affirmative action became necessary.

Q: Can you describe your first encounter with William Styron's *Nat Turner*?

Dr. Alvin F. Poussaint: Well, William Styron's *Confessions of Nat Turner* received wide publicity when it was published. It also received excellent reviews. Since I was involved in the movement, I knew about Nat Turner. I rushed to read it. I was appalled by the book. I felt it had so many things that were demeaning about Nat Turner: the fact that Styron never talked about Nat Turner's family; that in the novel Nat Turner only developed in relationship to white people who taught him; and the connection between his wish to be free and his attachment to this white teenager described as having silky, creamy, marble skin. It was full of white-worship language. It seemed unbelievable. Styron described Turner almost as a weak man, indecisive, not knowing what to do, fretting all the time. It just didn't sound real, even from the limited information that we had about Nat Turner. To me, it fell in an area of a lot of stereotypes about black men that were common all over the country, but particularly in the South. The racist film *Birth of a Nation* had the theme of a black man wanting to get power so he could get to the white woman.

Styron was denying the reality of the black experience, particularly in descriptions of Nat Turner with his own people. He was also distorting some of the historical facts. In reality, Nat Turner was married to a slave woman. That was part of his motivation, because she was separated from him and sold off to another plantation. That was one of the things that made him angry and visionary and caused him to start an uprising.

In Styron's novel, Nat Turner didn't come out as some heroic character that you wanted to emulate. Styron gave him sexual preoccupations. Why he put them all in, I don't know. But, they were Styron's preoccupations;

they weren't Nat Turner's. It was based on nothing that he read; it was how he imagined it. I don't know if he was unconsciously playing to the white psyche of the nation when he wrote it, because it was so well-received. He made it up and I felt it was a little bit of a slander and misrepresented and perpetuated certain myths in American culture.

Q: I wonder if you could link up your reaction to Nat Turner to the narrative of your involvement in the civil rights movement.

Dr. Alvin F. Poussaint: I am a psychiatrist, so I was thinking psychologically how things were. I think as a psychiatrist during the 1960s I began to understand more about how bigotry and racism works. I began to understand the psychological dynamics of it. I could sit and talk to a group of psychiatrists, white psychiatrists, and they would tell me that segregation was the best thing for the mental health of black and white people. They would think that way because they believed in segregation and the separation of the races and believed that blacks were inferior.

Southern whites had all kinds of stereotypes about black people. For example, no matter how hard they worked blacks in the field, they would call them lazy. It was always peculiar to me that one of the stereotypes about black people was that they were lazy. How could they be lazy when they were doing all that backbreaking work? I began to see some of these stereotype devices as psychological manipulations in the service of white supremacy. In other words, if whites call black people lazy, and black people actually come to believe that "my problem is that I'm lazy," then they would work harder and become more productive as slaves. So the stereotypes were ways of keeping blacks oppressed.

I could go to an all-black bar in Mississippi and white men regularly would come into the bar with black women and no one would say a word. It was not taboo. If a black man walked down the street with a white woman at that time in Jackson, Mississippi, they would have been killed. So they created a whole lot of this fantasy stuff. The rallying cry of the Ku Klux Klan was to protect sacred white womanhood. If you don't protect it, they believed we would have mongrelization of the race. Somehow it wasn't mongrelization of the race if white men had black children from black women; it was only mongrelization if black men had children with white women.

So this dynamic was very important psychologically in terms of keeping black people oppressed. It was a myth created to keep the white people mobilized. They were adamant about it and they lynched and killed over it. Emmett Till was murdered for eyeballing a white woman. He was 15 years old and they killed him. This shows you how fanatical they were. So, to see these stereotypes in *The Confessions of Nat Turner* by William Styron just fit right into that pattern that was part of the oppressive psychology they used against black people.

Q: Can you discuss the origins of your participation in the book *William Styron's Nat Turner: Ten Black Writers Respond?*

Dr. Alvin F. Poussaint: I think I was called by John Henrik Clarke. He asked me what I thought about Styron's book and I said I was appalled by some of the racial dynamics and the stereotypes in it. He asked me, as a psychiatrist, if I would write a short piece about what Styron was doing in this book with Nat Turner and the white/black relationships.

I think Styron took it to an extreme. He made it seem as if Nat Turner was searching for God and would find God in this white teenager, then he would be whole or something. He couldn't find God unless he repented the murder of this young teenager. He was going to find God through her, and he even says words to that effect near the end of the book as he is fantasizing about her in his jail cell. It is a preoccupation of Styron, that is what a black male would be fantasizing about in his jail cell the day before he is going to be hanged for insurrection. It feels and sounds demeaning.

I think that Styron made Nat Turner's longing for this teenage white girl, who was supposed to be so beautiful and smooth and silky, as his primary motivation for revolution. Somehow he really just didn't want to be free, but he wanted to have the opportunity to get between her legs in some way and find God and even uses words to that effect; that he would not have found God if he didn't have her and that she brought him to God. I think it is very bizarre that he would put that kind of dynamic in his story line. That is really part of a stereotype. I think it reinforced a stereotype in American culture about black men and the longing for white women, but he took it to really new levels. I didn't know you found God there. I think he portrayed Nat Turner as a weak, confused individual, not sure of himself, uncertain, clumsy, unorganized.

Q: Were you aware at the time that William Styron thought of himself as a liberal integrationist?

Dr. Alvin F. Poussaint: Yes. That is why I'm a little nice to him in my essay. I say that he may not have consciously known what he was doing. I knew he saw himself as a liberal and I knew he saw himself as a friend to James Baldwin—a man who supported the novel and said praiseworthy things about it. It wasn't accepted by most of the black intellectuals at the time. As you know, Baldwin himself, in a lot of his writings, was very preoccupied with the dynamics between whites and blacks. In some of the books he wrote, he talked about a black man becoming involved with a white woman.

Since no one was writing much about Nat Turner, or about any black revolutionaries, some people felt Styron's novel was a positive thing. Through the novel a slave insurrectionary was being recognized and was on the cover of a book for all of America to know there was a black slave who did rebel, even if they didn't read the book. So, maybe that was positive, in one sense. But, I think if whites read the book, they would come away with a kind of reinforced feeling about their own superiority. He was almost saying that Nat Turner did what he did almost out of emotional disturbance. This echoed an idea from the time of slavery. One white "psychologist" back then said that slaves who ran away from plantations were suffering from a mental disorder that he called "drapetomania," a kind of runaway mania. He said slaves who did that were mentally ill and needed to be therapeutically attended to, to keep them happy on the plantation. The whole image of the "crazy nigger" that they had in the South was a way to label a rebellious slave as insane.

Q: Do you think that your experience in the civil rights movement had an influence on the way you read the Styron novel?

Dr. Alvin F. Poussaint: Some of the humiliation I felt in the South made me feel more acutely what I saw Styron doing in the novel. I would have hated to be Nat Turner and then be seen in that way. Do you know what I mean? In other words, I was in Mississippi and all these other people were in Mississippi doing work for civil rights. Black men were not motivated to participate because they had a craving for white women.

Styron also portrayed Nat Turner as full of self-hatred. That is a dynamic that is frequently overplayed. In reality, Turner probably wanted to revolt because he was filled with pride and had glorified feelings about what black people were all about. He probably believed "I need freedom, I should be free." Styron also made it seem as if Turner wanted to be white. The novel even has some passages in which Nat Turner says things like "how white I felt when I did so-and-so." I thought that was very peculiar. In my own experience I never went through things where I felt and said, "Oh, how white I feel now; hey, that is great; I want to feel whiter and whiter."

Black people in the South saw white people as powerful. There were very real reasons for them to believe if you are white you have power over me. You can kill me; you can stop me from getting a job; you can run me out of state; and I have no protection. So, together with being impressed with the whiteness was the fear of the whiteness. If they came to a church because a white civil rights worker there wanted them to come, it was not only that they saw the white as superior, it was also because they saw the white as powerful. They also may have felt in some way that if a white person asked them to come, it was dangerous not to come. This is what I described in the hospital situation when the black people were afraid to sit on the white side even though the signs were down. It wasn't that they were thinking, "I wish I were white." Why didn't they go sit on the white side if they wanted to be white? They knew they were black and they were afraid of what white doctors and nurses would do to them if they didn't comply with segregation.

Q: How did people respond to your essay and the other essays in the *Ten Black Writers Respond* volume?

Dr. Alvin F. Poussaint: I remember it got much more attention than I expected. I expected we were going to publish this and people were going to ignore it or see it as just some whining, black men disagreeing. John Henrik Clarke felt there had to be a response, that people had to know there was a different perspective on this book. He collected the responses of a group of black intellectuals. He didn't tell me what to write.

I was surprised at how widely the book was distributed at the time and later. It is still used in classes. If students read Styron's *Confessions of Nat Turner*, they frequently also read *Ten Black Writers Respond* as a critique. I think that is good. I think it served its purpose to do that. It represented a new kind of consciousness and assertiveness on the part of blacks to say, "Why are you doing it this way? What is in your head? Why are you making this up this way? Why does it fit so neatly into stereotypes about black people, and images of superiority of white people, and the inadequacy of black people, and the emasculation of black people? Why didn't you imagine Nat Turner as a really strong character, not as a character all split up and torn up? Why did you make Turner less heroic?"

Q: How did William Styron respond to your critique?

Dr. Alvin F. Poussaint: Styron, to my knowledge, never officially responded to our critique. I think he just saw the essays in our volume as intolerant, off-the-wall, militant, fiery. He didn't like the idea of militance. He seems to have thought the race problem could be solved through integration, with whites allowing and recognizing the humanity of blacks.

I don't know if he really believed that he saw Nat Turner in all his human dimensions. What human dimensions? How did he know? Something was arrogant about it. Writers have a right to use their imaginations. But, at the same time, there has to be some humility too. How could he know what a black man was thinking who's been enslaved and is a revolutionary? I kept asking, "Where did he get this idea? Why does he think Nat Turner is thinking this? He says he uses the utmost in his imagination in writing the book. Well, then, what does he have to draw upon—that he's talked to James Baldwin before, and read some of his work?" It wasn't convincing to me. I don't think that he had been around that many black people and understood the black experience.

Q: Perhaps we could discuss some of the other specific ways in which you and the other ten black writers criticized Styron.

Dr. Alvin F. Poussaint: In the South, black people were never addressed with their last name. Whites would just call them by their first name. That was my experience regularly from white people, including law enforcers and public officials. When I was in Mississippi they wanted to call me "Alvin," even though I was a doctor. With regular black folks, even in records they kept in the welfare department or in the courts, they often only addressed them by their first names, as if they didn't have last names. I was very, very aware and conscious of that practice of dehumanizing black people by not giving them their full name. That is what the slave-holders did with their slaves and so on and so forth. This was part of white supremacy practice and racial etiquette to do that. So, in the book, when Styron is referring to Nat Turner only as "Nat," it just stirred up memories of that. I wondered if Styron was doing that in some unconscious way because he also is part of a culture that sees black people in terms of their first names and not their full names. I just raise that to indicate the complexity of what he was trying to do. I saw what he was doing, perceived it differently than perhaps what he meant it to be, or perhaps he did mean it to be, but was not aware of what he was doing. I just point this out to indicate the kind of minefields that may be in there psychologically.

Q: How did you react to the "homosexual" encounter in the novel in the scene between Nat Turner and Willis?

Dr. Alvin F. Poussaint: You have to remember that this was in 1967. When I read this episode I had the feeling that Styron was depicting something odd and deviant. That is what I felt. He even had Nat Turner refer to the encounter as a sin. In the context of the times, to describe such an encounter was to take away the "manhood" of the person. Even psychiatrists at that time believed that homosexuals lacked "manhood," that they were feminized, that they were some form of woman, and that they were weak. Styron seemed to be saying Nat Turner couldn't deal with his manhood, was passive, and really didn't want to be a killer. That is the way the American public saw it at the time too, certainly.

Q: One of the critical points you made in your critique of Styron's novel was that he failed to mention black people as significant figures in Nat Turner's life. Can you elaborate on this point?

Dr. Alvin F. Poussaint: I felt that considering that Nat Turner was a unique and special individual who was strong enough to be a revolutionary, it was wrong not to examine the sources of strength that came from his own black family and the other black people surrounding him. To see all of his realities and all of his learning in terms of his contact with white people struck me as very odd. Why did he obliterate Nat Turner's family? Why couldn't he talk about them? Maybe he didn't know how to talk about black families or black mothers and fathers in a home. That is a serious omission that implies an indifference or a lack of appreciation of the black experience and black people and the upbringing of children and where they get their strength.

Q: People today might wonder why Styron's novel created such controversy in 1967. After all, it was just a novel and not a history.

Dr. Alvin F. Poussaint: Historical novels have impact. When you read a historical novel and when you see historical films, you can't help but think that somehow this is true. This is the way it really happened. So, a lot of people read that book and took it as fact, not as a creation of Styron's imagination.

We have so few heroes from that period. Nat Turner was one of them. To see him defrocked symbolically by Styron was painful. If we had a wide variety of heroes and this was the way he treated one particular character among many, then probably people wouldn't have had the same reaction.

Q: How did you react to James Baldwin's comment that William Styron had begun to write "our common history"?

Dr. Alvin F. Poussaint: I did not agree with James Baldwin that Styron had begun to write our common history. I think Styron was writing his own fantasy about black people. It was not a book from a black perspective; it was all from a white perspective, one that was tainted with white supremacist kinds of attitudes.

Q: What does Nat Turner mean to you and to other African Americans today?

Dr. Alvin F. Poussaint: Nat Turner is a critical, important part of black history and American history. I think it is important for black kids and white kids to understand the truths of our past. They should not think that the slaves were passive and tolerated being enslaved. That is not the truth. Even the slaves who did not revolt certainly did not love slavery. Every bit of gospel music and folk music coming from the slaves always talked of freedom. The slaves sought freedom and escaped whenever they could and probably managed a lot of heroics we know nothing about.

Epilogue

Nat Turner in Hollywood

KENNETH S. GREENBERG

Nat Turner arrived in Hollywood in October 1967, when producer David Wolper paid $600,000 for film rights to the image of the slave rebel in William Styron's novel *The Confessions of Nat Turner*.[1]

Nat Turner departed from Hollywood in January 1970.[2] By then he had been much transformed. He was no longer William Styron's Nat Turner, but some other mixture of fact and fiction. An extraordinary series of events led to that departure. Overall, these events illustrate the deep and bitter racial divisions that made it virtually impossible for the nation to remember collectively its most important slave rebel during the 1960s, even in fictional Hollywood form. The dispute sometimes produced harsh and pointed debate—but at its most divisive moments the controversy generated a breakdown in language and in the ability of people to communicate across the racial divide. What made Nat Turner's passage through Hollywood such a disturbing event for our culture was less the expressions of anger that it produced than the moments of silence it generated.

The broad outlines of the rise and fall of Nat Turner in Hollywood can briefly be summarized. After the successful purchase of Styron's *Confessions of Nat Turner*, Wolper immediately sold the rights to Twentieth Century Fox and they, in turn, hired him to produce the film. This was to be a major production. Wolper recruited Norman Jewison to direct and James Earl Jones to play the starring role. Jewison had already dealt with racially sensitive issues in *In the Heat of the Night*, and Jones was fresh from his Broadway triumph in *The Great White Hope*.[3]

While Wolper was beginning to piece together the group to complete the *Confessions*, a wave of escalating outrage at the production began to develop within some segments of the black community. A number of African-American cultural and intellectual leaders had read Styron's novel and believed it contained an emasculated and demeaning image of the slave rebel. They feared that a major film based on Styron's *Confessions* would help sell copies of a book many considered "racist" and that it would imbed forever in the public imagination a misleading image of a great hero.

Louise Meriwether, later to become an important novelist but then working as a story analyst at Universal Studios, played the central role in organizing opposition to the film. She recruited actor and civil rights activist Ossie Davis to serve as a high-profile spokesperson, formed a small organizing group known as the Black Anti-Defamation Association (BADA), and then set out to transform the movie or to stop its production.[4]

Initially, Meriwether was unaware that John Henrik Clarke, a highly influential African-American historian, educator, and writer, had begun to solicit critiques of the Styron novel that soon would be published as *William Styron's Nat Turner: Ten Black Writers Respond.*[5] Her own outrage developed independently but was instantly shared by many others she asked to read the novel or to join her protest. Meriwether's criticism of the novel perfectly paralleled the critique developed by contributors to the Clarke volume. In fact, histories of that era should probably refer to "11 black writers" who responded to Styron—the ten men organized by Clarke and the one woman acting independently in Hollywood. Meriwether's letter to Wolper and Jewison, dated 26 March 1968, laid out the main lines of her critique. "Styron," she noted, "omitted, distorted and falsified history in order to convert Nat Turner from a bloody avenger fighting for freedom to just another black boy itching to fornicate with white women. Styron divests Turner of all his strength, fortitude and manhood, of his hatred for all slave masters and oppression. He castrates Nat mentally, physically and sexually."[6]

Meriwether was a skillful organizer and persuasive speaker who made effective use of a variety of tactics. She delivered a powerful presentation to a Los Angeles umbrella group of black activist organizations known as the Black Congress and won their support for her campaign. The Black Congress included representatives from the Urban League, the Black Panther Party, the NAACP, the Black Student Union, the Student Non-Violent Coordinating Committee, and virtually every other black activist group in the area—from the most conservative to the most radical.[7] She solicited and received celebrity endorsements from prominent figures including Leroi Jones, Godfrey Cambridge, Rap Brown, Stokely Carmichael, and Adam Clayton Powell, Jr. She also sent out press releases to black newspapers across the nation, requesting letters of support from readers—and scores responded.

One of Louise Meriwether's most effective tactics involved taking out a full-page advertisement that occupied the back page of the *Hollywood Reporter*. Addressed "To All Black Actors," it consisted of a statement from Ossie Davis declaring the Styron book to be "false to black history," "an insult by implication to black womanhood," and "dangerous." It concluded with a rousing call for a black boycott of the film. "For a black actor," Davis wrote, "a black man, to lend his craft, his body, and his soul to such a flagrant libel against one of our greatest heroes, would be to have one of us become an agent for the enemy against our own legitimate aspirations. It is quite possible I would despise such a man who would do such a thing." The names of nearly forty supporters and their organizations appeared below the letter.[8]

In the end, Jewison, Wolper, and Lew Peterson, a newly hired black screenwriter, met with Louise Meriwether and the other major organizers of the campaign against the Styron novel and film on at least two occasions. Wolper and his team wanted to know exactly what Meriwether demanded, and they began a dialogue. At some point before a final agreement could be completed in writing, Jewison dropped out of the project and director Sydney Lumet took his place.[9] It was Lumet and Wolper who eventually signed an extraordinary contract with the protesters. They capitulated to both of Louise Meriwether's demands—demands intended to disassociate the film from Styron's novel:

1. That the picture will project a positive image of Nat Turner as a black revolutionary. The motion picture will not be based solely upon "The Confessions of Nat Turner" by William Styron, but upon a variety of source materials, one of which will be the Styron book.
2. That the motion picture will bear a title other than "The Confessions of Nat Turner."

Louise Meriwether, in turn, agreed to cease all present and future "picketing, demonstrations and boycotts" against the film.[10]

While the central terms of the agreement had been settled at a meeting in December 1968 and announced to the press early in 1969, the final written document was not signed by all parties until May. Meanwhile, Lew Peterson completed the screenplay, and the film moved inexorably toward production. *Nat Turner* would be filmed in Southampton County, Virginia. Wolper hired an influential lawyer and descendant of a white survivor of the rebellion, Gilbert Francis, to win the consent of a complex local community divided along racial and political lines. With varying degrees of success, Francis spoke with "moderates" in the community as well as with people he described as "militants" among the blacks and "rednecks" among the whites. Yet just as Francis began to gather mules and farm implements, send out orders for construction, make arrangements with local motels, and lease various sites for filming, Twentieth Century

Fox canceled the production.[11] Fox was in economic trouble, and *Nat Turner* was one of several films they chose to shut down. While many participants in the project and in protests against the project (including Louise Meriwether and William Styron) had the impression that production had been stopped as a result of intense racial and political pressure, it was almost certainly closed down for economic reasons. By January 1970, Louise Meriwether had already reached final agreement with Wolper; and, within Virginia, most blacks and whites in Southampton County seemed eager for the start of production.

Regardless of why the film was never made, the conflict and turmoil along the path to production illustrated a deep racial rift in the culture— one that would certainly have resurfaced had the film been completed. However, what was most interesting and troubling about Nat Turner's visit to Hollywood was not all the anger and political maneuvering that accompanied him, but the silences that marked several places in his passage. These were silences that signified a breakdown in the ability of language to transmit meaning across a deep cultural divide. No voice seemed able to speak words understandable to all participants in the controversy.

One notable silence lurked in the gap between statements made about Styron's novel by leading literary figures of the time, and the reactions of Louise Meriwether and her supporters. During 1967 early copies of Styron's book had been sent to friends, reviewers, and critics for comment. The reactions were not simply positive—they were ecstatic. The private correspondence gushed with words of praise. Jason Epstein, Styron's first correspondent from Random House, called the book "miraculous." Robert Penn Warren wrote from France, telling Styron the novel was "terrific." Robert Silvers found it "marvelous and great, the best novel by an American in many years." For Joseph M. Fox it was "an incredible achievement" that left him "breathless." Willie Morris labeled it "a *great* book," "a work of such powerful impact that when I put down the last page I literally had to go outside and take a walk." It was "marvelous" for Arthur Schlesinger, Jr., and "the best work of fiction in this country since *Invisible Man*" for R. W. B. Lewis.[12] The private praise was publicly repeated in virtually every major American news and review publication.

However, within one year of these early reactions, Louise Meriwether's campaign against Styron's novel in Hollywood publicized the most extreme examples of a radically different set of comments about the novel. Leroi Jones concluded that "a white street gang has the same goals as the author." Stokely Carmichael described the book as "a joke to us black people." Rap Brown said it was a book of "lies," "deception," and "distortion" from the pen of a "hunkie."[13]

A deep silence occupied the space between those who labeled Styron's novel "marvelous" and those who called it "a joke." It would be incorrect to understand this disagreement as a debate. A debate involves conversation. The gap between William Styron and his most ardent critics did not at all involve interaction or engagement. The dispute was really about a clash of worldviews so profound that it did not lend itself to conversation. William Styron's defenders and his critics spoke different languages based on radically different racial, political, and literary assumptions. They lived in parallel worlds of meaning separated by a gap of silence.

Another area of silence surrounded David Wolper's interactions with a variety of interest groups wanting to shape the final film. Gilbert Francis of Southampton County, a key figure in preparing the county for the start of production, demanded a film that was historically accurate and not based solely on William Styron's novel. He was especially interested in supporting a film that would treat his white ancestors more favorably than had Styron. After he was hired by Wolper, Francis, in turn, had to convince local black and white residents from all parts of the political spectrum that the film would also satisfy their financial and political interests— that they and the county would make profits from cooperating with and participating in the production, and that the final film would vilify neither their master nor their slave ancestors.[14]

At the same time, Wolper needed to deal with the demands set forth by Louise Meriwether—or risk a boycott by some of the most talented black actors in the nation. Meriwether, like Francis, also demanded a historically accurate film not based solely on William Styron's novel. Finally, there was Styron himself, a man to whom Wolper had already paid $600,000, as well as the director Norman Jewison, who demanded the artistic freedom to sculpt the film as he saw fit.

One of the skills that made a man like David Wolper an effective producer was his ability to convince nearly everyone that he could look after their interests—even when those interests were completely incompatible. Wolper had several strategies for dealing with the people of Southampton County. First he sent down a charming advance man, Chico Day, to work with Gilbert Francis. Wolper himself largely stayed away from the county. That way, if for any reason local people became alienated from the production, he could step foreword to change key personnel or otherwise smooth out the controversy.[15] Wolper also allowed Francis to read the script, and he responded favorably to the request to treat the Francis family ancestors with respect. Francis, in turn, used all of his political skills and power, as well as Twentieth Century Fox's money (purchasing material, renting property, and hiring workers) to placate the wide spectrum of competing interests in the county.

At the same time that Wolper was pacifying Southampton County, he was also signing an agreement with Louise Meriwether. As with Gilbert Francis, he essentially promised Meriwether a film that would be historically accurate and not based solely on Styron's *Nat Turner*. The only person he alienated in all of these negotiations was William Styron himself—who

resented what he saw as Wolper's capitulation to Meriwether's black nationalist demands and, with some disgust, washed his hands of the entire
project.[16]

David Wolper's skillful juggling of competing interests depended on
silence. Louise Meriwether and Gilbert Francis never met, and probably
never even knew about each other. Wolper had promised each of them
"historical accuracy" and yet their visions of history were completely incompatible. Meriwether was devoted to the black consciousness movement
of the 1960s and Francis was devoted to preserving the good name of his
slave-owning ancestors. Wolper well understood that the promise of "historical accuracy" was a promise with remarkably little content. If Meriwether and Francis had engaged in conversations with each other they
almost certainly would have realized that Wolper could not have kept his
promises to both of them. The same was true for the white "rednecks"
and black "militants" that Gilbert Francis tried to placate in Southampton
County. Wolper and his agents could talk and make promises to all of the
competing interest groups, but his great juggling act would have been
disrupted if conversation rather than silence had prevailed.

A third important silence sits at the center of the turmoil over Styron's
novel and film. It is the silence of the great black novelist James Baldwin.
Baldwin was the only figure universally respected by all participants in the
controversy. He was also deeply involved at every level. Yet he never publicly gave full expression to his thoughts on the subject.

During the late fall of 1960, William Styron had heard about Baldwin's
need for housing and offered him indefinite use of a guest residence
adjacent to his home in Roxbury, Connecticut. Baldwin would write all
day and then often join Styron for dinner and drinks in the evening.
While the two were wary of each other at first, they soon formed a close
bond as they spent night after night drinking and talking to each other,
often until dawn.

Styron later wrote about Baldwin with deep warmth and affection, and
the feelings seem to have been reciprocated. The black man from Harlem
had a great deal to teach the white Virginian about race relations in America. They talked about their common roots in slavery—only one generation removed from their links to masters and slaves. Styron learned about
the profound sense of racial injustice and anger felt by Baldwin. This was
Styron's first close encounter with a powerful, intellectual, black man and
the experience changed him forever. At the time, Styron was just beginning serious work on *The Confessions of Nat Turner*, and Baldwin encouraged him in the project. Most significantly, it was Baldwin who urged
Styron to write in the voice of Nat Turner—to get into the mind of a slave
as a way of fully understanding him.[17]

Baldwin continued to support Styron even after he read the galley
proofs of the novel. He understood that it might be controversial for
Styron to have assumed the voice of a black man, but he considered the

attempt "courageous." "Styron," he told *Newsweek* magazine in October 1967, "is probing something very dangerous, deep and painful in the national psyche. I hope it starts a tremendous fight, so that people will learn what they really think about each other." Baldwin even lent words of support to the back cover of the novel, praising Styron as a man who "has begun the common history—ours."[18]

Yet as the controversy over Styron's novel deepened and as the attacks on the book became more pointed and virulent, Baldwin retreated into silence. He was admired by and friendly with many of the black intellectuals who attacked *The Confessions of Nat Turner*. He certainly understood and respected their position, but he would not betray his friend by joining the opposition. Nor did he feel comfortable developing an extended defense of Styron, other than to note that Styron had the right of any writer to imagine the mind and voice of another person.

At one point in 1968, at the height of the controversy over the Hollywood film, Baldwin moderated a debate between Ossie Davis and William Styron at a fundraiser for presidential candidate Eugene McCarthy. Counting both Styron and Davis to be his friends, he chose to keep himself out of their conflict. After a brief introduction, Baldwin could not or would not speak the words to bridge the great gap that separated the two men he so deeply admired and respected.[19]

The silences that accompanied Nat Turner on his journey through Hollywood continued long after the 1960s. Yet recently, interesting new voices from the world of film have begun to speak about the slave rebel. African-American director Spike Lee briefly became intrigued by the possibility of bringing William Styron's *Nat Turner* to the screen in the form of a movie made for television, but the project quickly faded for economic reasons. Charles Burnett, a black director, recently became the first person to tell the story of the way Americans have remembered Nat Turner—even including dramatized scenes from the Styron novel—in his documentary film *Nat Turner ~ A Troublesome Property*. This new interest of major African-American directors in Nat Turner suggests intriguing possibilities for the transformation of cultural meanings. Identical words and images carry different meanings depending on who gives them voice. Just as Thomas R. Gray, William Styron, and the "ten black writers" reshaped the historical Nat Turner as they tried to speak his words, so Spike Lee and Charles Burnett must inevitably transform Styron's and other images of Turner as they portray them on film. All of this may tell us nothing more about the historical Nat Turner, but it will almost certainly tell us something more about ourselves.

NOTES

INTRODUCTION

1. A substantial number of these documents can be found in Henry I. Tragle, comp., *The Southampton Slave Revolt of 1831: A Compilation of Source Material* (Amherst: University of Massachusetts Press, 1971).
2. Kenneth S. Greenberg, ed., *The Confessions of Nat Turner and Related Documents* (Boston: Bedford Books of St. Martin's Press, 1996).
3. Herbert Aptheker, *Nat Turner's Slave Rebellion* (New York: Grove Press, 1966).
4. William Sidney Drewry, *Slave Insurrections in Virginia (1830–1865)* (Washington, D.C.: The Neale Company, 1900), 26.
5. Herbert Aptheker, *American Negro Slave Revolts* (New York: Columbia University Press, 1943).
6. Thomas C. Parramore, *Southampton County, Virginia* (Charlottesville: University Press of Virginia, 1978).
7. Ibid., 121.
8. Vincent Harding, *There Is a River: The Black Struggle for Freedom in America* (New York: Vintage Books, 1983).
9. Louis P. Masur, *1831: Year of Eclipse* (New York: Hill and Wang, 2001).
10. Mary Kemp Davis, *Nat Turner Before the Bar of Judgment: Fictional Treatments of the Southampton Slave Insurrection* (Baton Rouge: Louisiana State University Press, 1999).
11. William Styron, *The Confessions of Nat Turner* (New York: Random House, 1967).
12. John Henrik Clarke, ed., *William Styron's Nat Turner: Ten Black Writers Respond* (Boston: Beacon Press, 1968).
13. Charles Joyner, "Styron's Choice: A Meditation on History, Literature, and Moral Imperatives," in *Southern Writers and Their Worlds*, ed. Christopher Morris and Steven G. Reinhardt (College Station: Texas A & M Press, 1996).

CHAPTER ONE

1. Orlando Patterson, *Slavery and Social Death: A Comparative Study* (Cambridge: Harvard University Press, 1982), 54–58; Michal Sobel, *The World They Made Together: Black and White Values in Eighteenth-Century Virginia* (Princeton: Princeton University Press, 1987), 157; Ira Berlin, *Many Thousands Gone: The First Two Centuries of Slavery in North America* (Cambridge: The Belknap Press of Harvard University Press, 1998), 112.
2. Patterson, *Slavery*, 120, 130, 173–74; Sobel, *The World*, 156–57; Eugene Genovese, *Roll, Jordan, Roll: The World the Slaves Made* (New York: Pantheon Books, 1974), 444–50; Charles Joyner, *Down by the Riverside: A South Carolina Slave Community* (Urbana: University of Illinois Press, 1984), 217–18; Herbert Gutman, *The Black Family in Slavery and Freedom* (New York: Pantheon Books, 1976), 185–201; Cheryll Ann Cody, "There Was

No 'Absalom' on the Ball Plantations: Slave Naming Practices in the South Carolina Low Country, 1720–1865," *American Historical Review* 92 (June 1987): 563–96; Orville Vernon Burton, *In My Father's House Are Many Mansions: Family and Community in Edgefield, South Carolina* (Chapel Hill: University of North Carolina Press, 1985), 165–66.

3. On the relationship between honor and names, see Kenneth S. Greenberg, *Honor and Slavery: Lies, Duels, Noses, Masks, Dressing as a Woman, Gifts, Strangers, Humanitarianism, Death, Slave Rebellions, The Proslavery Argument, Baseball, Hunting and Gambling in the Old South* (Princeton: Princeton University Press, 1996), 6–7, 41–43; and Bertram Wyatt-Brown, *Southern Honor: Ethics and Behavior in the Old South* (New York: Oxford University Press, 1982), 120–21, 122–25.

4. *Southampton County Will Book*, vol. 9, p. 254, "An Inventory and Appraisement of the Estate of Samuel G. Turner dcsd. taken this 4th day of March 1822," Library of Virginia.

5. *Southampton County Court Minute Book*, 1830–1835, p. 72, Library of Virginia.

6. Ibid., 72–124.

7. The development of surname usage for some people in slavery is discussed in Genovese, *Roll, Jordan, Roll*, 445; Sobel, *The World*, 159; and Peter Kolchin, *Unfree Labor: American Slavery and Russian Serfdom* (Cambridge: The Belknap Press of Harvard University Press, 1987), 209.

8. William Sidney Drewry, a local Southampton County historian writing in 1900, said that Nat Turner was "often" called Nat Travis in 1831. He probably heard this from local white residents with a folk memory of the events of 1831. But there does not exist any 1831 reference to Nat Turner as Nat Travis. William Sidney Drewry, *Slave Insurrections in Virginia* (Washington, D.C.: The Neale Company, 1900), 27.

9. Genovese, *Roll, Jordan, Roll*, 445; Joyner, *Down by the Riverside*, 221.

10. Genovese, *Roll, Jordan, Roll*, 445.

11. Many newspaper reports of the rebellion have been conveniently reprinted in Henry I. Tragle, comp., *The Southampton Slave Revolt of 1831: A Compilation of Source Material* (Amherst: The University of Massachusetts Press, 1971). References to "Nat" can be found on 67, 74, 93, 95, 137, and 138; references to "Nat Turner" are on 44, 58, 60, 87, 100, 123, 134, 135, 136, and 140; references to "Gen. Nat," "General Nat Turner," or the "General" are on 45, 48, 50, 55, 62, 70, 71, 92, 132, and 133; references to "Capt. Nat" can be found on 55, 80, and 95. Nat Turner is called "the Prophet" on 50 and the "Preacher Captain" on 52. In addition, one newspaper, in what was probably a misprint, called him "Ned the prophet or preacher," and another referred to him as "General Cargill," a mysterious reference repeated nowhere else in the documentary record. See Tragle, 49, 61.

12. Berlin, *Many Thousands Gone*, 95.

13. Tragle, *Southampton*, 45, 54.

14. Ibid., 66–72, 90–99.

15. African-American references to Nat Turner's name can be found in the rebel trial records in *Southampton County Court Minute Book*, 1830–1835, pp. 89, 96–98; and *Southampton County Court Judgments*, 1831, Case 34, Library of Virginia. This evidence is corroborated in the 30 August diary entry of Governor John Floyd in which he refers to "Nat, alias Nat Turner, by the Negroes called General." The relevant section of Floyd's diary can be found in Kenneth S. Greenberg, ed., *The Confessions of Nat Turner and Related Documents* (Boston: Bedford Books of St. Martin's Press, 1996), 105.

16. *Southampton County Minute Book*, 1830–1835, p. 121, Library of Virginia. The Southampton County Court did not invent this usage of "alias" for slaves who asserted surnames. It frequently appeared in notices for runaways. Sobel, *The World*, 159.

17. A copy of the reward notice can be found in Tragle, *Southampton*, 421–23.

18. *Journal of the Governor's Council*, 1831, pp. 114, 118, 150, Library of Virginia.

19. Edward Butts's receipt for the delivery of Nat Turner can be found in Tragle, *Southampton*, 425; the certification of the hanging is on 427.

20. Greenberg, *Confessions*, 39–58.

21. F. N. Boney, "The Blue Lizard: Another View of Nat Turner's Country on the Eve of the Revolution," *Phylon* 34, no. 4 (1970): 353.

22. Levi Waller testified that he heard the rebels refer to Hark as "Captain Moore." The name "Moore" seems to have come from Hark's former master. Waller also testified

that he heard Davy called "brother Clements." A letter from Southampton County dated 24 August and published in the 30 August issue of the *Richmond Enquirer* refers to Hark as "Gen. Moore." Tragle, *Southampton,* 45, 192, 194. Tragle misinterprets Levi Waller's testimony about the name "brother Clements" and erroneously suggests that it refers to Nelson. See 194, n. 61.

23. See, for example, the following speeches: William H. Brodnax, *The Speech of William H. Brodnax in the House of Delegates of Virginia, on the Policy of the State with Respect to its Colored Population, Delivered January 19, 1832* (Richmond: Thomas W. White, 1832), 10; John Thompson Brown, *The Speech of John Thompson Brown in the House of Delegates of Virginia on the Abolition of Slavery, Delivered Wednesday, January 18, 1832* (Richmond: Chas. H. Wynne, 1860; reprinted from pamphlet copy of 1832), 3; Henry Berry, *The Speech of Henry Berry in the House of Delegates of Virginia on the Abolition of Slavery* (n.p., n.d.), 2.

24. "Speech by Henry Highland Garnet, Delivered before the National Convention of Colored Citizens, Buffalo, New York, 16 August, 1843," in *The Black Abolitionist Papers,* vol. III, ed. C. Peter Ripley (Chapel Hill: The University of North Carolina Press, 1991), 409.

25. Douglass's references to "Nathaniel Turner" can be found in "A Black Hero," in *Douglass' Monthly,* August 1861, reprinted in *The Life and Writings of Frederick Douglass: The Civil War, 1861–1865,* vol. III, ed. Philip S. Foner (New York: International Publishers, 1950–1955, 134; "Vote the Regular Republican Ticket: An Address Delivered in Raleigh, North Carolina, on 25 July, 1872," reprinted in *The Frederick Douglass Papers: Series One: Speeches, Debates and Interviews, 1864–1880,* vol. 4, ed. John W. Blassingame and John R. McKivigan (New Haven: Yale University Press, 1991), 317. The reference to "General Turner" can be found in "The Significance of Emancipation in the West Indies: An Address Delivered in Canandaigua, New York, on 3 August 1857, reprinted in *The Frederick Douglass Papers: Series One: Speeches, Debates, and Interviews, 1855–1863,* vol. 3, ed. John W. Blassingame (New Haven: Yale University Press, 1985), 208. One Douglass speech does contain a reference to "Nat Turner," but this seems to be a typographical error. Elsewhere in the same speech the same name is repeated, but "Nat." is clearly marked as an abbreviation for "Nathaniel." See "Did John Brown Fail?: An Address Delivered in Harpers Ferry, West Virginia, on May 30, 1881," reprinted in *The Frederick Douglass Papers: Series One: Speeches, Debates, and Interviews, 1881–1895,* vol. 5, ed. John W. Blassingame and John R. McKivigan (New Haven: Yale University Press, 1992), 18, 29.

26. Charles L. Perdue, Jr., Thomas E. Barden, and Robert K. Phillips, eds., *Weevils in the Wheat: Interviews with Virginia Ex-Slaves* (Bloomington: Indiana University Press, 1980), 67, 76. It should be noted that the Allen Crawford quotation does not correctly identify the place at which Nat Turner was captured.

27. For references to frightening images of Nat Turner in the African-American folk tradition see F. Roy Johnson, *The Nat Turner Story* (Murfreesboro, N.C.: Johnson Publishing Company, 1970), 210–11.

28. Drewry, *Slave Insurrections.* The reference to John Brown is on 26. References to "Nat" and to white people as "Mr.," "Mrs.," "Colonel," or "General" are on nearly every page of the book. A reference to Nat Turner as "general" can be found on 35.

29. John Henrik Clarke, ed., *William Styron's Nat Turner: Ten Black Writers Respond* (Boston: Beacon Press, 1968).

30. Dr. Alvin F. Poussaint, interview with author, filmed at the Judge Baker Children's Center, Boston, February 2000. This interview was conducted as part of preparation for the documentary film *Nat Turner ~ A Troublesome Property*—a collaboration between Charles Burnett, Frank Christopher, and Kenneth S. Greenberg. The transcript is in possession of the author.

31. Ibid.

32. Alvin F. Poussaint, M.D., "The Confessions of Nat Turner and the Dilemma of William Styron," in *William Styron's Nat Turner: Ten Black Writers Respond,* ed. John Henrik Clarke (Boston: Beacon Press, 1968).

33. A revealing portrait of William Styron can be found in James L. West III, *William Styron: A Life* (New York: Random House, 1998), especially 315–95.

34. One newspaper account of the capture of Nat Turner does have him name himself. It

describes a scene in which Benjamin Phipps stumbles across the rebel leader in hiding and demands, "Who are you?" Turner then responds, "I am Nat Turner." However, this was likely an invention of the newspaper writer, intended for dramatic presentation. The same question and response is not reported in Thomas R. Gray's version of the episode or in other accounts of the capture. *Norfolk Herald,* 4 November 1831.

35. *Norfolk Herald,* 14 November 1831. Republished in the *Richmond Enquirer,* 18 November 1831. The abolitionist Thomas Wentworth Higginson searched for the lithographic image in vain in 1861.

36. William C. Parker's letter to Governor Floyd as well as Floyd's official reward notice can be found in Tragle, *Southampton,* 420, 423.

37. *Richmond Enquirer,* 8 November 1831.

38. Harriett Beecher Stowe, *Dred: A Tale of the Great Dismal Swamp* (New York: AMS Press, 1970; reprinted from the edition of 1856, Boston), 240.

39. Drewry, *Slave Insurrection,* 27.

40. John W. Cromwell, "The Aftermath of Nat Turner's Insurrection," in *Journal of Negro History,* vol. 5 (April 1920); reprinted in Tragle, *Southampton,* 371; Stephen B. Oates, *The Fires of Jubilee: Nat Turner's Fierce Rebellion* (New York: New American Library, 1975), 76.

41. Between 1997 and 2001, I worked with Frank Christopher and Charles Burnett on a documentary film entitled *Nat Turner ~ A Troublesome Property.* It included dramatic excerpts from William Styron's novel. As we cast for the part of Styron's Nat Turner, we searched for a description of the man in the book. Unable to find one, we then asked the author for guidance. Styron confirmed that he had no clear image of the face of the slave rebel as he wrote the book.

42. For examples of "blackness" as an issue for the "Ten Black Writers" see Clarke, *William Styron's Nat Turner,* 5, 30.

43. I have been exposed to James McGee's ideas in a series of conversations between 1997 and 2002. The content here was confirmed by telephone on 3 January 2002.

44. Greenberg, *Confessions,* 44, 46.

45. Tragle, *Southampton,* 140.

46. Todd L. Savitt, *Medicine and Slavery: The Diseases and Health Care of Blacks in Antebellum Virginia* (Urbana: University of Illinois Press, 1978), 292. Douglas R. Egerton, *He Shall Go Free: The Lives of Denmark Vesey* (Madison, Wis.: Madison House Publishers, 1999), 190 notes the dissection of the rebels after the Denmark Vesey insurrection of 1822.

47. Drewry, *Slave Insurrections,* 102.

48. The program and script of the "Southampton County Bi-Centennial 1749–1949" can be found at the Library of Virginia.

49. Frances Lawrence Webb, *Recollections of Franklin and Historical Sketches of Southampton County,* ed. John C. Parker (Franklin, Va.: Franklin Library, 1963), excerpted in Tragle, *Southampton,* 397.

50. *The Democrat,* 27 August 1902; The Leander Firestone biography can be found in *History of Franklin and Pickaway Counties, Ohio* (Cleveland, Ohio: Williams Brothers, 1880). Reference found at USGenWeb Archives for Ohio on the Internet.

51. "Dr. D. B. Miller to William Styron," 11 October 1967, William Styron Papers, Rare Book, Manuscript, and Special Collections Library, Duke University.

52. Greenberg, *Confessions,* 19.

53. "Robert B. Franklin to William Styron," 18 November 1968, William Styron Papers, Rare Book, Manuscript, and Special Collection Library, Duke University.

54. Cromwell, "The Aftermath of Nat Turner's Insurrection," reprinted in Tragle, *Southampton,* 378.

CHAPTER TWO

1. *Richmond Constitutional Whig,* 29 August 1831, in *The Southampton Slave Revolt of 1831: A Compilation of Source Material,* comp. Henry Irving Tragle (Amherst: University of Massachusetts Press, 1971), 53.

2. *Norfolk Herald,* 29 August 1831.

3. *Richmond Enquirer,* 2 September 1831.

4.   John Timothee Trezevant, *The Trezevant Family in the United States* (Columbia, S.C.: The State Company, 1914), 24; *Biographical Directory of the American Congress, 1774–1996* (Alexandria, Va.: CQ Staff Directories, 1997), 1961.

5.   *Southampton County Court Minute Book*, 20 June 1815, 18 May 1818, 16 May 1825, Library of Virginia.

6.   *Southampton County Court Minute Book*, 21 March 1827, Library of Virginia.

7.   *Richmond Compiler*, 24 August 1831, in *Norfolk American Beacon*, 27 August 1831, under news of 26 August

8.   Theodore Trezvant to editors, 31 October 1831, *Norfolk American Beacon*, 5 November 1831.

9.   *Southampton County Court Minute Book*, 21 August 1826, Library of Virginia. *Southampton County Personal Tax List*, Nottoway Parish, 1827, p. 13, Library of Virginia. *Southampton County Land Tax Book*, Nottoway Parish, 1827, pp. 17–18, Library of Virginia.

10. *Southampton County Circuit Superior Court Minute Book*, 1 September 1831, Southampton County Courthouse, Courtland, Va.

11. *Richmond Enquirer*, 30 August 1831.

12. William C. Parker to Bernard Peyton, 14 September 1831; William C. Parker to Gov. John Floyd, 1 October 1831, Executive Papers, Library of Virginia.

13. [Thomas Ruffin Gray], *To the Public* [1834], 8. The copy of this pamphlet in special collections of the Library of Virginia is missing the title page. The pamphlet concerns Gray's quarrel with Dr. Orris A. Browne of Southampton.

14. Deed, Thomas Gray to Thomas R. Gray, 4 June 1821, *Southampton County Deed Book* 18: 134, Library of Virginia; Thomas Parramore, *Southampton County, Virginia* (Charlottesville: University Press of Virginia, 1978), 51.

15. Deed, Thomas R. Gray to Richard Urquhart trustees, 17 May 1830, *Southampton County Deed Book* 21: 339, Library of Virginia.

16. *Southampton County Personal Property Tax List*, Nottoway Parish, 1831, p. 14, Library of Virginia. Gray again owned a horse by spring 1832.

17. List of taxable town lots, *Southampton County Land Tax Book*, Nottoway Parish, 1830, p. 27 Library of Virginia.

18. *Southampton County Court Minute Book*, 20 December 1830, Library of Virginia.

19. Brodnax's notes are in Southampton County Court, box 93, Judgments, 1831, Library of Virginia.

20. James W. Parker and William C. Parker were not related.

21. *Southampton County Land Tax Book*, St. Luke's Parish, 1827, pp. 17, 21, Library of Virginia.

22. Theodore Trezvant to editors, 31 October 1831, *Norfolk American Beacon*, 5 November 1831.

23. "Small Talk," *Raleigh Observer*, 3 November 1877.

24. Thomas R. Gray, *The Confessions of Nat Turner* (Baltimore: Lucas & Deaver, 1831), 15–16.

25. Theodore Trezvant to editors of the *Richmond Constitutional Whig*, 3 September 1831, *Richmond Constitutional Whig*, 6 September 1831, in *Norfolk American Beacon*, 10 September 1831.

26. Evidence on the Turner, Francis, Moore, and Travis families and slaves is drawn from the author's Southampton County biographical research files (hereafter cited as SCB). These files, in turn, are drawn from *Southampton County Land Tax Books, 1810–1839; Personal Property Tax Books, 1807–1836; Will Books, 1783–1852; Deed Books, 1808–1847; Register of Marriages, 1750–1854; County Court Minute Books, 1811–42*; genealogical sources and published family histories; and manuscript schedules of the *U.S. Census for Southampton, 1810–60*.

27. *Richmond Enquirer*, 2 September 1831.

28. "Inventory of estate for Joseph Reese," 20 November 1826, *Southampton County Will Book* 10: 180–81, Library of Virginia. Jack was listed as a "boy."

29. Jordan Barnes, who hired Jack in 1831, testified that Jack returned home Monday morning and told him of the Whitehead killings. *Southampton County Court Minute Book*, 5 September 1831, Library of Virginia.

30. Moses did not witness the attack at Henry Bryant's house or the assault on Trajan Doyel.

31. *Southampton County Court Minute Book*, 3, 5 September 1831, Library of Virginia.

32. *Richmond Constitutional Whig*, 3 September 1831, in *Norfolk Herald*, 7 September 1831. Pleasants was referring to Moses when he mentioned "a negro boy whom they carried along to hold their horses."

33. Moses testified at the trials of Davy Turner, Jack Reese, Nathan Blunt, Nathan Francis, Tom Francis, Davy Francis, and Lucy Barrow. He was listed as a witness in trial documents for Joe Turner, Matt Ridley, Jim Porter, Stephen Bell, and Sam Edwards, in Southampton County Court, box 93, Judgments, 1831, Library of Virginia.

34. *Southampton County Court Minute Book*, 18 October 1831, Library of Virginia. Virginia, Auditor of Public Accounts, List of Slaves and Free Persons of Color Received into the Penitentiary of Virginia for Sale and Transportation from the 25th June 1816 to the 1st February 1842; p. 7, box 1972, Condemned Blacks Executed or Transported, 1783–1865, Library of Virginia.

35. *Raleigh Register*, 8 September 1831.

36. *Richmond Compiler*, 3 September 1831, in *Richmond Enquirer*, 6 September 1831.

37. One other letter, by a woman who lived east of Jerusalem, referred to the arrival of an express from Cross Keys. See *Richmond Compiler*, 27 August 1831, in *Richmond Enquirer*, 30 August 1831.

38. Italics in original.

39. Jack Reese described the idea in these terms: "[T]hey intended to rise and kill all the white people." He said Hark had predicted that "as they went on and killed the whites the blacks would join them." *Southampton County Court Minute Book*, 3 September 1831, p. 89 Library of Virginia.

40. *Richmond Constitutional Whig*, 26 September 1831, in *Norfolk American Beacon*, 1 October 1831.

41. Gray, "Confessions," in *Confessions*, Greenberg, 19.

42. Ibid., 15.

43. Stephen B. Oates suggests that William C. Parker may have been the author; see *The Fires of Jubilee: Nat Turner's Fierce Rebellion* (New York: Harper and Row, 1975), 102. Henry I. Tragle suggests the author was Gray; see Tragle, "Styron and His Sources," *Massachusetts Review* 11 (1970): 144–47; reprinted in *Southampton Slave Revolt*, 406–8. Kenneth S. Greenberg makes a similar suggestion in *The Confessions of Nat Turner and Related Documents* (New York: Bedford Books of St. Martin's Press, 1996), 9–10.

44. Ibid., 10.

45. Ibid., 8.

46. In Gray, "Confessions," in *Confessions*, Greenberg. Nelson replaced Austin at Cabin Pond.

47. *Richmond Enquirer*, 30 September 1831. This fourth communication consisted of a letter dated 21 September and an attachment dated 24 September by the same author.

48. *Greensville County Circuit Superior Court, Order Book 1-C*, 16 September 1831, Greensville County Courthouse, Emporia, Va. This entry indicated that Judge Robert B. Taylor heard no cases on this day, merely entering into record rules of the court; no attorneys or prosecutors were named.

49. On 14 September, in transmitting a description of Nat Turner to the governor, Parker had reminded Governor Floyd of the "volunteer corps." Also on that day he wrote to Colonel Bernard Peyton, seeking his support for the "volunteer corps." William C. Parker to John Floyd, 14 September 1831; Parker to Peyton, 14 September 1831, box 321, Executive Papers, Library of Virginia.

50. O. A. Browne, Medical Account of T. R. Gray, September 1831, *Browne v. Gray*, Southampton County Court Records, box 39, Chancery Papers, 1835, Library of Virginia. Gray's father lay ill and dying during these weeks. Captain Gray wrote a will on 6 September and died before 19 September, when the will was proved. Browne's bill, which listed visits on the 19th and 20th, clearly was for services rendered to the son, not to the father.

51. *Richmond Enquirer*, 8 November 1831. The appearance of identical phrases in the 1 November letter and in *The Confessions* has been taken as evidence that Gray wrote the letter. (There were ten such identical phrases—"a shotgun well charged" and "a small light sword," for example.) The similarities in expression could indicate instead a shar-

ing of information and catch phrases between members of the courthouse circle. For an attribution of this letter to Gray, see Daniel S. Fabricant, "Thomas R. Gray and William Styron: Finally, A Critical Look at the 1831 Confessions of Nat Turner," *American Journal of Legal History* 37 (1993): 345.

52. The list of victims in the *Richmond Constitutional Whig* letter (dated 17 September in manuscript) followed an order close to the actual sequence of attacks, as did lists in the *Norfolk American Beacon* on 15 September 1831 and in *The Confessions.*

53. Gray, "Confessions," in *Confessions*, Greenberg, 3–5.

54. Ibid., 7–11.

55. Ibid., 11. Here Gray identified the white man for the first time by name. He was Etheldred T. Brantley, who resided in Cross Keys in 1831 as overseer for David Westbrook. *Southampton County Personal Property Tax List*, St. Luke's Parish, 1831, p. 11, Library of Virginia.

56. He mentioned the whipping in *Richmond Constitutional Whig*, 26 September 1831.

57. Gray, "Confessions," in *Confessions*, Greenberg, 11–18.

58. Ibid., 18.

59. Ibid., 19–21.

60. Ibid., 22–23.

61. Thomas C. Parramore, *Southampton County, Virginia* (Charlottesville: University Press of Virginia, 1978), 112.

62. The reviewer probably was editor Thomas Ritchie himself. Modern scholarly skepticism is expressed in Seymour L. Gross and Eileen Bender, "History, Politics and Literature: The Myth of Nat Turner," *American Quarterly* 23 (1971): 487–518; see also Mary Kemp Davis, *Nat Turner Before the Bar of Judgment: Fictional Treatments of the Southampton Slave Insurrection* (Baton Rouge: Louisiana State University Press, 1999), 63–76. The issue of authenticity reappeared in Tony Horwitz, "Untrue Confessions," *New Yorker*, 13 December 1999.

63. On slave confessions, see Thomas D. Morris, *Southern Slavery and the Law, 1619–1860* (Chapel Hill: University of North Carolina Press, 1996), 239–46; and Philip J. Schwarz, *Twice Condemned: Slaves and the Criminal Laws of Virginia, 1705–1865* (Baton Rouge: Louisiana State University Press, 1988), 53–54.

64. Gray, "Confessions," in *Confessions*, Greenberg, 7–11.

65. Biographical evidence in this and the next paragraph comes from SCB.

66. The revelation is described in Gray, "Confessions," in *Confessions*, Greenberg, 11.

67. The remarks about Travis are in Gray, "Confessions," in *Confessions*, Greenberg, 11.

68. William C. Parker wrote his description of Nat Turner with the aid of "persons acquainted with him from his infancy." Parker to Floyd, 14 September 1831, box 321, Executive Papers, Library of Virginia.

69. John Clark Turner's age appeared in U.S. Census, Manuscript Schedules, Southampton County, Va., 1850, p. 257, National Archives, Washington, D.C.

70. One link between Sarah Francis and the Turner Methodists was documented in 1811, when her husband helped to pay taxes on the acre given by Benjamin Turner. *Southampton County Land Tax Book*, St. Luke's Parish, 1811, listing for Nathan Turner, Jr., Samuel Francis, and others, p. 30, Library of Virginia.

71. Virginia, Auditor, List of Slaves Received into the Penitentiary, p. 7, box 1972, *Condemned Blacks Executed or Transported*, Library of Virginia.

72. The narrative begins in the final paragraph of Nat's recollections, on p. 11 of the original pamphlet, with Nat Turner saying, "And immediately on the sign appearing in the heavens." It concludes on p. 18, where he said, "I am here loaded with chains, and willing to suffer the fate that awaits me." The count of new details includes only new information presented from the perspective of Nat Turner. The number might vary with different definitions and methods but probably would not fall below 100 or rise above 125.

73. Inventory of estate for Samuel Francis, 27 May 1815, *Southampton County Will Book* 8: 379, Library of Virginia. Will was between 32 and 36 years old in 1831 and probably had been a slave of the Francis family his entire life.

74. Gray, "Confessions," in *Confessions*, Greenberg, 12.

75. Ibid., 12.
76. Ibid., 12–13. After the Whitehead events, Will Francis disappeared from Nat Turner's narrative. No other witnesses mentioned him, though it is possible that white authorities mistook statements about "Will" as references to Billy Artist, a free black man.
77. Events from the Whitehead farm through the Waller farm are in Gray, "Confessions," in *Confessions*, Greenberg, 14.
78. Gray, "Confessions," in *Confessions*, Greenberg, 14–15; *Southampton County Register of Marriages* 2:395, Library of Virginia. Rebecca Ivy and William Williams signed a marriage bond on 21 January 1829, with her father consenting. She was listed in the 1830 census as being between 15 and 20 years old. U.S. Census, Southampton, 1830, p. 259, National Archives.
79. Gray, "Confessions," in *Confessions*, Greenberg, 15.
80. Ibid., 18.
81. Ibid., 12.
82. *Richmond Constitutional Whig*, 26 September 1831.
83. *Southampton County Register of Marriages* 2: 402, 679; *U.S. Census, Southampton, 1830*, p. 260, National Archives. The existence of the Travis infant was not recorded in the census taken in the summer of 1830.
84. Gray, "Confessions," in *Confessions*, Greenberg, 14.
85. Ibid., 12.
86. *Oxford English Dictionary*, 2d ed., prepared by J. A. Simpson and E.S.C. Weiner (Oxford: Clarendon Press, 1989), s.v., "terror."
87. Gray, "Confessions," in *Confessions*, Greenberg, 18.

CHAPTER THREE

1. *The Confessions, op. cit.*, Thomas Gray, Baltimore, 1831, p. 4. Only coincidence is meant to be shown here, not "prenatal influence" which J. W. Cromwell sees—*Journal of Negro History*, Vol. 5 (1920) No. 2, April, "The Aftermath of Nat Turner's Insurrection," p. 208. The information on Vesey is in *An Account of some of the principal slave insurrections, and others, which have occurred, or been attempted, in the United States . . .* New York, 1860, by Joshua Coffin, p. 33.
2. The *National Intelligencer*, Washington, September 24, 1831.
3. The *Liberator*, October 1, 1831, Vol. I, p. 159.
4. Richmond *Enquirer*, October 25, 1831.
5. W. S. Drewry, *The Southampton Insurrection*, Washington, 1900, p. 173. Note 1.
6. *The Confessions. . . .* p. 11.
7. *The Confessions. . . .* p. 9.
8. In fact Drewry says that "Nat himself, up to the time of the insurrection had been faithful and highly trusted"; p. 28 of *The Southampton Insurrection, op. cit.*
9. B. B. Weeks, *Magazine of American History*, XXV, June, 1891, op. cit., p. 450 says that Turner repaid Joseph Travis' kindness by running away. Turner makes it clear that he ran away in 1825 and became the slave of Travis in 1830. From whom he ran away is not certain, but he certainly did not run away from Joseph Travis. *Confessions*, pp. 9, 11.
10. *The Southampton Insurrection*, Washington, 1900, by W. S. Drewry, p. 28. He does not say whom he is quoting. Similar, though not precisely the same words are used by Thomas Gray in the *Confessions*, p. 18.
11. J. C. Ballagh, *A History of Slavery in Virginia*, Johns Hopkins University Studies. . . . Extra Volume XXIV, Baltimore, 1902, p. 93.
12. The rest of this paragraph is taken from *The Confessions* passim. The quotations are on pp. 7, 8, 9. The first quotation is given by W. S. Drewry, *The Southampton Insurrection, op. cit.*, 29.
13. W. S. Drewry, *Ibid.*, p. 27; U. B. Phillips, *American Negro Slavery. . . .* New York, London, 1918, p. 480.
14. W. S. Drewry, *Ibid.*, pp. 26, 27; U. B. Phillips, Ibid., p. 480.
15. *The Confessions. . . .* Thomas Gray, Baltimore, 1831, p. 11.

16. For examples see *The Atlas*, New York, September 10, 1831, quoting the *Richmond Compiler* of August 29; J. C. Ballagh, *A History of Slavery in Virginia*, *op. cit.*, p. 93; *American Annual Register*, 1830–1831, Boston and New York, 1832, p. 349.

17. As examples see, The *National Intelligencer*, Washington, September 10, 1831; J. W. Cromwell, *Journal of Negro History*, Vol. 5, *op. cit.*, 209; Benjamin Brawley, *A Social History of the American Negro.* . . . New York, 1921, p. 141.

18. *New York Evening Post*, October 10, 1831.

19. *The Confessions.* . . . pp. 8–9.

20. *The Papers of Thomas Ruffin* collected and edited by J. G. de Roulhac Hamilton, Raleigh, North Carolina, 1918 (publication of the N. C. Historical Commission), Vol. II, p. 45.

21. Richmond *Enquirer*, August 30, 1831; editor of the Richmond *Constitutional Whig*, quoted by the *Atlas*, New York, Vol. 4, p. 7, September 17, 1831.

22. J. E. Cooke, *Virginia, A History of the People* (American Commonwealths, editor, H. E. Scudder), Boston, 1883, p. 486.

23. As examples, Richmond *Enquirer*, August 30, October 18, November 8, 1831.

24. *Journal of the House of Delegates of the Commonwealth of Virginia.* . . . 1831, Richmond, no pagination; the message is also in *Niles' Weekly Register*, XLI, 350, January 7, 1832.

25. Richmond *Enquirer*, November 26, 1831, quoting Raleigh Register (n.d.)

26. *Niles' Weekly Register*, XL, 455, August 27, 1831.

27. Article signed "A.G." in the *Free Enquirer*, New York, Vol. III, No. 47, September 17, 1831.

28. *ante*, note 24, *Niles' Weekly Register*, XLI, 350, January 7, 1832.

29. S. E. Morison, *The Life and letters of Harrison Gray Otis.* . . . Boston and New York, 1913, Vol. II, p. 260. (emphasis in original).

30. "The Morals of Slavery. . . ." in *The Pro-Slavery Argument.* . . . Chancellor Harper, Governor Hammond, Dr. Simms, and Professor Dew, Charleston, 1852, p. 223. Miss Martineau's statement is in her *Society in America*, New York and London, 1837, Fourth edition, Vol. I, p. 378.

31. A. B. Hart, *Slavery and Abolition 1831–1841* (Vol. 16 of the *American Nation* series, edited by A. B. Hart), N.Y. & London, 1906, pp. 217–218.

32. Hilary A. Herbert, *The Abolition Crusade and its consequences.* . . . New York, 1912, p. 60.

33. *Life, Travels and Opinions of Benjamin Lundy.* . . . *op. cit.*, Philadelphia, 1847, pp. 249, 247, also p. 237.

34. "Miscellaneous Papers 1672–1865" in *Collections of the Virginia History Society*, new series, VI, Richmond, 1887, p. 24 note 69.

35. *The Southampton Insurrection*, *op. cit.*, p. 150.

36. *The Education of the Negro prior to 1861.* . . . , New York and London, 1915, p. 163.

37. The *Liberator*, September 24, 1831, Vol. I, p. 155.

38. *History of the United States from the compromise of 1850*, New York, 1896, Vol. I, p. 57.

39. *Life and Letters of Harrison Gray Otis.* . . . Boston and N.Y., 1913, Vol. II, p. 261.

40. The *Liberator* (Boston), Vol. I, p. 143, September 3, 1831; quoted, in part, in *William Lloyd Garrison 1805–1879.* . . . , by his children, W. P. and F. J. Garrison, New York, 1885. Vol. I, p. 250.

41. J. Macy, *The Anti-Slavery Crusade.* . . . (Chronicles of America V. 28, edited by A. Johnson), New Haven, Toronto, London, 1921, p. 59 says this concerning Garrison; see also G. H. Barnes, *The Anti-Slavery Impulse 1830–1844.* . . . N.Y. & London, 1933, p. 51.

42. *The Confessions*, p. 9.

43. J. W. Burgess, *The Middle Period 1817–1858*, New York, 1918, p. 249.

44. Frederick Douglass' speech at Moorfields, England, May 12, 1846—". . . the better you treat a slave, the more you destroy his value as a slave. . . . as soon as the blow was not to be feared, then came the longing for liberty." C. G. Woodson, *Negro Orators and their Orations*, Washington, 1925, p. 162.

45. *The Confessions*, pp. 9, 10. Thomas Gray, Baltimore, 1831.

46. *Ibid.*, p. 11, quoted, not accurately, by W. S. Drewry, *The Southampton Insurrection*, Washington, 1900, p. 33.

47. In the Richmond *Enquirer* of November 8, 1831.

48. W. S. Drewry, *The Southampton Insurrection*, pp. 145–150; given also in J. E. Cutler, *Lynch*

Law, an investigation into the history of lynching in the United States, New York, London, Bombay, 1905, p. 93. This is contradicted by account in the *Atlas,* Vol. 4, p. 71, November 12, 1831, quoting the Petersburg *Intelligencer* (n.d.) ". . . not the least personal violence was offered to Nat. . . ." The eclipse is noted in *The Confessions,* p. 11.

49. "The Nat Turner Insurrection," W. H. Parker, in *Old Virginia Yarns,* V. 1, no. 1, January 1893, p. 18. (no title page—the above is written in pencil—copy in the Virginia State Library, Richmond).

50. *New York Evening Post,* August 26, 1831; S. B. Weeks, *Magazine of American History,* XXV, June, 1891, p. 451.

51. "The 100th Anniversary of the Turner revolt," by N. Stevens in *The Communist,* N.Y. August, 1931, Vol. X, No. 8, p. 739.

52. *The Southampton Insurrection,* W. S. Drewry, *op. cit.,* p. 157.

53. *The Confessions,* p. 12. This date is followed by all writers, except three. The exceptions are—(Samuel Warner) *Authentic and impartial narrative of the tragical scene which was witnessed in Southampton County (Virginia) on Monday the 22d of August last.* . . . New York, 1831; J. B. McMaster (who used Warner pamphlet) *A History of the People.* . . . Vol. VI, p. 73 (night of August 22) New York, 1906; F. B. Sanborn, *Life and Letters of John Brown.* . . . Boston, 1891 (date as August 23) p. 34, note 1.

54. *The Confessions,* p. 12 and 20. See also W. S. Drewry, *op. cit.,* p. 117

55. *History of the Negro race in America from 1619 to 1880.* . . . by George W. Williams, N.Y. 1883, Vol. II, 87–88; same speech quoted uncritically by H. P. Wilson, *John Brown soldier of fortune.* . . . Lawrence, Kansas, 1913, pp. 360–361.

56. Ante, *The Papers of Thomas Ruffin,* Vol. II, p. 45.

57. T. W. Higginson, "Nat Turner's Insurrection," *Atlantic Monthly,* August, 1861, Vol. 8, p. 176; W. S. Drewry, *The Southampton Insurrection,* Washington, 1900, p. 117.

58. W. S. Drewry, *op. cit.,* p. 117; p. 117 n. 2.

59. The *Atlas,* New York, September 10, 1831; *Encyclopedia Britannica,* 14th edition, Vol. 22, p. 628; W. S. Drewry, *op. cit.,* p. 59.

60. T. W. Higginson, *Atlantic Monthly,* August, 1861, *op. cit.,* pp. 180–181.

61. W. S. Drewry, *op. cit.,* pp. 35–74.

62. *Ibid.,* p. 36.

63. *The Autobiography of Lincoln Steffens,* complete in one volume, New York, 1931, p. 844.

64. *Richmond Enquirer,* November 8, 1831; T. W. Higginson gave this, without quotation marks, and as being stated by the editor of the *Enquirer.* The editor here was paraphrasing Turner. See *Atlantic Monthly,* V. 8, August, 1861, *op. cit.,* p. 176.

65. *Niles' Weekly Register* (Baltimore) XL, August 27, 1831, p. 456.

66. As examples, see *Ibid.,* XL, 455, 456; *Richmond Enquirer,* August 26, 1831; (S. Warner) *Authentic and impartial narrative.* . . . *op. cit.,* New York, 1831, p. 10.

67. *A History of the people of the United States.* . . . N.Y. 1906, p. 73.

68. *The Confessions.* . . . , p. 14 ff.

69. *Niles' Weekly Register* (speech of December 6, 1831), XLI, 350, January 7, 1832.

70. Richmond *Constitutional Whig,* August 29, 1831.

71. Quoted in The *Atlas,* New York, September 10, 1831.

72. Dated Raleigh, August 28, 1831, in *The Papers of Thomas Ruffin,* edited by J. G. de Roulhac Hamilton, Raleigh, 1918, Vol. II, p. 46.

73. As examples, see: T. W. Higginson, *Atlantic Monthly, op. cit.,* Vol. 8, p. 176; W. D. Weatherford and C. S. Johnson, *Race Relations.* N.Y. 1934, p. 271; Drewry, *op. cit.,* p. 96 (this is, however, contradicted by a statement on p. 86); U. B. Phillips, *American Negro Slavery.* . . . New York, London, 1918, p. 481.

74. *A History of Slavery in Virginia, op. cit.,* Baltimore, 1902, p. 93.

75. Quoting the editor of the Richmond *Constitutional Whig* in the *Atlas,* Vol. 4, p. 7, September 17, 1831.

76. *The Southampton Insurrection,* Washington, 1900, p. 65.

77. See: T. W. Higginson, *Atlantic Monthly, op. cit.,* p. 176; J. W. Cromwell, "The Aftermath of Nat Turner's Insurrection," *Journal of Negro History* (1920, Vol. V, p. 214).

78. In *Confessions,* p. 22; (S. Warner) *Authentic and impartial narrative.* . . . N.Y., 1831, the total is in the title—see bibliography.

79. As examples see: *Harper's Encyclopedia of United States History*. . . . N.Y., London, 1902, Vol. IX, p. 133; U. B. Phillips, *American Negro Slavery*. . . . N.Y. & London, 1918, p. 481; *Race Relations* by W. D. Weatherford, C. S. Johnson, *op. cit.*, N.Y. 1934, p. 271.

80. W. S. Drewry, *op. cit.*, p. 196.

81. *William and Mary College Quarterly Historical Magazine*, Vol. XXIV (first series) 1915, Richmond, p. 52.

82. J. W. Cromwell, *op. cit.*, *Journal of Negro History*, V. 214; *Anti-Slavery Manual*. . . . by Rev. LeRoy Sunderland, second edition, 1837, N.Y., p. 87; The *Atlas*, *op. cit.*, Vol. 4, p. 6, September 17, 1831: J. C. Ballagh, *History of Slavery in Virginia*, *op. cit.*, p. 93; G. M. Weston, *The Progress of Slavery in the United States*, Washington, 1857, p. 192; J. W. Burgess, *The Middle Period 1817–1858*, N.Y., 1898, p. 249; L. P. Stryker, *Andrew Johnson, a study in courage*, N.Y., 1929, p. 45—and others.

83. *Society in America, fourth edition*, New York, London, 1837, Vol. I, p. 378; J. K. Paulding, *Slavery in the United States*, N.Y., 1836, p. 192, also p. 56—the planter was George E. Harrison—*Virginia Magazine of History and Biography*, Richmond, XXVI, 1928, p. 277, n; N.Y., *Evening Post*, August 26, 1831.

84. Richmond *Enquirer*, August 26, 1831; *Niles' Weekly Register*, XL, 456, Aug. 27, 1831; *Ibid*, XLI, p. 4, September 3, 1831.

85. *Journal of the House of Delegates*. . . . 1831–1832, no pagination; this may be found in H. Wilson, *History of the rise and fall of the slave power in America*, Boston, 1872, Vol. I, p. 191.

86. *Atlantic Monthly*, August, 1861, Vol. 8, p. 174.

87. *The Southampton Insurrection*, *op. cit.*, p. 116.

88. "The participation of white men in Virginia Negro insurrections," *Journal of Negro History*, XVI, 1931, pp. 163–164. Chesterfield County is in the Piedmont district.

89. See letter of E. D. Guion to Thomas Ruffin, *Papers of Thomas Ruffin*, J. G. de Roulhac Hamilton, editor, p. 45; W. S. Drewry, *The Southampton Insurrection*, Washington, 1900, pp. 39–40; The *Atlas*, quoting editor of Richmond *Constitutional Whig*, Vol. 4, p. 7, New York, September 17, 1831.

90. *A History of Virginia from its discovery*, N.Y. & London, 1848, Vol. II, p. 441 (emphasis in original).

91. *American Negro Slavery*. . . . N.Y. and London, 1918, p. 481.

92. *The Confessions*, Thomas Gray, Baltimore, 1831, pp. 15, 16—the fact that seven or eight men were left at the gate is also given by W. S. Drewry, *op. cit.*, p. 62; J. W. Cromwell, *Journal of Negro History*, V, 211 (1920).

93. W. S. Drewry, *op. cit.*, p. 66.

94. Given in *The Atlas*, Vol. III, no. 52, September 10, 1831, N.Y.

95. "Federal Aid in domestic disturbances 1787–1903," H. C. Corbin and F. T. Wilson, *Senate Document* No. 209, 57th Cong., 2nd sess. (Vol. 15), Washington, 1903, pp. 56, 261.

96. *The Atlas*, September 10, 1831, Vol. III, No. 52, New York, quoting the *Richmond Compiler* of August 29th.

97. As examples; J. W. Cromwell, *Journal of Negro History*, V. 214; A. B. Hart, *Slavery and Abolition, 1831–41*, N.Y. & London, 1906, p. 218; U. B. Phillips, *American Negro Slavery*. . . . New York, London, 1918, 481.

98. S. Warner, *Authentic and Impartial narrative*. . . . , New York, 1831, p. 15; T. Gray, *The Confessions*. . . . Baltimore, 1831, p. 23.

99. *American Negro Slavery*, *op. cit.*, 481 note 76; J. C. Ballagh says 13, *A History of Slavery in Virginia*, *op. cit.*, Baltimore, 1902, p. 94.

100. As example see A. B. Hart, *op. cit.*, *Ibid.*, J. W. Cromwell, *op. cit.*, *Ibid.*

101. The capture is in *The Confessions*, p. 16; it has been very often, and, on the whole, accurately, retold. For the rumors, see *Richmond Enquirer*, October 18, 1831; *Niles' Weekly Register*, October 29, 1831, XLI, 162.

102. *The Confessions*, 16; in *The Communist*, X, 741, N. Stevens suggests he was given food by Negroes. No evidence of this has been seen.

103. W. S. Drewry, *The Southampton Insurrection*, Washington, 1900, p. 100, note 2, gives the entire sentence. What his source was is not known.

104. See, for example, New York *Evening Post*, November 19, 1831.

CHAPTER FOUR

1. Thomas R. Gray, "The Confessions of Nat Turner," in *The Confessions of Nat Turner and Related Documents*, ed. Kenneth S. Greenberg (Boston: Bedford Books of St. Martin's Press, 1996), 48. Henry Porter, tortured to death by his captors, is identified as a preacher in the *Haverhill (N.H.) Post*, 14 September 1831; Hark Travis, lately purchased by Mrs. Caty Whitehead, is said by the *Fayetteville (N.C.) Journal*, 31 August 1831, to have been a Baptist preacher and a ringleader. Four of the original six rebels were, according to the *Norfolk and Portsmouth Herald*, 29 August 1831, said to be preachers, though the fourth has not been identified. The terms preacher, minister, and exhorter were apparently used interchangeably for black religious leaders.

2. Gray, "Confessions," in *Confessions*, Greenberg, 48–49.

3. William S. Drewry, *The Southampton Insurrection of 1831* (1900; reprint, Murfreesboro, N.C.: Johnson Publishing Company, 1968), 25–39; *New York General Advertiser*, 1 September 1831; *Raleigh Register*, 18 September 1831; *Richmond Compiler*, 2 September, 1831; *Richmond Enquirer*, 30 August 1831; *Norfolk American Beacon*, 29 August 1831.

4. Gray, "Confessions," in *Confessions*, Greenberg, 49; *Niles' Weekly Register*, 3 September 1831.

5. Gray, "Confessions," in *Confessions*, Greenberg, 49; Drewry, *Southampton*, 37; Johnson, R. Roy, *The Nat Turner Story* (Murfreesboro, N.C.: Johnson Publishing Co., 1970), 93; *Richmond Constitutional Whig*, 26 September 1831.

6. Gray, "Confessions," in *Confessions*, Greenberg, 49; Drewry, *Southampton*, 37; *Courier and New York Enquirer for the Country*, 16 September 1831; *Richmond Constitutional Whig*, 8 September 1831; *Richmond Compiler*, 31 August 1831; *Commonwealth* v. *Moses*, Southampton County Judgments, 1830–1841, Library of Virginia.

7. Gray, "Confessions," in *Confessions*, Greenberg, 49; Drewry, *Southampton*, 36.

8. Gray, "Confessions," in *Confessions*, Greenberg, 49; Drewry, *Southampton*, 38; Johnson, *Nat Turner Story*, 54, 69.

9. Gray, "Confessions," in *Confessions*, Greenberg, 49; Drewry, *Southampton*, 40.

10. Drewry, *Southampton*, 40–41.

11. *Richmond Constitutional Whig*, 13 September 1832.

12. Gray, "Confessions," in *Confessions*, Greenberg, 49; Henry I. Tragle, comp., *Southampton Slave Revolt of 1831: A Compilation of Source Material* (Amherst: University of Massachusetts Press, 1971) 196–97.

13. Drewry, *Southampton*, 42, 66.

14. Gray, "Confessions," in *Confessions*, Greenberg, 50; *Niles' Weekly Register*, 3 September 1831.

15. Gray, "Confessions," in *Confessions*, Greenberg, 50; Drewry, *Southampton*, 43.

16. Gray, "Confessions," in *Confessions*, Greenberg, 50; Drewry, *Southampton*, 43–44.

17. Gray, "Confessions," in *Confessions*, Greenberg, 50; Drewry, *Southampton*, 44–45; Tragle, *Southampton*, 107.

18. Gray, "Confessions," in *Confessions*, Greenberg, 50; Drewry, *Southampton*, 44–45.

19. Gray, "Confessions," in *Confessions*, Greenberg, 48; *Richmond Constitutional Whig*, 26 September 1831.

20. Gray, "Confessions," in *Confessions*, Greenberg, 49.

21. Ibid., 40; Drewry, *Southampton*, 42, 55.

22. *New York Daily Advertiser*, 29 August 1831; *Courier and New York Enquirer for the Country*, 6 September 1831; *Richmond Constitutional Whig*, 29 August 1831; *New York Spectator*, 30 August 1831.

23. *Richmond Constitutional Whig*, 3 September 1831.

24. Ibid., 26 September 1831.

25. Gray, "Confessions," in *Confessions*, Greenberg, 50; Drewry, *Southampton*, 45–49; Tragle, *Southampton*, 98–201.

26. Drewry, *Southampton*, 47, 74, n. 2.

27. Gray, "Confessions," in *Confessions*, Greenberg, 50; Drewry, *Southampton*, 49–50; letter of Jo Ella to Emma, 28 August 1831, Mordecai Family Papers, Folder 56, no. 847, Southern Historical Collection, University of North Carolina, Chapel Hill; Peter Ed-

wards' petition for compensation, Legislative Petitions, Southampton County, 1825–1863, Library of Virginia.

28. Richmond *Enquirer*, 30 August 1831; Drewry, *Southampton*, 50–51; *Fayetteville (N.C.) Carolina Observer*, 7 September 1831.

29. *Richmond Constitutional Whig*, 26 September 1831; Drewry, *Southampton* 52–53.

30. Gray, "Confessions," in *Confessions*, Greenberg, 51; Drewry, *Southampton*, 51–52.

31. Gray, "Confessions," in *Confessions*, Greenberg, 50–51; statement of Levi Waller, Court Notes, Southampton County Judgments, 1820–1841. These are rough summaries of testimony by witnesses and participants.

32. Gray, "Confessions," in *Confessions*, Greenberg, 50–51; Drewry, *Southampton*, 56–58. Statement of Mrs. Whitehead's slave Wallace, Southampton County Judgments, 1820–1841.

33. Drewry, *Southampton*, 57–58; "Trial of Nat Turner," *Southampton County Court Minute Book*, 1830–1845, Library of Virginia.

34. Tragle, *Southampton*, 194; Drewry, *Southampton*, 59.

35. Gray, "Confessions," in *Confessions*, Greenberg, 51; Drewry, *Southampton*, 59.

36. Gray, "Confessions," in *Confessions*, Greenberg, 51; Drewry, *Southampton*, 60–61; *Boston Liberator*, 17 September 1831; *Norfolk Herald*, 26 August 1831; *Richmond Religious Herald*, 2 September 1831; *Commonwealth* v. *Nelson Williams*, Southampton County Judgments, 1820–1841.

37. Drewry, *Southampton*, 61; *Southampton*, 53; Samuel Warner, "An Authentic Narrative of the Tragical Scene," in Tragle, *Southampton*, 287.

38. Drewry, *Southampton*, 45; Thomas C. Parramore, *Southampton County Virginia* (Charlottesville: University Press of Virginia, 1978), 88.

39. Drewry, *Southampton*, 76–77; *Richmond Compiler*, 27 August 1831; *Courier and New York Enquirer for the Country*, 6 September 1831; *Richmond Enquirer*, 30 August 1831.

40. Drewry, *Southampton*, e.g., 41, 43–47, 59.

41. *Richmond Compiler*, 31 August 1831; Drewry, *Southampton*, 117; extract from Thomas Wentworth Higginson, "Nat Turner's Insurrection," in *Nat Turner*, ed. Eric Foner (Englewood Cliffs, N.J.: Prentice-Hall, 1971), 134.

42. *Richmond Compiler*, 27 August 1831; Drewry, *Southampton*, 63–64; Gray, "Confessions," in *Confessions*, Greenberg, 51.

43. Gray, "Confessions," in *Confessions*, Greenberg, 51; Drewry, *Southampton*, 63–64.

44. Stephen B. Oates, *The Fires of Jubilee: Nat Turner's Fierce Rebellion* (New York: New American Library, 1975), 100; Drewry, *Southampton*, 64–65; Gray, "Confessions," in *Confessions*, Greenberg, 51–52.

45. *Raleigh Observer*, 3 November 1877.

46. Gray, "Confessions," in *Confessions*, Greenberg, 51–52; *Niles' Weekly Register*, 26 August 1831, Johnson, *Nat Turner Story*, 119.

47. Gray, "Confessions," in *Confessions*, Greenberg, 51–52; Drewry, *Southampton*, 65; *Norfolk Herald*, 26 August 1831; *Niles' Weekly Register*, 3 September 1831.

48. Gray, "Confessions," in *Confessions*, Greenberg, 51-52; *Commonwealth* v. *Daniel*, Southampton County Judgments, 1830–1841, Library of Virginia.

49. Gray, "Confessions," in *Confessions*, Greenberg, 52.

50. Drewry, *Southampton*, 68–69.

51. Ibid., 71.

52. Ibid., 71–72; Tragle, *Southampton*, 182–83.

53. Gray, "Confessions," in *Confessions*, Greenberg, 52–53, 85; Drewry, *Southampton*, 70–71.

54. Gray, "Confessions," in *Confessions*, Greenberg, 53; Drewry, *Southampton*, 72.

55. Drewry, *Southampton*, 72–73; testimony of Shadrac Futrel and Mary, *Commonwealth* v. *Moses*, Southampton County Judgments, 1830–1841.

56. Gray, "Confessions," in *Confessions*, Greenberg, 53; Drewry, *Southampton*, 73; Trial of Moses, Southampton County Judgments, 1830–1841; petition no. 9915-E, estate of Thomas Fitzhugh, Legislative Petitions, Southampton County, 1825–1863.

57. Gray, "Confessions," in *Confessions*, Greenberg, 53; Drewry, *Southampton*, 69–70; Tragle, *Southampton*, 186–88.

58. Gray, "Confessions," in *Confessions*, Greenberg, 53; (*Tarborough*) *North Carolina Free Press*, 8 September 1831.

59. Gray, "Confessions," in *Confessions*, Greenberg, 94.

60. Petition for compensation by estate of Thomas Fitzhugh, 29 December 1831, Legislative Petitions, Southampton County, 1825–1863.

61. Drewry, *Southampton*, 76–77, 82–83.

62. *North Carolina Free Press*, 30 August 1831.

63. Gay Neale, *Brunswick County, Virginia, 1720–1975* (Clarksville, Va.: Brunswick County Bicentennial Committee, 1975), 206.

64. *New York Daily Advertiser*, 29 August 1831; *Halifax (N.C.) Roanoke Advocate*, 13 October 1831.

65. Drewry, *Southampton*, 48, 98, n. 1; *Richmond Constitutional Whig*, 3 September 1831.

66. *North Carolina Free Press*, 6 September 1831; *Roanoke Advocate*, 13 October 1831.

67. John Hill Wheeler, *Historical Sketches of North Carolina, from 1584 to 1851* (Philadelphia: Lippincott, Grambo and Co., 1851), 210; Statement of John Edwards, 28 November 1831, on behalf of petition by Richard Porter, Legislative Petitions, Southampton County, 1825–1863.

68. Statements of Joseph Joiner, John Womack, and Levi Waller on behalf of petition for compensation by Peter Edwards, Legislative Petitions, Southampton County, 1825–1863; petition of Piety Reese for compensation, Legislative Petitions, Southampton County, 1825–1863.

69. *New York General Advertiser*, 1 September 1831; *Haverhill (N.H.) Post*, 14 September 1831.

70. *New York Constellation*, 8 October 1831. Smith, a Haverhill, N.H., native, was a Dartmouth College alumnus and a tutor. See Gary M. Williams to author, 24 April 1979.

71. Testimony of A. P. Peete and Thomas Porter, 22 November 1831, on behalf of Levi Waller's petition for compensation. Legislative Petitions, Southampton County, 1825–1863.

72. *Haverhill (N.H.) Post*, 14 September 1831; Jo Ella to Emma [Mordecai?], 28 August 1831, Mordecai Papers, No. 847, Box 56 (1825–1851), Southern Historical Collection, University of North Carolina, Chapel Hill.

73. *Richmond Constitutional Whig*, 3 September 1831.

74. *New York General Advertiser*, 1 September 1831; *Greenfield (Mass.) Gazette*, 30 August 1831; Seymour L. Gross and Eileen Bender, "History, Politics and Literature: The Myth of Nat Turner," *American Quarterly* XXIII (October 1971): 515; Howard P. Gates, Jr., *American Philatelist* (June 1988): 528–529.

75. *Haverhill (N.H.) Post*, 14 September 1831.

76. Anonymous, *American Slavery as it is: Testimony of a Thousand Witnesses* (New York: American Anti-slavery Society, 1839), 91.

77. *Courier and New York Enquirer for the Country*, 13, 18 October 1831.

78. Thomas Borland to Gov. Montford Stokes, 13 September 1831, Governor's Letter Book, 1 June–31 October 1831, 30, North Carolina Division of Archives, Raleigh; *Roanoke Advocate*, 30 August 1831.

79. *Haverhill (N.H.) Post*, 14 September 1831; petition of Benjamin Blunt's Anthony, 20 December 1824, Legislative Petitions, Southampton County, 1825–1863.

80. Southampton County Judgments, 1830–1841; *Norfolk American Beacon*, 29 August 1831; *Liberator*, 5 November 1831; *New York Badger's Weekly Messenger*, 7 September 1831.

81. *Edenton (N.C.) Gazette and Farmer's Palladium*, 27 September 1821; *Richmond Compiler*, 8 October 1831.

82. *Courier and New York Enquirer for the Country*, 11 November 1831; *Norfolk American Beacon*, 5 November 1831.

83. *Norfolk American Beacon*, 13 November 1831; *Petersburg (Va.) Intelligencer*, 8 November 1831.

84. *Liberator*, 19 November 1831; *Norfolk American Beacon*, 2 November 1831; *Petersburg Intelligencer*, 4 November 1831; *Richmond Enquirer*, 8 November 1831.

85. *Richmond Enquirer*, 8 November 1831.

86. *Norfolk American Beacon*, 8 November 1831.

87. *Courier and New York Enquirer for the Country*, 17, 18 September 1831; W. C. Parker to John Floyd, 30 September 1831, Executive Papers, Gov. John Floyd, Library of Virginia.

88. Gray, "Confessions," in *Confessions*, Greenberg, 42–43. No other source of the era confirms Nat's astonishing facility with the king's English as employed in Gray's version.

89. *Norfolk Herald*, 14 November 1831; *Richmond Constitutional Whig*, 11 November 1831; *Raleigh (N.C.) Star*, 10 November 1831.

90. *Washington (D.C.) Globe*, 22 November 1831; *Norfolk American Beacon*, 24 November 1831; *Norfolk Herald*, 14 November 1831.

91. Gray, "Confessions," in *Confessions*, Greenberg, 41.

92. Ibid., 54–55.

93. Ibid., 54.

94. *Liberator*, 17 December 1831.

95. Thomas Gray's will of 6 September 1831 was probated 9 September 1831, Southampton County Will Book, 10: 343, County Clerk's Office, Courtland, Va. See "The Godwin Family," *Virginia Magazine of History and Biography* V (1898): 201–2. Thomas Gray's wife apparently died before 1820. See Southampton County Court Records, November Court, 1793, Library of Virginia.

96. *Southampton County Land Tax* 1829, 1830–1831, 1832; *Southampton County Personal Property Tax*, 1829, 1830–31, 1832, Library of Virginia.

97. *Southampton County Court Minute Book*, Library of Virginia. The guardianship was dated 16 July 1832.

98. He was licensed to practice law on 20 December 1830. *Southampton County Court Minute Book*, 1824–1830, pp. 220, 357, Library of Virginia; *Norfolk American Beacon*, 28 October 1831; *Norfolk Herald*, 27 August 1845.

99. *Norfolk Herald*, 27 August 1845.

CHAPTER FIVE

1. The following overview of America in the late 1820s is based on many sources, including: Robert Baird, *Religion in America* (New York, 1844); Charles I. Foster, *An Errand of Mercy: The Evangelical United Front, 1790–1837* (Chapel Hill: University of North Carolina Press, 1960); Sidney E. Ahlstrom, *A Religious History of the American People* (New Haven: Yale University Press, 1972); John B. McMaster, *A History of the People of the United States*, 8 vols. (New York: D. Appleton and Company, 1918–24), IV, V; Perry Miller, *The Life of the Mind in America* (New York: Harcourt, Brace & World, 1965); Alice Felt Tyler, *Freedom's Ferment: Phases of American Social History to 1860* (Minneapolis: University of Minnesota Press, 1944); George Dangerfield, *The Era of Good Feelings* (New York: Harcourt, Brace & World, 1963). Of course the interpretation is largely my own.

2. See for instance Helen Hunt Jackson, *A Century of Dishonor* (1885; rpt. Minneapolis: Scholarly Press, 1964), *passim*; Grant Foreman, *Indian Removal* (Norman: University of Oklahoma Press, 1953), *passim*. See also the excellent collection of documents on the dispossession in Virgil J. Vogel, ed., *This Country Was Ours: A Documentary History of the American Indian* (New York: Harper and Row, 1972).

3. On the Missouri Compromise debates, see Dangerfield, *The Era*, pp. 95–245; and Glover Moore, *The Missouri Controversy, 1819–1821* (Lexington: University of Kentucky Press, 1953), *passim*.

4. *Negro Population*, pp. 24–57. The internal slave trade is discussed fully in Frederic Bancroft, *Slave Trading in the Old South* (1931; rpt. New York: Frederic Ungar, 1959), pp. 19–66; also Robinson, *Slavery*, pp. 427–66.

5. *Negro Population*, pp. 24–57. Examples of the references are to be found, for instance, in Aptheker, *Slave Revolts*, pp. 18–45, and Tragle, *Southampton*, p. 17.

6. In dealing with the local attorney, Thomas Gray, and his version of Turner's *Confessions* (Tragle, pp. 300–21), we are faced with many problems. Tragle offers a helpful analysis of the document and its authenticity in the course of his sharp and telling criticism of the novelist William Styron, pp. 401–09. I suspect that there is much truth in the *Confessions*, that Gray inserts himself more than is helpful, and that Nat Turner conceals a good deal. Oates's biography, *The Fires of Jubilee*, is competent but flat, missing the mystery inherent in a man like Turner.

7. Tragle, *Southampton*, pp. 306–07.

8. *Ibid.*, pp. 308.

9. *Ibid.*

10. Indeed, there soon developed a belief among many blacks that Nat was endowed with
    the gift of healing; others said he had power to control the clouds. Such stories, clearly
    drawing on the lively traditions of Africa, only added to the young man's renown. See
    Tragle, *Southampton*, pp. 222, 420–21, 100, 309–10; Oates, *Fires*, pp. 35–41; Aptheker,
    Slave Revolts, pp. 294–95.

11. On Nat Turner's marital status, the documents and suggestions provided by Tragle
    (*Southampton*, pp. 90, 281, 327) are valuable; also Oates, *Fires*, pp. 29, 162–63, 308–09.

12. The millenarian setting of early nineteenth-century Christianity is discussed in H. Shel-
    ton Smith, Robert T. Handy, Lefferts A. Loetscher, eds., *American Christianity*, 2 vols.
    (New York: Charles Scribner's Sons, 1960), II, pp. 12, 16, 18; Nelson Burr, *A Critical
    Bibliography of Religion in America*, Vol. IV of James W. Smith and A. Leland Jamison, eds.,
    Religion in American Life, 4 vols. (Princeton: Princeton University Press, 1961), I, pp.
    326–27; Ahlstrom, *Religious History*, pp. 474–78.

13. Tragle, *Southampton*, p. 310; Herbert Aptheker, *Nat Turner's Slave Rebellion* (New York:
    Humanities Press, 1966), pp. 137–38; Oates, *Fires*, p. 41.

14. Robert Hayden, "Ballad of Nat Turner," *Selected Poems* (New York: October House,
    1966), pp. 72–74.

15. Tragle, *Southampton*; p. 92; Oates, *Fires*, p. 42.

16. Aptheker, *Slave Revolts*, p. 265. On the subject of these other uprisings, there is a helpful
    bibliography in Eugene D. Genovese, *Roll, Jordan, Roll: The World the Slaves Made* (New
    York: Pantheon, 1974), pp. 709–11; an important, expanded version of his treatment
    and of his bibliography on the subject is available in *From Rebellion to Revolution: Afro-
    American Slave Revolts in the Making of the Modern World* (Baton Rouge: Louisiana State
    University Press, 1979). See also Aptheker, *Slave Revolts*, p. 278.

17. The story of the shipboard suicides is found in Austin Bearse, *Reminiscences of Fugitive-
    Slave Law Days in Boston* (1880: rpt. New York: Arno Press, 1969), p. 9.

18. Aptheker, *Slave Revolts*, pp. 279–80; a continued movement of rebellion and resistance
    by Alabama outlyers in this period is confirmed by James B. Sellers, *Slavery in Alabama*
    (University: University of Alabama Press, 1950), pp. 282–83. Also see Franklin, *From
    Slavery*, pp. 210–11.

19. Unfortunately, we still have nothing more comprehensive on David Walker's life than
    Henry Highland Garnet's "A Brief Sketch on the Life and Character of David Walker,"
    first published in 1848 and reprinted in Herbert Aptheker, ed., *One Continual Cry: David
    Walker's Appeal to the Colored Citizens of the World* (New York: Humanities Press, 1965),
    pp. 40–44. A modern essay focusing especially on Walker's Boston years indicates a
    number of the pertinent questions about him: Donald M. Jacobs, "David Walker: Boston
    Race Leader, 1825–1830," *Essex Institute Historical Collections* 107 (January 1971), 94–
    107.

20. Garnet, "Brief Sketch," p. 41; *Freedom's Journal*, March 16, 1827; Jacobs, "David Walker,"
    pp. 95–97.

21. For examples of such words and their costliness, see Ira Berlin, *Slaves Without Masters*
    (New York: Pantheon, 1975), pp. 89–97, 336–38; Samuel Ringgold Ward, *Autobiography
    of a Fugitive Negro* (1855; rpt. Chicago: Johnson Publishing, 1970), p. 12; Robert S. Sta-
    robin, ed., *Blacks in Bondage: Letters of American Slaves* (New York: Franklin Watts, 1974),
    pp. 107–10. Moreover, persons like Nat Turner and Frederick Douglass could also testify
    to these realities.

22. For the dangers faced by black abolitionists in the North, see Aptheker, *Documentary*, I,
    220; Dorothy Sterling, ed., *Speak Out in Thunder Tones* (New York: Doubleday, 1973),
    pp. 132–36; Ward, *Autobiography*, pp. 35–37.

23. Quoted in Bracey et al., *Black Nationalism*, p. 25.

24. The text of the speech appeared in *Freedom's Journal*, December 19, 1828.

25. [Robert Alexander Young], *The Ethiopian Manifesto* (New York, 1829). The most readily
    available source of the full text is Sterling Stuckey, ed., *The Ideological Origins of Black
    Nationalism* (Boston: Beacon Press, 1972), pp. 30–38.

26. Stuckey, *Ideological Origins*, p. 30. In the light of Young's reference to Grenada as the source of the mulatto Messiah, a few alert twentieth-century black nationalists have noted that the mother of Malcolm X came to the United States from Grenada. However, internal evidence in the *Manifesto* suggests that Young was really pointing to himself as the promised deliverer. It is also important to note that, like so many similar manifestoes in the later black struggle, this one was addressed at least as fully to whites as to "Ethiopians."

27. There are several modern editions of the complete text of the *Appeal*. Among the most accessible are Charles M. Wiltse, *David Walker's Appeal* (New York: Hill and Wang, 1965), and Aptheker's *One Continual Cry*. Aptheker's introduction and footnotes are by far the most helpful; his text is used in this study.

28. Walker/Aptheker, pp. 64–65. Certainly the line of spiritual heirs reaches at least from Henry Highland Garnet to Malcolm X.

29. Walker/Aptheker, pp. 73–74.

30. *Ibid.*, p. 89.

31. *Ibid.*, p. 75. It is fascinating to note how directly Walker is related to the traditions of religious/political revolution. For instance, very similar sentiments were expressed by the Anabaptist revolutionary Thomas Muntzer during the German Peasants' War of the sixteenth century; see Guenther Lewy, *Religion and Revolution* (New York: Oxford University Press, 1974), p. vii. Also, many concepts and even certain stylistic aspects of the *Appeal* suggest that Walker had had access to the April 1804 proclamation by Jacques Dessalines, the Haitian liberator. See the Dessalines document in Drake, "Black Nationalism," pp. 28–35.

32. Drake, "Black Nationalism," p. 30.

33. Walker/Aptheker, pp. 83–85, 65–66.

34. Confidence in God's retributive justice is a constant in the literature of black struggle. Many of its modern manifestations were most deeply lodged in the teachings of the Nation of Islam and their foremost heretic, Malcolm X. Compare Malcolm X, *The Autobiography of Malcolm X* (New York: Grove Press, 1964), pp. 246, 370; Elijah Muhammad, *The Fall of America* (Chicago: Muhammad's Temple of Islam No. 2, 1973), pp. 52–55, 108–11; and Louis E. Lomax, *When the Word Is Given* (New York: New American Library, 1964), pp. 175–76.

35. Walker/Aptheker, pp. 76, 126–28. Again, Walker seems very close to Dessalines. Indeed, his description of whites as the "natural enemies" of black people is precisely the same as Dessalines's in the 1804 proclamation: Drake, "Black Nationalism," p. 29.

36. Walker/Aptheker, pp. 139, 140, n.

37. *Ibid.*, pp. 77–78.

38. *Ibid.*, pp. 93–94. Consciously or not, Walker, the church member, introduced here a pan-African parallel to the New Testament concept of the Christian Church as the indivisible "body of Christ."

39. *Ibid.*, p. 104.

40. *Ibid.*, pp. 137–38.

41. *Ibid.* In our own post-Montgomery Boycott generation, we have seen leaders and institutions as varied as Martin Luther King, Jr., Malcolm X, James Forman, the Nation of Islam, and the Urban League struggle mightily with the issue of what *would* be the appropriate restitution and reparations due to the black community.

42. Walker/Aptheker, pp. 45–50; William H. Pease and Jane H. Pease, "Document: Walker's *Appeal* Comes to Charleston: A Note and Documents," *JNH* 59 (July 1974), 287–92; H. E. Sterkx, *The Free Negro in Ante-Bellum Louisiana* (Rutherford, N.J.: Fairleigh Dickinson University Press, 1972), p. 98.

43. Quoted in Litwack, *North*, p. 234.

44. Walker/Aptheker, p. 43. Eventually the bounty on Walker was raised to $3,000.

45. *Ibid.*, pp. 45–50.

46. Aptheker, *Slave Revolts*, p. 290.

47. Walker/Aptheker, pp. 43–44. Jacobs, "David Walker," pp. 106–07, does not accept the poisoning theory, and raises an interesting question about Walker's age when he died.

48. Tragle, *Southampton*, p. xv. Oates, *Fires*, p. 51, identifies the marriage year as late 1829.

49. According to his *Confessions* (Tragle, p. 310), the four men named comprised the first group to whom Nat revealed his plans. By the time of the actual event, two more persons, Jack Reese and Will Francis, were included. See also Oates, *Fires*. pp. 52–53.
50. Tragle, *Southampton*, p. 310. The final words are quoted in G. Williams, *History of Negro Race*, II, 88. Williams knew and appreciated the oral traditions of the black community. This quotation may well have been reconstructed from such a source.
51. Tragle, *Southampton*, pp. 310–13. In addition, for all their lack of precision and accuracy, several contemporary newspaper reports suggest the impact of the event on the surrounding population. They are quoted in Tragle, pp. 31–72. See Oates, *Fires*, pp. 66–91.
52. On the poor supply of arms, see a contemporary statement quoted in Aptheker, *Nat Turner's Slave Rebellion*, p. 55.
53. On the involvement of the U.S. military, two different emphases appear in Aptheker, *Slave Revolts*, p. 300, and Tragle, *Southampton*, pp. 16–17. Also note Oates, *Fires*, p. 97.
54. Tragle, pp. 34, 69, 74–75, 92; Aptheker, *Nat Turner's Slave Rebellion*, pp. 60–62.
55. Aptheker, *Nat Turner's Slave Rebellion*, pp. 37–38.
56. [Samuel Warner], *Authentic and Impartial Narrative of the Tragical Scene . . . in Southampton County* (New York, 1831), p. 23. The Warner document is also reproduced in Tragle, *Southampton*, pp. 279–300.
57. Ira Berlin, "Documents: After Nat Turner, A Letter from the North," *JNH* 55 (April 1970), 144–51.
58. The wording of the formal charge against Nat Turner is found in the Minute Book of the Court of Southampton County. The more familiar formulation: ". . . making insurrection, and plotting to take away the lives of divers free white persons," is evidently Gray's own version: Tragle, *Southampton*, pp. 221, 318.
59. Tragle, pp. 221, 132, 317; Oates, *Fires*, p. 119.
60. G. Williams, *History of Negro Race*, II, 90.
61. Tragle, p. 7.

CHAPTER SIX

1. Kenneth S. Greenberg, "The Meaning of Death in Slave Society," in *Research in Law Deviance and Social Control: A Research Annual*, vol. 8, ed. Steven Spitzer and Andrew T. Scull (Greenwich, Conn.: JAI Press, 1986), 124; [John Hampden Pleasants], *Richmond Constitutional Whig*, 26 September 1831, quoted in *The Southampton Slave Revolt of 1831: A Compilation of Source Material*, comp. Henry I. Tragle (Amherst: University of Massachusetts Press, 1971), 95.
2. L. Minor Blackford, *Mine Eyes Have Seen the Glory: The Story of a Virginia Lady, Mary Berkeley Minor Blackford, 1802–1896, Who Taught Her Sons to Hate Slavery and Love the Union* (Cambridge: Harvard University Press, 1954), 25–29; [Thomas Roderick Dew], "The Abolition of Negro Slavery," *American Quarterly Review* XII (September 1832): 190–91; William Sidney Drewry, *The Southampton Insurrection* (1900; reprint, Murfreesboro, N.C.: Johnson Publishing Company, 1968), 110, 111.
3. [John Hampden Pleasants], *Richmond Constitutional Whig*, 29 August 1831, quoted in *Southampton*, Tragle, 54; Thomas R. Gray, *The Confessions of Nat Turner* (Baltimore: Lucas and Deaver, 1831), 5, 21; *Richmond Enquirer*, 27 September 1831, quoted in *Southampton*, Tragle, 100; *Norfolk Herald*, 4 November 1831, quoted in *Southampton*, Tragle, 134–35.
4. Herbert Aptheker, *Nat Turner's Slave Rebellion: Together with the Full Text of the So-Called "Confessions" of Nat Turner Made in Prison in 1831* (New York: Humanities Press, 1966), 37, and Aptheker, *American Negro Slave Revolts* (New York: International Publishers, 1963), 306; Stephen B. Oates, *The Fires of Jubilee: Nat Turner's Fierce Rebellion* (New York: Harper Perennial, 1990), 35, 27, 37; Kenneth S. Greenberg, "The Confessions of Nat Turner: Text and Context," in *The Confessions of Nat Turner and Related Documents*, ed. Greenberg (Boston: Bedford Books of St. Martin's Press, 1996), 16; Eric Foner, "Introduction," in *Nat Turner*, ed. Foner (Englewood, N.J.: Prentice-Hall, 1971), 2.

5.   Gray, "Confessions," in *Confessions*, Greenberg, 4, 7; Thomas C. Parramore explains how Thomas R. Gray had in the course of three years squandered his estate, losing all eight hundred acres and 21 slaves that he had held as recently as 1829. Penury seemed assured when he was disinherited by his father, who died weeks after the rebellion. Gray clearly hoped that royalties from *The Confessions* would help restore his fortune. Parramore, *Southampton County, Virginia* (Charlottesville: University of Virginia Press, 1978), 105–7; for the evidence of retribution taken against Nat Turner's wife, who was put "under the lash," even before his capture, see *Richmond Constitutional Whig*, 26 September 1831 in *Southampton*, Tragle, 92.

6.   Gray, "Confessions," in *Confessions*, Greenberg, 7.

7.   Ibid. These others may have included whites as well, although one wonders if Turner would not have mentioned the whites who thought he was a prophet specifically as a way to make his story more believable to his white interviewer.

8.   Frederick Douglass, *The Life and Times of Frederick Douglass, Written by Himself: His Early Life as A Slave, His Escape from Bondage, and His Complete History* (1892; reprint, New York: Collier Books, 1962), 79; Gray, "Confessions," in *Confessions*, Greenberg, 8.

9.   Gray, "Confessions," in *Confessions*, Greenberg, 8.

10. Gray, "Confessions," in *Confessions*, Greenberg, 8–9.

11. Gray, "Confessions," in *Confessions*, Greenberg, 9.

12. Gray, "Confessions," in *Confessions*, Greenberg, 9.

13. Eugene D. Genovese suggests that runaways may have made "the greatest contribution to the spirit of collective resistance" possible in the antebellum South. See Genovese, *Roll, Jordan, Roll: The World the Slaves Made* (New York: Vintage, 1976), 657. For a more detailed handling of runaway slaves' resistance, see John Hope Franklin and Loren Schweninger, *Runaway Slaves: Rebels on the Plantation* (New York: Oxford University Press, 1999).

14. Gray, "Confessions," in *Confessions*, Greenberg, 9. According to many historians of runaway slaves, it was not uncommon for runaways to rely upon aid from the black community. Kenneth Stampp, *The Peculiar Institution: Slavery in the Ante-Bellum South* (New York: Vintage, 1984), 115; Genovese, *Roll, Jordan, Roll*, 654.

15. Gray, "Confessions," in *Confessions*, Greenberg, 9.

16. Gray, "Confessions," in *Confessions*, Greenberg, 10.

17. See Luke 12:47; Gray, "Confessions," in *Confessions*, Greenberg, 9–10. Eric J. Sundquist suggests, "Here, Turner appropriates and overturns one of proslavery's favorite passages, transfiguring a text of racist subjugation into his own prophetic call to revolt." Given the context—Nat Turner was not fomenting rebellion but instead explaining his unforced return from an escape attempt—Turner's use of this passage from Luke's gospel seems to echo rather than subversively appropriate the message of the slaveholder's Christianity. See Sundquist, *To Wake the Nations: Race in the Making of American Literature* (Cambridge: Harvard University Press, 1993), 59.

18. Gray, "Confessions," in *Confessions*, Greenberg, 8–9, 10.

19. Douglas R. Edgerton's *Gabriel's Rebellion: The Virginia Slave Conspiracies of 1800 and 1802* (Chapel Hill: University of North Carolina Press, 1993), 56; Edward A. Pearson, ed., *Designs Against Charleston: The Trial Record of the Denmark Vesey Slave Conspiracy of 1822*, (Chapel Hill: University of North Carolina Press, 1999), 181, 244. On Gabriel's rebellion, see also James Sidbury, *Ploughshares into Swords: Race, Rebellion and Identity in Gabriel's Virginia, 1730–1810* (New York: Cambridge University Press, 1997). On Vesey, see also Edward A. Pearson, "Culture and Conspiracy in Denmark Vesey's Charleston," in Pearson, *Designs Against Charleston*; Peter P. Hinks, *To Awaken My Afflicted Brethren: David Walker and the Problem of Antebellum Slave Resistance* (University Park: Pennsylvania State University Press, 1997); Douglas R. Egerton, *He Shall Go Out Free: The Lives of Denmark Vesey* (Madison, Wis.: Madison House, 1999), 140–45; David Robertson, *Denmark Vesey: The Buried History of America's Largest Slave Rebellion and the Man Who Led It* (New York: Knopf, 1999); E. Horace Fitchett, "The Origin and Growth of the Free Negro Population of Charleston, South Carolina," *Journal of Negro History* 26 (October 1941): 421–37; and John Oliver Killens, ed., *The Trial Record of Denmark Vesey* (Boston: Beacon Press, 1970).

20. Gray, "Confessions," in *Confessions*, Greenberg, 11. As with most slave rebellions, the first allusions to the revolt were received with skepticism. Not until after the rebellion did the white community realize that they had been warned by some who knew of the plotting. For the first allusions to the Southampton plan that made it to the white community, see Casell Worrell's testimony in Nelson's trial. This overseer testified that Nelson warned him that "something would happen before long" on Thursday, three days before the rebellion began, Tragle, *Southampton*, 193. In contrast, three weeks before whites finally realized that Gabriel's Rebellion was serious, word had reached Governor James Monroe of "some plan of insurrection among the blacks," Egerton, *Gabriel's Rebellion*, 67. Likewise, Vesey's plot was first betrayed on 22 May 1822 almost two months before the day initially chosen for the rebellion to begin. Again, it took whites more than three weeks to recognize that there was a foundation to the earliest rumors. Egerton, *He Shall Go Out Free*, 154–62.

21. Gray, "Confessions," in *Confessions*, Greenberg, 10–11.

22. Ibid., 11.

23. Ibid., 11; Oates, *Fires* 40; *Richmond Enquirer*, 27 September 1831, quoted in Tragle, *Southampton*, 100.

24. Gray, "Confessions," in *Confessions*, Greenberg, 10, 11.

25. *Richmond Enquirer*, 27 September 1831, quoted in Tragle, *Southampton*, 100. See also Gray, "Confessions," in *Confessions*, Greenberg, 11.

26. Greenberg, *Confessions*, 11; Oates, *Fires*, 40.

27. *Richmond Constitutional Whig*, 26 September 1831, in Tragle, *Southampton*, 92; Gray, "Confessions," in *Confessions*, Greenberg, 11.

28. Stephen B. Weeks, *Southern Quakers and Slavery: A Study in Institutional History*, ed. Herbert B. Adams (Baltimore: Johns Hopkins University Press, 1896), 331–44; Parramore, *Southampton*, 50–53. In 1808 Barrow published *Involuntary, Unmerited, Perpetual, Absolute, Hereditary Slavery Examined; on the Principles of Nature, Reason, Justice, Policy, and Scripture* (Lexington, Ky.: D. and C. Bradford, 1808).

29. Parramore, *Southampton*, 72.

30. Ibid., 62, 63.

31. Trial of Davy in Tragle, *Southampton*, 194. Tragle misidentifies "brother Clements" as Nelson.

32. *Richmond Enquirer*, 18 October 1831, quoted in Tragle, *Southampton*, 123.

33. Trial of Nelson in Tragle, *Southampton*, 194. Ironically, the same evidence that was used to sentence Nelson to death was later used to minimize the latent black support for rebellion. A report written more than a month after the rebellion emphasized the "free use of spirits" as a recruiting tool and described the insurgents as "beastly drunk." *Richmond Constitutional Whig*, 26 September 1831, quoted in Greenberg, *Confessions*, 82, 84. See also Gray, "Confessions," in *Confessions*, Greenberg, 11–12; the trials of Davy, Stephen, and Curtis in Tragle, *Southampton*, 186–88, 194.

34. *Richmond Compiler*, 3 September 1831, quoted in Tragle, *Southampton*, 62; the trials of Lucy and Hark in Tragle, *Southampton*, 192, 208–9.

35. *Richmond Compiler*, 3 September 1831, quoted in Tragle, *Southampton*, 62; the trial of Isaac in Tragle, *Southampton*, 189.

36. The trials of Hardy and Barry Newsom in Tragle, *Southampton*, 202; Gray, "Confessions," in *Confessions*, Greenberg, 15; *Richmond Enquirer*, 30 August 1831, quoted in Tragle, *Southampton*, 45.

37. Gray, "Confessions," in *Confessions*, Greenberg, 11.

38. Ibid., 11.

39. Ibid., 12. Will was the only recruit whose motives were recorded in *The Confessions*.

40. Ibid., 12, 15.

41. Interestingly, in the trials, Turner is repeatedly referred to as "General." Never was he given a religious honorific such as Prophet or Preacher by any black involved in the rebellion. It was the whites, not the blacks, who focused upon Nat Turner's religious message.

CHAPTER SEVEN

1. James Sidbury, *Ploughshares into Swords: Race, Rebellion, and Identity in Gabriel's Virginia, 1730–1810* (Cambridge: Cambridge University Press, 1997), 76–77; Edward A. Pearson, ed., *Designs Against Charleston: The Trial Record of the Denmark Vesey Slave Conspiracy of 1822* (Chapel Hill: The University of North Carolina Press, 1999), 185; Albert E. Stone, *The Return of Nat Turner: History, Literature, and Cultural Politics in Sixties America* (Athens: University of Georgia Press, 1992), 416.

2. Eugene D. Genovese, *Roll, Jordan, Roll: The World the Slaves Made* (New York: Pantheon Books, 1974); Albert J. Raboteau, *Slave Religion: The Invisible Institution in the Antebellum South* (New York: Oxford University Press, 1978); Lawrence W. Levine, *Black Culture and Black Consciousness: Afro-American Folk Thought from Slavery to Freedom* (New York: Oxford University Press, 1977), chaps. 1, 3; Norrece T. Jones, Jr., *Born a Child of Freedom, Yet a Slave: Mechanisms of Control and Strategies of Resistance in Antebellum South Carolina* (Hanover, N.H.: Wesleyan University Press, 1990), chap. 5; Charles Joyner, *Down by the Riverside: A South Carolina Slave Community* (Urbana: University of Illinois Press, 1984), chap. 5; Sterling Stuckey, *Slave Culture: Nationalist Theory and the Foundations of Black America* (New York: Oxford University Press, 1987), chap. 1.

3. Brian Stock has traced analogous uses of spiritual writing in his analysis of heretics as "textual communities." See *The Implications of Literacy: Written Language and Models of Interpretation in the Eleventh and Twelfth Centuries* (Princeton: Princeton University Press, 1983), chap. 2 (esp. 88–101, 125–28, 405, and 502); and *Listening for the Text: On the Uses of the Past* (Baltimore: Johns Hopkins University Press, 1990), chaps. 2, 7. There are also important parallels with Stanley Fish's notion of "interpretive communities"; for the original formulation see *Is There a Text in This Class?: The Authority of Interpretive Communities* (Cambridge: Harvard University Press, 1980); the concept is further developed in the essays collected in *Doing What Comes Naturally: Change, Rhetoric, and the Practice of Theory in Literary and Legal Studies* (Durham: Duke University Press, 1989). Because Stock's notion of textual communities is more closely rooted in the historical practice of oppositional movements, rather than in processes of interpretation in the modern world, his discussion is closer than Fish's to what I am attempting here.

4. Gerald W. Mullin, *Flight and Rebellion: Slave Resistance in Eighteenth-Century Virginia* (New York: Oxford University Press, 1972), 159–60; and Douglas R. Egerton, *Gabriel's Rebellion: The Virginia Slave Conspiracies of 1800 and 1802* (Chapel Hill: University of North Carolina Press, 1993), 20, 51–52, 179–82. I have made the contrary case in more detail than I do here in *Ploughshares*, esp. chap. 2.

5. This is a reiteration of a point made in different places by Winthrop D. Jordan and Kenneth S. Greenberg: that to make sense of the evidence that has survived from slave resistance, historians must listen to the silences in the record. See Jordan, *Tumult and Silence at Second Creek: An Inquiry into a Civil War Slave Conspiracy* (Baton Rouge: Louisiana State University Press, 1993), throughout (esp. chap. 2); Greenberg, ed., *The Confessions of Nat Turner and Related Documents* (Boston: Bedford Books of St. Martin's Press, 1996), 10–13.

6. The only report of this conversation that survives is in Ben Woolfolk's confession. Woolfolk (and several other conspirators) gave confessions to authorities in hopes of gaining leniency. The confessions recorded much more detail about the conspiracy than did routine courtroom testimony. In fact, there is no mention of this discussion either in the trial record from Woolfolk's trial or in trial records of other conspirators against whom Woolfolk testified for the state. Martin quoted a condensed and slightly changed version (changed either by him or by Woolfolk in the retelling) of Lev. 26: 6–8. Woolfolk's confession and a substantial, but far from comprehensive, selection of documents relating to Gabriel's conspiracy can be found in *Calendar of Virginia State Papers and Other Manuscripts, 1652–1869, Preserved in the Capitol at Richmond*, 11 vols., ed. William Price Palmer and Henry W. Flournoy (Richmond: R. F. Walker, 1875–93) 9:140–74. For a fuller discussion of sources, see Sidbury, *Ploughshares*, 57, n. 3.

7. Much secondary literature asserts that the story of Israel's deliverance from Egyptian slavery was fundamental to slave Christianity, and it is clear that such was often the case

(see Levine, *Black Culture*, chap. 1, esp. 33: "[slaves] extended the boundaries of their restrictive universe backward until it fused with the world of the Old Testament"; and the analysis of Vesey below). But Nat Turner's *Confessions* indicates that he found much more inspiration in the New Testament (see Eric Sundquist, *To Wake the Nations: Race in the Making of American Literature* [Cambridge: The Belknap Press of Harvard University Press, 1993], 70–79).

8.   James M. Stayer, *The German Peasants' War and Anabaptist Community of Goods* (Montreal: McGill-Queens University Press, 1991); John K. Thornton, *The Kongolese Saint Anthony: Doña Beatriz Kimpa Vita and the Antonian Movement, 1684–1706* (Cambridge: Cambridge University Press, 1998).

9.   Sidbury, *Ploughshares*, pt. 2 (esp. chaps. 5, 6), though the focus there is on their success in overcoming these shortcomings.

10. Pearson, *Designs*, Introduction (esp. 39–77); Bernard Powers, *Black Charlestonians: A Social History, 1822–1885* (Fayetteville: University of Arkansas Press, 1994); Philip D. Morgan, "Black Life in Eighteenth-Century Charleston," in *Perspectives in American History*, n.s., 1 (1984), 187–232; Janet Duituman Cornelius, *"When I Can Read My Title Clear": Literacy, Slavery, and Religion in the Antebellum South* (Columbia: University of South Carolina Press, 1991), 8–9 (for unreliability of figures on slave literacy).

11. Pearson claims (as have other scholars) that the debates in question were those held in Congress during the Missouri controversy. Michael Johnson argues that there is little evidence to support this claim and that the debates were more likely state house debates regarding manumission law. Michael P. Johnson, "The Making of a Slave Conspiracy: Denmark Vesey and His Coconspirators" (unpublished manuscript in possession of author). I thank Michael Johnson for allowing me to consult his essay prior to its publication.

12. See Pearson, *Designs*, Introduction, for an account of Vesey's background (esp. 17–39); Mary L. Beach to Elizabeth L. Gilchrist, 5 July 1822: 324 ("voluminous" papers); 189, 190, 231, 238 (knowledge of Haiti); 214–15 (knowledge of Missouri Compromise); 258 (Gell).

13. Douglas R. Egerton, *He Shall Go Out Free: The Lives of Denmark Vesey* (Madison, Wis.: Madison House, 1999) is the best account of the conspiracy; see also Peter P. Hinks, *To Awaken My Afflicted Brethren: David Walker and the Problem of Antebellum Slave Resistance* (University Park: Pennsylvania State University Press, 1997), chap. 2 for the history of the Charleston African Methodist Episcopal (AME) congregation and the fullest analysis of its role in the Vesey conspiracy. The church was torn down in the wake of the conspiracy's repression and the AME Church was kept out of Charleston until after Emancipation. For primary source indications of the role of the AME Church, see (among many possible citations) Pearson, *Designs*, 166–67, 182, 216, 217, 235.

14. Martha Proctor Richardson to Dr. James Screven, 6 July 1822, in *Designs*, ed. Pearson, 325. Hinks, *To Awaken*, 37–38, 261–64.

15. Mary L. Beach to Elizabeth L. Gilchrist, 5 July 1822 in *Designs*, ed. Pearson, 323 (emphasis in original). Beach admitted Vesey's claim but insisted that "the good man did it to accommodate it to their understanding."

16. Ibid., 279. ("It is evident, that you are totally insensible of the divine influence of that Gospel, 'all whose paths are peace.' It was to reconcile us to our destinies on earth, and to enable us to discharge with fidelity, all the duties of life, that those holy precepts were imparted by Heaven to fallen man.")

17. Michael Johnson, "The Making of a Slave Conspiracy," shows that Vesey did not, in fact, receive a trial, so he may not have been given a chance to explain or defend himself.

18. *Carolina Gazette*, 28 September 1822 in *Designs*, ed. Pearson, 348. Emphasis in original. The summary is accurate—or, to be more precise, it accords with the recorded trial testimony—in its general outline. I discuss some of the trial testimony in more detail below.

19. It is interesting that the brief citation that Martin used in arguing with Ben Woolfolk also came from the Pentateuch, while Gabriel made an allusion to the less-immediately hopeful text of Daniel when he was attempting to escape after the conspiracy had been

betrayed (see Sidbury, *Ploughshares*, 78–79 for Gabriel's allusion to Daniel, though I do not make this point there).

20. For the most recent analysis of the role of Exodus in antebellum black religious thought, see Eddie S. Glaude, Jr., *Exodus!: Religion, Race, and Nation in Early Nineteenth-Century Black America* (Chicago: University of Chicago Press, 2000). Glaude focuses on religious thought among northern free blacks rather than among southern slaves.

21. Pearson, *Designs*, 329 (Bacchus Hammet), 336 (John). In Hammet's confession the clerk breaks off from Hammet's voice to include (in brackets as shown) "[The passages alluded to were Exodus 1st Chpt. & 21st Chpt., 16th verse also 19th Chpt. Isaiah and 14th Zachariah (*sic*) 1 & 3rd. verses etc]."

22. Exodus 21 was not the only Scripture cited by the rebels, nor do I want to argue that it should somehow be given magical priority over the others. Conspirators made reference to the books of the prophets, to the apocryphal (within Anglican tradition) book of the prophet Tobit, and to a number of secular texts. A full-blown analysis of Vesey's textual world would need to draw the links among the references to legislative debates, to the letters to and about Haiti, and to even vaguer references to "a book about the complexion of people" (Pearson, *Designs*, 336–37).

23. Pearson, *Designs*, 348 (*Gazette*), 279 (magistrates).

24. Ibid., 168 (quote). Variations on this point were made in numerous trials (e.g., 181, 185, 186, 191).

25. It is worth noting that the trial records for all three of these events consist of court clerks' summaries of testimony (rather than of question-and-answer verbatim transcripts). In Virginia these records were created in response to a law dating from the 1790s that required the governor and his council to review the trials of slaves convicted of capital offenses; as a result there is often no record of the testimony given in trials of slaves that resulted in acquittal, and the trial records that were created focused on the offenses for which the defendants had been convicted (e.g., the act of joining a conspiracy or the act of committing a murder) rather than on any broad explanatory background for the defendant's act. See note 27 below for sources that discuss the making of the text of Turner's *Confessions*.

26. The standard narrative history of the rebellion is Stephen B. Oates, *The Fires of Jubilee: Nat Turner's Fierce Rebellion* (New York: New American Library, 1975). See Stone, *Return*, for a discussion of Turner's place in American culture generally; Stone is most interested in the place of Turner in popular accounts—especially in the controversy surrounding William Styron's novel—but he relates those controversies to historiography in interesting and insightful ways. Also see Greenberg, *Confessions*, esp. 26–31, for a discussion of the paucity of analytical historical work on Turner. Greenberg's collection and Henry I. Tragle, comp., *The Southampton Slave Revolt of 1831: A Compilation of Source Material* (Amherst: The University of Massachusetts Press, 1971) have compiled and made easily available a wide range of source material about the rebellion. Sundquist, *To Wake the Nations*, chap. 1 provides a literary scholar's reading of Turner's *Confessions* and is among the most insightful work available on Turner.

27. Tragle, *Southampton*, 90–99; Greenberg, *Confessions*, 78–87. See Greenberg's Introduction (esp. 7–14) for a discussion of the creation of the text of Turner's *Confessions* with attention to this letter (9–11); also Sundquist, *To Wake the Nations*, 37–41 for the creation of Turner's *Confessions*. I will not discuss the complications in the creation of the text of Turner's *Confessions* because I have nothing to add to the analyses of Greenberg and Sundquist.

28. The text of *Confessions* is available in many places, including those volumes by Tragle and Greenberg. I have used the appendix to Stone, *Return*. This quote is on 414–15; Turner's text is Matthew 6:33.

29. Though I have not always used Sundquist's terminology, this paragraph relies on his brilliant reading of the *Confessions* in *To Wake the Nations*, chap. 1 (esp. 72–75, 79–81).

30. Stone, *Return*, 415–17. For a different reading of Turner's hieroglyphics, see Grey Gundaker, *Signs of Diaspora, Diaspora of Signs: Literacies, Creolization, and Vernacular Practice in African America* (New York: Oxford University Press, 1998), 178–81. My colleague

Howard Miller pointed out to me the weird parallel between Turner's invocation of "hieroglyphics"—if the term is his rather than that of his recorders—and Joseph Smith's claim that God communicated with him through "reformed Egyptian."

31. Stone, *Return*, 417–18, 420–21.

32. Tragle, *Southampton*, 70 (tricks), 92 (prophet), 80 (Baptists), 135 (Scriptures).

33. Peter H. Wood, " 'Jesus Christ Has Got Thee at Last': Afro-American Conversion as a Forgotten Chapter in Eighteenth-Century Southern Intellectual History," *The Bulletin of the Center for the Study of Southern Religion* 3 (1979), 1–7, points out that searching theological discussions must have occurred in slave quarters when enslaved people began to turn to Christianity during the late eighteenth century. The records of these insurrectionary acts underscore that such discussions continued throughout the antebellum era. Genovese, *Roll, Jordan, Roll*, 250–70, provides the crucial start to this discussion in his analysis of the role of slave preachers in creating a sense of the black nation.

34. The sole source for this struggle is William S. White, *The African Preacher: An Authentic Narrative* (Philadelphia: Presbyterian Board of Publication, 1849), 61–66. This is a biography of "Uncle Jack," the "African Preacher," who was one of the disputants. The account is slanted toward Jack's position, and all quotes are from this account.

35. The allusion is to the quite heated disputes of the time about the theology of Alexander Campbell, a white Baptist. The specific content of Alexander Campbell's preaching does not, however, appear to play any role in this dispute.

36. Seeing slave Christianity this way helps make sense of the varieties of Christian belief that both black and white northern missionaries found in the South during Reconstruction. See Leon F. Litwack, *Been in the Storm So Long: The Aftermath of Slavery* (New York: Vintage Books, 1980), chap. 9 (esp. 456–62); Eric Foner, *A Short History of Reconstruction, 1863–1877* (New York: Harper and Row, 1990), 40–42.

CHAPTER EIGHT

1. Thomas R. Gray, "The Confessions of Nat Turner," in *The Confessions of Nat Turner and Related Documents*, ed. Kenneth S. Greenberg (Boston: Bedford Books of St. Martin's Press, 1996), 45. This interpretation follows the lead of Donald R. Wright, *African Americans in the Early Republic, 1789–1831* (Arlington Heights, Ill.: Harlan Davidson, 1993), 108, who rightly observes that Styron's long shadow "hinder[s] the task of recreating the historical Turner." Styron's characterization of Turner as a "nut" appears in *Conversations With William Styron*, ed. James L. West (Jackson: University Press of Mississippi, 1985), 100, and Arna Bontemps's comments come from his *Black Thunder: Gabriel's Revolt, Virginia 1800* (1936; reprint, Boston: Beacon Press, 1968), xii. For a superb discussion of Turner's numerous fictional incarnations, see Mary Kemp Davis, *Nat Turner Before the Bar of Judgment: Fictional Treatments of the Southampton Slave Insurrection* (Baton Rouge: Louisiana State University Press, 1999).

   I wish to thank Alan Gallay, Stanley Harrold, Graham Russell Hodges, Melissa A. Maestri, Monique Patenaude, and Donald R. Wright for their kind comments and suggestions.

2. West, *Conversations With Styron*, 100. Perhaps the most compelling question is not whether Turner stood outside of the American mainstream, but why those who fought *for* liberty—from Nat Turner to John Brown—are so often depicted as mentally unstable, while those who employed the hangman's noose in the cause of unfree labor— specifically Virginia governors James Monroe, John Floyd, and Henry A. Wise—are not similarly treated by modern historians and novelists.

3. Styron quoted in *New York Times Book Review*, 8 October 1967, in *The Southampton Slave Revolt of 1831: A Compilation of Source Material*, comp. Henry I. Tragle (Amherst: University of Massachusetts Press, 1971), 399; *Richmond Enquirer*, 30 August 1831, in *Southampton*, Tragle, 44; *Norfolk Herald*, 25 September 1800; Anna Haynes Johnson to Elizabeth Haywood, 28 June 1822, Haywood Papers, Southern Historical Collection, University of North Carolina.

4. William S. Drewry, *The Southampton Insurrection* (Washington: The Neal Company, 1900), 37.

5. *Norfolk Herald*, 4 November 1831, in Tragle, *Southampton*, 134–35; James Curtis Ballagh, *A History of Slavery in Virginia* (Baltimore: Johns Hopkins University Press, 1902), 94 n. 2.

6. Gray, "Confessions," in *Confessions*, Greenberg, 46; Tony Horwitz, "Untrue Confessions," *New Yorker*, 13 December 1999, 84; Vincent Harding, *There Is a River: The Black Struggle for Freedom in America* (New York: Harcourt Brace, Jovanovich, 1981), 79.

7. Merton L. Dillon, *Slavery Attacked: Southern Slaves and Their Allies* (Baton Rouge: Louisiana State University Press, 1990), 150–51; Herbert Aptheker, *American Negro Slave Revolts*, 5th ed. (New York: International Publishers, 1983), 296 n. 13; Edward Ball, *Slaves in the Family* (New York: Farrar, Straus and Giroux, 1998), 268.

8. Peter P. Hinks, *To Awaken My Afflicted Brethren: David Walker and the Problem of Antebellum Slave Resistance* (University Park: Pennsylvania State University Press, 1997), 160–61.

9. Joao Jose Reis, *Slave Rebellion in Brazil: The Muslim Uprising of 1835 in Bahia* (Baltimore: Johns Hopkins University Press, 1993), 49–50, 135.

10. Robert L. Paquette, *Sugar Is Made With Blood: The Conspiracy of La Escalera and the Conflict Between Empires Over Slavery in Cuba* (Middletown, Conn.: Wesleyan University Press, 1988), 242–43.

11. Michael Craton, *Testing the Chains: Resistance to Slavery in the British West Indies* (Ithaca: Cornell University Press, 1982), 296; Mary Reckford, "The Jamaica Slave Rebellion of 1831," *Past and Present* 40 (July 1968): 113.

12. Archibald H. Grimke, *Right on the Scaffold, or, The Martyrs of 1822* (Washington: The Academy, 1901), 12; Lionel Kennedy and Thomas Parker, eds., *An Official Report of the Trials of Sundry Negroes, Charged With an Attempt to Raise an Insurrection in the State of South Carolina* (Charleston: J. R. Schenck, 1822), 17–18.

13. Confession of Enslow's John, no date, William and Benjamin Hammet Papers, Duke University Library; Examination of Benjamin Ford, 26 June 1822, Records of General Assembly, Governor's Messages, South Carolina Department of Archives and History. See also Douglas R. Egerton, *He Shall Go Out Free: The Lives of Denmark Vesey* (Madison, Wis.: Madison House, 1999), chap. 5.

14. Examination of William Paul, 19 June 1822, Records of General Assembly, Governor's Messages, South Carolina Department of Archives and History; Gray, "Confessions," in *Confessions*, Greenberg, 46.

15. *Richmond Enquirer*, 15 November 1831, in Tragle, *Southampton*, 139; Aptheker, *American Negro Slave Revolts*, 299 n. 24; Gray, "Confessions," in *Confessions*, Greenberg, 48.

16. *Richmond Enquirer*, 27 September 1831, in Tragle, *Southampton*, 100. By transforming Turner into a charlatan and a fraud, this writer clearly hoped to disassociate Turner from Christianity, as if there could be no possible connection between the two.

17. Eugene D. Genovese, *From Rebellion to Revolution: Afro-American Slave Revolts in the Making of the Modern World* (Baton Rouge: Louisiana State University Press, 1979), 45; Stephen B. Oates, *The Fires of Jubilee: Nat Turner's Fierce Rebellion* (New York: Harper and Row, 1975), 54–55; Alison Goodyear Freehling, *Drift Toward Dissolution: The Virginia Slavery Debates of 1831–1832* (Baton Rouge: Louisiana State University Press, 1982), 36–81; Abel P. Upshur to Francis Gilmer, 7 July 1825, Francis Gilmer Papers, University of Virginia.

18. Gilbert C. Din, *Spaniards, Planters, and Slaves: The Spanish Regulation of Slavery in Louisiana, 1763–1803* (College Station: Texas A&M University Press, 1999), 154; Douglas R. Egerton, *Gabriel's Rebellion: The Virginia Slave Conspiracies of 1800 and 1802* (Chapel Hill: University of North Carolina Press, 1993), 34–49; *Fredericksburg Virginia Herald*, 9 May 1800; Testimony of Prosser's Sam at trial of Jack Ditcher, 29 October 1800, Executive Papers, Negro Insurrection, Library of Virginia.

19. Reis, *Slave Rebellion*, 53; James Hamilton, *An Account of the Late Intended Insurrection Among a Portion of the Blacks of the City* (Charleston: A. E. Miller, 1822), 42.

20. Craton, *Testing the Chains*, 277–78; Emilia Viotti da Costa, *Crowns of Glory, Tears of Blood: The Demerara Slave Rebellion of 1823* (New York: Oxford University Press, 1994), xv, 205.

21. Gad Heuman, *"The Killing Time": The Morant Bay Rebellion in Jamaica* (Knoxville: University of Tennessee Press, 1994), 35–36; Mary Reckford, "Jamaica Slave Rebellion of 1831"; Richard Frucht, ed., *Black Society in the New World*, 110.

22. Craton, *Testing the Chains*, 269; Da Costa, *Crowns*, xviii, 217; Oates, *Fires*, 3.

23. William W. Freehling, *The Road to Disunion: Secessionists at Bay, 1776–1854* (New York: Oxford University Press, 1990), 179–80; Eugene D. Genovese, *Roll, Jordan, Roll: The World the Slaves Made* (New York: Pantheon Books, 1974), 594–95.

24. Genovese, *From Rebellion to Revolution*, 48–49; Wright, *African Americans*, 114. Oates, *Fires*, 78, also suspects that Turner "expected God to guide him after the insurrection began."

25. Testimony of Prosser's Ben at trial of Prosser's Gabriel, 6 October 1800, Executive Papers, Negro Insurrection, Library of Virginia; *Fredericksburg Virginia Herald*, 23 September 1800; James Thomson Callender to Thomas Jefferson, [misdated 13] 18 September 1800, Jefferson Papers, Library of Congress.

26. Confession of Rolla Bennett, 25 June 1822, in Kennedy and Parker, eds., *Official Report*, 68; Mary Lamboll Beach to Elizabeth Gilchrist, 5 July 1822, Beach Letters, South Carolina Historical Society.

27. *Richmond Constitutional Whig*, 26 September, 1831, in Tragle, *Southampton*, 95. Tragle theorized that the letter was written by attorney Thomas R. Gray, see 406–9. An earlier edition, *Richmond Constitutional Whig*, 3 September 1831, in Tragle, *Southampton*, 67, also suggests that "the Village of Jerusalem [was] the immediate object of the movement."

28. Genovese, *From Rebellion to Revolution*, 8; *Norfolk Herald*, 4 November 1831, in Tragle, *Southampton*, 135. In this, Turner was similar to John Brown, who believed that if he could temporarily "conquer Virginia, the balance of the Southern states would nearly conquer themselves, there being such a large number of slaves in them." See Stephen B. Oates, *To Purge This Land With Blood: A Biography of John Brown* (Amherst: Harper and Row, 1970), 278–79.

29. Quoted in Tony Horwitz, "Untrue Confessions," 86–87; E. P. Thompson, *The Making of the English Working Class* (New York: Pantheon Books, 1963), 168.

30. Gray, "Confessions," in *Confessions*, Greenberg, 45, 54; George P. Rawick, *From Sundown to Sunup: The Making of the Black Community* (Westport: Greenwood Publishing Company, 1972), 74–75; Trial of Jim and Isaac, 22 September 1831, in Tragle, *Southampton*, 214.

31. Peter H. Wood, "Nat Turner: The Unknown Slave as Visionary Leader," in *Black Leaders of the Nineteenth Century*, ed. Leon Litwack and August Meier (Urbana: University of Illinois Press, 1988), 34–35; Hinks, *To Awaken*, 168; Samuel Warner, *Authentic and Impartial Narrative of the Tragical Scene Which Was Witnessed in Southampton County*, in Tragle, *Southampton*, 289.

32. Da Costa, *Crowns*, 202; *Norfolk American Beacon*, 29 August 1831, in Tragle, *Southampton*, 49. (the correspondent talked "with one of the ring leaders who is mortally wounded and will probably die tonight." Hark was wounded at Dr. Blount's, according to the *Richmond Constitutional Whig*, 3 September 1831, in Tragle, *Southampton*, 68.); Drewry, *Southampton*, 37.

33. J. L. C. to unknown, 1802, Slave Collection, 1748–1856, North Carolina State Archives; *Niles' Weekly Register*, 14 September 1822.

34. Testimony of Prosser's Ben at trial of Gregory's Charles, 12 September 1800, Executive Papers, Negro Insurrection, Library of Virginia; Gray, "Confessions," in *Confessions*, Greenberg, 48.

35. Oates, *Fires*, 54; Reckford, "Jamaican Slave Rebellion of 1831," 116; Gray, "Confessions," in *Confessions*, Greenberg, 48; Wood, "Nat Turner," in *Black Leaders*, Leon Litwack and August Meier, 27; Stanley Harrold and John McKivigan, *Antislavery Violence* (Knoxville: University of Tennessee Press, 1999), 6.

36. *Richmond Constitutional Whig*, 26 September 1831, in Tragle, *Southampton*, 93, 96.

37. Richard Jones to William Prentis, 2 January 1802, Executive Papers, Library of Virginia; Testimony of Smith's Abram at trial of Booker's Sancho, 23 April 1802, Executive Papers, Pardon Papers, Library of Virginia; Da Costa, *Crowns*, 207; Gray, "Confessions," in *Confessions*, Greenberg, 51–52.

38. Testimony of Ben Woolfolk at trial of Gabriel, 6 October 1800, Executive Letterbook, Library of Virginia; Deposition of Turner's Isaac, June 1802, Slave Collection, 1748–1856, North Carolina State Archives; Thomas O. Ott, *The Haitian Revolution, 1789–1804* (Knoxville: University of Tennessee Press, 1973), 48; Confession of Enslow's John, no date, William and Benjamin Hammet Papers, Duke University Library.

39. *Norfolk American Beacon,* 29 August 1831, in Tragle, *Southampton,* 50. (A photograph of the intersection taken by Drewry can be found in *Southampton,* Tragle, 165.)

40. *Richmond Enquirer,* 8 November 1831, in Tragle, *Southampton,* 137.

41. Wood, "Nat Turner," in *Black Leaders,* Leon Litwack and August Meier, 27; Warner, *Authentic and Impartial Narrative,* in Tragle, *Southampton,* 296; *Richmond Constitutional Whig,* 26 September 1831, in Tragle, *Southampton,* 92. Although the evidence regarding Turner's wife is circumstantial at best, there can be little doubt that she existed. Tragle, *Southampton,* 327, n. 2, discovered that at the time Samuel Turner's estate was liquidated in 1822, a young slave named Cherry was sold to Giles Reese, and this may have been the unnamed woman mentioned by Warner and the *Richmond Constitutional Whig.*

42. Thomas Wentworth Higginson, *Travellers and Outlaws: Episodes in American History* (Boston: Lee and Shephard, 1889), 292.

CHAPTER NINE

1. Kenneth S. Greenberg, ed., *The Confessions of Nat Turner and Related Documents* (Boston: Bedford Books of St. Martin's Press, 1996), 48; *Ash's Pocket Almanac,* quoted in the *Saturday Bulletin,* 5 February 1831.

2. *Diary of Sarah Connell Ayer* (Portland: Lefavor-Tower Company, 1910), 312; *Boston Evening Gazette,* 12 February 1831; *Richmond Enquirer,* 15 February 1831.

3. Greenberg *Confessions,* 48; *Boston Evening Transcript,* 18 August 1831.

4. Many of the newspaper accounts of Turner's insurrection are compiled in Henry I. Tragle, comp., *The Southampton Slave Revolt of 1831: A Compilation of Source Material* (Amherst: The University of Massachusetts Press, 1971). Parenthetic page numbers refer to this edition. *Niles' Weekly Register,* 10 September 1831, 77; *Alexandria Gazette,* September 1831, 88.

5. *Richmond Constitutional Whig,* 26 September 1831, 92; *Richmond Enquirer,* 27 September 1831, 102.

6. *Liberator,* 1 January 1831.

7. William Lloyd Garrison, *An Address Delivered Before the Free People of Color in Philadelphia, New York, and other Cities* (Philadelphia: Stephen Foster, 1831), 3, 8, 10–13, 14–15; Wendell Phillips Garrison, *William Lloyd Garrison* (Boston: The Century Company, 1885), I: 260.

8. Sean Wilentz, ed., *David Walker's Appeal* (New York: Hill and Wang, 1995).

9. *Liberator,* 29 January 1831; 22 January 1831.

10. *Liberator,* 8 January 1831.

11. *Liberator,* 14 May and 28 May 1831.

12. Walter M. Merrill, ed., *The Letters of William Lloyd Garrison* (Cambridge: Belknap Press of Harvard University Press 1971). I: 113; *Liberator,* 3 September 1831.

13. *Richmond Enquirer,* 27 September 1831, p. 101; Merrill, *Letters,* I; *Liberator,* 10 September 1831.

14. Merrill, *Letters,* I: 113; *Liberator,* 17 December 1831; *Liberator,* 1 October 1831.

15. *Liberator,* 10 September and 1 October 1831.

16. *Free Enquirer,* 17 September 1831, 380.

17. [Thomas R. Dew] "Abolition of Negro Slavery," *American Quarterly Review* 12 (September 1832), 245.

18. John Floyd, diary entry for 27 September, reprinted in Tragle, *Southampton,* 255–56.

19. Jane Randolph quoted in Alison Goodyear Freehling, *Drift Toward Dissolution: The Virginia Slavery Debate of 1831–32* (Baton Rouge: Louisiana State University Press, 1982), 6.

20. Floyd to James Hamilton, 19 November 1831, in Tragle, *Southampton,* 275–76; Floyd diary in Tragle, 261–62.

21. *Richmond Enquirer,* 17 December 1831.

22. Ibid., 19 January 1832.

23. Ibid., 21 January 1832; 24 January 1832.

24. *Speech of John Thompson Brown* (Richmond: T. W. White, 1832), 5, 15, 18, 21.

25. *Richmond Enquirer*, 24 January 1832; 28 January 1832.
26. "The Kentucky Resolutions" in *The Portable Thomas Jefferson*, ed. Merrill Peterson (New York: Viking Press, 1975), 281; "Notes on the State of Virginia" in Ibid. 186.
27. Edward Coles to Thomas Jefferson Randolph, 29 December 1831 in *William and Mary Quarterly*, 2nd Series, vol. 7 (1927): 105–7.
28. *The Speech of Thomas J. Randolph in the House of Delegates of Virginia on the Abolition of Slavery* (Richmond: Samuel Shepherd and Company, 1832); *Richmond Enquirer*, 28 January 1832. On 2 September 1829, Garrison proclaimed in the *Genius of Universal Emancipation*: "the question of expediency has nothing to do with that of right and it is not for those who tyrannize to say when they may safely break the chains of their subjects."
29. *Speech of Thomas J. Randolph*, 8–9.

CHAPTER TEN

1. William Sidney Drewry, *The Southampton Insurrection* (Washington, D.C.: The Neale Company, 1900), 51, 58–59.
2. Henry I. Tragle, comp., *The Southampton Slave Revolt of 1831: A Compilation of Source Material* (Amherst: University of Massachusetts Press, 1971), 177–228 for inclusive trial records; summation of trial records on 229–45; Artist and his wife are mentioned on 227. See also Thomas C. Parramore, *Southampton County, Virginia* (Charlottesville: University Press of Virginia, 1978); Parramore says that Artist was a mulatto and that his wife was named Cherry, 95; he mentions Artist's possible suicide on 102.
3. Tragle, *Southampton*, 177–228 for trial records; 15 for statistics. In 1830 the county had 7,756 slaves: 3,563 were women. There were only 3,191 white women in the population.
4. For Lucy, see Tragle, *Southampton*, 208; for total executed see Stephen B. Oates, *The Fires of Jubilee: Nat Turner's Fierce Rebellion* (New York: Harper and Row, 1975), 125; for the total number of females executed in Virginia, see James Sidbury, *Ploughshares into Swords: Race Rebellion and Identity in Gabriel's Virginia, 1730–1810* (Cambridge: Cambridge University Press, 1997), 221, n. 3.
5. Tragle, *Southampton*, 177–228 for inclusive records; for reference to transportation of certain condemned slaves, see Philip J. Schwarz, *Slave Laws in Virginia* (Athens: University of Georgia Press, 1966), 99, 104.
6. For Delsey's trial record, see Tragle, *Southampton*, 183; for supplementary sources, see Drewry, *Southampton*, 70; F. Roy Johnson, *The Nat Turner Insurrection, Together with Thomas R. Gray's The Confession, Trial and Execution of Nat Turner as a Supplement* (Murfreesboro, N.C.: Johnson Publishing Co., 1966), 106–7.
7. Tragle, *Southampton*, 183, 194, 214, 227.
8. Drewry, *Southampton*, 26; Tragle, *Southampton*, 14; Michael Mullin, *Africa in America: Slave Acculturation and Resistance in the America South and the Caribbean, 1786–1831* (Urbana: University of Illinois Press, 1994), 261; Daniel W. Crofts, *Old Southampton: Politics and Society in a Virginia County, 1834–1869* (Charlottesville: University Press of Virginia, 1992), 5.
9. Drewry, *Southampton*, 58–59; Oates, *Fires*, 83–85; see also, Waller's testimony in Tragle, *Southampton*, 221–22.
10. Drewry, *Southampton*, 58–59. Cf. at Nat Turner's trial, Waller reportedly testified that "he saw [not heard] his family murdered," Tragle, *Southampton*, 222.
11. For the number of Blunt's slaves, see Parramore, *Southampton*, 95; Drewry, *Southampton*, 70.
12. Cf. Parramore argues that the slaves had guns, but he does not place them "at the side of the house," *Southampton*, 96.
13. Drewry, *Southampton*, 53–54; Johnson, *Nat Turner*, 92, 172, 209 n. 14.
14. Drewry, *Southampton*, 48.
15. Oates, *Fires*, 96.
16. L. Minor Blackford, *Mine Eyes Have Seen the Glory: The Story of a Virginia Lady, Mary Berkeley Minor Blackford, 1802–1896, Who Taught Her Sons to Hate Slavery and to Love the Union* (Cambridge: Harvard University Press, 1954), 24; Anne Firor Scott, *The Southern Lady:*

From Pedestal to Politics, 1830–1930 (Chicago: University of Chicago Press, 1970), 51; Drewry, *Southampton*, 62; Tragle, *Southampton*, 68–69.

17. For quotation, see Blackford, *Mine Eyes*, 25; for the entire section, see 25–29.
18. Ibid., 28.
19. Ibid., 24.
20. Ibid., 27–28.
21. Drewry, *Southampton*, 62; Tragle, *Southampton*, 68.
22. Tragle, *Southampton*, 68–69.
23. Charles L. Perdue, Jr., Thomas E. Barden, and Robert K. Phillips, comps. and eds., *Weevils in the Wheat: Interviews with Virginia Ex-Slaves* (Charlottesville: University Press of Virginia, 1976; reprint, Bloomington: Indiana University Press, 1980), 75; For all-black interviewers in Virginia, see Sharon Ann Musher, "Contesting 'The Way the Almighty Wants It': Crafting Memories of Ex-slaves in the Slave Narrative Collection," *American Quarterly* 53 (March 2000): 9.
24. Oates, *Fires*, 20; Perdue, Barden, and Phillips, *Weevils*, 75–76.
25. Perdue, Barden, and Phillips, *Weevils*, 76. The phrase "stands in fear" alludes to Kenneth Stampp's title (chap. 4, "To Make Them Stand in Fear") in *The Peculiar Institution: Slavery in the Antebellum South* (New York: Vintage Books, 1956), 141.
26. M. M. Manring, *Slave in a Box: The Strange Career of Aunt Jemima* (Charlottesville: University Press of Virginia, 1998), 8, 19.
27. Henry Louis Gates, Jr., and Nellie Y. McKay, gen. eds., *The Norton Anthology of African American Literature* (New York: W. W. Norton and Company, 1997), 285.
28. Tragle, *Southampton*, 403–4. Thomas R. Gray, *The Confessions of Nat Turner* (Baltimore: Lucas and Deaver, 1831).
29. Gray, "Confessions," in *Confessions*, Greenberg, 7–8; Mary Kemp Davis, *Nat Turner Before the Bar of Judgment: Fictional Treatments of the Southampton Insurrection* (Baton Rouge: Louisiana State University Press, 1999), 74; Oates, *Fires*, 158, n. 4.
30. Lucy Mae Turner, "The Family of Nat Turner," *Negro History Bulletin* 18 (March 1955): 127–58; 155–58.
31. Oates, *Fires*, 8–11.
32. Ibid., 13, 29.
33. Oates, *Fires*, 29, 163 n. 22; Tragle, *Southampton*, 24; Tony Horwitz, "Untrue Confessions," *The New Yorker*, 13 December 1999, 85.
34. Oates, *Fires*, 53; cf. 162 n. 21; Tragle, *Southampton*, 92; cf. Oates *Fires*, 102; Tragle, *Southampton*, 417; Gray, "Confessions," in *Confessions* Greenberg, 3.
35. Davis, *Nat Turner*, 232; Sidbury, *Ploughshares*, 90–92; Douglas Egerton, *He Shall Go Out Free: The Lives of Denmark Vesey* (Madison, Wis.: Madison House Publisher, 1999), 134–35.

CHAPTER ELEVEN

1. Petersburg, Virginia, *Intelligencer* quoted in Richmond *Enquirer*, November 22, 1831. Thomas Gray's interviews with Nat Turner, the key source for practically everyone who has written on the subject, are published as Thomas R. Gray, *The Confessions of Nat Turner, the Leader of the Late Insurrection in Southampton County, Va., As Fully and Voluntarily Made to Thomas R. Gray, in the Prison Where He was Confined, and Acknowledged by Him To Be Such When Read before the Court of Southampton . . .* (Richmond: Thomas R. Gray, 1831). Gray's *Confessions* have been widely reprinted, including in John Henrik Clarke, ed., *William Styron's Nat Turner: Ten Black Writers Respond* (Boston: Beacon Press, 1968), 93–118; Henry Irving Tragle, ed., *The Southampton Slave Revolt of 1831: A Compilation of Source Material including the Full Text of the Confessions of Nat Turner* (Amherst, Mass.: University of Massachusetts Press, 1971, rpt. New York, 1973), 300–321, and in John B. Duff and Peter M. Mitchell, eds., *The Nat Turner Rebellion: The Historical Event and the Modern Controversy* (New York: Harper and Row, 1971), 11–30. See also Thomas Wentworth Higginson, "Nat Turner's Insurrection," *Atlantic Monthly*, 8 (August, 1861), reprinted in his

Travellers and Outlaws (Boston: Lee and Shepard, 1889), reprinted as *Black Rebellion* (New York: Arno Press, 1969), 207; William Sidney Drewry, *The Southampton Insurrection* (Washington, 1900), 98–102; John W. Cromwell, "The Aftermath of Nat Turner's Insurrection," *Journal of Negro History* 5 (1920), 212–34.

2. C. Vann Woodward was the first, I believe, to call attention to Nat Turner as "a kind of Christ-figure. Consider his age, his trade as a carpenter, his march on Jerusalem, his martyrdom." See C. Vann Woodward and R. W. B. Lewis, "The Confessions of William Styron," an interview with William Styron on November 5, 1967, in *Conversations with William Styron*, ed. James L. W. West, III (Jackson: University Press of Mississippi, 1985), 88 (hereinafter cited as *Conversations*) and C. Vann Woodward, "Confessions of a Rebel: 1831," *New Republic*, October 7, 1967, 26. Throughout Styron's oeuvre, essential humanity depends on an *imitation Christi*, according to John Douglas Lang, "William Styron: The Christian Imagination" (Ph.D. diss., Stanford University, 1975). Styron, however, constructed his Nat Turner as "an avenging Old Testament angel" and explicitly eschewed Christian parallels. "I avoided mention of Christ as much as I could throughout the book," he said. "I really saw Nat as a man profoundly motivated by the empathy he feels with the old prophets, Ezekial, Jeremiah, Isaiah."

3. James Jones and William Styron, "Two Writers Talk It Over," *Esquire* 60 (July, 1963), 58, reprinted in *Conversations*, 43; Phyllis Meras, "Phyllis Meras Interviews William Styron," *Saturday Review* (October 7, 1967), 30.

4. Benna Kay Kime emphasizes the sheer technical virtuosity of Styron's narrative techniques in "A Critical Study of the Technique of William Styron" (Ph.D. diss., Tulane University, 1971).

5. Meras, "Interviews William Styron," 30. According to Henry Grady Morgan, Jr., Styron's novels all represent the world as a prison and imprisonment as the human condition from which there is no escape. See his "The World as a Prison: A Study of the Novels of William Styron" (Ph.D. diss., University of Colorado, 1973). Sandra M. Peterson sees Turner's testimony to Gray in Styron's *Confessions* as part of a continuum from Puritan confessional literature through *The Scarlet Letter, Billy Budd,* and *An American Tragedy* in her "The View from the Gallows: The Criminal Confession in American Literature" (Ph.D. diss., Northwestern University, 1972). W. A. Kort explores connections between what he called "the resources of confessional fiction" and "the phenomenon of a revolutionary act" in "*The Confessions of Nat Turner* and the Dynamic Revolution," in *Shriven Selves: Religious Problems in Recent American Fiction* (Philadelphia: Fortress Press, 1972), 116–40.

6. Styron, *The Confessions of Nat Turner* (New York: Random House, 1966), 35. Hereinafter cited in the text within parentheses as *CONT*.

7. *CONT*, 132.

8. *CONT*, 123, 135, 169.

9. *CONT*, 232.

10. *CONT*, 127–98, 169–98.

11. *CONT*, 156–57, 191.

12. *CONT*, 211ff.

13. *CONT*, 287.

14. *CONT*, 157.

15. *CONT*, 258–59, 279–80.

16. *CONT*, 259–60.

17. *CONT*, 260.

18. *CONT*, 55–56.

19. *CONT*, 250.

20. *CONT*, 366–71, 381–94, 48, 109, 348.

21. *CONT*, 371–81, 95, 92, 91.

22. *CONT*, 401–402.

23. *CONT*, 403.

24. Meras, "Interviews with William Styron," 30.

25. Meras, "Interviews with William Styron," 30.

26. C. Vann Woodward, "Clio with Soul," *American Historical Review* 75 (1970), 712. One

interesting early review was that of Philip Rahv in the *New York Review of Books*. "I think that only a white Southern writer could have brought it off," Rahv gushed. "A Northerner would have been too much 'outside' the experience to manage it effectively." Then he added that "a Negro writer, because of a very complex anxiety not only personal but social and political, would have probably stacked the cards, producing a mood of unnerving rage and indignation, a melodrama of saints and sinners." Rahv's comments were not only patronizing; they were prophetic of the rage and indignation to follow. See his "Through the Midst of Jerusalem," *New York Review of Books*, October 26, 1967, 6–10.

27. See, for example, Herbert Aptheker, "A Note on the History," *The Nation*, October 16, 1967, 375–76; Herbert Aptheker and William Styron, "Truth and Nat Turner: An Exchange," *The Nation*, April 22, 1968, 543–47; and Vincent Harding and Eugene D. Genovese, "An Exchange on Nat Turner," *New York Review of Books*, November 7, 1968, 35–37. Richard Gilman was one of the few critics who ventured a dissenting literary judgment: "Nat Turner seems to me a mediocre novel," he wrote, "not a beautiful or even well-written work of fiction which happens to contain historical inaccuracies or perversions of historical truth." See his "Nat Turner Revisited," *The New Republic*, April 27, 1968, 23–32. In his *The Return of Nat Turner: History, Literature, and Cultural Politics in Sixties America* (Athens: University of Georgia Press, 1992), Albert E. Stone summarizes the controversy and echoes the criticism with uncritical approval, adding to it his own prosecution of the author as a manipulative opportunist in pursuit of fame and fortune.

28. Albert Murray, "A Troublesome Property," *The New Leader*, December 4, 1967, 18–21; *William Styron's Nat Turner: Ten Black Writers Respond*, ed. John Henrik Clarke (Boston: Beacon Press, 1968), hereinafter *TBWR*.

29. Alvin Poussaint, "*The Confessions of Nat Turner* and the Dilemma of William Styron," *TBWR*, 21; Ernest Kaiser, "The Failure of William Styron," *TBWR*, 63; Vincent Harding, "You've Taken My Nat and Gone," *TBWR*, 29, 20; John Oliver Killens, "The Confessions of Willie Styron," *TBWR*, 43–44; Lerone Bennett, Jr., "Nat's Last White Man," *TBWR*, 5.

30. Harding, "You're Taken My Nat and Gone," *TBWR*, 26. Styron departs here from his principal primary source, Gray's *Confessions*. See Gray, *Confessions*, in *TBWR*, 100.

31. Bennett, "Nat's Last White Man," *TBWR*, 8–9; Gray's *Confessions* have been widely reprinted, most notably as an appendix to *TBWR*, 99–100; *CONT*, 132. See also F. Roy Johnson, *The Nat Turner Slave Insurrection* (Murfreesboro, N.C.: Johnson Publishing Co., 1966), 228–30.

32. Kaiser, "Failure of William Styron," *TBWR*, 56; Gray, "Confessions," in *TBWR*, 99, 102; Johnson, *Nat Turner Insurrection*, 232–33. As early as 1965 Styron had expressed his enthusiasm for what he called Erikson's "brilliant study of the development of the revolutionary impulse in a young man, and the relationship of this impulse to the father figure." It apparently led him to surmise that "Nat Turner's relationship with his father (or his surrogate father, his master) was tormented and complicated, like Luther's." See William Styron, *This Quiet Dust and Other Writings* (New York: Random House, 1982), 16.

33. Poussaint, "Dilemma of William Styron," *TBWR*, 18–19; Bennett, "Nat's Last White Man," *TBWR*, 9.

34. John A. Williams, "The Manipulation of History and of Fact: An Ex-Southerner's Apologist Tract for Slavery and the Life of Nat Turner; or, William Styron's Faked Confessions," *TBWR*, 48; Killens, "Confessions of Willie Styron," *TBWR*, 36–37.

35. Poussaint, "Dilemma of William Styron," *TBWR*, 21; Killens, "Confessions of Willie Styron," *TBWR*, 40; Bennett, "Nat's Last White Man," *TBWR*, 11, 6. The main charges are summarized in Eugene D. Genovese's spirited defense of Styron, "The Nat Turner Case," *New York Review of Books*, September 12, 1968, 34–37; reprinted as "William Styron before the People's Court" in his *In Red and Black: Marxian Explorations in Southern and Afro-American History*, 2nd ed. (Knoxville: University of Tennessee Press, 1984), 204, 210. But see also James M. McPherson, preface to Thomas Wentworth Higginson, *Black Rebellion* (New York, 1969), xi; and Johnson, *Nat Turner Insurrection*, 239.

36. Harding, "You've Taken My Nat and Gone," *TBWR*, 28; Bennett, "Nat's Last White

Man," *TBWR*, 13; Mike Thelwell, "Back With the Wind: Mr. Styron and the Reverend Turner," *TBWR*, 88–89, *CONT*, 107–108, 370, 390.

37. Bennett, "Nat's Last White Man," *TBWR*, 13–15; Gray, *Confessions* in *TBWR*, 107–108.

38. Bennett, "Nat's Last White Man," *TBWR*, 15; Loyle Hairston, "William Styron's Nat Turner—Rogue-Nigger," *TBWR*, 67.

39. Kaiser, "Failure of William Styron," *TBWR*, 63; Harding, "You've Taken My Nat and Gone," *TBWR*, 29.

40. Bennett, "Nat's Last White Man," *TBWR*, 4; Kaiser, "Failure of William Styron," *TBWR*, 64; Poussaint, "Dilemma of William Styron," *TBWR*, 21.

41. Styron's pre-*Confessions* attitude toward critics is indicated in an interview with Madeleine Chapsal in *L'Express*, March 8, 1962, 26–27, reprinted as "Interview," in *Conversations*, 23–24. The text of the Southern Historical Association panel discussion is reprinted as Ralph Ellison, William Styron, Robert Penn Warren, and C. Vann Woodward, "The Uses of History in Fiction" in *Conversations*, but the words alone hardly recapture the ambience of the experience. Styron's exchange with his critic is on p. 122. Ellison declared of Styron, "One thing that I know is that he isn't a bigot, he isn't a racist." And Woodward declared that Styron in the *Confessions* "comes very close, indeed, given the license of the novelist, to doing what the historian does in reconstructing the past." See "The Uses of History in Fiction," 116, 131.

42. Styron, author's note in *Confessions*, vii; Styron, introduction to *This Quiet Dust*, 4; Barzelay and Sussman, "William Styron," 24–25, reprinted in *Conversations*, 95; James L. W. West III, "A Bibliographer's Interview with William Styron," *Costerus*, N. S. 4 (1975), 13–29, reprinted in *Conversations*, 209.

43. Barzelay and Sussman, "William Styron," 94; Robert Canzoneri and Page Stegner, "An Interview with William Styron," in *Conversations*, 67–68; Bertram Wyatt-Brown, review of Stone's *Return of Nat Turner*, in *Journal of Southern History* 59 (1993), 587. Styron had earlier said that he intended the "meditation on history" tag "to take the curse of the label 'historical novel' off the book, because it has regrettably acquired a pejorative connotation." See Woodward and Lewis, "Confessions of William Styron," 86. Robert Penn Warren, writing on the same subject, notes in the foreword to the revised edition of his *Brother to Dragons*, that "a poem dealing with history is no more at liberty to violate what the writer takes to be the spirit of history than it is at liberty to violate what he takes to be the nature of the human heart." See Robert Penn Warren, *Brother to Dragons*, rev. ed. (New York: Random House, 1979), quoted in C. Vann Woodward, *The Future of the Past* (New York: Oxford University Press, 1989), 233.

44. Eugene D. Genovese, "The Nat Turner Case," *New York Review of Books*. September 12, 1968, 34–37; reprinted as "William Styron before the People's Court," in his *In Red and Black*, 200–217. Pagination is to "William Styron before the People's Court." The quote is on p. 202.

45. Genovese, "William Styron before the People's Court," 203–204; "William Styron on *The Confessions of Nat Turner*," 100: William W. Freehling, *The Road to Disunion: Secessionists at Bay*, 1776–1854 (New York: Oxford University Press, 1990), 180–81. Nat had told Gray that the young slaves looked up to him and chose him as their leader because of his ability to read. See Gray, "Confessions," in *TBWR*, 100–101. See also Johnson, *Nat Turner Insurrection*, 231. The contemporary press did not hesitate to convict Nat Turner of cowardice. According to the *Richmond Enquirer*, the rebel leader "acknowledges himself a coward, and says, he was actuated to do what he did, from the influence of fanaticism." After his capture, the paper noted, he had become "convinced that he has done wrong, and advises all other Negroes not to follow his example." See the *Richmond Enquirer*, November 8, 1831, in Duff and Mitchell, eds., *Nat Turner Rebellion*, 37. On Thomas Gray, see the new revelations in Thomas C. Parramore, *Southampton County, Virginia* (Charlottesville: University Press of Virginia, 1978).

46. Genovese, "William Styron before the People's Court," 206–207; David Walker, *Appeal in Four Articles, Together with a Preamble to the Coloured Citizens in the World, but in Particular, and Very Expressly, to those of the United States of America* (1829–1830), quoted in Genovese, *In Red and Black*, 207.

47. Killens, "Confessions of Willie Styron," *TBWR*, 41; John Floyd, governor of Virginia, to

James Hamilton, Jr., governor of South Carolina, November 19, 1831, in Duff and Mitchell, eds., *Nat Turner Rebellion*, 43.

48. To say that the Elkins thesis proved controversial is to understate. His concentration camp analogy drew fire from the right while his Sambo characterization drew fire from the left. Elkins acknowledged that the system worked less efficiently in practice than in theory. "It was possible for significant numbers, of slaves, in varying degrees, to escape the full impact of the system and its coercions upon personality," he wrote. "For all such people there was a margin of space denied to the majority; the system's authority-structure claimed their bodies but not quite their souls." Nevertheless, he insisted that harsh systems have harsh effects. See Stanley M. Elkins, *Slavery: A Problem in American Institutional and Intellectual Life* (Chicago: University of Chicago Press, 1959), 86. For examples of the response to Elkins, see Ann J. Lane, ed., *The Debate over Slavery* (Urbana: University of Illinois Press, 1971).

49. Stanley M. Elkins, *Slavery: A Problem in American Institutional and Intellectual Life*, 2nd ed. (Chicago: University of Chicago Press, 1963), ix, 81–89; Ulrich B. Phillips, *American Negro Slavery* (New York: D. Appleton, 1918); and his *Life and Labor in the Old South* (Boston: Little, Brown, 1929), quotation on 217.

50. Bennett, "Nat's Last White Man," *TBWR*, 7, 4; Ernest Kaiser, "The Failure of William Styron," *TBWR*, 50–65; Williams, "Manipulation of History," *TBWR*, 45–49; and Killens, "The Confessions of Willie Styron," *TBWR*, 34–44.

51. William Styron, "Truth and Nat Turner: An Exchange," *The Nation*, April 22, 1968, 545; Eugene D. Genovese, "The Nat Turner Case," *New York Review of Books*, September 12, 1968, 34–37; Barzelay and Sussman, "William Styron," 106.

52. Higginson, "Nat Turner's Insurrection," 169; Barzelay and Sussman, "William Styron," 106; Howard Meyer, *Colonel of the Black Regiment: The Life of Thomas Wentworth Higginson* (New York: W. W. Norton, 1967), 156.

53. William Sidney Drewry, *The Southampton Slave Insurrection* (Washington: Neale Co., 1900), also published as *Slave Insurrection in Virginia, 1830–1865*; Canzoneri and Stegner, "Interview with William Styron," 68. There were more recent secondary sources as well. Herbert Aptheker, for instance, maintained that another of Nat Turner's sons, Gilbert, had become a respected citizen of Zanesville, Ohio, and had died there a decade before Styron was born. And Lucy Mae Turner, who claimed to be Nat Turner's granddaughter, had published an article on the Turner family in 1955. See also Herbert Aptheker, "Truth and Nat Turner: An Exchange," *The Nation*, April 22, 1968, 543. Interestingly enough, Aptheker rejects Drewry's book as "untruthful" on most questions, but believes Drewry's report of Nat's wife and son. See also Lucy Mae Turner, "The Family of Nat Turner," *Negro History Bulletin* 18 (March, 1955), 127–32; and Stephen B. Oates, *Fires of Jubilee: Nat Turner's Fierce Rebellion* (New York: Harper and Row, 1975), 32.

54. Unsigned communication to Richmond *Constitutional Whig*, September 17, 1831, in Duff and Mitchell, eds., *Nat Turner Rebellion*, 35. Genovese revised his sentence in the second edition of his collection of essays, *In Red and Black*, to read, "The evidence for Turner's alleged black wife is slim and not beyond challenge." See Genovese, "William Styron before the People's Court," 210.

55. William Styron, "Truth and Nat Turner: An Exchange," *The Nation*, April 22, 1968, 547; Woodward and Lewis, "Confessions of William Styron," 90.

56. Gray, "Confessions," in *TBWR*, 105.

57. Winthrop D. Jordan, *Tumult and Silence at Second Creek: An Inquiry into a Civil War Slave Conspiracy* (Baton Rouge: Louisiana State University Press, 1993), 154–56; Richmond *Constitutional Whig*, August 29, 1831. Jordan, after examining all extant issues of the *Richmond Enquirer* for August and September, 1831, found not even any intimation of rape on the part of Turner's rebels. Nor were there any hints of rape in such newspapers as the Boston *Columbian Sentinel*, the Albany *Argus*, the New York *Post*, the Harrisburg *Chronicle*, the Milledgeville *Federal Union*, or the Mobile *Register*, all of which quoted at length from Virginia newspapers. See also Robert N. Elliott, "The Nat Turner Insurrection as Reported in the North Carolina Press," *North Carolina Historical Review* 38 (1961), 1–18.

58. Higginson, "Nat Turner's Insurrection," 175–77; Jordan, *Tumult and Silence,* 155. Walter White, in his 1929 study of lynching, reported that the issue of interracial sex was distorted by what he called a "conspiracy of semi-silence into an importance infinitely greater than the actual facts concerning it would justify." That silence, he said, was the result of a willful blindness to "the historical fact the rape of black women by white men during and after slavery," combined with what he called "a hallucinatory frenzy" about the craving for and rape of white women by black men, which, he said, "exists more in fantasy than in fact." That silence, he said, prevented many Southerners from any kind of response except one of "berserk rage." See Walter White, *Rope and Faggot: A Biography of Judge Lynch* (New York: Arno Press, 1969), 54–55.

59. Drewry, *Southampton Insurrection,* 117; Jordan, *Tumult and Silence,* 155–56.

60. *CONT,* 368; Gray, "Confessions," in *TBWR,* 105–106; Woodward and Lewis, "Confessions of William Styron," 89; Genovese, "William Styron before the People's Court," 204; Bennett, "Nat's Last White Man," *TBWR,* 15. See also Johnson, *Nat Turner Slave Insurrection,* 235–36. Styron said in a 1965 interview that "one of the things about this Negro, Nat Turner, is that he took it upon himself to do this incredible thing, to slaughter a lot of white people, which for an American Negro was probably the most prodigious and decisive act of free will ever taken." Nat Turner, he said, "couldn't deal with the violence that he himself had ordained, so to speak, and this is part of my story. I think it's very central to the book—the idea of what happens when a man boldly proposes a course of total annihilation and starts to carry it out and finds to his dismay that it's not working for him. I think it's unavoidable in an honest reading of Nat Turner's confessions that he himself was almost unable to grapple with violence, to carry it out successfully." According to Styron, "the Nat Turner I created (and perhaps the Nat Turner I believe might have existed), failed for the very reason of his humanity." See Jack Griffin, Jerry Hornsy, and Gene Stelzig, "A Conversation with William Styron," in *Pennsylvania Review* I (Spring, 1965), reprinted in *Conversations,* 57; Canzoneri and Stegner, "Interview with William Styron," 69; Ben Forkner and Gilbert Schricke, "An Interview with William Styron," *Conversations,* 194.

61. Bennett, "Nat's Last White Man," *TBWR,* 12, 15; J. Floyd to J. Hamilton, Jr., November 19, 1831, in Duff and Mitchell, eds., *Nat Turner Rebellion,* 44; Higginson, "Nat Turner's Insurrection," 181; unsigned communication [presumably from Governor John Floyd] to Richmond *Constitutional Whig,* September 17, 1831, in Duff and Mitchell, eds., *Nat Turner Rebellion,* 35; Gray, "Confessions," in *TBWR,* 104, 115, 113.

62. Johnson, *Nat Turner Insurrection,* 235–36; J. Floyd to J. Hamilton, Jr., November 19, 1831, in Duff and Mitchell, eds., *Nat Turner Rebellion,* 44.

63. Bennett, "Nat's Last White Man," *TBWR,* 7; Poussaint, "Dilemma of William Styron," *TBWR,* 17–18; Kaiser, "Failure of William Styron," *TBWR,* 63, 65; Killens, "Confessions of Willie Styron," *TBWR,* 36 passim. The contributors to *TBWR* misstate some facts, which it might be best to assume were consequences of zeal rather than malice: Styron's *Confessions* received neither unqualified praise from white reviewers nor unqualified opprobrium from black reviewers. Nor was their charge true that no blacks were invited to review Styron's *Confessions.*

64. Styron, introduction to *This Quiet Dust,* 6.

65. Vincent Harding, "You've Taken My Nat and Gone," *TBWR,* 29. Among the most significant collections and analyses of authentic field-recorded African-American folklore are Roger D. Abrahams, *Deep Down in the Jungle: Negro Narrative Folklore from the Streets of Philadelphia* (Hatboro, Pa.: Folklore Associates, 1964) and his "Trickster, the Outrageous Hero," in *Our Living Traditions,* ed. Tristram Potter Coffin (New York: Basic Books, 1968); Roger Bastide, *African Civilisations in the New World,* trans. Peter Green (New York, 1971); J. Mason Brewer, *Humorous Tales of the South Carolina Negro* (Orangeburg: South Carolina State College, 1945); and his "John Tales," *Publications of the Texas Folklore Society* 21 (1946), 81–104, A[bigail]. M. H. Christensen, *Afro-American Folk Lore Told Round Cabin Fires in the Sea Islands of South Carolina* (Boston: J. P. Cupples, 1892); Daniel J. Crowley, ed., *African Folklore in the New World* (Austin: University of Texas Press, 1977); Richard M. Dorson, *American Negro Folk Tales* (Greenwich, Conn.: Fawcett, 1967); Alan Dundes, "African and Afro-American Tales," in *African Folklore,* ed. Crowley, and his

"African Tales among the North American Indians," *Southern Folklore Quarterly* 29 (1965), 207–19; Ambrose E. Gonzales, *The Black Border: Gullah Stories of the Carolina Coast* (Columbia: The State Publishing Co., 1922); Zora Neale Hurston, "High John de Conquer," *American Mercury* 57 (1943), 450–58; and her *Mules and Men* (Philadelphia: J. P. Lippincott, 1935); Bruce Jackson, ed., *The Negro and His Folklore in Nineteenth Century Periodicals* (Austin: University of Texas, 1967); Guy B. Johnson, *Folk Culture on St. Helena Island, South Carolina* (Chapel Hill: University of North Carolina Press, 1930); Charles Colcock Jones, Jr., *Negro Myths from the Georgia Coast* (Boston: Houghton-Mifflin Co., 1888); Lawrence W. Levine, *Black Culture and Black Consciousness; Afro-American Folk Thought from Slavery to Freedom* (New York: Oxford University Press, 1977), esp. pp. 81–135; Harry C. Oster, "Negro Humor: John and Old Marster," *Journal of the Folklore Institute* 5 (1968), 42–57; Elsie Clews Parsons, *Folk-Lore of the Antilles, French and English* (Cambridge: Harvard University Press, 1923), her *Folk-Lore of the Sea Islands, South Carolina* (Cambridge: Harvard University Press, 1923), and her *Folk-Tales of Andros Island, Bahamas* (Cambridge: Harvard University Press, 1918); *South Carolina Folk Tales,* compiled by Workers of the Writers' Program of the Work Projects Administration in the State of South Carolina (Columbia: University of South Carolina, 1941); and Sterling Stuckey, "Through the Prism of Folklore: The Black Ethos in Slavery," *Massachusetts Review* 9 (1968). According to Eugene D. Genovese, "there is little evidence of a revolutionary folk tradition among the southern slaves of the kind that Palmares inspired among the slaves of the Brazilian northeast." He believes that the reason "no powerful tradition emerged" was simply that neither the Turner rebellion nor such other revolts as the Stono Rebellion, Gabriel's Rebellion, or the Denmark Vesey Revolt ever "achieved an appropriate size or duration." See his *Roll, Jordan, Roll: The World the Slaves Made* (New York: Pantheon, 1974), 596–97.

66. Henry Clay Bruce, *The New Man: Twenty-Nine Years a Slave. Twenty Nine Years a Free Man: Recollections of H. C. Bruce* (York, Pa.: P. Anstadt and Sons, 1895), 25–26; Allen Crawford, North Emporia, Va., interviewed by Susie R. C. Byrd, June 25, 1937, in Charles L. Perdue, Jr., Thomas E. Barden, and Robert K. Phillips, *Weevils in the Wheat: Interviews with Virginia Ex-Slaves* (Charlottesville: University Press of Virginia, 1976), 75–76. Cf. Gray, "Confessions," *TBWR*, 105–108.

67. Fannie Berry, Petersburg, Va., interviewed by Susie R. C. Byrd, February 26, 1937, in Perdue, *Weevils in the Wheat*, 35; Linda Brent [Harriet Jacobs], *Incidents in the Life of a Slave Girl,* ed. Lydia Maria Child (Boston: author, 1861), p. 102. The standard modern edition is Harriet Jacobs, *Incidents in the Life of a Slave Girl,* ed. Jean Fagan Yellin (Cambridge: Harvard University Press, 1987).

68. Charity Bowery, interviewed by Lydia Maria Child, in her "Charity Bowery," *The Liberty Bell: By Friends of Freedom,* ed. Maria W. Chapman (Boston: American Anti-Slavery Society, 1839), 42–43; James Lindsay Smith, *Autobiography of James Lindsay Smith, including, also, Reminiscences of Slave Life, Recollections of the War, Education of Freedmen, Causes of the Exodus, etc.* (Norwich: Press of the Bulletin, 1881), 162–65.

69. Jacobs, *Incidents in the Life of a Slave Girl,* 98–99; Allen Crawford, in Perdue, *Weevils in the Wheat,* 75–76; Henry Box Brown, *Narrative of the Life Henry Box Brown, Written by Himself* (Boston: Samuel Webb, 1852) 19; Jacobs, *Incidents in the Life of a Slave Girl,* 102.

70. Allen Crawford, in Perdue, *Weevils in the Wheat,* 75–76.

71. Bowery interviewed by Lydia Maria Child, 42; Jamie Parker, *Jamie Parker, the Fugitive; Related to Mrs. Emily Pierson* (Hartford: Brockett, Fuller, and Co., 1851), 16–17.

72. "The real Nat Turner as opposed to the one I created were and are two different people," Styron acknowledged to an interviewer in 1974. See Ben Forkner and Gilbert Schricke, "An Interview with William Styron," *Southern Review* 10 (1974), 923–34, reprinted in *Conversations,* 192–93.

73. Peter Nicholas Corodimas, "Guilt and Redemption in the Novels of William Styron" (Ph.D. diss., Ohio State University, 1971); Ardner Randolph Cheshire, Jr., "The Theme of Redemption in the Fiction of William Styron" (Ph.D. diss., Louisiana State University, 1973). An earlier study, Jonathan Baumbach's "The Theme of Guilt and Redemption in the Post Second World War Novel" (Ph.D. diss., Stanford University, 1961) points to themes of guilt and redemption in Styron's *Lie Down in Darkness* along with selected

works by Saul Bellow, Ralph Ellison, Bernard Malamud, Wright Morris, Flannery O'Connor, J. D. Salinger, and Robert Penn Warren. Styron concedes that "the themes of all my books do somehow revolve around the idea that people act out of selfish and willful and prideful motivations without realizing that the universe is fairly indifferent and doesn't care, and that more often than not these willful acts will result in some kind of catastrophe, especially if they're directed in terms of violence against other people." See Forkner and Schricke, "Interview with William Styron," *Conversations*, 191.

74. William Styron, *The Long March* (New York: Random House, 1952); William Styron, *Set This House on Fire* (New York: Random House, 1960). "Mannix was a total figment of my imagination," Styron told an interviewer in 1977. "That part did not really happen. Nor did he really exist." See Michael West, "An Interview with William Styron," in *Conversations*, 223. Kinsolving's affinity for alcohol may be semiautobiographical. Styron denies ever having written a line under the influence of alcohol, but says that having "a few drinks" allows the writer "to think in this released mode" in a way that "often gives you very new insights" and "certain visionary moments" that are "very valuable." See Hilary Mills, "Creators on Creating: William Styron," in *Conversations*, 241. Styron's indebtedness to theologian Paul Tillich is stressed by Rohart Detweiler in his "William Styron and the Courage to Be," in *Four Spiritual Crises in Mid-Century American Fiction* (Gainesville: University Press of Florida, 1964), 6–13. Nancy Carter Goodley emphasizes the influence of Christian existentialist Søren Kierkegaard on what she calls the "strongly affirmative and Christian" theology of Styron's work in her "All Flesh is Grass: Despair and Affirmation in *Lie Down in Darkness*, (Ph.D. diss., American University, 1975).

75. William Styron, *Lie Down in Darkness* (Indianapolis: Bobbs-Merrill, 1951). Styron recalled in an interview that "if that final monologue of Peyton has any intensity, it might be due to the fact that I was monstrously oppressed" at the time by what he was certain would be a bad time. He had been called up for active duty in the U.S. Marine Corps. He had served two and a half years during the Second World War and had remained in the Reserves. "I was called up in 1951 at the very height of the Korean War. I was just finishing *Lie Down in Darkness*, and I was working against time because I wanted to get the thing done before I went back in to the marines." See Griffin, Hornsy, and Stelzig, "Conversation with William Styron," in *Conversations*, 52.

76. Styron, *Lie Down in Darkness*, 394–95.

77. According to the Ten, "Styron's selection of 'factual' and psychological material speaks for itself." Of course. So does it for all writers, whether of fiction or fact, not excluding the Ten Black Writers themselves. Bennett, "Nat's Last White Man," *TBWR*, 4; Kaiser, "Failure of William Styron," *TBWR*, 64. Eudora Welty, *One Writer's Beginnings* (Cambridge: Harvard University Press, 1983), 110–11; Poussaint, "Dilemma of William Styron," *TBWR*, 21; Forkner and Schricke, "Interview with William Styron," 192–93; Meras, "Interviews William Styron," 30. Welty—writing of Miss Eckhart, the piano teacher in her *The Golden Apples*—adds that "there wasn't any resemblance in her outward identity." Welty notes carefully, "What animates and possesses me is what drives Miss Eckhart, the love of her art and the love of giving it, the desire to give it until there is no more left." It was not in the character "as she stands solidly and almost opaquely in the surround of her story, but in the making of her character out of my most inward and most deeply feeling self, I would say I have found my voice in my fiction" (*One Writer's Beginnings*, III).

78. William Styron, "Jimmy in the House," *New York Times Book Review*, December 20, 1987, 30.

79. James Baldwin, *Go Tell It on the Mountain* (New York: Alfred A. Knopf, 1953), 27; James Baldwin, "Everybody's Protest Novel," in his *Notes of a Native Son* (Boston: Beacon Press, 1955; reprint 1964), 21.

80. Baldwin, *Go Tell It on the Mountain*, 228.

81. James Baldwin, *Another Country* (New York: Dial Press, 1962), 22.

82. Baldwin, "Everybody's Protest Novel," 13–23; Styron, "Jimmy in the House," 30.

83. Richard Wright, *Native Son* (New York, 1940), 17, 101; James Baldwin, "Many Thousands Gone," in *Notes of a Native Son*, 29.

84. *CONT*, 172, 349, 255–56.

85. Baldwin, *Another Country*, 22; Wright, *Native Son*, 81–85, 108; Eldridge Cleaver, *Soul on Ice* (New York: McGraw-Hill, 1968), 14.

86. Wright, *Native Son*, 108–109, 101.

87. Ralph Ellison, *Invisible Man* (New York: Random House, 1952), 7–8.

88. Herman Melville, "Benito Cereno," in his *Piazza Tales* (New York: Dix and Edwards, 1856). "Benito Cereno" is based on an actual slave mutiny that took place on board a Spanish ship off South America in 1799.

89. Harriet Beecher Stowe, *Dred: A Tale of the Great Dismal Swamp* (Boston: Phillips, Sampson, and Co., 1856). *Dred* is less concerned with the black rebel of the dismal swamp than with the interlocking relationships among an interracial family, like that of Thomas Sutpen in Faulkner's *Absalom, Absalom!* According to Higginson, "Mrs. Stowe's 'Dred' seems dim and melodramatic beside the actual Nat Turner." See his "Nat Turner's Insurrection," 209.

90. Arna Bontemps, *Black Thunder* (New York: Macmillan, 1936), 82. As a matter of fact, Styron had planned to write his Nat Turner novel "from an omniscient point of view, from many reactive standpoints, such as that of one of the white victims, one of the farmer types." But "it just didn't seem right to me," and he eventually realized that he would have to "risk leaping into a black man's consciousness. Not only did I want the risk alone—which was an important thing, to see if it could be done—but by doing so, I thought I could get a closer awareness of the smell of slavery." Filtering through "the consciousness of the 'I', the first person," he hoped, "would somehow allow you to enter the consciousness of a Negro of the early decades of the nineteenth century." He added that "if you start finding out about Nat, discovering things about Nat, well, of course, every passage, every chapter, every section is kind of a revelation both for yourself and for Nat." See Canzoneri and Stegner, "Interview with William Styron," *Conversations*, 69–70, and Brazelan and Sussman, "William Styron on *The Confessions of Nat Turner*," *Conversations*, 103.

91. Styron, *This Quiet Dust*, 247. Of course, the Faulkner influence on Styron, as on virtually all Southern writers, is palpable—as both god and demon. "Writers as disparate as Flannery O'Connor and Walker Percy have expressed their despair at laboring in the shadow of such a colossus," Styron has written, "and I felt a similar measliness" (*This Quiet Dust*, 292). It is interesting to ponder how Nat Turner might have fared in Faulkner's hands. John A. Williams suggests that he might well have resembled the cold, unremitting Lucas Beauchamp of *Go Down, Moses* and *Intruder In the Dust*. See Williams, "The Manipulation of History," in *TBWR*, 48.

92. See F. Garvin Davenport, Jr., *The Myth of Southern History: Historical Consciousness in Twentieth-Century Southern Literature* (Nashville: Vanderbilt University Press, 1970), 131–70; Richard H. King, *A Southern Renaissance: The Cultural Awakening of the American South, 1930–1955* (New York: Oxford University Press, 1980), 72–76, 231–41, 277–86; Daniel Joseph Singal, *The War Within: From Victorian to Modernist Thought in the South, 1919–1945* (Chapel Hill: University of North Carolina Press, 1982), 339–72; C. Vann Woodward, "History in Robert Penn Warren's Fiction," in his *The Future of the Past*, 221–34.

93. Peter H. Wood, "Nat Turner: the Unknown Slave as Visionary Leader," in *Black Leaders of the Nineteenth Century*, ed. Leon Litwack and August Meier (Urbana: 1988), 37–39.

94. Styron, *This Quiet Dust*, 9–34. The quotes are on pp. 10, 12, 11, 14. The essay, "This Quiet Dust," was originally published in *Harper's*, April, 1965; Granville Hicks, "Race Riot, 1831," *Saturday Review*, October 7, 1967.

95. Ellison et al., "The Uses of History in Fiction," *Conversations*, 128, 130, 142; C. Vann Woodward, "Fictional History and Historical Fiction," *New York Review of Books*. November 16, 1987, 38. According to Roland Barthes, "myth is constituted by the loss of the historical reality of things: in it, things lose the memory that they once were made." See his *Mythologies* (London: Paladin, 1973), 134–42. The quotation is on p. 155. See also Tony Bennett, "Text, Readers, Reading Formations," *Literature and History* 9 (1983).

96. Ralph Ellison, "Twentieth-Century Fiction and the Black Mask of Humanity," in his *Shadow and Act* (New York: Random House, 1953), 42–43; Willie Lee Rose, *Slavery and Freedom* (New York: Random House, 1982), 169; Ellison, *The Invisible Man*.

97. Ellison, "Twentieth-Century Fiction," in *Shadow and Act*, 43; Kaiser, "Failure of William Styron," *TBWR*, 56; Killens, "Confessions of Willie Styron," *TBWR*, 36; Genovese, "William Styron before the People's Court," 203–204. Genovese points out that the novelist's depiction of Nat Turner shared many characteristics with the historical Toussaint L'Ouverture, the successful black revolutionary of Saint Domingue. A "privileged" bondsman, Toussaint led his own master's family to safety, remained aloof from the violence while his fellow slaves put the North Plain to the torch. "Not being a statue," he writes, Toussaint possessed "all the frailties and contradictions common even to the greatest of men" (204–205).

98. Styron, *This Quiet Dust*, 13; Ralph Ellison, introduction to *Shadow and Act*, xi–xxiii; Meras, "Interviews William Styron," 30; Richard Wright, *White Man Listen!* (New York: Doubleday, 1957), 108–109 (emphasis mine).

99. Toni Morrison, *Playing in the Dark: Whiteness and the Literary Imagination* (Cambridge: Harvard University Press, 1992), 11–12; James Baldwin, "Many Thousands Gone," *Partisan Review* 18 (1951), 673–74; William Faulkner, "A Letter to the Leaders of the Negro Race," in his *Essays, Speeches and Public Letters*, ed. James B. Meriwether (New York: Random House, 1956), 110.

100. According to Styron, while writing the *Confessions*, he came to realize that his protagonist was "ignorant of his own pride, was ignorant of his own undertaking, was ignorant of the enormity of what he was doing—mainly this horrible act of violence in the name of retribution which—well meant or not—resulted in catastrophe not only for himself and of course the white people, but especially for his own people, the blacks." See Forkner and Schricke, "Interview with William Styron," *Conversations*, 191. Such unrecognized overweening pride is, of course, what Aristotle called the "tragic flaw" in his *Poetics*.

101. Joel Williamson, *The Crucible of Race: Black-White Relations in the American South Since Emancipation* (New York: Oxford University Press, 1984), 522.

EPILOGUE

1. *Variety*, 19 October 1967; *Hollywood Reporter*, 19 October 1967.
2. *New York Post*, 27 January 1970.
3. *Variety*, 15 January 1968; 3 February 1969; *New York Times*, 9 February 1969.
4. The story of the protest against the Wolper film can be found in letters and other documents in the Louise Meriwether Papers, private collection.
5. Louise Meriwether to John Oliver Killens, 13 July 1968; Louise Meriwether to John Henrik Clarke, 5 December 1968, Louise Meriwether Papers.
6. Louise Meriwether to David Wolper and Norman Jewison, 26 March 1968, Louise Meriwether Papers.
7. Interviews with Ayuko Babu and Louise Meriwether from the documentary film *Nat Turner ~ A Troublesome Property*, produced and written by Frank Christopher and Kenneth S. Greenberg, directed by Charles Burnett.
8. *Hollywood Reporter*, 18 April 1968.
9. *Variety*, 6 February 1969.
10. Copies of the agreement can be found in the Louise Meriwether Papers.
11. The involvement of Gilbert Francis in the Nat Turner film project is documented in the Gilbert Francis Papers, private collection.
12. Quotations can be found in letters dated 11 February 1967; 8 June 1967; 9 June 1967; 22 March 1967; 21 February 1967; 27 July 1967; and 29 August 1967 in the William Styron Papers, Rare Book, Manuscript, and Special Collections Library, Duke University.
13. Quotations from a broadside found in the Louise Meriwether Papers.
14. Gilbert Francis Papers.
15. Gilbert Francis's relations with Chico Day are chronicled in the Gilbert Francis Papers. See also Elizabeth Francis's interview from the documentary film *Nat Turner ~ A Troublesome Property*.
16. *New York Post*, 27 January 1970; William Styron's interview from the documentary film *Nat Turner ~ A Troublesome Property*.

17. William Styron, "Essay on James Baldwin published in London *Observer*," William Styron Papers, Rare Book, Manuscript, and Special Collections Library, Duke University.
18. *Newsweek*, 16 October 1967.
19. A tape of the debate between William Styron and Ossie Davis can be found in the William Styron Papers, Rare Book, Manuscript, and Special Collections Library, Duke University.